POETRY, PLACE, AND GENDER

Helen Damico at the Mouth of Truth (portico of the Church of Santa Maria in Cosmedin, Rome) July 1997. Photo courtesy of Christopher Kleinhenz.

Medieval Institute Publications is a program of
The Medieval Institute, College of Arts and Sciences

WESTERN MICHIGAN UNIVERSITY

POETRY, PLACE, AND GENDER

STUDIES IN MEDIEVAL CULTURE
IN HONOR OF HELEN DAMICO

Edited by
Catherine E. Karkov

MEDIEVAL INSTITUTE PUBLICATIONS
Western Michigan University
Kalamazoo

Library of Congress Cataloging-in-Publication Data

Poetry, place, and gender : studies in medieval culture in honor of Helen Damico / edited by Catherine E. Karkov.
    p. cm.
 Includes bibliographical references and index.
 ISBN 978-1-58044-127-8 (casebound : alk. paper)
 1. Literature, Medieval--History and criticism 2. Civilization, Medieval, in literature. 3. English poetry--Old English, ca. 450-1100--History and criticism. 4. Gender identity in literature. 5. Place (Philosophy) in literature. I. Karkov, Catherine E., 1956- II. Damico, Helen.
 PN671.P64 2009
 809.1'02--dc22

              2009032924

Contents

ABBREVIATIONS

ANQ	*American Notes and Queries*
ASE	*Anglo-Saxon England*
ASPR	Anglo-Saxon Poetic Records
CCCC	Corpus Christi College Cambridge
CCCM	Corpus Christianorum, Continuatio Medievalis
CCSL	Corpus Christianorum Series Latina
CSASE	Cambridge Studies in Anglo-Saxon England
CSEL	Corpus Scriptorum Ecclesiasticorum Latinorum
EEMF	Early English Manuscripts in Facsimile
EETS	Early English Texts Society
EHD	*English Historical Documents c. 500–1042*, ed. Dorothy Whitelock. London: Eyre and Spottiswoode, 1968.
e.s	extra series
HE	*Bede's Ecclesiastical History of the English People*, ed. B. Colgrave and R. A. B. Mynors. Oxford: Clarendon Press, 1969.
Jnl.	Journal
Ker	*Catalogue of Manuscripts Containing Anglo-Saxon*, ed. N. R. Ker. Oxford: Clarendon Press, 1957
n.s	new series

OED	Oxford English Dictionary
OEN	*Old English Newsletter*
o.s	ordinary series
PL	*Patrologia Latina*, ed. J. P. Migne (Paris, 1844–65); Supplemental series ed. A. Hammon and L. Guillaumin (Paris, 1958–74)
PMLA	*Proceedings of the Modern Language Association of America*
s.a.	sub anno
TCBS	*Transactions of the Cambridge Bibliographical Society*

Introduction

Patrick W. Conner

In 1997, four of the people whose work is included in this collection sat in July sunlight at a round, white, wrought-iron table on the flagstone veranda next to a sapphire-bright Mediterranean Sea at the posh Villa Igeia just outside Palermo. Helen Damico was the fifth member of the party, and it is an image of her on that afternoon that comes to mind as I write this introduction to these studies by which an assembly of distinguished scholars now honors her career. In addition to Helen were Catherine Karkov, Kevin Kiernan, George Brown, and I. Catherine and George had come with Helen, having taken the long way around Sicily to get to Palermo, the rest of us learned over very fine martinis. In going around the island, they had driven to Girgenti to seek out the birthplace of Luigi Pirandello, because Helen, who had been an actress, had once played in *Six Characters in Search of an Author*, and she wanted to visit the home of its playwright, a man who had led a life completely reversed from her own. He had begun with philology and discovered theater. She had begun with theater and discovered philology.

When the Nobel Prize for Literature was awarded to Pirandello in 1934, Göran Liljestrand of the Caroline Institute said, in praising his work, "society is a higher unit of life than the individual; it has a greater complexity and involves adjustments of different kinds." While drama may play the individual off against society, using one to illuminate the other as Pirandello so often did, philology seeks to catalog the complexities and adjustments that society derives from individuals and their manifold identities. This is what Helen Damico has understood in all of her work from *Beowulf's Wealhtheow and the Valkyrie Tradition*, sometimes called "the first feminist book on Old English literature," right through to her indispensable edited collection, *Medieval Scholarship: Biographical Studies on the Formation of a Discipline*. That is why Helen, on the one hand, sought the mythic roots of the woman in the hall; the trace of such a history gives both Wealtheow and the poem of *Beowulf* the texture of social complexity and the attendant adjustments a view from a woman's perspective requires. And that is why, on the other hand, Helen has seen the importance of drawing together critical biographies of the great medieval scholars, because scholarship is

1

the means whereby we nudge ourselves to adjust the histories by which we live. These essays offered in Helen's honor will lead us to adjust a few more such histories. They are, like Helen's pursuits, far-ranging, and they touch her interests in Old Norse and later medieval literatures, as well as Old English poetry. But literature alone is not large enough to contain all of Helen's interests. For years, she organized an annual symposium at the University of New Mexico bringing together papers on art, archaeology, and history as well as poetry and prose, and her support for such interdisciplinary concerns is reflected in the contents of this volume, too, where archaeologists, art historians, palaeographers, and liturgists have combined their talents to probe a wide range of issues including those of poetry, place, and gender.

Éamonn Ó Carragáin has made a career of exploring the liturgical, doctrinal, and theological aspects of Benedict Biscop's monasteries at Monkwearmouth and Jarrow, where, as he has repeatedly shown, the desire for *imitatio Romae*, to imitate Rome, illuminates the degree of orthodoxy practiced by the English church at a time when communications and travel were difficult, and it was not always easy to know the authoritative position on religious matters that were being altered and adjusted quite frequently at distant Rome. The study offered here, "The Wearmouth Icon of the Virgin (A.D. 679): Christological, Liturgical, and Iconographic Contexts," discusses the icon of the Virgin that Benedict Biscop brought from Rome to Wearmouth along with several other images in the fall of 689. Why, Ó Carragáin asks, was this image given prominence at Wearmouth by being placed above the altar, with the apostles arranged on either side of it? He concludes that the cult of the Virgin was developed at Wearmouth to articulate the Church's understanding of Christ's nature and achievement. He demonstrates how the Virgin is referenced by the Mass and the Creed, and how she is implicated in the contemporary debate between the positions that Christ had only a divine will (Monotheletism) and that he possessed both divine and human wills (Dyotheletism), perfectly in harmony with each other so that his human will never contradicted his divine will.

To place the icon of the Mother of God centrally above the altar at Wearmouth was to connect the monastery at the place of the Mass with a visual reminder of the doctrine of the Virgin Birth, which the third canon of the Lateran Council in 649 had given a new emphasis, and the act attests to Wearmouth's participation in the central Christological debate of the later seventh century. Ó Carragáin traces the wider import of this doctrine in the history of the feast of the Annunciation, which had only recently been promulgated by Rome, and which created the liturgical difficulty of celebrating Christ's Incarnation at the same time as the Church was commemorating the Passion, a difficulty solved in Rome by creating a Mass for the Annunciation which would allude to the essential unity of that feast and of the Easter events in admixing of Christ's divine and human wills.

The second paper informed by the liturgy is "*The Dream of the Rood* at Nones on Good Friday" by Sarah Larratt Keefer. Keefer traces the development of the Good Friday Veneration of the Cross ceremony, which originated possibly as early as the fourth century, was continuously elaborated in Francia, and was completed in the *Regularis Concordia* tradition with the *Depositio Crucis* described therein. She shows how these developments inform *The Dream of the Rood*. More specifically, it is the Office rites at Nones of Good Friday which she finds encoded into the words of the poem. Keefer points out that the nature of meditation is such that we do not have to worry that the poem does not create a kind of versified parallel of the liturgy. "*The Dream of the Rood* could not have been an attempt to recapture the sequence of the Veneration synaxis but instead to encapsulate those parts of the service that rise in the memory in order to form a suitable devotion deriving from the act of *meditatio*," she notes. The parallels, however, are indeed instructive.

The Dream of the Rood is one of the great gifts of Anglo-Saxon literature to the English literary tradition. I remember being moved by it as a young man taking my first Old English course, the effect being more powerful than my ignorance of Old English style and rhetoric could negate. I am not surprised that Keefer finds the liturgy in it. What else has so honed these words and images to cut through to one's very soul, as they do in this poem?

In "Prophetic Vision in *The Dream of the Rood*," Thomas N. Hall takes an epistemological approach to elucidating the dreamer's vision of the cross, asking to what extent the dynamic and paradoxical vision of the cross can be explained by the medieval concepts of seeing and knowing, and what may be the place of visionary experience within that epistemology. Hall is drawn especially in his study to Gregory the Great's *Homilies on Ezechiel* for Gregory's analysis of the nature of prophecy and its relation to visionary experience. Hall is not undertaking a source study, and does not conclude that the *Homilies on Ezechiel* were known to the poet of *The Dream of the Rood*. Rather, he wishes to suggest that the visionary state is, for Gregory, not merely prophetic of the future, but revelatory of things hidden in all times simultaneously, including the past and the present as well as the future. A prophet, therefore, sees whole what others see only in part, which means that allegorical meanings coexist with literal meanings in the prophet's understanding, whereas the rest of us tend to compartmentalize these into discrete categories. Furthermore, "the Holy Spirit does not express outwardly through language all at once what it reveals inwardly to the heart of the prophet in a single instant." Hall relates Gregory's sense of knowing through prophecy to Albert Rothenberg's studies on "janusian thinking," the ability to hold two contradictory—indeed, antithetical—ideas in mind at once. He applies these ideas to the dreamer's vision in the first twenty-three lines of *The Dream of the Rood*, suggesting that the poet's fragmented set of discrete visionary elements at the opening of the poem is a result of the failure of language to communicate the atemporal visionary experience. Certainly, it is difficult to speak atemporally in English, where the verb is always marked for tense in every finite use of it and where the temporally unmarked infinitive is always governed by a finite verb. Hall concludes this remarkable essay with the observation that accounts of such visionary experience are to be connected with the theological principle of the hypostatic union of the human and the divine, which, for Christians, exists only in the person of Christ, the ultimate prophet in the very sense Gregory has advanced in his *Homilies on Ezechiel*.

In "*Þyle* as Fool: Revisiting *Beowulf*'s Hunferth," Leslie A. Donovan, Helen's colleague at the University of New Mexico, offers an exhaustive study of the figure of Hunferth in *Beowulf* with roots in some sort of institutionalized Loki figure and moving toward the figure of the court jester or fool. This very smart analysis is not the narrative of an evolution, but, instead, it documents a point on the evolutionary path of the figure, pointing out the contradictions to any single picture of the figure of Hunferth and challenging easy assumptions about this pivotal character. Donovan sees Hunferth as an early court functionary who used words to protect, improve, and entertain the court, who may have been both a warrior and a poet, and whom philologists have linked with the pagan priesthood. In Hrothgar's *þyle*, however, Donovan discovers a type of early court figure "whose attributes still can be seen as vestigial remnants in the later fools and jesters."

In "The *nathwylc* Scribe and the *nathwylc* Text of *Beowulf*," Kevin Kiernan returns to the topic that caused intense discussions and immense controversy when, in 1981, he teased out the implications of the blurred texts on folio 179. Kiernan considered folio 179 to have been created when the second scribe of *Beowulf* scraped and rewrote material over the original text on the recto and verso of folio 179 to create a link between the tale of Beowulf's youthful exploits and his old age and death. The implication of that idea was that the text was still being created at the time the manuscript was written, which allowed Kiernan to date the final composition of the poem to the creation of the manuscript itself, which he argues may have been as late as the reign of King Cnut.

While folio 179 remains a key to understanding the production of the manuscript, Kiernan is now persuaded that the hand which Julius Zupitza claimed to be a later "freshen[ing] up" of the faded leaf and which Carl Berkhout has identified with the hand of Laurence Nowell, is in fact the work of a third scribe contemporary with the two main scribes of the manuscript. The rare Old English pronoun *nathwylc* appears twice on folio 179 in the hand of the new scribe whom Kiernan therefore labels "the *nathwylc* scribe." He demonstrates that the leaf was dampened to soften the ink shortly after it was originally written, that it was scraped, and that the *nathwylc* scribe then rewrote this portion of the poem. That the preparation of the new page was not quite suited to preserving the new text in the way the rest of the leaves have maintained the writing upon them explains its condition today, where letters have literally fallen off its surface. Kiernan asserts that this hypothesis better explains why only portions of the dominant text survive than the idea that bits were freshened up inconsistently. A modern application of reagent to areas of the leaf most difficult to read has further obscured what the *nathwylc* scribe wrote there, but an impressive array of digital tools, originally developed by Kiernan and Emil Iacob as "Edition Production & Presentation Technology" (EPPT) and now called "Image-based XML" (IBX), provide strong visual support to give credence to the interpretations of the physical data that he offers here.

The implications of his argument are intriguing. The third, or *nathwylc*, scribe not only rewrote folio 179 but also seems to have made corrections in other parts of the manuscript. What role did he (not impossibly "she") play in the organization of this scriptorium? What was the poem's attraction in the monastic scriptorium that it demanded the coordinated efforts of three scribes? As Kiernan continues to create support for dating the *Beowulf* we have to the dating of its manuscript and to implicate a wider range of persons and resources in its creation, the stronger the context becomes for works like Helen Damico's historicist study of Queen Emma as a model for Wealtheow.

In his contribution to the volume, Paul E. Szarmach writes that St. Æðeldreda got what is now known as "very good press." Bede created her first vita in his *Historia ecclesiastica*, her narrative was given special attention in the Old English translation of Bede's great history, an epitome of her life was created for the Old English martyrology, and Ælfric included her in his *Lives of the Saints*. In "Æðeldreda in the *Old English Bede*," Szarmach looks in great detail at how the creator of the Old English version of the *Historia ecclesiastica* altered Bede's version of the vita, and Szarmach attempts to recover the translator's intentions behind those alterations in an incipient effort to begin a reassessment of the full context in which the Old English Bede was published.

Bede's treatment of Æðeldreda amounts to another exercise in writing an *opus geminatum*. Bede had already composed a prose life to accompany Paulinus of Nola's verse life of St. Felix, and added a verse life to his own prose life of St. Cuthbert, so this complex genre that required the twinning of a subject in both prose and verse treatments might well be behind his prose treatment of the English saint in *Historia ecclesiastica* 4.19 followed in *Historia ecclesiastica* 4.20 by a fifty-four line hymn in abcedarian elegiac serpentines which Alcuin considered *praeclari* or "splendid". In spite of the rhetorical tour de force Bede presented in his verses on St. Æðeldreda, the Old English translator of the *Historia ecclesiastica* chose not to render them at all, and to offer no indication that they were ever there. Apparently, this translator would have agreed with Hamlet's mother that "more matter with less art" was required. Nevertheless, Szarmach shows how his translation may have anticipated, in small points of style, structure, and specific renderings, the reception of the established cult of Æðeldreda, who came to be regarded as one of the three major English saints of the twelfth century, in league with Cuthbert and Edmund.

Appropriate to a collection with "gender" in its title, Szarmach also examines the position of Æðeldreda, rather than Hild, as Bede's epitome of womanly virtue. Hild may suit our tastes today as a proper feminist, with her political aptitude and administrative abilities, but for Bede's time Æðeldreda is the proper model of womanhood, representing chastity as the productive virtue that Spenser would again declare it to be eight hundred years later in the character of Britomart. Æðeldreda gains power in her monastery through abasement and humility, and this leads Bede to offer up *praeclarissimi* verses to her, but as her history continued outside Bede's book, the Old English translator had to make decisions about representing a personage as well established in his time as George Washington has become in our own. His interaction with Bede's text thus offers perspective on other accounts in Bede and the many forces at work in the shape their continuing presentation would take.

Katherine O'Brien O'Keeffe's "Goscelin, the *Liber confortatorius*, and the Library of Peterborough" examines Goscelin of Saint-Bertin's *Liber confortatorius*, an instructional work that he wrote for Eve of Wilton after she departed for reclusion in Angers, ca. 1080, partly as a tract on the consolation provided by the saints—especially women saints—for Eve and partly to console himself at her leaving. O'Keeffe sets herself the daunting task of determining where Goscelin took up residence while he wrote the *Liber confortatorius* by matching his pattern of citations against a library inventory (Oxford, Bodleian Library, Bodley 163, fols. 250–51) that Michael Lapidge assigned to Peterborough. It's a difficult business, as she admits, haunted by the problem of identifying the exact exemplar of any text. Since one must depend upon replication of error in the copy texts merely to suggest a connection, proving one is all but impossible. Furthermore, as O'Keeffe admits, Lapidge's argument for assigning the bifolium booklist in MS Bodley 163 to Peterborough is not certain.

All of these shortcomings are admitted, however, and I draw further attention to them here, because it is appropriate to emphasize that the case is not fully proven. And yet, O'Keeffe's contribution to Goscelin studies here is immense. She has initiated work that will bear significant fruit as a full and careful text-historical account of the *Liber confortatorius* is constructed, by O'Keeffe herself, I should hope; she has moreover added to the study of monastic libraries and their use that many of us have been attempting to enlarge during the last decade or so. We can now say that Goscelin most likely used the library at Peterborough where he was resident while composing his masterpiece of epistolary treatise; for the first time we have a place to stand and a reason to stand there, until someone offers a better solution to the problem.

In "The Lady and the Vine: Putting the Horsewoman on the Hilton of Cadboll Cross-slab into Context," Kellie S. Meyer examines another Valkyrie-like figure, the "Pictish Queen" depicted on the Hilton of Cadboll cross-slab. The stone exists in two parts, the upper, main part now surviving in the National Museum of Scotland. This part of the monument was broken from its place at St. Mary's Chapel just outside of Hilton of Cadboll in 1676 and defaced in an effort to make it into a tombstone for Alexander Duff and his three wives, although it was never used as such. In 2001, the bottom of the stone was excavated at St. Mary's Chapel and is being conserved on site.

Of special interest on the cross-slab is the prominent position of the female rider, as well as the presence of trumpeters, and Meyer suggest that these modifications to a standard hunt scene create a multilayered stone text that compliments a unique inhabited vine-scroll on the stone. A wide range of biblical and exegetical tableaux are called to mind if the so-called hunt scene in fact figures a wedding ceremony. The lady may be a secular bride, or an anchoritic "Bride of Christ," or even the "Bride of Revelations," while the angels blow the last trump at the second coming and Last Judgment. As Meyer notes, the scene reifies the idea of a covenant, commemorating perhaps a secular marriage, religious vows, or the profound covenant between Christ and (wo)mankind. This is a wonderful, ambitious interpretation of the iconographic program of the cross-slab, one that challenges the simplistic notion that the Ruthwell and Bewcastle crosses both preceded and initiated the development in Northumbria of Christian imagery, which then spread to Pictish works, and one that suggests a complexity of interpretations that is perhaps only matched at Ruthwell and Bewcastle.

David N. Klausner offers "Petitionary Poetry in Old English and Early Welsh: *Deor, Widsið, Dadolwch Urien*" in a petition of his own to widen the genre of petitionary poetry. Indeed, Klausner's essay offers exactly the sort of problem that Helen herself loves to take on, because it suggests another way of thinking about an established problem. One would assume that petitionary poetry would simply refer to a poem that asks for something, e.g., money, land, the hand of your daughter. The fourteenth-century Welsh *canu gofyn* does just this; it asks for a material object. But the Welsh tradition also includes the earlier *dadolwch*, where the patron is asked for something more abstract, such as reconciliation or reinstatement to a position of favor, a situation easily paralleled in *Deor*. Might we not bracket both traditions under a single genre of the petitionary poem? Certainly, there was poetry in early Britain in which a request was made of a patron, and there seems to be no need to restrict this genre to Wales, given the presence of *Deor* and *Widsið*. It may be that Anglo-Saxon poems are subtler in how they go about framing the petition than are the Welsh poems, requests being made implicitly and not explicitly, but that should not exclude them from the tradition.

In "Revisiting Anglo-Scandinavian Settlement and Sculpture," Christopher D. Morris of the University of Glasgow's Department of Archaeology examines the relationship of Anglo-Scandinavian sculpture to the evidence for landholding and settlement at estate-centers and vills. My summary of this article cannot justly represent the detail Morris provides in both words and images. The most dramatic evidence, however, for such generalizations as he is willing to make derives from the remarkable evidence at Socceburg or modern-day Sockburn on Tees in the Tees Valley. Between the beginnings of an important eighth-century ecclesiastical site at Sockburn and its later recordation in the eleventh century as having reverted to the community, high status secular patrons of Scandinavian origin or extraction presided there. The question is open as to whether this Scandinavian presence derived from the post-876 or post-918 periods of Scandinavian control in this area, but Morris submits that the site probably functioned as a secular estate for an aristocratic follower of the Scandinavian ruler Raegnald in the tenth century. Although we have no surviving documentary record, Scandinavian or Anglo-Scandinavian rulers left their imprint (and maybe even their portraits, Morris suggests) in a grand collection of sculpture, the foundation of which still survives. These survivals represent the contribution of sculpture to our understanding of settlement and landholding in the north of England as Scandinavians and English vied for eminent domain.

Coming to praise Helen not of Troy but of Albuquerque, Roberta Frank writes in the headnote to her contribution in words that almost cry out to be clothed in hexamerate dactylics: "Greece may have nurtured Helen, America may have embraced her, but it was the North and its poetry, pounding with the surge of the Atlantic, that won her heart." Thus, "The *Málsháttakvæði* or 'Proverb Poem' Englished" is a most appropriate offering to the author of *Beowulf and the Valkyrie Tradition*. The rhythmic, pounding *Málsháttakvæði* is a collection of gnomic materials and allusions to mythical tropes, vignettes, and "situations." It is difficult not to find something to like in a poem with lines like these: "A prince should be especially brave. / A frog can croak in the marshes," which offers a motto to any number of our present leaders. "A dog is shaped for barking" recalls Alexander Pope's notion of wit as what was "ne'er so well expressed"; and the enigmatic predication that "The living man always rejoices in a cow" begs careful analysis of the sort we find in Benjamin's Franklin's "Advice to a Young Man."

The *Málsháttakvæði* was composed in Orkney in the early thirteenth century and it is found in the Codex Regius, famous for its copy of Snorri's *Edda*. It is, in fact, a wonderful example of the tradition that we find in Old English poems like *Deor* or *Precepts*, poems whose essence derives from pithy mouthfuls of traditional material woven into a single composition. To my mind, the concluding statement of *Wulf and Eadwacer*—"what is destroyed with ease never could be strong. Thus our story together"—gives closure to the thin and allusive narrative, exploits a register that both signifies the speaker's voice and reverberates with a sympathetic counselor's words, and leaves a modern reader with an overwhelming sense of the enduring power of what is candidly simple. Frank's authoritative translation of *Málshát-takvæði* is another demonstration of such disarming simplicity, most unusual among skaldic poems; it is, as she writes, "unparalleled, unforgettable, and worth sampling."

George Hardin Brown's "From the Wound in Christ's Side to the Wound in His Heart, Progression from Male Exegesis to Female Mysticism" traces the history of a change in the iconography of Christ's Crucifixion from the detail of his passion to the symbol of his sacrifice. In poetry and art of the West, it is an important change, most famously in modern times echoed by T. S. Eliot in *The Wasteland*: "Come into the shadow of this red rock, and I will etc." In the vernacular of the Anglo-Saxons, we find it in *The Dream of the Rood*, and—I might add—in *The Descent into Hell*.

In the eleventh and twelfth centuries, the devotions of monks, pedants, and divines who tended to create the rhetoric of Christian religious practice underwent a major change from the thoughtful rumination proposed in the Benedictine Rule to the graphic emotive mysticism that we identify with later medieval mystics, such as Julian of Norwich. In the earlier periods, the wound in Christ's side merely opened his body in a symbolic way to allow access to grace, but in the later period, the wound in his side implied a wound in his heart, so that the source of his life and symbol of his love are driven back onto humanity.

Richard K. Emmerson's "Translating Images: Image and Poetic Reception in French, English, and Latin Versions of Guillaume de Deguileville's *Trois Pèlerinages*" is part of a longer project in which Emmerson studies the intersection of linguistic and visual materials in late medieval manuscripts in order to appreciate how several groups of readers did in fact read these poems. In this essay, he restricts his analysis to the popular fourteenth-century poetic trilogy in French, English, and Latin, Guillaume de Deguileville's *Trois Pèlerinages*, asking how the language, genre, layout, and illustration of such medieval texts were designed for their audiences. Guillaume's pilgrimage poems, like Chaucer's poetry and much other fourteenth-century writing, were most likely originally intended to be read aloud to their audience, and by the sixteenth century they were sufficiently eminent to appeal to readers in the new medium of print. In the fifteenth century, however, they were received in new linguistic and generic versions in an array of manuscripts. In Yorkshire, Carthusians assembled a humble miscellany including the poems of Deguileville's *Trois Pèlerinages* on the low end of the presentation spectrum, while a deluxe Latin book proclaiming itself designed for the duke of Bedford represents the high end of this spectrum during that period. Along the way, we might note a didactic Middle English translation for an anonymous lady on the one hand and a textless cycle of pictures in a book of hours produced for a wealthy duchess on the other.

In our more textually conservative time, we are perhaps surprised to discover how malleable a text could be in earlier periods. Not only might the text be translated into another language but a designer might choose how much or how little of a text would be copied and illuminators might substitute artistic renderings for whole blocks of text, thus meeting the needs of their differing audiences. Emmerson argues that such reworking was as significant to the needs of the fifteenth century as were later changes made for readers of printed editions.

The calamitous fourteenth century witnessed the Hundred Years' War, the plague known as the Black Death, the Great Schism, and in England the peasants' revolt and the abdication of King Richard II. On the other hand, the century marks the year in which Dante found himself midway through this life's journey and wrote about it as reflected through the three realms of the afterlife; it marks the year of the first Papal Jubilee, as well as the first year of the new century. In his essay, "Dante's Views on Judaism, Christianity, and Islam: Perspectives from the New (Fourteenth) Century," Christopher Kleinhenz examines "the infamous 'pageant of the Church': a moving allegorical tableau representing a thousand years of vicissitudes of the Church, from its early persecutions to its final physical and spiritual debasement in Avignon." Through all of this, Dante maintained, Kleinhenz argues, a degree of equanimity towards both Jews and Muslims. It was Christian decadence and anarchy that evoked his disapprobation, and it was suggesting corrections to these things that called forth his finest rhetoric. Dante knew that what was wrong with Christianity—and therefore with his own culture—could not be laid at the door of Islam or Judaism. Even though, in the *Inferno*, Mohammad and Ali are seen as schematics and punished though the continuous cleaving of their bodies most foully described, yet when in *Paradisio* Thomas Acquinas speaks of an attempt by St. Francis of Assisi to convert Muslims, he speaks in terms of fertility and growth, suggesting that "Islam, though yet too proud, will someday be ripe for conversion, and unity in the Christian flock will be reestablished." While such a sentiment patronizes Muslims in today's religiously conflicted world, we must nevertheless allow that Dante's position on the religions of the Book is much more complex than we are used to attributing to the Middle Ages.

Thus, much is covered, and much is adjusted in these essays that we thought we had already settled. But as we have learned over and over from Helen Damico, there is always a little something more to say, something more to note and remember and add to the way we look at things—things such as gender, place, and poetry—in all their manifestations.

THE WEARMOUTH ICON OF THE VIRGIN (A.D. 679): CHRISTOLOGICAL, LITURGICAL, AND ICONOGRAPHIC CONTEXTS

ÉAMONN Ó CARRAGÁIN

In autumn 679, Benedict Biscop returned from Rome to Wearmouth, to the monastery which five years before in 673–74, he had founded and dedicated to St. Peter.[1] On the long journey from Rome, Benedict had been accompanied by Ceolfrid, who was to succeed him as abbot, and by a Roman abbot, John, also called *archicantator*, that is, 'archcantor'. John was the precentor, responsible for the liturgy and its chant, at St. Peter's on the Vatican.[2] In his *Historia abbatum*, Bede gives us an extensive list of the pictures Benedict Biscop brought back for his new monastery:

> Quintum, *picturas* imaginum sanctarum quas ad ornandam aecclesiam beati Petri apostoli, quam construxerat, detulit; imaginem uidelicet beatae Dei genetricis semperque uirginis Mariae, simul et duodecim apostolorum, quibus mediam eiusdem aecclesiae testudinem, ducto a pariete ad parietem tabulato praecingeret; imagines euangelicae historiae quibus australem aecclesiae parietem decoraret; imagines uisionum apocalipsis beati Iohannis, quibus septentrionalem aeque parietem ornaret, quatinus intrantes aecclesiam omnes etiam litterarum ignari, quaquauersum intenderent, uel semper amabilem Christi sanctorumque eius, quamuis in imagine, conteplarentur aspectum; uel dominicae incarnationis gratiam uigilantiore mente recolerent; uel extremi discrimen examinis, quasi coram oculis habentes, districtius se ipsi examinare meminissent.[3]

> (Fifthly, he brought back many holy pictures of the saints to adorn the church of St Peter he had built: a painting of the Mother of God, the

---

1. The standard work on the history and archaeology of monasticism at Wearmouth and Jarrow is now Cramp, *Wearmouth and Jarrow*. The present paper, which argues that the Wearmouth iconographic program of 679 is best understood in relation to the achievements of two monks from the Latin West (Benedict Biscop and John the Archcantor) and two from the Greek East (Maximus the Confessor and Theodore of Tarsus and Canterbury) is offered in celebration of Helen Damico, whose scholarly and administrative achievements have united the best qualities of the Eastern (Greek) and Western (Latin) traditions.

2. On the visit of John the Archcantor to Northumbria, see the recent discussion in Ó Carragáin, *Ritual and the Rood*, pp. 81–93, 223–28.

3. Bede, *Historia abbatum*, ch. 6, in *Venerabilis Baedae opera historica*, ed. Plummer, 1: 369–70.

Blessed Mary Ever-Virgin, and one of each of the twelve apostles which
he fixed round the central arch on a wooden entablature reaching from
wall to wall; pictures of incidents in the gospels with which he decorated
the south wall, and scenes from St John's vision of the apocalypse for the
north wall. Thus all who entered the church, even those who could not
read, were able, whichever way they looked, to put themselves more firmly
in mind of the Lord's Incarnation and, as they saw the decisive moment
of the Last Judgement before their very eyes be brought to examine their
conscience with all due severity.)[4]

In this account, Bede naturally gives pride of place to the pictures nearest the altar. When they entered St. Peter's church at Wearmouth visitors
might well have turned to left or right to admire the narrative images on
the south or north walls; but, as they advanced towards the altar, the iconic
image of the Mother of God, flanked by (smaller?) icons of the twelve apostles, would have been directly before their eyes.[5] This essay examines the
question of why, from autumn 679, these particular icons were given such
prominence in the chancel at Wearmouth.

In recent times, there has been excellent discussion of the way in which
the icons of the Virgin and the apostles may have been arranged.[6] Paul
Meyvaert demonstrated that the icons were panel paintings, and that Bede
used the word *tabulatum* to refer to wood- or plank-work, whether horizontal or vertical.[7] Meyvaert argued that the *tabulatum* consisted simply of
the paintings themselves, rather than of a wooden arch or frame to which
they might have been attached. He also argued that all thirteen icons were
arranged in a single horizontal row, stretching across the chancel or sanctuary arch, even though he himself had emphasized that *tabulatum* could
refer to vertical as well as to horizontal rows.[8] Meyvaert also demonstrated
that the panels must have been placed on, or close to, the chancel arch.
Rosemary Cramp has shown that the altar was probably forward of this
arch, which opened on to "the *porticus* of the Blessed Peter, to the east of
the altar" ("in porticu beati Petri, ad orientem altaris") in which Benedict
would later be buried. To this eastern *porticus* the bones of abbots Eoster-

4. Trans. in *Age of Bede*, ed. Farmer, pp. 190–91.

5. Kitzinger, "Interlace and Icons," pp. 6–7.

6. See, for example, George Henderson, *Bede and the Visual Arts*, pp. 5 and 13–18; and
Meyvaert, "Bede and the Church Paintings."

7. Meyvaert, "Bede and the Church Paintings," pp. 70, 73.

8. Meyvaert, "Bede and the Church Paintings," pp. 72–73: "Bede is thinking of a straight
line of panelling. . . . the word *tabulatum* itself does not tell us whether it was in a vertical or
a horizontal position."

wine and Sigfrid would also be translated, to join those of Benedict Biscop, in 716, or soon after.[9] Meyvaert saw that if all the icons were arranged in a single horizontal row across the arch from wall to wall they must have been rather small: as the church was some nineteen feet wide, each panel must have been, on average, only about seventeen inches wide.[10] Richard Gem reassessed Meyvaert's argument and concluded that "the *tabulatum* could have been a transverse wall of planks screening the sanctuary, while the *testudo* could be the entrance arch through the screen or, more probably, an altar canopy immediately beyond the screen. In this alternative arrangement the panel paintings would have been hung upon the screen structure—possibly in imitation of a Roman *cancellus* screen with a columnar superstructure on which icons were hung."[11]

Both in the arrangement suggested by Meyvaert (a horizontal row of icons spanning the chancel arch), and even more clearly in either of the two arrangements suggested by Gem (either along the vertical sides and horizontal top of a wooden frame for the chancel arch or on the columns and across the top of an altar canopy or ciborium), it is clear that the icon of the Virgin must have been the central feature of the sequence. The most probable arrangement has been succinctly described by Rosemary Cramp: "Another interpretation of the passage could be that the figures on their individual boards were placed on the wall dividing the nave and chancel and that Mary was in the high central position over the central opening, flanked on either side by the apostles."[12] In the arrangements proposed by Gem, the icon of the Virgin might have been flanked on each side by one or more icons of the apostles. It is likely that the horizontal row, just under the top of the chancel arch, would have included the most senior among them: St. Peter and his brother Andrew. The remaining apostle-icons might have been arranged in two vertical sequences, mounted either on each side of the wooden screen at the chancel arch, flanking the entrance to the altar area, or on an altar canopy or ciborium: presumably on its two

9. Bede, *Historia abbatum*, ch. 18, in *Venerabilis Baedae opera historica*, ed. Plummer, 1:394. On this layout of the area around the altar of St. Peter's basilica at Wearmouth, see Cramp, *Wearmouth and Jarrow*, 1:66–71; on the eastern *porticus* see Ó Carragáin, "Term *Porticus*," pp. 32–34; Cramp, *Wearmouth and Jarrow*, 1:70.

10. Meyvaert, "Bede and the Church Paintings," pp. 74–76; see also Cramp, *Wearmouth and Jarrow*, 1:33.

11. Gem, "Documentary References to Anglo-Saxon Painted Architecture," pp. 2–3; but, as we have seen above, Cramp proposes that the altar was before the chancel arch, and so in front of the icons.

12. Cramp, *Wearmouth and Jarrow*, 1:32.

columns nearest the nave. For example, if the Virgin was flanked only by
Peter and Andrew on the horizontal row (either on the wooden *tabulatum*
directly over the chancel entrance or at the top of an altar canopy), each
of the two vertical sequences of icons would have comprised five icons. If
a greater number of apostle-icons was placed on the horizontal row, each
vertical sequence might have had only four or even three icons.

Whether the icons were arranged as argued by Meyvaert, by Gem, or
by Cramp, it is clear that the icon of the Mother of God would have been at
the center of the sequence. Henceforth, any group of clerics proceeding up
the nave at St. Peter's towards the altar in front of the chancel area, or any
congregation standing or kneeling in the nave, is likely to have seen the
altar visually surmounted by an icon that celebrated Christ's Incarnation
within the Virgin's womb. Benedict Biscop ensured that, from the autumn
of 679, during each Mass a congregation at St. Peter's would have closely
associated the altar, at which the Passion of Christ was made present in
liturgical action, with an icon of the Virgin Mary, Mother of God.

The Mass provided a particularly suitable context, both for the icon
of the Virgin and for those of the flanking apostle-icons. At each Roman
Mass, before the consecration, the *Communicantes* prayer was recited.[13] This
included a list of saints that began with the Virgin Mary and proceeded
with a list of twenty-four other saints: the twelve apostles (including Paul
as one of the apostles) and twelve other saints, including five of the earliest
successors of St. Peter as bishops of Rome:[14]

> Communicantes, et memoriam venerantes, in primis gloriosae semper
> Virginis Mariae, Genetricis Dei et Domini nostri Iesu Christi, sed et bea-
> torum apostolorum ac martyrum tuorum, Petri et Pauli, Andreae, Jacobi,
> Joannis, Thomae, Jacobi, Philippi, Bartholomaei, Matthaei, Simonis et
> Thaddaei: Lini, Cleti, Clementis, Xysti, Cornelii, Cypriani, Laurentii,
> Chrysogoni, Joannis et Pauli, Cosmae et Damiani: et omnium Sanctorum
> tuorum; quorum meritis precibusque concedas, ut in omnibus protectio-
> nis tuae muniamur auxilio. Per eundem Christum Dominum nostrum.
> Amen.

---

13. This prayer occurs both in the Old Gelasian sacramentary (the manuscript which
survives, which was written in France about 750, supplements the list with a further nine,
mainly Gallican, saints) and in the Gregorian sacramentaries: see *Liber Sacramentorum*, ed.
Mohlberg, Siffrin, and Eisenhöfer, p. 184, par. 1246; *Sacramentaire grégorien*, ed. Deshusses,
1:88, par. 7. The text of the prayer given here corresponds to the Gregorian version.

14. On the structure and history of the prayer, see Kennedy, *Saints of the Canon of the
Mass*, pp. 97–148.

(In union with the whole church, we honor Mary, the ever-virgin mother
of Jesus Christ our Lord and God, the apostles and martyrs Peter and
Paul, Andrew, James, John, Thomas, James, Philip, Bartholomew, Matthew, Simon and Jude; we honor Linus, Cletus, Clement, Sixtus, Cornelius, Cyprian, Lawrence, Chrysogonus, John and Paul, Cosmas and
Damian, and all the saints. May their merits and prayers gain us your
constant help and protection. Through Christ our Lord. Amen.)

One wonders whether the Wearmouth set of apostle-icons might not possibly, like the *Communicantes* prayer, have been headed, not only by St. Peter,
but also by St. Paul, "the least of the Apostles" (I Corinthians 15:9). Most
of the ancient Roman apse-mosaics paired Peter with Paul, in the context
of the altar, and therefore a set that included St. Paul would be normal
for Rome.[15] To include Paul as "companion" to St. Peter would have anticipated Benedict's founding (from 681/2), of Wearmouth's twin monastery,
St. Paul's at Jarrow (formally dedicated on April 23, 685).[16]

To associate an icon of the Mother of God with apostle-icons was also
to recall the creeds, and so the faith of the Church. All the credal formulae
recited or taught at Wearmouth would have stated that Christ was "born of
the Virgin Mary."[17] By their very nature, confessional creeds were understood to encapsulate the pure faith of the apostles, and neither to add
nor to subtract from that faith.[18] The Creed was not yet sung at Mass, but
credal formulae were central to the ceremonies of the catechumenate and
baptism.[19] At the end of his life, in 734, Bede would urge Bishop Ecgbert
of York to ensure that each Northumbrian Christian should be taught the
Creed and the Our Father: he himself had by then given vernacular trans-

---

15. For the iconography of the early Roman apse mosaics, see Ihm, *Programme der christlichen Apsismalerei*.

16. On the early history and architecture of St. Paul's see Cramp, *Wearmouth and Jarrow*,
1:139–295.

17. See Kelly, *Early Christian Creeds*, p. 102 (Old Roman Creed: "qui natus est de Spiritu
sancto et Maria virgine": for discussion of this clause, see pp. 146–49); p. 297 (the Constan-
tinopolitan Creed accepted at the Council of Chalcedon, often known, inaccurately, as "the
Nicene Creed": "and was incarnate from the Virgin Mary and became man"); p. 402 (the
late seventh-century Creed in the Antiphonary of Bangor: "conceptum de Spiritu sancto,
natum de Maria virgine"); this, an elaboration of the Old Roman Creed, is similar to the
slightly later Creed known as the Apostles' Creed, p. 369 ("qui conceptus est de Spiritu
sancto, natus ex Maria virgine").

18. As the title "Apostles' Creed" implies (Kelly, *Early Christian Creeds*, pp. 1–6, 52–61).

19. Kelly, *Early Christian Creeds*, pp. 30–61; de Puniet, "Trois homélies catéchétiques";
trans., *Documents*, ed. Whitaker, pp. 174–77 (Old Gelasian), p. 201 (*Ordo Romanus XI*).

lations of the Latin texts to priests ignorant of Latin.[20] Since the fourth century, the Our Father had come to be recited at each Mass.[21] The liturgy of Lent was centered on the rites of initiation, of which an important element was the "handing on" to the catechumens of the Our Father, the Creed, and the four gospels. During the lenten catechumenate, the Church was seen as a Virgin mother, eagerly looking forward to bringing her catechumens to new birth from the womb of the font. The catechumenate, a time of spiritual growth in the womb of the Church, was seen to reenact the growth of Christ in the womb of the Virgin. But when in baptism the neophytes came forth to new life from the womb of the font, during the Easter Vigil, they were immediately brought to the altar to receive Communion. Thus, the true climax of the rites of initiation was seen to be eucharistic participation in the Body of Christ.[22] As the Virgin Mary and the apostles were united at each Mass in the *Communicantes* prayer, and as the catechumenate (understood as a new birth in the virginal womb of the Church) involved the "handing on" of the Creed and culminated in the reception of the Eucharist, it made good symbolic sense visually to associate the altar area with icons of the Virgin and the apostles.

Benedict Biscop made his icon of the Mother of God the visual climax not only of the sequence on or near the chancel arch but of the whole iconographic program for his new church. From the earliest Christian traditions, celebration of the Eucharist was understood to have important eschatological implications: it was seen as a pledge which Christ had left to his body the Church that he, the head of that body, would reveal himself in glory at the Parousia: as St. Paul had put it, "as often as you eat this bread and drink the cup, you proclaim the Lord's death until he comes" (I Corinthians 11:26).[23] Benedict's program included paintings of episodes from the gospels on the south wall of the church, and as we have seen the catechumenate included a ceremony in which the gospels were symbolically "handed on" to the catechumens. Opposite these scenes, there was a set of eschatological scenes on the north wall. Within Benedict's lifetime, Roman

---

20. Bede, *Letter to Ecgbert*, section 5, in *Venerabilis Baedae opera historica*, ed. Plummer, 1:408–9 (text), 2:380–81 (notes); trans. in *EHD*, ed. Whitelock, pp. 737–38.

21. Jungmann, *Mass of the Roman Rite*, 2:277–93.

22. *Documents*, ed. Whitaker, p. 204, par. 103 (translating *Ordo XI*). This document makes it clear that even infants were given Communion directly after being baptized: see the discussion of the catechumenate and infant baptism in Ó Carragáin, "Between Annunciation and Visitation," pp. 158–59 and n. 69; Ó Carragáin, *Ritual and the Rood*, pp. 120–79.

23. See Wainwright, *Eucharist and Eschatology*.

liturgical developments had begun to connect Christ's nativity still more intimately to his imminent return in glory. In the second half of the seventh century, the liturgists of the papal *schola cantorum* at the Lateran gradually gave definitive shape to the Roman version of the season of Advent. They elaborated that season as a carefully structured penitential season before Christmas, the midwinter feast of Christ's Incarnation.[24] The Roman Mass-readings for Advent had been systematized by the mid-seventh century. They made it clear that in Advent the Church prepared to celebrate, not only Christ's incarnation at Bethlehem, but also his return in glory at the end of human history.[25] Eschatological themes were particularly important on the second Sunday of Advent, when the pope went in procession from the Lateran to celebrate solemn Mass at the basilica known as Hierusalem. That basilica provided an appropriate setting for celebrating the eschatological dimension of Advent: images of the heavenly Jerusalem, and of the signs of approaching Judgment, dominated its Mass-chants and readings.[26] The gospel was taken from St. Luke (21:25–33): "There will be signs in the sun, the moon, and the stars, and on the earth distress among the nations."[27] The sentence in which Bede summed up the devotional impression which the Wearmouth iconographic program made on himself and his community encapsulates the themes of the Roman Advent: the icons encouraged all who entered the monastic church to "put themselves more firmly in mind of the Lord's Incarnation and, as they saw the decisive moment of the Last Judgement before their very eyes be brought to examine their conscience with all due severity."[28] Bede clearly understood the icon of the Virgin to be central to the whole iconographic program in the church.

Benedict Biscop's decision to place his new icon of the Mother of God in a significant relationship to the altar of St. Peter's had particular relevance to the situation of the English Church in autumn 679. For a genera-

---

24. McKinnon, *Advent Project*, pp. 125–53.

25. McKinnon, *Advent Project*, pp. 146–53. McKinnon argued convincingly that the Lateran *schola cantorum* did not complete its task of composing elaborate chants for Advent until the reign of Pope Sergius (686–701). However, he makes it clear that their work was based on earlier, less formal, Roman traditions of Advent, reflected for example in the earliest gospel-capitulary, now preserved in Würzburg: McKinnon, *Advent Project*, pp. 147–49 and table 8 on p. 148.

26. McKinnon, *Advent Project*, tables on pp. 130 and 138.

27. Lenker, *Westsächsische Evangelienversion*, p. 342, no. 259.

28. Bede, *Historia abbatum*, ch. 6, quoted in n. 3 above.

tion, the question of whether Christ had a human will had led to schism between Constantinople and Rome: in 679 it had become possible for the young English Church to play an active part in resolving the schism. Ten years before, in 669, Benedict Biscop had accompanied Theodore of Tarsus from Rome for his installation as archbishop of Canterbury, after which Biscop had worked for two years with Theodore as abbot of the monastery of St. Peter's at Canterbury.[29] Theodore's appointment to Canterbury ensured that, under his leadership, the English Church would quickly attain a new awareness of its place within the universal Christian Church. On his return to England, Benedict Biscop on September 17, 679, attended a Church synod at Hatfield.[30] The synod was important: Archbishop Theodore of Canterbury, considered to be the greatest living expert on the Monothelete controversy, presided. Pope Agatho had sent Abbot John the Archcantor as his special representative. On September 17, 679, the Council of Hatfield solemnly stated the faith of the English Church that Christ, as well as participating fully in the divine will that he shared with the Father and the Holy Spirit, had a separate, fully human will distinct from though coherently united with the divine will; it rejected the heresy of Monotheletism, which had denied that Christ had a will of his own.

In the 630s, Monotheletism had been espoused, primarily for political reasons, by the imperial administration at Constantinople. The emperor Constans II had issued a formal command (*Typos*: 'edict' or 'order') forbidding any further discussion of Christ's human will. The pope, Theodore (642–49), refused to accept the *Typos*; it seems likely that before his death he had already planned a Roman synod which would formally state the theological reasons why the *Typos* was heretical. It was left to his successor, Pope Martin I, a native of Todi in Umbria, to execute and be executed for Theodore's defiant policy. Martin, who was consecrated on July 5, 649, without waiting for the customary permission of the emperor, immediately convoked the planned synod at his episcopal basilica, the Lateran (October 6–31, 649). The Lateran Synod duly rejected Monotheletism and proclaimed the reality of Christ's human will. Rudolf Riedinger has shown that the formal acts of the Lateran Council were drafted in Greek, probably in advance of the council and possibly before the death of Pope Theodore, under the direction of the great Greek theologian, Maximus

29. Lapidge, "Career of Archbishop Theodore," pp. 26–27.
30. Chadwick, "Theodore"; Cubitt, *Anglo-Saxon Church Councils*, pp. 20–21, 27; *Councils*, ed. Haddan and Stubbs, 3:141–60; Ó Carragáin, *Ritual and the Rood*, pp. 79–83, 225–28.

the Confessor.[31] It has been argued that Theodore of Tarsus was one of the team of Greek-speaking monks who helped Maximus to draft the acts; it is possible that, in addition, Theodore attended the Lateran Council and signed its acts.[32] By 679 Theodore was considered to be the greatest expert in the West on the theological issues raised by the monothelete heresy: in 680 Pope Agatho was to write to the emperor Constantine IV that the only person in the Latin West who had a full understanding of the complex issues relating to the monothelete controversy was Theodore, "the philosopher and archbishop of Great Britain."[33] The acts of the Lateran Council, taken as a whole, provided a definitive synthesis of the theology of Christ's human will and courage, which Maximus the Confessor had developed: to that theology it gave the authority of a synod presided over by the pope who by 679 had come to be accepted by the Church in East and West as a martyr for the faith.

The emperor Constans knew that doctrinal dissent could easily become a focus for political dissent, thus Roman defiance must quickly be quashed. The way in which Constans's first plan to do this misfired demonstrates how real was the danger to the unity of the Empire, which had in the previous decade lost so many Christian provinces to Islamic aggression. Constans gave the task of asserting his authority to Olympius, his exarch at Ravenna, who arrived at Rome when the Lateran Council was still in session: but when Olympius saw how strong the opposition to Monotheletism was, even among the Greek community and the army at Rome, he refused to carry out the imperial orders and set himself up as the independent ruler of Italy. Beat Brenk has argued that much of the seventh-century decoration of Santa Maria Antiqua must have been carried out in the pontificates of Theodore and Martin, and especially in the brief period (October 649 to summer 653) when Olympius ruled Rome as an independent city confident in its public opposition to Monotheletism.[34] Within Rome, Santa Maria was of clear political as well as ecclesiastical importance: it stood in the shadow of the imperial palace on the Palatine and near the

---

31. *Concilium Lateranense*, ed. Riedinger, pp. xxvii–xxviii.
32. Lapidge, "Career of Archbishop Theodore," pp. 21–23.
33. Lapidge, "Career of Archbishop Theodore," p. 23.
34. Brenk, "Kultgeschichte versus Stilgeschichte"; Brenk, "Papal Patronage." The present account of the monothelete crisis complements and corrects that in Ó Carragáin, *Ritual and the Rood*, p. 227, written when, not yet having read the recent studies by Brenk, I did not understand the importance of the exarch Olympius for understanding the seventh-century frescoes in Santa Maria Antiqua.

Greek quarter (*schola Graeca*), and provided a basilica in the Forum Romanum for the Greek community of Rome. The separation from the Empire
of an independent Italy only ceased when in summer 652 Olympius, on
campaign to expel Arab invaders from Sicily, died of fever. A new exarch,
Theodore Calliopas, was quickly sent to reassert imperial authority in Italy;
he entered Rome on June 15, 653. In vain did Pope Martin, seriously ill,
claim refuge by placing his portable bed or stretcher before the altar in
the Lateran: on the morning of Monday, June 17, Theodore arrested him
there in the basilica.[35] Maximus the Confessor was also arrested; both
were taken separately as prisoners to Constantinople, tried, and finally
martyred: Pope Martin on September 16, 655, the last pope to suffer martyrdom; Maximus the Confessor on August 13, 662. By the late 670s, however, Constans II's son and successor, Constantine IV, had decided to reject
Monotheletism, and in this way to restore theological unity to the Church
in East and West. Pope Agatho (678–81) welcomed the imperial offer of
reconciliation, and requested the Churches of the West to discuss the matter and to send their conclusions to Rome. The responses were to form
part of a considered Western reply, to be reported at the Sixth Ecumenical
Council, held at Constantinople in 681, which would put an end to the
monothelete schism. The synod of Hatfield was, thus, of considerable ecumenical significance. Benedict Biscop and John the Archcantor brought
to Wearmouth a copy of the Latin acts of the Lateran Council of 649. The
acts were deposited in the library of Benedict's new monastery, and the
synod of Hatfield solemnly declared that the English Church accepted the
teaching of the Lateran Council. That council had declared that Christ
"willed and effected our salvation at once divinely and humanly" ("utpote
volentem et operantem Divine et humane nostram salutem").[36] Its tenth
canon declared that in Christ two wills, divine and human, were *cohaerenter
unitas* 'coherently united'; the eleventh canon in addition affirmed that
in Christ two principles of action, divine and human, were also *cohaerenter
unitas*.[37]

The coherent unity between Christ's divine will and his human will
was a crucial issue: monothelete theologians had objected that, if Christ

---

35. For the political importance of Roman opposition to Monotheletism, see Bertolini,
Roma, pp. 329–50.
36. Prologue to the Acts, *Councils*, ed. Haddan and Stubbs, 3:146; *Concilium Lateranense*,
ed. Riedinger, p. 367.
37. *Councils*, ed. Haddan and Stubbs, 3:148; *Concilium Lateranense*, ed. Riedinger, p.
375.

had a human will, it must at times have been in conflict with the divine will in which he shared.[38] The opponents of Monotheletism stressed that Christ, uniquely among humans, never acted in conflict with the divine will. In a new dogmatic formula, the third canon of the Lateran Council proclaimed that Christ was uniquely incorruptible because he had been born without corruption from the Virgin Mary: "If anyone refuses to confess in accordance with the holy Fathers that the holy ever-virgin immaculate Mary is literally and truly Mother of God, inasmuch as in this last age she conceived without seed, of the Holy Spirit, and brought forth without corruption [*incorruptibiliter genuisse*] the very one who is literally and truly God the Word born of God the Father before all ages, her virginity remaining inviolate after this birth as well—let him be condemned."[39]

Because it was essential to the anti-monothelete position to stress that Christ's courage was incorruptible, even to the death on the Cross, precisely because he had been conceived and born without corruption, a new devotion to Christ's Incarnation, and so to his Virgin mother, was central to Roman opposition to Monotheletism: Per Jonas Nordhagen and Beat Brenk have shown how central this new devotion was to the seventh-century frescoes in Santa Maria Antiqua.[40] This provides one context, among several, within which to understand why, in the two generations (between the 630s and the 680s) during which Monotheletism was a living issue, Roman basilicas gradually introduced four new feasts of the Virgin and commissioned a notable amount of Marian iconography (in particular images of the Annunciation).[41] Henceforth, Rome would celebrate Christ's virginal birth, not only at the Nativity (December 25) but on February 2, the feast of the Christ's presentation in the Temple (celebrated from the 630s); on

---

38. Hurley, "Born Incorruptibly," p. 230, points out that this is the first objection that the patriarch Pyrrhus raised against Maximus the Confessor in his debate with Maximus at Constantinople in 641 (PG 91:291A).

39. Trans. Hurley, "Born Incorruptibly," p. 216; for the Latin text of the canon, see *Councils*, ed. Haddan and Stubbs, 3:146; for the Greek and Latin texts, *Concilium Lateranense*, ed. Riedinger, pp. 370–71.

40. Nordhagen, "Earliest Decorations in Santa Maria Antiqua"; Brenk, "Kultgeschichte versus Stilgeschchte"; Brenk, "Papal Patronage," relates the several new paintings of the Annunciation in Santa Maria Antiqua in this period to the defense of orthodoxy against Monotheletism, because "the Annunciation is the scene *Par excellance* that focuses on the human and the divine will of Christ" (p. 77).

41. I do not wish to argue that the new feasts should be understood simply as a reaction to Monotheletism, simply that the new feasts, introduced primarily for liturgical and devotional reasons, were nevertheless also consistent with the Christological and political concerns of the Roman Church in these two generations.

August 15, the feast of the Virgin's death (Dormition; later, Assumption) (from the 650s); on March 25, the feast of the Annunciation of the Lord (from the 660s); and finally, on September 8, the feast of the Nativity of the Virgin (from the 670s).[42] All four feasts, including a number of the readings assigned to them, were imported from Constantinople. Educated Roman clerics must have seen it as ironic that these recent liturgical innovations at Constantinople strengthened devotion to Christ's human birth from the Virgin Mother of God and thus reinforced the orthodox, and Roman, theological position: that Christ's incorruptible will stemmed from his human birth, in which his divine nature, begotten from the Father before all ages, became indissolubly united "as two [natures] in one flesh" (cf. "dua in carne una" [Genesis 2:24]) to his human body and his human nature, in and of the *thalamus* (bridal chamber) of Mary's womb.[43] By 679, Benedict Biscop and John the Archcantor would have been familiar with at least three of the new feasts: the Purification (February 2), the Annunciation (March 25), and the great *sollemnitas Sanctae Mariae* (her death, *Natale* into heaven, or Dormition: August 15).[44]

The acts of the Lateran Council begin with a memorable affirmation that Christ's unique Incarnation from the Virgin was central to the defense of Christian orthodoxy against Monotheletism. The acts record that, in his opening address to the council, Pope Martin explicitly associated the members of the council, the pastors of the Church, with the shepherds to whom on Christmas night the angels proclaimed the Incarnation of Christ. Pope Martin used the formula that would appear in the third canon of the council: "conceived without [male] seed, he went forth from the Virgin without corruption" ("sine semine conceptus incorrupte de uirgine processit"). In his speech, Pope Martin expanded on Gregory the Great's use of the etymology of the place-name Bethlehem: *domus panis* 'house of bread'. Gregory had made a close connection between Bethle-

---

42. For a table showing the approximate dates on which each of the four feasts was introduced into the papal and presbyteral rites at Rome, see Frénaud, "Culte de Nôtre-Dame," p. 184.

43. On Christ's divine and human births, reaffirmed by the fourth canon of the Lateran Council, see Ó Carragáin, *Ritual and the Rood*, pp. 61 and 82; on Mary's womb as *thalamus* in which divinity was wedded to humanity (Psalm 18/19:6) see ibid, pp. 322–23.

44. Mary Clayton has demonstrated that there was considerable confusion and error about the new feasts in England: significantly, the only insular writer who seems to have known all four accurately in the early eighth century, and whose account has come down to us, was Bede: Clayton, *Cult of the Virgin*, pp. 30–40.

hem, the "living bread" of the Eucharist, and Christ filling the minds of the faithful with spiritual food:

> Qui bene etiam in Bethleem nascitur; Bethleem quidem domus panis interpretatur. Ipse namque est qui ait: Ego sum panis uiuus qui de caelo descendi. Locus ergo in quo Dominus nasceretur, domus panis ante uocatus est, quia futurum profecto erat, ut ille ibi per materiam carnis appareret, qui electorum mentes interna satietate reficeret.

> ([Christ] is fittingly born in Bethlehem; for Bethlehem is interpreted as meaning "house of bread." For it is he who says "I am the living bread who has come down from heaven." Therefore, the place in which the Lord would be born was earlier called "house of bread," because it was to come about that he would there appear in the materiality of flesh, who would replenish the minds of the chosen ones with an inner fullness.)[45]

In the acts of the Lateran Council, Pope Martin establishes a similar chain of associations. The council gathers at the Lateran within a "spiritual Bethlehem"; the Catholic Church, in which the spiritual shepherds preserve their flock by teaching true doctrine about Christ's Incarnation from the Virgin and his eucharistic presence as Agnus Dei (Lamb of God):

> Euangelicus et *omnibus hominibus salutaris* (Titus 2:11) sermo, qui secundum uirtutem suae diuinae praedicationis *orbis terrarum fines* (cf. Romans 10:18, Psalm 18:5) conplexus est, uolens manifare ministros et praedicatores sollicitos esse nos dumtaxat, qui Christiani populi pastoris suscipere meruimus officium et sacerdotii diuinae incarnationis summaeque dispensationis, per quam nostram adsumens mirificae renouauit naturam, demonstrauit, sicut nostis, reuerentissimi fratres, *pastores uigilantes et conseruantes custodias noctis* (Luke 2:8), tunc uidelicet quando sine semine conceptus incorrupte de uirgine processit ipse qui propter nos incarnatus est deus. quibus et testatur euangelista dicens: *et festinantes uenerunt et uidentes cognouerunt de uerbo quod quod dictum est eis, et omnes qui audierunt mirati sunt de his quae dicta sunt a pastoribus.* quos et *gloria domini* e caelo *refulsit* et *multitudo militiae caelestis laudantium dominum et dicentium: gloria in altissimis deo et in terra pax hominibus bone uoluntatis* (Luke 2:16–18). Cum quibus oportet et nos praecipue, propter quos haec eadem scripta sunt, *conseruantes* cum summa uigilantia et sollicitudine *custodias* (Luke 2:8) de ouile nobis commisso, id est creditis nobis a domino populis in huius saeculi nocte, conuenientes *in unum intellectum eundemque sensum* (I Cor. 1:10), sicut dicit beatus Paulus apostolus, ac si in aliquam spiritalem *Bethleem* (Luke 2:8), quae est catholica dei et apostolica ecclesia, in qua

---

45. Gregory the Great, *Homiliae in Evangelia*, p. 54, Homily VIII, lines 8–13. Translation mine.

ipse *panis uitae* (cf. John 6:35) firmius conlocatur, quatenus cognoscere
et intendere in eo *sermonem* inmaculatae fidei debeamus, quem firmius
roborantibus nobis per traditas apostolicas paternasque promulgationes
ipsa domini gloria cum *militia caeleste* (Luke 2:9) et laudibus *enitescat* atque
mirentur et in nobis deum miraculorum *omnes qui audiunt* de pio nostro
studio sinceram in domino plenitudinem (cf. Luke 2:13).

(The gospel teaching, saving for all men, through the power of its divine
preaching has encompassed the ends of the earth: it wishes to produce
caring ministers and preachers. We have deserved to assume the office of
the shepherd of the Christian people, and to exercise the office of priesthood of the divine Incarnation. The highest dispensation, who in taking
on our nature wonderfully renewed it, showed forth, as you know, most
reverend fathers, shepherds waking and keeping the watches of the night.
This happened at the time when he, who was conceived without [male]
seed came forth without corruption from the Virgin: God, who for our
sake became incarnate. The evangelist bears witness to these events, saying *and they came in haste and, seeing, understood what had been said to them,
and all who heard wondered at what the shepherds had said. For the glory of the
Lord shone round about* them from heaven, *and a multitude of the heavenly
host, praising the Lord and saying: Glory to God in the highest and peace on
earth to men of goodwill.* It particularly behoves us, for whom these things
were written, to *keep guard* with great vigilance and care over the flock
entrusted to us, that is, over the peoples whom the Lord has committed
to our care, during the night of the present age. It behoves us to gather
together in one spirit and understanding, as the blessed apostle Paul says,
as though into a spiritual *Bethlehem,* which is the catholic and apostolic
Church, in which he, *the bread of life,* is safely placed: this means that, in
that Church, we should know, understand and express the true faith. *The
glory of the* same *Lord* is strengthened and shines forth in us, together with
the heavenly host and its praises, through the declarations of the Apostles
and of the Fathers; and all those who hear of the fullness of the Lord
through our zeal are amazed at the God of miracles.)[46]

To associate the icon of the Mother of God with the altar at St. Peter's Wearmouth was to provide the monastery with a visual reminder of the doctrine
of the Virgin Birth, a doctrine to which the third canon of the Lateran
Council had recently given a new and authoritative formulation. To place
the icon of the Virgin at the center of a set of icons of the apostles made it
clear that the Virgin Birth corresponded, in the words of Pope Martin, to
what the apostles had handed down and the Fathers proclaimed ("traditas apostolicas paternasque promulgationes"). The icon of the Virgin, and
the flanking icons of the apostles, together attested to Wearmouth's (and

---

46. *Concilium Lateranense,* ed. Riedinger, p. 11, lines 11–28.

Northumbria's) commitment to orthodoxy in the central Christological debate of the later seventh century.

Placing the icon of the Mother of God in the visual perspective of the altar at Wearmouth established a striking visual relationship between an image of the Incarnation and the altar at which, at every Mass, Christ's Passion was made present. Such a link between Incarnation and Passion was consonant with the liturgical thought of John the Archcantor, who in the winter of 679–80 taught the monks of Wearmouth the liturgical traditions of the Vatican.[47] In the 670s, the Vatican liturgists had composed their own special Mass for the new feast of the Annunciation. The Annunciation nearly always fell during Lent or Holy Week, and this posed a serious liturgical problem: how could the joy of Christ's Incarnation be celebrated properly in the season that prepared for his Passion? Of all the basilicas of the Western Church, only St. Peter's on the Vatican worked out an explicit theology to justify celebrating the Annunciation during Lent. Their Mass was entitled *Adnuntiatio Domini et Passio Eiusdem*; its Offertory prayer stated that the Mass was offered "on account of the Incarnation and likewise the Passion of our Redeemer Jesus Christ"; and its Collect, a masterpiece of liturgical thought, explicitly related the Incarnation to the Passion:

> Gratiam tuam quaesumus domine mentibus nostris infunde, ut qui angelo nuntiante Christi filii tui Incarnationem cognouimus, per passionem eius et crucem ad resurrectionis gloriam perducamur: qui tecum.[48]

> (We beseche thee, Lorde, powre thy grace into our heartes; that, as we haue knowen Christ, thy sonnes incarnacion, by the message of an Angell; so by hys crosse and passion, we maye be brought into the glory of his resurreccion; Through the same Christ our Lorde.)[49]

The strikingly original liturgical thought of the Vatican Mass drew on the ancient traditions of St. Martin's basilica at Tours. Since the late

---

47. See Ó Carragáin, "Ruthwell Crucifixion Poem," pp. 20–21; Ó Carragáin, *City of Rome*, pp. 16–20; Ó Carragáin, *Ritual and the Rood*, pp. 85–93.

48. *Liber Sacramentorum*, ed. Mohlberg, Siffrin, and Eisenhöfer, p. 29, no. 385. That the prayer *Gratiam tuam* might, seeing that it comes from the Vatican in the 670s, possibly have been composed by John the Archcantor himself, was first argued by Ó Carragáin, "Rome, Ruthwell, Vercelli."

49. I give the translation by Thomas Cranmer, who assigned the prayer as Collect for the Annunciation (Lady Day, 25 March), in the first prayer book of Edward VI: see Church of England, *First and Second Prayer Books of Edward VI*, p. 185. The history of this English prayer is discussed in Ó Carragáin, "Annunciation of the Lord," pp. 349–50, 364–78; Ó Carragáin, *Ritual and the Rood*, pp. 359–62.

fifth century, the monks at Tours had celebrated an annual vigil on March 27, to commemorate the anniversary of Easter. In addition to this commemoration of the anniversary of Easter, they also celebrated Easter in the normal way, as a moveable feast: but that Paschal Vigil was celebrated at the cathedral within the city, while the anniversary, on March 27, was celebrated in the basilica where St. Martin's body lay, outside the town walls. The idea that March 27 was the anniversary of Easter was calculated from the ancient Christian tradition, recorded from the second century (Tertullian, Hippolytus), that Christ had died on March 25, the spring equinox in the Julian calendar.[50] Thus, to justify celebrating the Annunciation during Lent, the Vatican liturgists turned to an ancient Christian tradition that had been given liturgical expression at Tours for almost two centuries. It was natural at that period for the Vatican to seek inspiration in Tours: the liturgy at St. Peter's was in the care of the monks of the monastery of St. Martin, which stood on the slope of the Vatican Hill, just outside the apse of the basilica. John the Archcantor, precentor of St. Peter's, was also abbot of St. Martin's. To celebrate March 25 as the anniversary of both the Annunciation of the Lord and his Passion was an idea which monks of St. Martin's would think of, and which would particularly appeal to John, their abbot. It is possible that, in the 670s, a short period before he set off with Benedict Biscop for Wearmouth and Hatfield, John himself as archcantor or precentor may have composed the Mass "Gratiam tuam." John, Benedict Biscop, and Ceolfrid visited Tours on the way to England, because John naturally had a particular devotion to St. Martin, patron of his own monastery on the Vatican.[51] John the Archcantor would certainly have appreciated the way in which Benedict visually associated the altar at Wearmouth with an icon commemorating the Incarnation.

What did Wearmouth's image of the Mother of God look like? It is impossible to be sure: at Rome itself, where at least six major early icons have survived, the chief characteristic of the group is its variety, both in size and in iconographic detail.[52] Ernst Kitzinger argued that the icons of the

---

50. Roll, *Towards the Origins of Christmas*, pp. 63–66, 79–106; Talley, *Origins of the Liturgical Year*, pp. 91–99.

51. Bede, *Historia abbatum*, ch. 6 (see n. 3 above); the present paragraph summarizes the argument of Ó Carragáin, "Rome, Ruthwell, Vercelli," pp. 62–73, where documentation of its hypothesis will be found.

52. Five of the early icons are reproduced and discussed in Amato, *Vera Effigie Mariae*. The variety of the early Roman icons has been emphasized by Belting, *Likeness and Presence*, pp. 63–73.

Mother of God and apostles on the Cuthbert Coffin, and the related icon of the Mother of God in the Book of Kells, may both have been inspired by the Wearmouth icons; his brilliant hypothesis may provide the best clue to the appearance of the Wearmouth icons.[53] Perhaps more useful are the three visual analogues that Rome provides for the way in which Benedict placed his Marian icon at Wearmouth in the visual perspective of the altar. Two of these analogues come from Santa Maria Maggiore on the Esquiline; the third from the Greek church, Santa Maria Antiqua in the Forum Romanum. The basilica of Sancta Maria on the Esquiline (later to be known as Santa Maria Maggiore), built in the second quarter of the fifth century, was the oldest basilica dedicated to the Mother of God in the Latin West. It was always particularly associated with Bethlehem: the Vigil Mass on Christmas Eve had been celebrated there since the mid-fifth century (while the Day Mass of Christmas had already been celebrated at St. Peter's since the mid-fourth century, when the feast first began to be celebrated in Rome). In the symbolic topography of the stational system, in which the pope celebrated Mass at particular basilicas on set days throughout the year, Sancta Maria was Rome's symbolic "Bethlehem."[54] In the period of the monothelete controversy, which was also the period of the Arab conquest of Jerusalem and Bethlehem, this association was strengthened. By the 640s, a chapel adjoined to the north or right side of the basilica (as one faced the altar) was believed to contain relics of the crib at Bethlehem. Because of this chapel and its cult of the crib, by the mid-seventh century the whole basilica had become known as Sancta Maria ad Praesepe (Saint Mary's at the Crib). Though Bethlehem had recently fallen to the forces of Islam, the most important feature of Bethlehem, the relics of Christ's crib, were understood to be safely in Rome, where they could always receive the cult that was their due.

The apse of Santa Maria Maggiore, above and behind the altar, was destroyed and rebuilt between 1288 and 1292. The mosaic of the thirteenth-century apse shows Christ crowning Mary Queen of Heaven. We do not know what the iconography of the original apse mosaic was like: it is most likely to have had an image of Christ in Glory at its center, but it is not impossible that the apse may have contained an image of the glori-

53. Kitzinger, "Coffin-Reliquary," pp. 263–65.

54. Baldovin, *Urban Character of Christian Worship*, pp. 148, 157; de Blaauw, *Cultus et Decor*, 1:57–66; Saxer, *Sainte-Marie-Majeure*, pp. 109–79.

fied Virgin Mary as *Theotokos* (mother of God).[55] The great chancel arch
viewed from the nave provides a visual frame for the altar and a transition
between the apse and the nave, and still preserves its fifth-century mosaics:
these provide the most important and extended fifth-century narrative iconography of Christ's incarnation, Epiphany, and flight into Egypt.[56] Possibly the fifth-century apse, but more probably the mosaic Incarnation-cycle
on the fifth-century arch over and behind the altar, may have inspired
Benedict Biscop to place his icons as a visual frame for the altar at St.
Peter's, Wearmouth. It seems possible that Benedict brought his icons to
Wearmouth so that, from autumn 679, the altar area of his new St. Peter's
should visually "cite" or recall that of the first and greatest Marian basilica
of the Western Church.

At Wearmouth, of course, there never was an apse: it seems likely the
icons hung, not only above the altar and behind it, but over and around
the arch that led to the "porticus Sancti Petri": in effect, to a separate chapel. If so, Santa Maria Maggiore possibly provided a second analogue for
Benedict's liturgical thought. Santa Maria Maggiore possessed, and still possesses, a revered icon of the Mother of God. Although the icon has been
much "restored," repainted, and revarnished over the centuries, it is possible that the original may date from the sixth century.[57] Until the end of
the thirteenth century, an icon (which may not have been the present one)
hung over the "Porta Reginae" (the 'Queen's Door'), which led from the
aisle to the fifth-century baptistery which adjoined the south or left wall of
the basilica.[58] The surviving sources that describe the icon as placed over the

55. For the hypothesis that the apse mosaic portrayed Christ in Glory see de Blaauw,
Cultus et Decor, 1:355–56; Saxer, *Sainte-Marie-Majeure*, pp. 50–51 (both studies have bibliogra-
phies of earlier discussions); for the hypothesis that the apse portrayed the glorified Virgin
Mary, see Andaloro and Romano, "L'immagine nell'abside," pp. 100–102 (with bibliography). Andaloro and Romano provide a good plate of the present apse showing clearly its
relation to the chancel arch (p. 99, fig. 76).

56. For a good synthesis of the iconography of the fifth-century mosaics in Santa Maria
Maggiore see Gandolfo, "La Basilica Sistina," and color plate pp. 110–11.

57. On the dating of the original icon, and its relation to the icon at present venerated
in the basilica, see Wolf, *Salus Populi Romani*, pp. 26–28; followed by Saxer, *Sainte-Marie-
Majeure*, pp. 201–2.

58. The "Porta Reginae" was opposite the space between the seventh and eighth pillars
from the entrance-door: see Wolf, *Salus Populi Romani*, pp. 103–5, who is followed by de Blaauw,
Cultus et Decor, 1:408, and 2: fig. 18, at C: "battistero e palazzo." In the Middle Ages there was
more than one icon in Santa Maria Maggiore: for discussion of the icons see Saxer, *Sainte-Marie-
Majeure*, pp. 94–95; Brenk, "Kultgeschichte versus Stilgeschichte," pp. 988–93. Howe, "Antoniazzo Romano," argued that the icon over the "Porta Reginae" was a different one from that at
present preserved in the basilica. Howe is followed by Andaloro, "L'Icona della Vergine," p. 124.

threshold (limen) of the baptistery date from the thirteenth century.[59] But to place a Marian icon over the entrance to a baptistery implies early theology, given classic expression by Pope St. Leo I. In a sermon preached at St. Peter's on Christmas Day 452, Leo closely associated the womb of the Virgin, in which humanity and divinity were united forever in the person of Christ, with the baptismal font, in which Christians became members of the body of Christ, and so were henceforth forever united to God: "He placed in the font of Baptism that very origin which he had assumed in the Virgin's womb. He gave to the water what he had given to his Mother. For, the same power of the Most High and overshadowing of the Holy Spirit (Luke 1:35) that caused Mary to bear the Saviour makes the water regenerate the believer."[60]

To place an icon of the Virgin over the archway that led to the baptistery was to provide a striking visual equivalent of this idea.[61] To approach the archway and cross the threshold of the baptistery, as the clergy and neophytes did for baptisms at Sancta Maria ad Praesepe during the Easter Vigil, was symbolically to proceed from the Virgin to the font: the spatial progression implied that the overshadowing of the Holy Spirit, which caused Mary to bear the Savior, now brings the neophytes to new birth from the font. If, as seems likely, an icon had already been hung over the threshold of the baptistery before the seventh century, we can be sure that educated English priest-monks like Wilfrid and Benedict Biscop would have seen the theological significance of where it was placed.[62]

---

59. Bartholomeus Tridentinus, *Liber epilogorum* (1244): "imago Virginis est in dextra parte ad fontes, quae dicitur 'Regina Coeli'" (the image of the Virgin is on the right side at the baptistery, which is called "Queen of Heaven") as printed in Wolf, *Salus Populi Romani*, p. 329 no. 18; Durandus, *Rationale divinorum officiorum* (written 1291–95), vol. 6, 89 (*De septem diebus post Pascha*): see *Guillemi Duranti*, ed. Davril and Thibodeau, CCCM 140A, p. 463, lines 58–60: "Premissa ymago in ecclesia Beate Marie maioris in Vrbe super limen baptisterii servatur, quam Romani Reginam uocant." (The aforesaid image in the church of Blessed Mary Major in Rome is kept over the threshold of the baptistery, which the Romans call the Queen.)

60. Leo the Great, Sermon 25, Section 5 in *Sermons*, trans. Freeland and Conway, p. 103, from *Sancti Leonis Magni*, ed. Chavasse, CCSL 138, p. 123: "Originem quam sumpsit in utero Virginis, posuit in fonte baptismalis, dedit aquae quod dedit matri: uirtus enim Altissimi et obumbratio Spiritus sancti, quae fecit ut Maria pareret Saluatorem, eadem facit ut regeneret unda credentem." This theme recurs throughout Leo's Christmas sermons: see the references in Ó Carragáin, "Between Annunciation and Visitation," p. 170, n. 90.

61. Slightly to the left, as one faces the high altar; see de Blaauw, *Cultus et Decor*, 2: fig. 18, at 11 ("Altare dell'icona della Vergine"). The baptistery was torn down in the late thirteenth or early fourteenth centuries to provide accommodation for the canons of the basilica: ibid., 1:408, 413.

62. The cult of the icon of Sancta Maria was closely connected with Easter and with the Old Roman antiphon *Regina Coeli laetare*, alleluia, sung during Easter Week: Durandus, *Rationale divinorum officiorum*, vol. 6, 89, 3: CCCM 140A, pp. 462–63; Wolf, *Salus Populi Romani*, pp. 107–14.

From autumn 679, in the words of Pope Martin at the Lateran Council (according to the acta which Benedict Biscop had just placed in the library), St. Peter's became an image of the "spiritual Bethlehem, which is the Catholic and Apostolic Church, in which he, the bread of life, is safely placed: this means that, in that Church, we should know, understand and express the true faith." The central tenets of that faith were expressed, not only by painted images, but by architectural space. At Wearmouth, Benedict Biscop placed his new icon of the Incarnation over the entrance to the eastern funerary chapel in which he presumably planned that he, the founder-abbot, should be buried. Christians believed that "as often as you eat this bread and drink the cup, you proclaim the Lord's death until he comes"; and that, "for as all die in Adam, so all will be made alive in Christ. But each in his own order: Christ the first fruits, then at his coming, those who belong to Christ" (I Corinthians 15:22–23). Thus the Eucharist, celebrated at the eastern altar towards which the congregation faced, was a pledge of the resurrection of the body, "for as the lightening comes from the east and flashes as far as the west, so will be the coming of the Son of Man. Wherever the corpse is, there will the eagles gather" (Matthew 24:27–28).[63] By placing the icon in a close visual relationship to the archway leading to the eastern funerary *porticus*, Benedict may have been thinking in similar terms to Leo the Great, that "the same power of the Most High and overshadowing of the Holy Spirit that caused Mary to bear the Saviour makes the water regenerate the believer." All educated Christians knew that "we have been buried with [Christ] by baptism into death, so that just as Christ was raised from the dead by the glory of the Father, so we too might walk in the newness of live" (Romans 6:4). The placing of the Marian icon at or near the transition between the altar and eastern *porticus* provided a visual and spatial equivalent for the synthesis of Christian experience that the Vatican collect for the new feast of the Annunciation had also recently encapsulated: "that, as we haue knowen Christ, thy sonnes incarnacion, by the message of an Angell; so by hys crosse and passion, we maye be brought into the glory of his resurreccion; Through the same Christ our Lorde."[64] The eastern funerary *porticus*, beyond the altar, used

---

63. On the eucharistic significance of Matthew 24:28, "ubi fuerit corpus illuc congregabuntur aquilae," see Ó Carragáin, *Ritual and the Rood*, pp. 145–46.

64. The first prayer book of Edward VI, Collect for March 25, quoted above. I do not of course wish to argue that Benedict Biscop was thinking of this prayer when planning the layout of St. Peter's; rather that St. Peter's and the Vatican *Gratium tuam* prayer each

space to symbolize the hope that participation in Christ's risen and glorified body, central to the Eucharist, was a pledge which would be redeemed
in the Resurrection of the body and life everlasting.[65]

Rome provides a third visual analogue for Benedict's decisive act. It
seems likely that, by the 640s, the apse mosaic of the Greek basilica of
Santa Maria Antiqua in the Roman Forum, represented the Mother of
God.[66] Beat Brenk has argued that the apse and its decoration may have
formed part of Pope Theodore's campaign against Monotheletism (642–
49). Probably in the brief period in which, in alliance with Pope Martin,
the exarch Olympius ruled an independent anti-monothlete Rome (October 649 to summer 653), the pope had the sixth- and early seventh-century
frescoes on the wall on either side of the apse, behind the altar, painted
over with a new series of portraits of Fathers of the Church. Traces of some
of these portraits remain: to the left of the apse as one faces the altar and
the absidal wall, Pope Saint Leo the Great and the Eastern saint Gregory Nazianzen; to the right, the Eastern saints Basil the Great and John
Chrysostom. These figures were about life-size, and as the four saints were
placed above a painted imitation-marble dado about one meter high, they
overlooked the *presbyterium*: they were clearly intended to be impossible
to miss.[67] Each of the four Fathers of the Church, flanking the apse and
overlooking the *presbyterium*, held a scroll on which a Greek text supporting
Dyotheletism was inscribed: these were chosen from among the proof-texts

---

independently provides a classic late seventh-century synthesis of the idea that the Incarnation, Passion, and Resurrection of Christ together formed a unified sacrament or mystery:
a pattern of religious experience in which Christians hoped to share. On seventh-century
understanding of the concepts of *sacramentum* and *mysterium* see Ó Carragáin, *Ritual and the
Rood*, pp. 120–26.

65. On the rationale for Benedict's decision to be buried east of the altar, see also
Ó Carragáin, "Term *Porticus*," pp. 31–33.

66. The apse was given a new fresco, representing Christ in Majesty, under Pope Paul
I (757–67), and practically no trace remains of the original absidal fresco: but the greatest
student of the Santa Maria Antiqua paintings, Per Jonas Nordhagen, accepted that "the
decoration of 650 probably included the apse as well" ("Earliest Decorations in Santa Maria
Antiqua," p. 61); and later fully accepted "the suggestion presented by earlier authors that it
had as its centre a figure of the Virgin, although Grüneisen's reconstruction of this figure as
a 'Maria Regina' is not substantiated by any visible remains" ("S. Maria Antiqua," p. 93). For
a clear recent summary of the phases of decoration in the apse area of Santa Maria Antiqua,
see Osborne, "Images of the Mother of God," pp. 138–40.

67. Nordhagen, "S. Maria Antiqua," pp. 97–100: height of the figures to the right of
the apse, including frames, ca. 190 cm. Distance from the floor to the height of the eyes
of the two saints: 283 cm. (ibid., p. 97); Ó Carragáin, *Ritual and the Rood*, p. 229 and pls.
13(a)–(b).

for Christ's human will read out at the Lateran Council of 649. This allows us to date the new program precisely to 649–53, and to be confident that it was intended to proclaim the opposition of the Roman Church to Monotheletism.[68] Soon after Pope Martin had been deposed and the monothelete crisis was still at its height, Benedict Biscop and Wilfrid, two intelligent and zealous young English monk-clerics, first visited Rome (Benedict was already ordained; Wilfrid would be ordained on his return to England). They are not likely to have missed the prominent frescoes, in the altar area of one of the most important churches in or near the Roman Forum, by which Pope Martin had recently publicized his rejection of Monotheletism. Though neither would have been able to read the Greek inscriptions for themselves, their bilingual Roman clerical friends could have informed them what the portraits, and inscriptions, implied: that in the political crisis then raging the emperor Constans was attacking ancient Christian traditions to which Rome held true.[69]

At Wearmouth, Benedict flanked his icon of the Mother of God with icons, not of the Fathers of the Church, but of the apostles. The theological statement implied by these apostle-icons was, however, consistent with, and possibly inspired by, Pope Martin's Fathers of the Church: as we have seen, the creeds, considered to encapsulate the faith of the apostles, stated that Christ had been born of the Virgin Mary. Credal formulae were of particular interest at Hatfield, the first synod to add to the Creed the "Filioque" clause, which stated that the Holy Spirit proceeds from God the Son as well as from God the Father.[70] It is possible that Pope Martin's program of frescoes in the *presbyterium* or altar area of Santa Maria Antiqua had a wider influence on Benedict's choice of icons for the Wearmouth program.

---

68. Transcriptions and discussion of sources in Gordon Rushforth, "Church of S. Maria Antiqua," pp. 68–72. All these texts are in Greek, even that taken from the Latin Tome of Leo the Great who is also labeled in Greek "the Pope of Rome."

69. The frescoes at Santa Maria Antiqua have survived because the basilica was abandoned and filled in with earth when ruined by an earthquake in the ninth century; it was excavated early in the last century.

70. Kelly, *Early Christian Creeds*, p. 363, comments on how odd it is that the *Filioque* should first be proclaimed at a synod presided over by an Eastern theologian, Theodore of Tarsus and Canterbury. Chadwick, "Theodore," pp. 88, 93–95, explained the Hatfield statement in the context of the monothelete controversy: Maximus the Confessor, martyred hero of the struggle against Monotheletism, had accepted the phrase. Chadwick also suggests that the acceptance of the *Filioque* at Hatfield may stem from tensions between Theodore and Wilfrid of York: Hatfield may have enabled Theodore to rebut accusations by Wilfrid that Theodore, as a Greek-speaking theologian, did not fully go along with the Western theological traditions which had first justified the *Filioque*.

As we have seen, the icons on the southern wall of St. Peter's, Wearmouth, provided "imagines euangelicae historiae," images of events in the gospels. Pope Martin's program of decoration on the side walls of the *presbyterium* at Santa Maria Antiqua also included scenes from the life and Passion of Christ: for example, traces survive of a "Carrying of the Cross to Calvary."[71] In placing narrative scenes of the events of scripture along the nave walls of his new church, Benedict was making it more like the great basilicas of Rome: not only Santa Maria Antiqua but Sancta Maria ad Praesepe (where the greater part of the fifth-century mosaic panels still survive along the walls of the nave), St. Peter's, and St. Paul's.[72] The iconographic campaigns of Benedict Biscop were innovative, impressive, and, as far as we can judge, influential. As we have seen, Ernst Kitzinger argued that they influenced the apotropaic iconography of the coffin provided in 698 for the body of St. Cuthbert by the allied monastery of St. Peter's, Lindisfarne; while the present writer has argued that later (perhaps 710–50) they inspired, directly or indirectly, the rich iconographic program of the Ruthwell Cross.[73]

To conclude: Benedict Biscop's decision in 679, to visually frame the altar area of St. Peter's with icons of the Mother of God flanked by the apostles, was both a clear example of *imitatio Romae* and a relevant response to the major Christological issue which that year faced the Catholic Church in East and West. In particular, it was consistent with the canons of the Lateran Council of 649, as reiterated in September 679 by the synod of Hatfield. Bede's descriptions of the monastic churches at Wearmouth make it clear that, from autumn 679, that monastery was the chief center in England of liturgical devotion to the Mother of God: far more advanced, in this regard, than any other English establishment of which we have evidence. We can safely conclude that, at Wearmouth and later at Jarrow, Benedict's concern with *decor* went hand in hand with that concern with *cultus* that had led him to persuade Pope Agatho to allow John the Archcantor to be the papal representative at Hatfield.[74] Benedict was determined that the man

---

71. Nordhagen, "S. Maria Antiqua," pp. 100–103.

72. See de Blaauw, *Cultus et Decor*, 1:348–49 (on Santa Maria Maggiore); 2:461–63 (on St. Peter's). For recent discussion of this Roman phenomenon, see Tronzo, "Shape of Narrative," (on St. Paul's, pp. 466–87).

73. Kitzinger, "Coffin-Reliquary," pp. 263–65; Kitzinger, "Interlace and Icons," p. 7; Ó Carragáin, *Ritual and the Rood*, pp. 92–93, 246–47, 297–98.

74. This sentence alludes to the title of de Blaauw's great work, *Cultus et Decor*. On Benedict persuading Pope Agatho to let him have Abbot John because of his liturgical and musical expertise, see Bede, *Historia abbatum*, ch. 6, in *Venerabilis Baedae opera historica*, ed. Plummer, 1:369.

responsible for the liturgy sung in the presence of St. Peter's body at Rome would teach the monks at Wearmouth *viva voce* during the winter of 679–80, in order to ensure that Wearmouth would celebrate the most authentic liturgy which a monastery dedicated to St. Peter could possibly have. It is reasonable to assume that Benedict Biscop and his successors, Ceolfrid and Hwaetberht, continued to keep up to date with new liturgical ways to celebrate the mystery of Christ's incarnation: for example, with the later decision of Pope Sergius I (686–701) to organize the four Marian feasts, which between the 630s and the 680s had come into the Roman liturgy at different forms and with a variety of formularies, into a unified set of feasts within the papal stational liturgy, each marked by solemn processions from the Roman Forum to Sancta Maria ad Praesepe.[75] Before he next set off for Rome in 682, Benedict had constructed at Wearmouth a separate chapel dedicated to the Mother of God. On his final return to Wearmouth, in 686 or 687, Benedict brought icons for this Marian chapel: "He brought back paintings of the life of Our Lord for the chapel of the Holy Mother of God which he had built within the main monastery [i.e., Wearmouth], setting them, as its crowning glory, all the way round the walls."[76] Once more at Wearmouth, as in the monastic church of St. Peter, the cult of the Virgin was associated with the life of her Son. As Bede understood and reported them, Biscop's commissions consistently placed the cult of Mary in the context of the whole faith of the Church, as proclaimed by the evangelists and the apostles. No doubt his Roman experiences since the monothelete crisis of the early 650s made Benedict sensitive to the importance of keeping his community in touch with the best in recent Christological thought, as expressed in the acts of the Lateran Council which he had just acquired for the monastic library. His close friendship with a first-rate liturgist like John the Archcantor and a first-rate theologian like Theodore of Canter-

---

75. Sergius's processions were known to Bede, who in *De temporum ratione* gave a coherent and historically convincing account of the development of the new Marian feasts at Rome: see Clayton, *Cult of the Virgin*, pp. 36–37.

76. Bede, *Historia abbatum*, ch. 9: "Nam et tunc dominicae historiae picturas, quibus totam beatae Dei genitricis, quam in monasterio maiore fecerat, aecclesiam in gyro coronaret, adtulit." Trans. *Age of Bede*, ed. Farmer, p. 194; see *Venerabilis Baedae opera historica*, ed. Plummer, 1:373 (text) and 2:362 (notes). Rosemary Cramp points out that Bede's phrase "in gyro" "could mean that this church was centrally planned, although the passage need not necessarily have this meaning, but it does seem to indicate that St. Mary's was treated as an individual building and so was probably a free-standing structure" (*Wearmouth and Jarrow*, 1:33; thus she "would no longer suggest that the Wearmouth eastern annexe was the chapel dedicated to St. Mary." This chapel remains so far unlocated (1:71).

bury, one-time colleague of Maximus the Confessor, evidently encouraged Benedict to make Wearmouth a leading English center for the fast-developing liturgical cult of the Virgin Mary who "brought forth without corruption the very one who is literally and truly God the Word born of God the Father before all the ages." But Benedict probably developed that cult for good pastoral reasons also: to articulate in visual terms the Church's understanding of the faith of the apostles, so that even the illiterate could "recall with a more wide-awake mind the grace of the Lord's Incarnation" ("dominicae incarnationis gratiam uigilantiore mente recolerent"), and could by using their eyes and their sense of symbolic space become more aware of the everyday sacramental means by which each monastic or secular member of the Wearmouth community, who had come to know the Incarnation of Christ the son of God by the message of an angel, might, by his Passion and Cross, be brought to the glory of the Resurrection.

THE DREAM OF THE ROOD
AT NONES ON GOOD FRIDAY

SARAH LARRATT KEEFER

For generations, the Vercelli Book's *The Dream of the Rood*[1] has enticed its readers into speculation about its composition. Art historians, archaeologists, literary critics, and cultural historians have all fallen under its spell; their efforts have ranged from attempts at dating the poem's original form (a matter of some contention, since the term "original" cannot readily be agreed upon) to establishing a context for its relationship with both the Ruthwell Cross[2] and the Brussels reliquary cross.[3] In fact, any effort to understand this magnificent "dream-vision" more completely will lead the reader into a labyrinth of structural, thematic, and ideological complexities.[4]

We cannot be sure of how to ascertain or date the earliest form of that poem which we recognize by its editorial title *The Dream of the Rood*. The Ruthwell Cross lapidary poem is clearly an early relation to it, or perhaps even the avatar for it, and the lines on the more contemporary Brussels reliquary cross are likely descended from a common ancestor. Éamonn Ó Carragáin believes that there were many recensions of this poem-model, some shorter and others longer; such a theory makes the sole extant text of the poem preserved in the late tenth-century Vercelli Book simply a redaction of an earlier version that dates perhaps from as early as the seventh

---

The following study was first presented as a paper in May 2002 at the International Congress on Medieval Studies at Kalamazoo and seeks to honor the scholarship and academic vision of Helen Damico, who has set new standards by which to appreciate the culture of Anglo-Saxon England.

1. Vercelli, Biblioteca Capitolare CXVII, fols. 104v–106r: see Ker, *Catalogue*, no. 394, pp. 460–64. Text of *The Dream of the Rood* taken from *Vercelli Book*, ed. Krapp, pp. 61–65.

2. For a wide-ranging study of this important Northumbrian monument, see *Ruthwell Cross*, ed. Cassidy.

3. A late tenth- or early eleventh-century cruciform reliquary preserved in the Cathedral of Saint Michel and Saint Gudule, Brussels. Its text reads "Rod is min nama. Geo ic ricne cyning / bær byfigynde, blode bestemed / þas rode het æþlmær wyrican and Aðelwold hys beroþor / Criste to lofe for ælfrices saule hyra beroþor" (http://www.georgetown.edu/labyrinth/library/oe/texts/a41.html). See also *Golden Age of Anglo-Saxon Art*, ed. Backhouse, Turner, and Webster, cat. no. 75.

4. For only one of many such attempts, see Keefer, "'Either/And.'"

century.[5] This theory cannot, however, be proven one way or another, and only serves to further the mystery surrounding the poem.

In many ways, an exploration of *The Dream of the Rood*'s origins comes most naturally to a liturgical source scholar, familiar enough with the language of church ritual to hear its resonance whenever that occurs in other milieus. However, one of the earliest studies of liturgical influences on this poem was inconclusive: "no hymn or piece of liturgy seems to have furnished [the poet of *The Dream of the Rood*] a model, and nothing could be more different in spirit and manner than his work and the type of hymn probably accessible to him."[6] Subsequent scholars have moved beyond Patch, showing the way for a wider range of scholarship and exploring *The Dream of the Rood* in the cultural context of public Christian practice. In the 1960s and 1970s, John Fleming[7] and Rosemary Woolf[8] laid the groundwork for examining the poem more closely, both from monastic and doctrinal vantage points. It does not, however, open its secrets easily nor indeed evenly: the more one looks, the more one sees, moving out into increasingly disparate dimensions as a result of that scrutiny. Éamonn Ó Carragáin has devoted a lifetime of academic investigation to a study of this poem, in its relationship both to the Ruthwell Cross poem and to the influence on it of late seventh-century Roman ecclesiastical culture.[9] Elaine Treharne has explored the colors and shapes of Holy Baptism to be found within its lines.[10] So it seems that there are many possible and indeed overlapping influences of church ritual at work in *The Dream of the Rood*; but this is perhaps to be expected. The life of the church was a vivid tapestry, alive with narrative and image, its music and texts interwoven into phrases to form part of the matrix of each individual memory.

The poet of this poem was beyond any doubt a Christian, though whether a new convert or of long standing, a baptismal candidate or an established believer creatively seeking to relocate his faith into the climax of the catechumens' experience of the last days of Holy Week, is not entirely clear.[11] From the sophistication of *The Dream of the Rood* poet's writing, I am

---

5. Ó Carragáin, "Sources or Analogues."

6. Patch, "Liturgical Influence," p. 233.

7. Fleming, "*Dream of the Rood* and Anglo-Saxon Monasticism."

8. Woolf, "Doctrinal Influences."

9. Ó Carragáin, "Rome, Ruthwell, Vercelli."

10. Treharne, "'Hiht waes geniwad.'"

11. While I do not exclude the possibility of a female poet, I follow the traditional identification of the poet as male.

inclined to consider him a member of the Christian faithful and not a
convert, although much has been made of the unusual depiction of Christ
in Germanic heroic terms. The piece could as easily have been written as
inspiration for new converts, either Danish or Viking and thus familiar
with such a presentation of a hero, and it seems likely, from the layering
of liturgical resonance present in the poem, that its author was steeped in
Christian rite and ritual, rather than approaching it for the first time. This
essay, then, will add the suggestion of another layer of liturgical influence
to those already set out by scholars who precede me. I propose the Good
Friday Nones Office ritual of the Veneration of the Cross as one of the
main inspirations at work on the version of the poem found in the Vercelli
Book. In the course of this study, I will introduce the Veneration service,
compare its components to *The Dream of the Rood* in some detail, and finally
consider what conclusions, if any, can be drawn from what we have read.

The Veneration of the Cross is a fascinating composite synaxis—or
non-eucharistic church ritual—which originated with the practice of the
faithful in Jerusalem at least as early as the fourth century.[12] It is possible to
trace its development from a simple act of adoration through to an increasingly dramatic and performative service by the mid-ninth century in some
of the monastic centers in northern or northeastern Francia.[13] The heart
of the Office is that part of the Good Friday devotions, celebrated at Nones
or three o'clock in the afternoon by individual acts of adoration; this ritual
consisted of the veneration of a relic of the True Cross preserved in a gold
and silver reliquary. That rite reached Rome after the fourth century, and
acquired new synactic addenda and detail as it spread into France and
Germany. Some time during the late eighth century, the reliquary, possibly
cruciform in shape, appears to have been replaced by a processional cross,
which is then imagined by the congregation to be the True Cross itself.[14]

Along with this new level of congregational involvement came affirmation of the imagined transformation in the words and chant of the antiphon *Ecce Lignum Crucis* together with Psalm 118, *Beati inmaculati*. These
were originally sung during the act of adoration, but were then moved
ahead of it, both for greater dramatic effect in focusing on the cross to be
venerated (this *is* the wood of the cross: come let us adore it) and because

---

12. For a complete history of the development of the Veneration of the Cross ritual in
Western Europe, see Keefer, "Veneration of the Cross."

13. See for example the service laid out in Einsiedeln, Stiftsbibliothek Cod. 235 (CCM
VII.1, 171–82), described in Keefer, "Performance of the Cross."

14. Keefer, "Performance of the Cross."

other rituals were added to replace them. Two new antiphons, another psalm, and a hymn were now sung during the act of adoration: in this way, during each individual prostration before the processional cross, the suppliant could readily imagine it towering overhead as the True Cross would have towered over those at its foot on Calvary, because of the scene so dramatically created by the words of *Crucem Tuam Adoramus* and *Dum Fabricator Mundi* (see Appendix I).

Nor was this all: perhaps as a result of innovative design within the monastic centers in the north of Francia, the entrance and exit of the processional cross were embellished and dramatized. By at least the mid-ninth century, the cross acquired the voice of Christ in the words of the *Improperia* (or Reproaches), which precentors and the choir answered with the *Trisagion*, sung first in Greek and then in Latin. In the elaborate English *Regularis Concordia* tradition, a final element, the *Depositio Crucis* was added; here, at the end of the ritual, the cross was reshrouded and laid in a representation of the sepulcher as if it were the body of Christ, and monks were set to keep vigil in pairs over this *scena* until Easter Sunday (Appendices I and II lay out the ritual, and compare its most sophisticated forms).

The Veneration service is therefore unusual in that it developed dramatic roles sung by groups of synactic performers that involved the unfolding of a narrative tableau through station and procession, with individual prostrations and prayers forming *actiones adorationis* carried out at the same time that antiphons and hymns were sung by the choir and precentors. Within a canonical framework constructed for the faithful, the entire synaxis would have re-created the scene on Calvary at Nones that first Good Friday: it was charged with solemn emotion, devastatingly effective because its ritual language was focused intently on the single visible emblem of the processional cross at its center. It thus becomes a "you are there" experience, the ultimate goal of every act of contemplative meditation on the events of Jesus Christ's life.

If my theory has any merit, then the poet of *The Dream of the Rood* likely had some experience of this intensely moving performance that made up the Veneration of the Cross. Such an experience could then have triggered a deliberate revisitation of that ritual's effect, perhaps as an act of personal devotion. There are three distinct aspects of the Good Friday ritual that served in part to construct *The Dream of the Rood*: (i) the unfolding drama of processional cross become *lignum crucis*; (ii) the performance proper, with the processional cross *in loco salvatoris* identified as the speaker of Christ's words of the *Improperia* sung by the deacons carrying it; and (iii) the echoes of the service itself in the language of the poem. However, from a liturgist's perspective, we may also examine *The Dream of the Rood* for a possible snapshot of the Veneration synaxis as it could have been experienced by the poet. If the poem is in fact earlier than 970, this examination should fill in our understanding of those forms of the Veneration of the Cross, known to the Anglo-Saxons, which predate its earliest but still uncertain English witnesses from the Reform period. However, dating again becomes an issue to bear in mind: I use the word "uncertain" because we can only assume that the *ordo* for the Veneration, from the eleventh-century texts of the *Regularis Concordia*, is an accurate reflection of practice in the 970s. Apart from these two manuscripts that purport to record the proceedings of the synod as it was held in the previous century, the sole service-book evidence that we have for the Veneration of the Cross ritual in Anglo-Saxon England at all resides in two newly edited texts of it, neither of them dating from any earlier than the 1060s.[15]

The entire drama of *The Dream of the Rood* is carried out while the Visionary is prostrate before the Cross that appears before him. That it is said to be "swefna cyst," the "best of dreams," happening while all other "reordberende" are sleeping, suggests not an actual experience of the Veneration ritual at Good Friday Nones but a re-created one, deemed perhaps to be a *visio* because it occurred as a result of meditation after Compline or around Nocturns. The central act of adoration with the antiphons that accompany it could thus be seen in the poem to encompass all the chants of the Good Friday service, even those that are performed before the prostrations. The poem might therefore be taken as a dramatization of an intensified, recollected *actio adorationis*, conflating all the elements of the Veneration service, with their import, into a reimagined prostration: "ic þær licende lange hwile / beheold hreowcearig Hælendes treow" (lines 24–25).

Let us compare the opening rubrics from the Veneration service and the first glimpse of the Rood in the poem, to see if any correlation is evident. At the beginning of the Veneration ritual, the veiled *crux gemmata* or processional cross moves forward during the three stations of the *Improperia* and *Trisagion* in the more complex of the *Ordines Romani*:[16]

---

15. Keefer, "Veneration of the Cross," pp. 173–76.
16. See for instance, OR XXXI, 46 in *Ordines Romani*, ed. Andrieu, 3:498.

Eall þæt beacen wæs
begoten mid golde;   gimmas stodon
fægere æt foldan sceatum . . .
    Ne wæs ðær huru fracodes gealga
ac hine þær beheoldon   halige gastas,
men ofer moldan,   ond eall þeos mære gesceaft . . .
    Geseah ic wuldres treow
wædum geweorðod . . . (lines 6–8a, 10b–12, 14b–15a)

(All that bright symbol was covered with gold; gems stood lovely at the surfaces of the earth . . . Nor indeed was it in that place the gallows of wicked-
ness . . . But holy spirits beheld it there, [and] men upon earth and all this
bright creation . . . I saw the tree of glory adorned with clothing . . .)

At this stage, we should consider the antiphon known as the *Trisagion* from the Veneration of the Cross service, where the people of God
acknowledge their guilt, as the *Improperia* are sung,

Agios o theos, agios ischiros, agios athanathos: eleison himas!
Sanctus deus, sanctus fortis, sanctus et inmortalis: miserere nobis!
(Holy God, holy and mighty, holy and immortal: have mercy upon us!)[17]

Lines 13–14 of *The Dream of the Rood* present a similar contrast between
the Cross of Christ standing as an inexorable representation of humanity's
betrayal of their Savior, and the Visionary's shamed self-awareness of his
guilt as a sinner, for whose transgressions the Crucifixion took place:

Syllic wæs se sigebeam,   and ic synnum fah
forwundod mid wommum.

(Glorious was the victory-tree, and I stained with sin, wounded with iniquities)

"Eall þæt beacen wæs / begoten mid golde; gimmas stodon fægere æt
foldan sceatum" (6b–8) suggests a jeweled cruciform reliquary, seen in
Ordo Romanus XXIII from the mid-eighth century,[18] or perhaps a *crux gemmata* as processional cross;[19] this "engel Dryhtnes" (9b) is truly a messenger
of the Lord, both for the Visionary-poet who would have it speak to him
directly and also for those taking part in the Good Friday Veneration. The
latter hear the words of the *Improperia* which are intended as Christ's words

17. All Veneration of the Cross texts taken from Appendix I, ultimately from Cambridge, Corpus Christi College MS 422, pp. 315–18. Translations mine.
    18. OR XXIII, in *Ordines Romani*, ed. Andrieu, 3:271.
    19. OR XXIV, in *Ordines Romani*, ed. Andrieu, 3:293.

from the Cross; yet they see, not Christ but a man-shaped and possibly even life-sized cruciform image, representing both his body and the means of his death, and it is this representation that advances in dramatic stations while the *Improperia* are sung. If this is indeed a processional cross that is veiled, it is not (yet) the gallows-tree (*lignum crucis*) of Golgotha, "ne wæs ðær huru fracodes gealga" (line 10b), but instead, as the focal point of the Good Friday procession, it commands the attention of everyone present: "ac hine þær beheoldon halige gastas / men ofer moldan and eall þeos mære gesceaft" (lines 11–12).

The Visionary's self-reference as "synnum fah" (line 13b), "stained with sin," conveys the same ideological relationship to the "syllic sigebeam" (line 13a) as the *Trisagion* which was sung by precentors and choir members in the two canonical tongues of the Church: "Holy God, holy and mighty, holy and immortal, have mercy upon us." The Visionary reaffirms the vision of the tree of glory as "wædum geweorðod" (line 15a), and this problematic description of "adorned with clothing," taken together with "shining with joys, decked out with gold, possessed of gems" makes excellent sense if we envision a shrouded processional *crux gemmata* as it is moved from station to station in the early part of the Veneration service.

Let us continue by comparing the unveiling of the processional cross on Good Friday with the Visionary's perception of that which lies beneath the clothing that shrouds the Rood. With the removal of the veil from the processional cross after the *Trisagion*, we hear the antiphon *Ecce Lignum Crucis*: "Ecce lignum crucis in quo salus mundi pependit; uenite adoremus" (Behold! the wood of the Cross, on which hung the salvation of the world. Come let us adore). In the poem we read:

> Hwæðre ic þurh þæt gold   ongytan meahte
> earmra ærgewin,   þæt hit ærest ongan
> swætan on þa swiðran healfe . . .
>   Geseah ic þæt fuse beacen
> wendan wædum and bleom;   hwilum hit wæs mid wætan bestemed,
> beswyled mid swates gange,   hwilum mid since gegyrwed. (lines 18–20,
> 21b–23)

> (Nevertheless, through the gold I might perceive the ancient torment of the wretched, [such] that it first began to sweat blood on the right side . . . I saw that shining beacon change its garments and color: at times it was drenched with wet, soaked with the flow of blood, at times adorned with treasure.)

"Hwæðre" ("nevertheless"), the Visionary begins to see through the outer appearance of the tree, such that "þæt fuse beacen / wendan wædum and bleom" (lines 21b–22): just as the focus of the ritual is the processional *crux* likely adorned with gems which at the same time is proclaimed the actual cross on which Christ died, so the Rood of the poem changes its garments and color, now rough and stained with blood, now adorned with treasure. At the end of the *Improperia* and *Trisagion*, the processional cross is unshrouded, often dramatically,[20] and is revealed to the eyes of the congregation with the triumphant antiphon *Ecce Lignum Crucis* (Behold! the wood of the cross). This pronounces the change from artifact to fact and from representation of the cross to the actual cross itself, confirming sacred time renewed within the drama of the synaxis. The poet would not have been able to express the simultaneous polysemy of the ritual in ways other than linear within the medium of written text; words must fall in a sequence which in turn determines the sequence of meaning that an audience receives. This might account for the adverbial *hwilum* marking the shift from one incarnation of the Rood to the other in terms of time rather than simultaneity.

We turn back now to the *Improperia* intended as the words of Christ from the cross with which the Good Friday ritual actually begins, and compare them to the first appearance of Christ in the poem:

> Popule meus quid *feci tibi* aut in quo *contristaui te*? responde mihi.
> (O my people, what have I done to you or in what have I aggrieved you? Answer me.)

> Quia *eduxi te* de terra egipti, parasti crucem saluatori tuo
> (Because I have led you from the land of Egypt, you have prepared a cross for your Savior.)

> Quia *eduxi te* per desertum quadraginta annos et manna *cibaui te* et *introduxi* in terram satis optimam, parasti crucem saluatori tuo.
> (Because I have led you through the desert forty years and fed you on manna and brought you to a land of plenty, you have prepared a cross for your Savior.)

> Quid ultra *debui facere* mala et non *feci ego* quidem *plantaui te* uinea mea fructu decoram et tu facta est mihi nimis amara aceto namque framea potasti et lancea perforasti latus saluatori tuo.
> (What further evil am I supposed to have done which I have not done? for I planted you as my lovely and fruitful vine and you have made for me vinegar bitter as a sword which you gave me to drink, and with a lance you have pierced the side of your Savior.)[21]

---

20. OR XXXI, in *Ordines Romani*, ed. Andrieu, 3:498.
21. Taken from Cambridge, Corpus Christi College MS 422, pp. 315–16. Italics mine.

Compare these words to the first appearance of Christ in the poem:

> Geseah ic þa Frean mancynnes
> efstan elne micle   þæt he me *wolde* on *gestigan* . . .
> *Ongyrede* hine þa geong hæleð . . .
>   Gestah he on gealgan heanne
> modig on manigra gesyhðe,   þa he *wolde* mancyn *lysan.*
> Bifode ic þa me se beorn *ymbclypte.* (lines 33b–34, 39–42a)

(I saw then the Lord of mankind hasten with great zeal, such that he wished to ascend upon me . . . Then the young hero stripped himself . . . he mounted the high gallows, courageous in the sight of many, when he wished to redeem mankind. I trembled when the warrior embraced me.)[22]

The processional cross has now "spoken" the words of the *Improperia* as if in Christ's voice, and has been proclaimed the Tree itself, "in quo salus mundi pependit" (on which hung the salvation of the world); the speaking Rood of the poem has its heroic Christ hasten with zeal, "þæt he me wolde on gestigan" (line 34b) . . . "þa he wolde mancyn lysan" (line 41b), (that he would ascend on me . . . when he would redeem mankind). But where the ritual's antiphon has the Savior hang—*pependit,* a static or at least neutral verb—the poem has him *efstan* (line 34a) 'hasten', *gestigan* (lines 34b, 40b) 'ascend', *hine ongyran* (line 39a) 'strip himself', and *ymbclypan* (line 42) 'embrace', all verbs of self-determination, with the Cross the passive recipient while Christ remains the active, heroic redeemer. Nevertheless, Christ's control of the events of Good Friday[23] may yet contain some echo of the *Improperia* that began the Veneration synaxis. There we hear Christ's "voice" pronouncing many self-determining verbs—*feci tibi* (I have done to you), *contristavi te* (I have grieved you), *eduxi te* (I have led you out of), *cibavi te* (I have fed you), *introduxi te* (I have brought you into), *plantavi te* (I have planted you)—with each of these contributing to a clear sense of Christ as agent in the synaxis, even within his own Crucifixion.

The spectacle of the cross prompts both the congregation on Good Friday and the audience of the poem to consider the results of God's salvation of humanity: "Crucem tuam adoramus domine et sanctam resurrec-

---

22. Italics mine.

23. In early Anglo-Saxon art, Christ was depicted as reigning from the Tree as King rather than hanging from it as Corpus: for reference to this see Coatsworth, "Iconography of the Crucifixion," vol. 1, chap. 6 (pp. 108–29); see also Coatsworth, "Decoration of the Durham Gospels," esp. pp. 58–62; and Coatsworth, "'Robed Christ.'"

tionem tuam laudamus et glorificamus; ecce enim propter crucem uenit gaudium in uniuerso mundi" (We adore thy cross, O Lord, and praise and glorify thy holy Resurrection; it is indeed because of the cross that joy of the world came for all creation).

> Is nu sæl cumen
> þæt me weorðiað   wide and side
> men ofer moldan,   ond eall þeos mære gesceaft,
> gebiddaþ him to þyssum beacne . . .
> Iu ic wæs geworden   wita heardost,
> leodum laðost,   ærþan ic him lifes weg
> rihtne gerymde,   reordberendum. (lines 80b–83a, 87–89)

(A time is now coming when men upon earth and all this glorious creation shall worship me far and wide, commend themselves to this sign . . . Once I was made the bitterest of torments most hateful to people, before I opened for them, for the voice-bearers, the right road to life.)

Creation in turn is called upon to adore this act of redemption in the antiphon *Crucem Tuam Adoramus*, and to revere the cross, by which joy came into the entire world, "enim propter crucem venit gaudium in universo mundi." The Rood tells the Visionary that a time is coming when "men ofer moldan and eall þeos mære gesceaft" (line 82), a perfect mirror of that earlier line 12, will commit themselves in prayer to the Cross, "gebiddaþ him to þyssum beacne" (line 83a). So where before in line 11 they watched (*beheoldon*), now in line 83a, as a result of what they have experienced of the mystery of the Crucifixion, they will adore. Joy has indeed come into the entire world, for where before the Cross was a death sentence, it has now become "lifes weg / rihtne . . . reordberendum" (the right way to life for voice-bearers [lines 88b–89]).

Éamonn Ó Carragáin has made a masterful association of Mary and the cross, alike in obedience to God's will on March 25, on which in certain years both Good Friday and the feast of the Annunciation will fall, and he suggests the seventh-century Mass for use when liturgical commemorations occur upon the same day as the ultimate source for both the Ruthwell lapidary poem and *The Dream of the Rood* itself.[24] I would propose another source, not in place of but in addition to this Mass of Christ's Passion and Annunciation, for one of the most pervasive images of the poem, that of the Rood being honored above all other trees:

---

24. Ó Carragáin, "Rome, Ruthwell, Vercelli," pp. 62–71.

Hwæt, me þa geweorþode   wuldres ealdor
ofer holmwudu,   heofonrices weard!
Swylce swa he his modor eac,   Marian sylfe,
ælmihtig god   for ealle menn
geweorðode   ofer eall wifa cynn (lines 90–94)

(Behold, the Prince of Glory then honored me over all trees of the wood,
the Guardian of heaven, just as Almighty God his mother also, Mary herself, did honor for all humanity, above all womankind.)

These lines may also bear some traces of an influence that is still earlier
than the Feast of Christ's Passion and Annunciation: the great Veneration
hymn, *Pange Lingua Gloriosi*, ascribed to Venantius Fortunatus and therefore written in the late sixth century:

Crux fidelis inter omnes arbor una nobilis
nulla silua talem profert fronde flore germine
dulce lignum dulce clauum dulce pondus sustinet.

(Faithful cross, unique and honored tree among all others: no wood
bears another such flower among its leaves and branches; the dear timber
supports sweet nails and a beloved weight.)

"Hwæt, me þa geweorþode wuldres ealdor / ofer holtwudu, heofonrices
weard" (lines 90–91) could plausibly derive from the first line of this verse
antiphon repeated before each *Pange Lingua Gloriosi* hymn verse proper:
"crux fidelis inter omnes arbor una nobilis" (faithful cross, unique and
honored tree among all others) matches well with "me þa geweorþode wuldres ealdor / ofer holumwudu" (Behold, the Prince of Glory has honored
me over all trees of the wood).

The experience of the Crucifixion leading to an adoration of the
cross involves all of creation in both the Veneration synaxis and *The
Dream of the Rood*. The antiphon *Dum Fabricator Mundi* tells us that "terra
motus enim factus fuerit magnus quia mortem filii dei clamabat mundus
se sustinere non posse" (all the great earth was shaken because it cried
out at the death of the Son of God which it could not bear). The Rood
recounts that "Weop eal gesceaft, / cwiðdon Cyninges fyll: Crist wæs
on rode" (all creation wept, bewailed the fall of its King: Christ was on
the cross [lines 55b–56]). This singular accordance seems astonishingly
persuasive, and is significant, because the *Dum Fabricator* was a relative
latecomer to the Veneration service and appears original to the Gallic
West of the ninth century. Therefore, if any kind of dependence is to be
posited between the Veneration of the Cross and *The Dream of the Rood*,

the poem as we have it in the Vercelli Book must likely be later than the mid-800s.[25]

Our theorized equation between poem and synaxis does not of course run as a parallel construction, but we have already noted that this can be explained by the process of meditation itself. *The Dream of the Rood* could not have been an attempt to recapture the sequence of the Veneration synaxis but instead to encapsulate those parts of the service that rise in the memory in order to form a suitable devotion deriving from the act of *meditatio*. With such a caution in mind, we must now use what we can and cannot find in the poem, and what we can and cannot explain about those presences or absences, to try to imagine the Veneration of the Cross synaxis that *The Dream of the Rood* poet might have experienced.

The history of the Veneration synaxis's development is complicated. To name only a few extant examples of the fullest form of the service with which we are dealing, we must consider mid-ninth century France, as Appendix II demonstrates. The earliest full version appears in a French service book, Paris, Arsénal MS 227, commonly known as the Pontifical of Poitiers but probably written at the monastery of Saint-Pierre de Rebais or Bourges between 860–70.[26] A very similar design of Veneration synaxis from a century later is preserved in Paris, Bibliothèque nationale de France, MS Latin 12052, the tenth-century "Ratoldus" sacramentary of around 970 which is a compilation of a number of disparate sources copied into a single book for Abbot Ratoldus at Corbie.[27] There is, however, no reason to assume any direct lines of influence between the two: in the ninth century, there was a trend within monastic centers of the north of Francia to expand and develop the Veneration ritual into the more elaborate form found in the *Regularis Concordia*, so this tendency may have been more common within that monastic milieu than extant recorded witnesses can show us.[28]

The mid-eleventh century texts in London, British Library, MSS Cotton Faustina B.iii and Tiberius A.iii are the only complete recensions left to us today that record the provisions made at the *Regularis Concordia* synod held in the 970s, more than half a century earlier. The Veneration of the Cross preserved in these recensions differs from the continental versions

---

25. The earliest appearance of the *Dum Fabricator Mundi* antiphon is in Paris, MS Arsénal 227, dated 860–70. See Keefer, "Veneration of the Cross," pp. 149–50.

26. Edited in *Cosiddetto Pontificale di Poitiers*, ed. Martini.

27. *Sacramentary of Ratoldus*, ed. Orchard.

28. Keefer, "Performance of the Cross."

of "Poitiers" and "Ratoldus" in three distinct areas. It lacks their prescribed Psalms 118 and 66 and instead indicates the recitation of the seven penitential psalms; its celebrant's third adoration prayer, *Deus omnipotens Iesu Christi qui tuas manus propter nos*, was evidently original to the synod since it only appears in service books from the late tenth century and afterwards; and it makes provision for the *Depositio Crucis* unlike any other version of this synaxis prior to it.

While the Faustina and Tiberius manuscripts preserve the *ordo* of the Veneration service, with antiphons only in incipit form, two independent service-book witnesses from the second half of the eleventh century present a better picture of the way it was performed in Anglo-Saxon England. A fragmentary Triduum *libellus* on four binding leaves in Oxford, Bodleian Library, Bodley 120 gives us the full text of the *Improperia* and *Trisagion*, the *Ecce Lignum Crucis* and the incipit for Psalm 118, and all but the last verse of the *Pange Lingua Gloriosi* with its verse-antiphon *Crux fidelis*. A more complete synaxis appears in the pages of Cambridge, Corpus Christi College MS 422, which has all of the antiphons and the hymn in full text, both psalms in incipit form, and the four antiphons for the *Depositio Crucis* at its close. Neumes accompany the antiphons, and the Veneration service in this book looks to have been laid out for a singer and not a celebrant.

It is instructive to examine *The Dream of the Rood* against the various designs of these Veneration services, to see if one lies closer to it than another. Of the English and continental service books, antiphoners, customaries, and *ordines* that I have studied, only the eleventh-century witnesses for the *Regularis Concordia* exclude both Psalms 118 and 66, and I can find no evident echo of these two psalms in the Old English poem. However, neither psalm has exactly to do with the theme of Good Friday, and both would have been well-known to at least a monastic poet, were that the case here, so that he would have been familiar with them in other contexts entirely. It is of course also possible that these psalms were not included in the Veneration that he might have known, and that would point us back to the synaxis in the Faustina and Tiberius manuscripts. However, these texts provide instead for the seven penitential psalms to be recited in between the three prayers of adoration, and I cannot find any clear traces in the poem of those psalms either. Once again, much the same explanation would apply; the seven penitential psalms were also prescribed for daily recitation as well as for Good Friday. The presence or absence of psalm material is thus not conclusive either way in helping us to further the theory of a Veneration of the Cross ritual lying somewhere behind *The Dream of the Rood.*

A consideration of the three prayers of adoration might be in order if we were to suppose that *The Dream of the Rood* poet were a priest who would have used these prayers, and not a cantor, a master of the catechumenate, or simply a literate congregation member instead. However, we have limited evidence for these prayers in the English service books from the period. We have already seen that the Veneration service in CCCC 422 makes it look very much like a copy used by a singer whose role was to chant the antiphons and sing the hymn, as it is heavily neumed and has no adoration prayers. The Triduum *libellus*, of which the Bodley 120 binding leaves are the sole remainder, would of course have drawn its material from both a sacramentary for Maundy Thursday and Good Friday, and a pontifical for the baptismal rites of Holy Saturday; indeed, text from the *Orationes Solemnes* preceding the Veneration are evident on one of the fragments, but the leaves are so tattered that all of Maundy Thursday, everything after the last verse of *Pange Lingua Gloriosi* on Good Friday and much of Holy Saturday is missing. So while this *libellus* would have been used by a celebrant in orders, we lack the important evidence of *acta adorationis* prayers in this book.

All we know, therefore, of the three *acta adorationis* prayers used in England by a celebrant comes from the *Regularis Concordia* texts of the Veneration ritual, and these were painstakingly explored by Lilli Gjerløw fifty years ago.[29] Of the three prayers in Faustina B.iii and Tiberius A.iii, the first, *Domine Iesu Christi adoro te in cruce ascendentem* also appears in "Ratoldus." It is however older than the tenth century: a variant form appears a century earlier in "Poitiers," while a much expanded version is included in the ninth-century Book of Cerne. Both this first *Regularis Concordia* prayer and the second, *Domine Iesu Christe, gloriosissime conditor mundi* which it again shares with both "Poitiers" and "Ratoldus," were also copied into the Galba Psalter before it was brought to England perhaps in the reign of Æthelstan,[30] and they appear in later service books as well. It seems evident that versions of these two prayers were so widely used as private devotions that any echoes of them in *The Dream of the Rood* would again be inconclusive for imagining a Veneration service as a source for the poem. The third

---

29. Gjerløw, *Adoratio Crucis.*

30. I am grateful to Dr. Michelle Brown for her help in reading these texts in this manuscript; see also Deshman, "Galba Psalter."

and unique prayer in the *Regularis Concordia* manuscripts, *Deus omnipotens Iesu Christi qui tuas manus propter nos*, is unremarkable for any features that might stand out as influential, and no evidence of it is discernible in the poem. Prayers are not going to help us out here either.

Finally, we reach the *Depositio Crucis* at the end of the Veneration ritual in the *Regularis Concordia*: it has been the subject of an exhaustive study by Solange Corbin.[31] Its first historical attestation occurs in Faustina B.iii and Tiberius A.iii, at least seventy years after the synod, and in them it looks very much like an interpolation that interrupts the sequence of the *ordo* at that point. However, on stylistic and theological grounds, Lucia Kornexl believes this section of the *Regularis Concordia* instead to be an insertion that was made by Æthelwold himself, shortly after the synod.[32]

It begins by describing a practice that is not part of the *ordo* but only a suggestion "for the strengthening of the faith of unlearned common persons and neophytes,"[33] and it continues on to describe what can only be termed a "set design" that is intended to represent the sepulcher in which Christ was buried. Into this construct, the now-reshrouded cross is placed, while the deacons who carry it sing the first three of four antiphons:

> In pace in idipsum dormiam et requiescam.
> (In peace itself shall I sleep and take my rest.)
>
> Habitabit in tabernaculo tuo requiescet in monte sancta tua.
> (He will dwell in your tabernacle, he will rest on your sacred mountain.)
>
> Caro mea requiescet in spe.
> (My body will rest in hope.)

The committal of the cross to the tomb is described as being "ac si Domini nostri Ihesu Christi corpore sepulto" or, in Old English, "swylce DNIC lichaman gebyrgedum"[34] (as if it were the burial of our Lord Jesus Christ's body); once completed, the deacons sing the final antiphon *Sepulto Domino*: "Sepulto domino signatum est monumentum ponentes milites qui custodirent eum" (The Lord having been buried, the monument was sealed, setting soldiers there who guarded it).

This "sepulcher" was then to be guarded from Nones Good Friday until Easter Sunday's Mass of the Resurrection by pairs of monks who were

---

31. Corbin, *Deposition liturgique du Christ.*

32. *Regularis Concordia*, ed. Kornexl, pp. clxx–clxxvii, and in private correspondence.

33. *Monastic Agreement*, ed. and trans. Symons, ch. 46, p. 44.

34. *Regularis Concordia*, ed. Kornexl, §46, pp. 95–96.

to recite psalms continuously. The presence of the four *Depositio* antiphons in CCCC 422 shows that the *Depositio* concluding the Veneration synaxis was a performative part of the Good Friday Nones service at least in later eleventh-century Winchester or Sherborne.

The drama of the Veneration synaxis was likely effective enough for me to suggest that, had *The Dream of the Rood* poet seen a *Depositio Crucis* in the service he may have experienced, there would be signs of it, even over against the Gospel account of Christ's burial. Compare the description of the *Depositio* from the *Regularis Concordia*:

> On that part of the altar . . . there shall be a representation as it were of a sepulchre, hung about with a curtain, in which the holy Cross, when it has been venerated, shall be placed in the following manner: the deacons who carried the Cross before shall come forward and, having wrapped the Cross in a napkin there where it was venerated, they shall bear it thence, singing the antiphons . . . when they have laid the Cross therein, in imitation as it were of the burial of the Body of our Lord Jesus Christ, they shall sing the antiphon *Sepulto Domino* . . . let brethren be chosen by twos and threes . . . who shall keep faithful watch [excubias fideles exerceant], chanting psalms[35]

with the pertinent lines in *The Dream of the Rood*:

> Hnag ic hwæðre þam secgum to handa . . .
>   Ongunnon him þa moldern wyrcan
> beornas on banan gesyhðe;   curfon hie ðæt of beorhtan stane . . .
>   Ongunnon him þa sorhleoð galan
> earme on þa æfentide . . .
> Reste he ðær mæte weorode (lines 59b, 65b–66, 67b–68a, 69b)
>
> (Nevertheless I bowed to the hands of the men . . . They began to make for him a sepulcher, the men within the sight of the slayer, they carved that from bright stone . . . They began to sing for him then a dirge, wretched in the eventide . . . he rested there with little company.)

Can we in fact see anything of this ritual in the poem? We have the Rood giving the body of Christ over to the "secgas" (line 59b), his followers, who abandon the Cross drenched with blood (lines 61b–62a) and, in its presence, carve a sepulcher from bright stone for their crucified Lord: "Ongunnon him þa moldern wyrcan / beornas on banan gesyhðe, curfon hie ðæt of beorhtan stane" (lines 65b–66). The Rood itself remains in place

---

35. *Monastic Agreement*, ed. and trans. Symons, ch. 46, p. 46.

with the other two crosses in mourning after the burial, "Hwæðere we ðær greotende gode hwile / stodon on staðole" (lines 70–71a) while the body in the tomb grows cold, "hræw colode" (line 72b), and then they are hewn down and cast into a pit, "Þa us man fyllan ongan / ealle to eorðan . . . bedealf us man on deopan seaþe" (lines 73b–74a, 75a).

I am suspicious about a few details in *The Dream of the Rood* that an influence of the *Depositio Crucis* might possibly explain. Lines 65b–66 describe Christ's followers carving the bright stone with the Cross standing present at station on Calvary, thus creating a new on-site construction in order to make a tomb (*moldern*) for the crucified Lord. Stone does not cut this rapidly (especially with the imminent time constraints of the Passover Sabbath, mentioned specifically in both Luke 23:54 and John 19:42) so this detail in the poem is at a substantial remove from the Gospel accounts of the newly prepared sepulcher that has *already* been hewn of stone and was not specifically intended for Jesus Christ.[36] Yet the poem reads "ongunnon him þa moldern wyrcan" and the pronoun "him" can only be masculine singular dative, referring back to *Dryhten* of line 64a. The tomb in the poem is for Christ, just as the representation of the tomb in the *Depositio Crucis* is for the processional cross in its role of Corpus Christi.

In all of the Gospel accounts, those who lay Christ's body in the tomb depart promptly thereafter. In the poem, we are told that they begin to sing a dirge, *sorhleoð* there, 'wretched in the evening'—the time at which the *Depositio Crucis*, after the Nones service proper but before the Mass of the Pre-Sanctified, would have occurred. In late March or April, the light would be fading from the sky by four o'clock or four-thirty in England, and it would be evening indeed. When they do abandon the tomb, they leave their Lord at rest there with little company, "reste he ðær mæte weorode." While these lines have commonly been interpreted as *litotes*, a different explanation for them might appear in the final *Depositio Crucis* antiphon, sung once the cross has been ritually interred in the sepulcher representation: "Sepulto domino signatum est monumentum ponentes milites qui custodirent eum" (when the Lord was buried, the tomb was sealed and soldiers were placed there who guarded him). This antiphon, originally from Nocturns of Holy Saturday, derives from Matthew 27:66 but does not quote it directly: the ablative absolute *Sepulto Domino* is not part of the Gospel

---

36. In Matt. 27:60 it is called Joseph of Arimathea's own tomb, "et posuit illud in monumento suo novo quod exciderat in petra," while in Mark 15:46, Luke 23:53, and John 19:41 it is simply a new tomb in whom no one has yet been laid.

narrative, which instead refers to guards being placed at the tomb on the day *after* Good Friday, "altera autem die" (Matt. 27:62). But logical use of the Nocturns antiphon was made by the *Depositio Crucis*'s *ordo*, in its provision for a pair of monks at vigil from Vespers of Good Friday until Easter Sunday morning. It is therefore possible that line 69b, "reste he ðær mæte weorode," is not *litotes* at all, but instead a way of indicating the Gospel's solitude of Christ's burial and the *Depositio Crucis*'s vigilant monks, "excubias fideles exerceant."

If there is any merit to my suggestion that *The Dream of the Rood* owes a debt of influence to the Veneration of the Cross ritual, then I am also justified in searching for the particular design of the ritual which influenced the poem. From the foregoing then, I consider the synaxis most likely to have affected the composition of *The Dream of the Rood* as it stands in the Vercelli Book to resemble that which is presented in the *Regularis Concordia* witnesses of the eleventh century, barring only the presence of the seven penitential psalms whose absence may nevertheless be explained in the way I have set out above. To this end, any elements of the Veneration of the Cross within the poem could again raise the question of dating for both the liturgical and poetic materials.

If we can assume such a connection between the two, we must reason as follows. Since chapter 46 of the *Regularis Concordia* containing the *Depositio Crucis* is likely an insertion, then, given the late tenth-century dating of the Vercelli Book which is our *terminus ad quem* for *The Dream of the Rood* as we know it, the *Depositio Crucis* can only have been added within a very short time after the synod itself, and is indeed very probably from Æthelwold's own hand, as Kornexl suggests. Thus, if the *Depositio Crucis* is original to the *Regularis Concordia* synod, then *The Dream of the Rood* as we have it in the Vercelli Book would likely belong to the period of the Benedictine Reform as well.

APPENDIX I

1. *Improperia (Reproaches) and Trisagion*

A veiled processional cross is brought forward by two deacons who halt for three stations; at each of these, one antiphon from the *Improperia* is sung. In reply, two precentors sing the *Trisagion* in Greek, which the choir repeats in Latin. The *Improperia* are intended as Christ's words from the cross to his faithless people; the *Trisagion*, the shamed response of the Church in its two canonical tongues.

> Popule meus quid feci tibi aut in quo contristaui te? responde mihi.
> (O my people, what have I done to you or in what have I aggrieved you? Answer me.)

> Quia eduxi te de terra egipti, parasti crucem saluatori tuo.
> (Because I have led you from the land of Egypt, you have prepared a cross for your Savior.)

> *Agios o theos, agios ischiros, agios athanathos: eleison himas!*
> *Sanctus deus, sanctus fortis, sanctus et inmortalis: miserere nobis!*
> (Holy God, holy and mighty, holy and immortal: have mercy upon us!)

> Quia eduxi te per desertum quadraginta annos et manna cibaui te et introduxi in terram satis optimam, parasti crucem saluatori tuo.
> (Because I have led you through the desert forty years and fed you on manna and brought you to a land of plenty, you have prepared a cross for your Savior.)

> *Agios o theos, agios ischiros, agios athanathos: eleison himas!*
> *Sanctus deus, sanctus fortis, sanctus et inmortalis: miserere nobis!*

> Quid ultra debui facere mala et non feci ego quidem plantaui te uinea mea fructu decoram et tu facta est mihi nimis amara aceto namque framea potasti et lancea perforasti latus saluatori tuo
> (What further evil am I supposed to have done which I have not done? For I planted you as my lovely and fruitful vine and you have made for me vinegar bitter as a sword which you gave me to drink, and with a lance you have pierced the side of your Savior.)

> *Agios o theos, agios ischiros, agios athanathos: eleison himas!*
> *Sanctus deus, sanctus fortis, sanctus et inmortalis: miserere nobis!*

2. *Ecce Lignum Crucis*

In some traditions, the cross is partly unveiled at each station of the *Improperia*, while in others it is unshrouded only at the last one: but after the third Trisagion response, the antiphon sung by the full choir proclaims "Ecce lignum crucis" (behold! the wood of the cross) and in the imagina-

tive gaze of the beholder, the *crux gemmata* which has been the processional cross becomes the rough-hewn tree of Golgotha and takes up station
before the altar.

> Ecce lignum crucis in quo salus mundi pependit; uenite adoremus.
> (Behold, the wood of the cross, on which hung the salvation of the world.
> Come let us adore.)

3. *Crucem Tuam Adoramus and Dum Fabricator Mundi*

The action of the synaxis then divides, with the celebrant coming forward
to prostrate himself in *adoratio* before the cross and recite three private
prayers; the choir members await their own individual acts of *adoratio*, turn
and turn about, while singing the antiphons that begin "Crucem tuam
adoramus" and "Dum fabricator mundi," often accompanied by some or
all verses of Psalms 66 and 118. The inclusion or exclusion of these psalms
may be determined by the number of the faithful who wish to follow suit
with *actiones adorationis* of their own.

> Crucem tuam adoramus domine et sanctam resurrectionem tuam lauda-
> mus et glorificamus;
> (We adore thy cross, O Lord, and praise and glorify thy holy Resurrec-
> tion;)
>
> ecce enim propter crucem uenit gaudium in uniuerso mundi.
> (It is indeed because of the cross that joy of the world came for all cre-
> ation.)
>
> Dum fabricator mundi mortis supplicium pateretur in cruce clamans
> uoce magna tradidit spiritum
> (While the Creator of the world suffered punishment on the cross, crying
> in a great voice he gave up the spirit)
>
> et ecce, uelum templi scissum est, monumenta aperta sunt,
> (and behold, the veil of the temple was torn, graves were opened,)
>
> terra motus enim factus fuerit magnus quia mortem filii dei clamabat
> mundus se sustinere non posse;
> (all the great earth was shaken because it cried out at the death of the
> Son of God which it could not bear;)
>
> aperto ergo militis lancea latere cruxi dei exiuit
> (then the side of the crucified deity was opened with a soldier's lance)
>
> exiuit sanguis et aqua in redemptionem salutis nostre
> (and forth came blood and water for the redemption of our welfare.)

4. *Crux Fidelis Antiphon (eighth verse of Pange Lingua Gloriosi)*

Then follows the great Parasceve hymn ascribed to Venantius Fortunatus,

Pange Lingua Gloriosi, and it is the complete version of this hymn that is sung at Good Friday Nones, with its eighth strophe "Crux fidelis inter omnes" repeated after each verse proper as an antiphon functioning within the hymn-framework.

> Crux fidelis inter omnes arbor una nobilis
> (Faithful cross, unique and honored tree among all others,)
>
> nulla silua talem profert fronde flore germine
> (no wood bears another such flower among its leaves and branches,)
>
> dulce lignum dulce clauum dulce pondus sustinet.
> (the dear timber supports sweet nails and a beloved weight.)

5. *Depositio Crucis Antiphons in CCCC 422 (from Pss. 4:9, 14:1, 15:9 and Matt. 27:66)*

Seen earlier in the English tradition than in any other record, we find the last dramatic element of this synaxis, the *Depositio Crucis*, wherein the *crux gemmata* turned *lignum crucis* is now given its third role as Corpus Christi. It is reshrouded and ritually interred in a representation of the sepulcher near the altar to a series of four sung antiphons more commonly used for Holy Saturday.

> In pace in idipsum dormiam et requiescam.
> (In peace itself shall I sleep and take my rest.)
>
> Habitabit in tabernaculo tuo requiescet in monte sancta tua.
> (He will dwell in your tabernacle, he will rest on your sacred mountain.)
>
> Caro mea requiescet in spe.
> (My body will rest in hope.)
>
> Sepulto domino signatum est monumentum ponentes milites qui custodirent eum.
> (The Lord having been buried, the monument was sealed, setting soldiers there who guarded it.)

APPENDIX II

Comparison Chart for Veneration of the Cross Synaxis

* = incipit only

Arsénal 227 ca 860	B.N. 12052 ca 960	Concordia synod ca 970 texts s xi	CCCC 422 s xi[3?]	Bodley 120 i–iv s xi[3?]
Improperia Trisagion	Improperia* Trisagion*	Improperia* Trisagion	Improperia Trisagion	Improperia Trisagion
Ecce lignum	Ecce lignum*	Ecce lignum*	Ecce lignum	Ecce lignum
Ps 118: Beati inmaculati*	Ps 66: Deus misereatur*	—	Ps 66: Deus misereatur*	Ps 118: Beati inmaculati*
Crucem tuam adoramus*	Crucem tuam adoramus*	Crucem tuam adoramus*	Crucem tuam adoramus	—
Ps 66: Deus misereatur*	Ps 118: Beati inmaculati*	—	Ps 118: Beati inmaculati*	—
O crux splendidior*	Adoramus crucis*	—	—	—
Dum Fabricator*	Dum Fabricator*	Dum Fabricator*	Dum Fabricator	—
Pange lingua + Crux fidelis	Pange lingua + Crux fidelis*	Pange lingua + Crux fidelis*	Pange lingua + Crux fidelis	Pange lingua + Crux fidelis
—	—	Depositio Crucis: -In pace in idipsum* -Habitabit* -Caro mea requiescat -Sepulto Domino	Depositio Crucis: In pace in idipsum Habitat Caro mea requiescat Sepulto Domino	<lacuna>
Mass of Presanctified	Mass of Presanctified	Mass of Presanctified	—	<lacuna>
Super omnia ligna*	—	—	—	

Prophetic Vision in *The Dream of the Rood*

Thomas N. Hall

A persistent challenge for readers of *The Dream of the Rood* is figuring out what to make of the dreamer's initial vision of the cross, a kaleidoscopic array of images which the dreamer struggles to relate and which students of the poem have had difficulty describing, much less explaining. The passage in question reads as follows, paired with Bradley's prose translation:

> Hwæt! Ic swefna cyst   secgan wylle,
> hwæt me gemætte   to midre nihte,
> syðþan reordberend   reste wunedon!
>   Þuhte me þæt ic gesawe   syllicre treow
> on lyft lædan,   leohte bewunden,
> beama beorhtost.   Eall þæt beacen wæs
> begoten mid golde.   Gimmas stodon
> fægere æt foldan sceatum,   swylce þær fife wæron
> uppe on þam eaxlegespanne.   Beheoldon þær engel dryhtnes ealle,
> fægere þurh forðgesceaft.   Ne wæs ðær huru fracodes gealga,
> ac hine þær beheoldon   halige gastas,
> men ofer moldan,   and eall þeos mære gesceaft.
>   Syllic was se sigebeam,   ond ic synnum fah,
> forwunded mid wommum.   Geseah ic wuldres treow,
> wædum geweorðode,   wynnum scinan,
> gegyred mid golde;   gimmas hæfdon
> bewrigene weorðlice   wealdendes treow.
> Hwæðre ic þurh þæt gold   ongytan meahte
> earmra ærgewin,   þæt hit ærest ongan
> swætan on þa swiðran healfe.   Eall ic wæs mid sorgum gedrefed,
> forht ic wæs for þære fægran gesyhðe.   Geseah ic þæt fuse beacen
> wendan wædum ond bleom;   hwilum hit wæs mid wætan bestemed,
> beswyled mid swates gange,   hwilum mid since gegyrwed. (lines 1–23)[1]

(Listen! I want to recount the most excellent of visions, and what I dreamed in the middle of the night when voiceful mortals lay abed. It seemed to me that I saw a wondrous tree spreading aloft spun about with light, a most magnificent timber. The portent was all covered with gold; beautiful gems appeared at the corners of the earth and there were also

---

1. Quotations from the poem are taken from *Vercelli Book*, ed. Krapp, pp. 61–65.

five upon the cross-beam. All the beautiful angels of the Lord throughout the universe gazed thereon; certainly it was not the gallows of a criminal there, but holy spirits gazed thereon, men across the earth and all this glorious creation. Magnificent was the cross of victory and I was stained with sins, wounded by evil deeds. I observed that the tree of glory, enriched by its coverings, decked with gold, shone delightfully. Gems had becomingly covered the Ruler's tree. However, through the gold I could discern the earlier aggression of wretched men, in that it had once bled on the right side. I was altogether oppressed with anxieties; I was fearful in the presence of that beautiful sight. I observed the urgent portent shift its coverings and its hues; at times it was soaked with wetness, drenched by the coursing of blood, at times adorned with treasure.)[2]

This passage presents a number of interpretive difficulties that all revolve around the basic question: What exactly is the dreamer seeing? If we begin by thinking of this passage as a set of descriptive elements that follows a deliberately ordered sequence, it appears that the dreamer first sees a single cross, then he sees a second cross through the first, then he sees one cross change in its outward appearance until it becomes the other, then he sees the two crosses alternate in a seemingly recurrent pattern that shifts back and forth from one image to the next while holding both in view at once, so that even the number of crosses becomes problematic (is he seeing one or two?). The passage is so numbingly obscure that when prompted to say something intelligent about it in the classroom, many of us fall back on the not very helpful strategy of praising the poet's ability to manipulate imagery in original and evocative patterns. Thus Mitchell and Robinson, in the introduction to their classroom edition of the poem, register their admiration for the poem's "startling effects such as the gory, talking cross whose drops of blood surrealistically congeal into beautiful gems and then become blood again," a detail which they attribute to the poem's "imaginative poeticizing of theological issues."[3]

But it is not as though the passage has escaped careful analysis from a variety of perspectives. Michael Swanton, following Howard Patch, saw the shifting or dual identities of the cross as an allusion "to the changing colours appropriate to different seasons of the church year. A plain wooden Cross, blood-red, the colour of death . . . was carried during Lent until Good Friday, while on Easter Sunday a magnificent and richly jew-

---

2. Bradley, *Anglo-Saxon Poetry*, p. 160.
3. Mitchell and Robinson, *Guide to Old English*, p. 257.

elled Cross appeared."[4] Other readers have seen the vision as informed
by conventions of medieval reliquary decoration and crucifixion iconography.[5] Rosemary Woolf appealed to Christological doctrine in proposing
that the juxtaposition of the imagery of triumph and of suffering in the
opening vision and of the soteriological concepts of victory and sacrifice
in the prosopopoeia that follows depends on the theological principle of
communicatio idiomatum, which holds that "since Christ's person was a unity,
the properties of both natures [divine and human] could be ascribed to
it."[6] Richard Payne associates the dual image with the appearance of Christ
as the Word of God on a white horse in Revelation 19:11–13, where he is
described as "clothed with a garment sprinkled with blood," preparing to
lead the final battle against the Beast and the kings of earth. Payne writes
that "the dual appearance of the Cross in *The Dream of the Rood*, like its
counterpart in Revelation, suggests the paradoxical coexistence of Christ
in glory and Christ crucified."[7] More recently, David Johnson has suggested
that the vision of the cross is fundamentally eschatalogical, a prefiguration
of the Last Judgment, and that the twofold appearance of the cross reflects
the common medieval belief that at the Last Judgment Christ will reveal
himself in different ways to the blessed and the damned. As explained by
Augustine, and as echoed repeatedly in Old English literature, when all
of humanity assemble at Judgment Day, the blessed will see Christ shining
in glory, while the damned will see him covered with blood and showing
his wounds. In *The Dream of the Rood*, Johnson argues, the dreamer's vision
remains ambiguous because his own salvation is not yet assured, and he

---

4. *Dream of the Rood*, ed. Swanton, p. 111. Patch ("Liturgical Influence," p. 249) earlier
asserted that this passage alludes to "the method of changing the style of the cross between
Lent and Easter" from the use of a blood-red cross during Lent, to an ornamental cross on
Palm Sunday, to a *crux de christallo* on Easter day.

5. The poem's relation to medieval crucifixion iconography is most fully examined
in Raw, "*Dream of the Rood*." See also Schwab, "Das Traumgesicht vom Kreuzesbaum"; and
Raw, *Anglo-Saxon Crucifixion Iconography*, pp. 136–37, 167–68, and 178–79. On the cross as
reliquary, see Mahler, "*Lignum Domini*." Comparisons with the iconography of the Ruthwell
Cross have been advanced by numerous scholars, including Fleming, "*Dream of the Rood* and
Anglo-Saxon Monasticism," pp. 43, 54, 60; Burlin, "Ruthwell Cross"; Brian Roberts, "Some
Relationships between *The Dream of the Rood* and the Cross at Ruthwell"; and Ó Carragáin,
Ritual and the Rood. Similar attempts have been made to interpret the poem's runic counter-
part inscribed on the Ruthwell Cross in light of crucifixion iconography: see Ó Carragáin,
"Ruthwell Crucifixion Poem," and Ó Carragáin, *Ritual and the Rood*.

6. Woolf, "Doctrinal Influences," pp. 139–40; repr. in her *Art and Doctrine*, p. 32. On the
concept of *communicatio idiomatum*, see further K. Forster, "Idiomenkommunikation."

7. Payne, "Convention and Originality," p. 335.

does not yet know which of the two visions will be his on Judgment Day. The double vision of the cross thus serves as a warning that the fate of the soul is uncertain, and the dreamer's realization of this fact is instrumental in his conversion at the end of the poem.[8]

One of the most illuminating and, to my mind, intellectually satisfying approaches to this passage was advanced by Robert Wright in a 1986 Duke University dissertation on the problem of ineffability in medieval literature. In a chapter on *The Dream of the Rood* and Dante, Wright begins by comparing the vision of the cross in the Old English poem to Dante's vision of the griffin in canto 31 of the *Purgatorio*, where the griffin, a traditional symbol for Christ, is depicted as a gleaming creature fashioned from two animals, half lion and half eagle, shining like the sun in a mirror, now with the one, now with the other nature:

> Come in lo specchio il sol, non altrimenti
> la doppia fiera dentro vi raggiava,
> or con altri, or con altri reggimenti.
> Pensa, lettor, s'io mi maravigliava,
> quando vedea la cosa in sè star queta,
> e nel'idolo suo si trasmutava. (*Purgatorio* XXXI.121–26)
>
> (As the sun in a mirror, so was the twofold animal gleaming therewithin, now with the one, now with the other bearing. Think, reader, if I marveled when I saw the thing stand still in itself, and in its image changing.)[9]

Like the vision of the cross in *The Dream of the Rood*, Dante's representation of the griffin is structured paradoxically around concurrent yet alternating symbols of Christ's two natures, simultaneously divine and human, and both visions can be explained, Wright suggests, in terms of the Christological doctrine of the hypostatic union as propounded by the Council of Chalcedon in 431. As a foundational statement for the church's teaching concerning the person of Christ, this doctrine maintained that Christ possessed "two natures, unconfusedly, immutably, indivisibly, inseparably [united]."[10] Wright proposes that the visions in Dante and the Old English poem are both informed by precisely this theological tenet in their attempt to represent the "mysterious concurrence of unity and duality in the

---

8. David Johnson, "Old English Religious Poetry."
9. Dante Alighieri, *Divine Comedy*, ed. and trans. Singleton, 2:346–47.
10. Robert Wright, "Art and the Incarnate Word," p. 193.

Incarnation."[11] But in addition, Wright goes further by pointing out that the theological mystery depicted in *The Dream of the Rood* is strikingly analogous to twentieth-century attempts to define the nature of metaphorical language, particularly as formulated by I. A. Richards and later elaborated by Max Black and Paul Ricoeur. According to this school of thought, a metaphor is engendered by the simultaneous presence of two constituent elements, a vehicle and a tenor, which cooperate in an inclusive meaning. A metaphor is consequently paradoxical and tensional, and the meaning produced in a metaphor lies not in the tension between the terms but in their predicative union. In Wright's reading, the vision of the cross in *The Dream of the Rood* accordingly functions as a metaphor for the Incarnation in which the interaction of tenor and vehicle, the union of two natures, is depicted visually and dynamically.[12]

These critical approaches to the dreamer's opening vision are by no means the end of the story when it comes to attempts to make sense of this troublesome passage, but they do suffice to indicate the range of approaches—grounded in liturgical, iconographic, theological, linguistic, and philosophical arguments—that have been put forward in criticism of *The Dream of the Rood*, and they are sufficiently representative of the interpretive history of the poem to provide a useful point of departure for further discussion. I should begin by saying that for all the arguments that have been brought to bear on this passage, the one question I find curiously absent from discussions of the dreamer's opening vision is its relation to medieval concepts of vision. By this I do not mean the poem's relation to medieval dream psychology, nor to the literary genre of the *visio*, which have more than occasionally attracted attention in discussions of the poem.[13] The question I wish to pose instead is simply how the dreamer's vision of the cross relates to early medieval concepts of the process of seeing and knowing. To what extent can the dynamic and paradoxical vision of the cross be explained by the nature of vision itself, and more importantly, is there a particular kind of vision to which it can be compared?

Visionary experience takes many forms in medieval thought but before the twelfth century is rarely defined or conceptualized beyond the

---

11. Robert Wright, "Art and the Incarnate Word," p. 195.
12. Robert Wright, "Art and the Incarnate Word," p. 201.
13. Notable forays into this territory include Burrow, "Approach to the *Dream of the Rood*"; Hieatt, "Dream Frame and Verbal Echo"; Szarmach, "Ælfric, the Prose Vision, and *The Dream of the Rood*"; Sola Buil, "Dream Vision"; Galloway, "Dream-Theory"; and Harbus, "Dream and Symbol."

familiar categories delineated by Augustine, Macrobius, and Calcidius.[14] An important but generally unacknowledged exception to this rule is the series of remarks on the relationship between prophetic vision and prophetic language in Gregory the Great's *Homilies on Ezechiel*.[15] Perhaps not as well known today as some of Gregory's other writings such as the *Dialogues*, the *Pastoral Care*, and the *Moralia in Job*, the *Homilies on Ezechiel* were first preached to the monks at Gregory's home foundation of St. Andrew's in Rome in 593 and 594, then at the monks' request were revised and collected eight years later and presented to Bishop Marinianus of Ravenna in the form in which they survive today.[16] To Anglo-Saxonists, these homilies will be familiar at least indirectly from the legend related in the Whitby *Life of Gregory* that they were dictated to Gregory by the Holy Spirit in the form of a white dove perched on his shoulder, an image that became a standard feature of the iconography of Gregory the Great throughout the Middle Ages.[17] Historically the *Homilies on Ezechiel* are of interest because they record Gregory's deeply anxious reflections on the Lombard siege of Rome in 593, a short-lived attack on the city that was brought to an end through a treaty which Gregory himself negotiated with the Lombard leader Agilulf. But these homilies are important as well for their probing and (so far as I know) unprecedented analysis of the nature of prophecy and its relation to visionary experience. As a preliminary step toward explicating the theophanic vision that opens the Book of Ezechiel, Gregory devotes the whole of the first homily to an examination of the nature of prophecy and pro-

14. Studies of patristic and medieval theories of visionary experience have multiplied rapidly in recent years and are too numerous to cite in full here, but important milestones include Miles, "Vision"; Kathryn Lynch, *High Medieval Dream Vision*; Kruger, *Dreaming in the Middle Ages*; Hamburger, "Speculations on Speculation"; Hahn, "*Visio Dei*"; Camille, "Before the Gaze"; Biernoff, *Sight and Embodiment*; Newman, "What Did It Mean to Say 'I Saw'?"; and Noble, "Vocabulary of Vision."

15. The following quotations from Gregory's homilies are taken from *Grégoire le Grand*, ed. and trans. Morel, by book, homily, and section; English translations are mine. For brief but valuable discussions of these texts, see Neuss, *Das Buch Ezechiel*, pp. 91–100; Lieblang, *Grundfragen der mystischen Theologie*; and Lieb, *Visionary Mode*, pp. 257–62. An English translation is available by Gray, *Homilies of Saint Gregory*.

16. On the dates of the collection see Morel, *Grégoire le Grand*, 1:10–11; and Markus, *Gregory the Great and His World*, p. 16.

17. *Earliest Life of Gregory the Great*, ed. and trans. Colgrave, pp. 120–22 (ch. 26). For the iconographic tradition that associates Gregory with the dove, see Croquison, "Origines de l'iconographie Grégorienne"; *Bibliotheca Sanctorum*, ed. Caraffa et al., 7:278–81 and 286; and *Lexikon der christlichen Ikonographie*, ed. Kirschbaum and Braunfels, 6:436–38. On the currency of Gregory's homilies in England through the early twelfth century, see Hall, "Early English Manuscripts."

phetic language. To Gregory's way of thinking, an act of prophecy involves much more than a present anticipation of future events: it is instead a revelation of things hidden in all temporal dimensions, including past and present, a form of visionary gnosis without temporal boundaries or restrictions. There are moments, Gregory says, when the spirit of prophecy will touch the prophet's heart on issues concerning past, present, and future all at once, and the prophet will experience a vision that involves multiple temporalities simultaneously (*Hom.* I.i.1). To illustrate his point, Gregory provides a reading of the encounter between the Virgin Mary and Elizabeth in the first chapter of the Gospel of Luke, where according to Gregory, Elizabeth utters a prophecy that concerns past and present as well as future events. In Luke's account of this scene, when Mary journeys into the hill country to greet her cousin, the unborn John the Baptist acknowledges Christ's approach by leaping in his mother's womb. Elizabeth becomes filled with the Holy Spirit and says to Mary, "Blessed art thou among women, and blessed is the fruit of thy womb. . . . And blessed art thou that hast believed, because those things shall be accomplished that were spoken to thee by the Lord" (Luke 1:42,45). In Gregory's interpretation of this passage, Elizabeth prophesied for the past when she revealed her knowledge that Mary had heard and believed Gabriel's promise (in Luke 1:26–38), she prophesied for the present in showing that she knew that the Son of God was at that moment dwelling in Mary's womb, and she prophesied for the future by affirming that God's promises to Mary would later be fulfilled (*Hom.* I.i.8). In this way Elizabeth demonstrated that the knowledge she acquired from the Holy Spirit pertained to more than one temporal realm but was nevertheless revealed to her in a single prophetic instant.

In turning to the text of Ezechiel, Gregory discerns far greater subtleties in the relation between prophecy and time and in the prophet's capacity to see what those who lack the prophet's visionary ability cannot. The Book of Ezechiel, he observes, begins with the word *et* ("Et factum est in tricesimo anno"), and because the word *et* is grammatically construed as a conjunction, its grammatical function requires that it mediate between two things and join those two things together. In Gregory's reading of this opening verse, there must be something preceding that initial word *et* which we as readers cannot perceive because we come to the text with our physical eyes alone. The prophet, on the other hand, can see what precedes the word *et* because he beholds a deeper *interior* meaning with his spiritual eyes, and that *interior* meaning is joined together (*coniuncta*) in the prophet's mind to an *exterior* meaning through the agency of a conjunction far more powerful than the word *et*. In the mind of the prophet, Gregory explains, spiritual realities and physical realities are inextricably joined, and the prophet's intimate vision (*uisio intima*) enables him to see the two realities simultaneously. Between the *interior* word which the prophet alone sees and the *exterior* word which he utters in the form of a prophecy, the connection is so close that he is unable to detect the movement from one to the other, and the two come to him as a unified whole (*Hom.* I.ii.2).[18]

Elsewhere in the *Homilies on Ezechiel* this idea that the prophet sees whole what others see only in part proves important to Gregory because it illuminates the relationship between allegorical and literal meanings, which coexist in the prophet's imagination and in the biblical text but which we as readers tend to analyze as discrete categories.[19] In a number of other passages, however, this claim for the integrative and totalizing power of prophetic vision also leads Gregory to a series of observations on the inevitable breakdown of language in its attempt to capture the essence of an ineffable or transcendent vision. In Book I Homily 6, he makes an effort to account for the fact that the "wheel with four faces" in Ezechiel 1:15 is introduced *after* the description of the four living creatures, even though according to Gregory's own interpretation of this passage, the wheel is meant to symbolize the Old Testament while the four living creatures represent the four evangelists.[20] One might expect these images to be presented in reverse order, so that the symbol of the Old Testament precedes that of the New, but as Gregory explains:

> Quamuis sit adhuc aliud quod in hac descriptione considerari debeat, quia prophetiae spiritus sic intra semetipsum anteriora et posteriora simul colligit, ut haec simul prophetae lingua proferre non possit. Sed ampla quae uidet de dispertitis sermonibus emanat, et nunc ultima post prima, nunc uero prima post ultima loquitur. Vnde Hiezechihel propheta sub figura sanctae uniuersalis Ecclesiae, et euangelistarum gloriam per quatuor animalium similitudinem uidit, et tamen repente illa subiungit, quae anterioribus temporibus gesta sunt, ut patenter indicet simul se uidisse quod carnis lingua non sufficeret simul dicere. (*Hom.* I.vi.11)

---

18. The Gregorian concept of interiority is examined by Aubin, "Intériorité et extériorité"; Dagens, *Saint Grégoire le Grand*, pp. 133–244; and Evans, *Thought of Gregory the Great*, p. 45.

19. See Morel, *Grégoire le Grand*, 1:16–19.

20. The association of the four beasts in Ezechiel's vision with the four evangelists goes back to Irenaeus: see Metzger, *Canon of the New Testament*, p. 263; and O'Reilly, "Patristic and Insular Traditions of the Evangelists," p. 55.

(There is yet another factor that needs to be taken into account in this arrangement, for the spirit of prophecy unites within itself earlier events and later ones, so that the language of the prophet is incapable of presenting them all at once. But the vastness that he witnesses is expressed in fragmented language, and he will sometimes say what comes first and then what comes next, while at other times he will relate a later event before what precedes it. Thus within this figuration the prophet Ezechiel beheld the glory of the holy catholic church and of the evangelists through the similitude of the four living creatures, and yet he abruptly connects them with events that took place at an earlier time so that he might clearly indicate that he has seen in an instant what human language is unable to express all at once.)

The prophet's inward vision, in other words, encompasses past and present without distinction and without sequential ordering, and the seemingly inverted presentation of the symbols in the opening chapter of Ezechiel can be understood as a sort of distortion effect that results when the multiple dimensions of Ezechiel's unified spiritual vision are forced to accommodate human conceptions of time. The failure of language to render the prophet's vision again becomes an issue in Homily 8, where the challenge of explicating another difficult verse prompts Gregory to consider the physical process involved in translating a prophetic vision into human language:

> quia sanctus Spiritus in corde prophetarum, quod simul ostendit intus, non simul eicit per linguam foras. Aqua quippe scientiae qua prophetantis animus repletur, in contemplatione uehementer exuberat. Sed quia angustum est spiritui omne os hominis, id est foramen carnis, ad explendam illam immensitatem quae conspicitur, proferendo lingua uariatur. (*Hom.* I.viii.5)[21]

(for the Holy Spirit does not express outwardly through language all at once what it reveals inwardly to the heart of the prophet in a single

---

21. The image recalls a passage in Cassian's *Conferences* IX.25 on the nature of the highest form of prayer, which similarly transcends human language and pours forth like a river or fountain. According to Cassian, this type of prayer "transcends all human understanding and is distinguished not, I would say, by a sound of the voice or a movement of the tongue or a pronunciation of words. Rather, the mind is aware of it when it is illuminated by an infusion of heavenly light from it, and not by narrow human words, and once the understanding has been suspended it gushes forth as from a most abundant fountain and speaks ineffably to God, producing more in that very brief moment than the self-conscious mind is able to articulate easily or to reflect upon" (*John Cassian. The Conferences*, pp. 345–46; cf. *Iohannis Cassiani Conlationes XXIIII*, ed. Petschenig, pp. 272–73).

instant. For the water of knowledge that replenishes the mind of the prophet gushes forth with great force in contemplation. But because the human mouth, the aperture of the flesh, is too narrow for the spirit, when he attempts to capture the immensity that he perceives and give utterance to it, his language breaks up.)

These remarks on the relation between prophetic vision and prophetic language form only a minor subtheme in Gregory's *Homilies on Ezechiel*, and they are presented so briefly that it is difficult to claim they make up a significant component of Gregory's thought. Yet in spite of their brevity, they are remarkable for the sheer novelty of their approach to the subject of visionary experience since they are so clearly independent of the traditional categories of medieval faculty psychology and Macrobian dream theory. As is typical of Gregory's writing, his thoughts on this subject rest on a strong Augustinian foundation, and an obvious model for a portion of these remarks is Augustine's distinction that for God, who exists outside of time, all things happen at once, whereas for humans, events succeed one another in time; however, Gregory appears to be original in transferring this distinction to the realm of prophecy. Gregory is also probably influenced to some degree by the Augustinian notion of spiritual vision—the vision of symbols and images with corporeal shape but without corporeal substance, as in St. John the Divine's visions in the Apocalypse—but once again Gregory raises issues concerning the relation of vision to language, time, and prophecy that Augustine never takes up in quite the same way.[22] Gregory's analysis of prophetic vision in the *Homilies on Ezechiel* is even to be distinguished from his own remarks elsewhere about the prophetic function of dreams (expressed most succinctly in the *Dialogues* IV.50),[23] the spiritual function of artistic images,[24] and the kind of contemplative visionary experience that leads to the threshold of a vision of God, the aspect of

---

22. Gregory's various debts to Augustine are traced by Courcelle, *Confessions de saint Augustin*, pp. 225–31; Butler, *Western Mysticism*, pp. 106–7; and Dagens, *Saint Grégoire le Grand*, pp. 178–84. For Augustine's elaborate theory concerning three different types of visionary experience—corporal, spiritual, and intellectual, each corresponding to one of the three heavens visited by St. Paul—see his *De Genesi ad litteram* XII.2–27, pp. 380–422.

23. See Godden, "Were It Not That I Have Bad Dreams," pp. 108–13.

24. Gregory's thoughts concerning the spiritual function of artistic images are most famously expressed in his two letters of July 599 and October 600 to Bishop Serenus of Marseilles, *S. Gregorii Magni Registrum Epistolarum*, pp. 768 and 873–76 (*Epp.* IX.209 and XI.10). See the discussion by Chazelle, "Pictures, Books, and the Illiterate"; Camille, "Gregorian Definition Revisited"; Chazelle, "Memory, Instruction, Worship"; and Kessler, *Spiritual Seeing*, pp. 114–16 and 120–24.

Gregory's thought that proved most crucial for the later development of medieval mysticism.[25]

Within the context of patristic and medieval visionary theory, Gregory's views are without close parallel, but it is instructive to observe that his analysis of the nature of prophetic vision corresponds surprisingly well to a more recent attempt to explain the relationship between visionary experience and artistic creativity. This explanation appears in the writings of Albert Rothenberg, a Yale psychiatrist who published a series of studies during the 1970s and 1980s on the nature of the creative process. After conducting over two thousand hours of interviews with scientists, artists, and writers, including a number of well-known figures such as Robert Penn Warren and Arthur Miller, Rothenberg found that a significant number of these highly successful creative individuals claim to have hit upon a particularly bold or innovative idea at the moment when they were able to hold two contradictory or antithetical concepts in mind at once, a phenomenon which he labeled janusian thinking (after the two-faced Roman god Janus).[26] Rothenberg found that writers who engage in janusian thinking tend to explore the nexus between ideas and their opposites, and their writings are characterized by a preoccupation with "conflict, irony, tragic tension, and aesthetic ambiguity."[27] "In the janusian process," Rothenberg explains,

> multiple opposites or antitheses are conceived simultaneously, either as existing side by side or as equally operative, valid, or true. In an apparent defiance of logic or of physical possibility, the creative person consciously formulates the simultaneous operation of antithetical elements or factors and develops those formulations into integrated entities and creations. It is, as I said, a leap that transcends ordinary logic. What emerges is no mere combination or blending of elements: the conception contains not only different entities, but also opposing and antagonistic elements that are experienced and understood as coexistent. As a self-contradictory structure, the janusian formulation is surprising when seriously posited.

---

25. For discussion of Gregory's teachings concerning contemplation and contemplative vision, see Ménager, "Contemplation d'après saint Grégoire le Grand"; Lieblang, *Grundfragen der mystischen Theologie*, pp. 99–170; Ménager, "Divers sens du mot 'contemplatio'"; Butler, *Western Mysticism*, pp. 87–92, 171–88; Dagens, *Saint Grégoire le Grand*, pp. 176–78, 211–12, 254–64; McGinn, *Presence of God*, pp. 50–79; and McGinn, "Contemplation in Gregory the Great."

26. This idea was first put forward by Rothenberg in "The Process of Janusian Thinking in Creativity."

27. Rothenberg, *Creativity and Madness*, p. 16.

Although it usually appears modified and transformed in the final product, it leaves the mark of implicit unexpectedness and paradox on the work.[28]

As an example, Rothenberg cites the case of the poet Richard Wilbur, who reported to Rothenberg that he came upon the idea for a poem one day when he was walking on a beach and noticed some rocks along the sand. These rocks had a smooth appealing texture like human skin but were hard and heavy and had the potential to be used as violent weapons. "The idea that the rocks were at once sensual objects as well as weapons led to a conception of the simultaneous operation of sex and violence in the world, and Wilbur elaborated those aspects in the final version of this poem."[29] A more intriguing example is the case of Albert Einstein, who at a crucial period in his career was struggling to adapt Isaac Newton's theory of gravitation to fit his own principle of special relativity. In 1905 Einstein had succeeded in formulating his Special Theory of Relativity, which holds that the physical laws of nature (such as the speed of light) are the same for all frames of reference, but he was unable to show how this theory applies to Newton's laws of gravitation. The breakthrough to this impasse came one day when Einstein was suddenly able to imagine the plight of a person falling from the roof of a house. From the perspective of this observer in free fall there exists no gravitational field in his immediate environment, so that if he releases an object during the fall, that object will remain in a position of rest relative to the observer, even though both observer and object are in the process of falling and are subject to the pull of the earth's gravitation. The observer and object are thus simultaneously at rest and in motion, both subject to the law of gravity and free from the effects of gravity at the same time. Einstein's ability to envision this paradoxical situation provided him with the concrete example he needed to modify Newton's theories to accommodate his own theory of relativity. It was a decisive step toward Einstein's development of the General Theory of Relativity published in 1915, and it was an idea he later referred to as "the happiest thought of my life."[30] In this and many other cases which Rothenberg relates at length, the sudden discovery of an inspirational new idea comes about when an individual is able to visualize two antithetical concepts in operation at once.

---

28. Rothenberg, *Creativity and Madness*, p. 15.
29. Rothenberg, *Creativity and Madness*, p. 16.
30. Rothenberg, *Creativity and Madness*, pp. 14–15.

In some cases, Rothenberg also found that this yoking together of opposing or contradictory ideas that lies at the heart of the janusian process is accompanied by a second, related type of thought process which Rothenberg labeled "homospatial thinking." In homospatial thinking, as the term suggests, two or more discrete entities are conceived of as occupying the same physical space.[31] Several of the artists, writers, musicians, and scientists whom Rothenberg interviewed report that they came up with their most creative ideas by superimposing two or more images or hearing multiple sounds simultaneously. The Nobel Prize–winning microbiologist Fuller Albright explained that he made a critical discovery when he imagined himself superimposed on a living cell; and the mathematician Henri Poincaré wrote that he made the essential connection that permitted him to develop his Fuchsian geometric series when he was lying awake in bed one night with a barrage of ideas storming through his head, and suddenly "two of them coalesced, so to speak, to form a stable combination." By morning all the details were in place and he had succeeded in completing the first class of Fuchsian geometric functions.[32] Several of the cases Rothenberg cites are of poets who explain that they arrived at certain metaphors by imagining two images sharing the same space at once, and as Rothenberg writes, "the homospatial process is a prime factor in the production of poetic metaphors."[33] Einstein's idea of the observer falling from a roof likewise exemplifies homospatial thinking since the two contradictory phenomena of being subject to gravity and having no gravitational field occur in the same space. Like Gregory's prophet, then, these creative individuals experience a revelation or discovery of some kind that is characterized by the perception of multiple realities that occur simultaneously, at times occupying the same physical location.

In *The Dream of the Rood*, the vision of the cross conforms in a number of ways to the definition of prophetic vision advanced by Gregory and to the nature of the creative process as analyzed by Rothenberg. The dreamer

---

31. Rothenberg, *Creativity and Madness*, p. 25. The homospatial process was first formulated and discussed in a series of articles by Robert S. Sobel and Albert Rothenberg, "Artistic Creation as Stimulated by Superimposed versus Separated Visual Images"; Rothenberg and Sobel, "Creation of Literary Metaphors"; Rothenberg, "Artistic Creation as Stimulated by Superimposed versus Combined-Composite Visual Images"; and Rothenberg, "Creativity and the Homospatial Process."

32. Rothenberg, *Creativity and Madness*, p. 30.

33. Rothenberg, *Creativity and Madness*, pp. 27, 26. For similar types of abstract thinking that involve the uniting of opposites, see Torrance, *Why Fly?* pp. 220–21.

tells us first of all that the vision was revealed to him in a single dream—
the best of dreams—but in his poetic retelling of that dream the vision of
the cross refracts into a cluster of distinct yet overlapping images. In the
terms made available by Gregory, the dreamer experiences a single coherent vision which, in the process of being put into language, devolves into
a fragmented set of discrete visionary elements. The vision comes to the
dreamer at a single time, "to midre nihte," but his efforts to express that
vision in words for the benefit of the "reordberend" results in a failure of
language to capture the intensity and magnitude of the divine revelation,
and it becomes instead a scatter of broken images. In his description of
the cross's shifting appearance, moreover, it is difficult to tell when the
dreamer has a single image in sight and when the two dominant images
merge or coalesce, so that like Ezechiel, and like Rothenberg's creative
subjects, the dreamer sees more than one thing at a time. In Gregory's
formulation, the dreamer's visionary ability permits him to see multiple
realities simultaneously. In Rothenberg's terms, "opposites or antitheses
are conceived simultaneously, either as existing side by side or as equally
operative, valid, or true." For the dreamer, the cross is both separately and
simultaneously a sign of glory and passion, an emblem of Christ's divinity and mortality. If, as others have supposed, the vision of the cross is
meant to recall typologically and iconographically both the Crucifixion
and the Last Judgment, then the vision can also be said to embrace events
from multiple temporalities, the hallmark of prophetic vision as defined by
Gregory.[34] The dreamer even states in lines 18–20 that he was able to perceive the "earmra ærgewin" by looking "þurh þæt gold," as if by gazing at
the golden cross he was able to peer through one temporality into another.
But the images are not fixed or static, and although both images appear
to be present in lines 18–20, they are said to shift back and forth in lines
21–23, so that as in Dante's vision of the griffin, the images are paradoxically concurrent yet alternating. The vision is dynamic and transformative.
It redefines itself even as the dreamer is describing it, and the difficult and

---

34. Another visionary experience that seems to reflect this aspect of Gregory's notion
of prophetic vision is ascribed to St. Guthlac in ch. 43 of Felix's *Vita*, where Guthlac abounds
in the spirit of prophecy ("Coepit . . . Guthlac prophetiae spiritu pollere") and is endowed
with the ability to see events from one temporality through another: "In tantam enim gratiae divinae spiritus in eo pollebat, ut absentia praesentibus et futura praeteritis ut praesen-
tia arbitraretur" (So greatly did the spirit of divine grace abound in him that he discerned
absent things by things present, and future things by the past, as though they were present)
(*Felix's Life of Saint Guthlac*, ed. and trans. Colgrave, pp. 132–35).

contradictory images that comprise it attest to the dreamer's inability to communicate the richness of his vision.[35]

I do not think it necessary to conclude that the dreamer in *The Dream of the Rood* should be ranked in a class of creative visionaries together with Einstein, or even that the poem's author was familiar with Gregory's *Homilies on Ezechiel*, but I do wish to suggest that the types of visionary experience examined by Gregory and Rothenberg provide useful analogies for the phenomenon described in the opening vision. These accounts of prophetic vision and of the visionary dimension of artistic creativity both express in visionary terms the same mystical idea embodied in the theological principle of the hypostatic union. They offer illuminating and apposite corollaries for an influential model for the nature of metaphorical language. And perhaps most important, they do not negate or oversimplify the poem's own ineffable qualities. For as another theorist of visionary experience has remarked, "A great work of art is like a dream; for all its apparent obviousness it does not explain itself and is always ambiguous."[36]

---

35. One other passage in the poem that involves an overlay of two distinct images held in suspension simultaneously is the cross's statement at line 101, "Deað he þær byrigde" (he tasted death there), where the pronoun *he* can refer both to Adam (named in the previous line) and Christ (referred to in the following half-line), who are thereby linked syntactically and typologically. For an elaboration of this argument, see Irvine, "Adam or Christ?" Robert DiNapoli finds a similar double vision at play in the Exeter Book poem *The Order of the World*, where the phrase "dryhtnes duguðe" (the Lord's host) at line 48a refers at once to the angels and the stars: see DiNapoli, "Heart of the Visionary Experience," pp. 103–4.

36. Jung, "Psychology and Literature," p. 104.

ÞYLE AS FOOL: REVISITING *BEOWULF*'S HUNFERTH

LESLIE A. DONOVAN

Beowulf's þyle, Hunferth, occupies not only a special place near the king but also a special place in the poem's critical history as probably its most discussed minor character.[1] Apart from Hrothgar, Hunferth is the first person in the hall to address the hero, his silence is noted in the climactic description of Grendel's dismembered arm, and his presence is spotlighted in the hall scene following Beowulf's victory over Grendel. He is also the only character to offer Beowulf practical aid in the form of a sword, presented as the hero is about to dive into the mere in search of Grendel's mother. Further, when returning the sword to Hunferth, Beowulf praises it with gracious and complimentary words, even though the sword was ineffective against the merewife. Hunferth is the son of a noble ("Ecglafes bearn" [line 499]), sits at Hrothgar's feet ("þe æt fotum sæt" [line 500]), utters words that bear martial connotations ("beadurune" [line 501]), feels great vexation about Beowulf ("micel æfþunca" [line 502]), speaks to Beowulf in an apparently blunt and disparaging fashion (lines 506–28), is accused of drunkenness ("beore druncen" [line 531]), is called the bane or slayer of his brothers ("broðrum to banan wurde" [line 587]), has a wit that is strong ("þeah þin wit duge" [line 589]), has a trusted spirit ("ferhþe treowde" [line 1166]), possesses a great mind or spirit ("mod micel" [line 1167]), wields a strong skill ("eafoþes cræft" [line 1466]), loses glory ("dome forleas" [line 1470]), and is widely renowned ("widcuðne" [line 1489]).[2] For nearly a century, these ambiguous and seemingly contradictory details of a minor character, who is dealt with directly in only 137 of the poem's 3,182 lines, have generated substantial critical comment, confusion, and speculation.[3]

---

1. My own fascination with Hunferth and his possible relationship to the court fool began in 1983 when I was a graduate student enrolled in my first *Beowulf* seminar, taught by Helen Damico, whose career this volume honors. Helen's passion for the epic and dedication to teasing out the literary and historical heritage of the poem's minor characters, as evidenced in her crucial study of Wealhtheow, inspired me both to look closely at Hunferth for my class project and to pursue a career in Old English literature. While the results of my effort here can never match the scope and importance of Helen's work, I offer this study in affection and gratitude for the immense personal and professional debt I owe her.

2. References to *Beowulf* are taken from Klaeber's *Beowulf and the Fight at Finnsburg.* All translations are my own, unless otherwise noted.

3. A useful summary of the most important criticism on Hunferth appears in Bjork, "Digressions and Episodes," pp. 205–8.

Based on his introductory speech, typically considered to be motivated by the *þyle*'s "pronounced envy"[4] of the hero, Hunferth has been perceived as affrontive, quarrelsome, and insolent. Scholars interpret the enigmatic *þyle*'s function in the poem variously as a pagan priest, Christian allegory of Discord, malevolent figure, jealous thane, or an ineffectual champion,[5] and have characterized his words to Beowulf as "attack[s]," [6] "invidious insults,"[7] and "abusive remarks."[8] Others understand him as providing a negative balance in the poem, an antithesis or artistic foil[9] to Beowulf, or as "a self-regarding, narcissistic parody of the hero."[10] To James L. Rosier, Hunferth is not only the prototype of the treacherous counselor found throughout Germanic legend but also a "drunkard, scurrilous accuser, fratricide, and coward."[11] He perceives a remarkable similarity between Grendel and Hunferth in that "both are associated with Cain, the one by the deed of fratricide, the other in lineage; both are consigned to hell and both disrupt the joy of the hall, [H]unferð by his battle-rune, and Grendel by physical assault."[12] Craig R. Davis expresses a similar sentiment when he claims Hunferth "is the serpent in the heart of Heorot. In [H]unferth burns the hateful spirit which now haunts the hall."[13] Yet, while these studies present neatly designed arguments, readings that insist on Hunferth as an emblem of diabolical intention and inspiration may be too narrowly focused.

Surely if Hunferth were intended to be the poem's archvillain, his sword Hrunting would not have been so generously praised by the poet and its loan so graciously accepted by Beowulf. Further, any possible past treachery against his brothers has not apparently made Hunferth less respected in the court; he still sits at the feet of the lord, holds an acknowledged court title, and speaks freely to hall-guests. Also significant is the fact that Hun-

---

4. Eugene Green, *Anglo-Saxon Audiences*, p. 99.

5. Listed in the order presented, these arguments appear in: Hollowell, "Unferð the *Þyle*"; Bloomfield, "*Beowulf* and Christian Allegory"; Nagy, "Reassessment"; Gingher, "Unferth Perplex"; and Fajardo-Acosta, "Intemperance, Fratricide and the Elusiveness of Grendel."

6. Nelles, "Beowulf's sorhfullne sið," p. 306.

7. Lee, *Gold-Hall and Earth-Dragon*, p. 62.

8. Gingher, "Unferth Perplex," p. 19.

9. See, for example: Pope, "*Beowulf* 505, 'gehedde'"; and Oglivy, "Unferth: Foil to Beowulf?"

10. Lee, *Gold-Hall and Earth-Dragon*, p. 215.

11. Rosier, "Design for Treachery," p. 4.

12. Rosier, "Design for Treachery," p. 7.

13. Davis, *Beowulf and the Demise of Germanic Legend*, p. 111.

ferth's jibes at Beowulf elicit no obvious disapproval from Hrothgar or any other members of his hall. Viewed alongside arguments for Hunferth as a villainous figure, such evidence highlights what Ted Irving has called the "serious trouble [we have] discovering a way to make the different aspects of his behavior consistent with each other."[14] Nevertheless, I suggest that the seemingly contradictory elements associated with Hrothgar's *pyle* may be resolved if we seriously consider Hunferth in the tradition of the court fool or jester.[15]

Modern readers are most accustomed to either the mentally deficient fool or the wise character who pretends foolishness popularized by Shakespeare and other late authors.[16] Historically, these members of society held their positions by right of a broad spectrum of characteristics including clinical idiocy, insanity, social ineptitude, dwarfism, radical individuality, ingenious wit, and improvisational skill.[17] Court fools are best known to contemporary readers as figures dressed in motley, wearing caps with bells, who are either silly creatures to be pitied because of mental deficiencies or savants like Lear's fool, who conceal wisdom in the guise of nonsense. Such fools of the late Middle Ages and the Renaissance bear little surface resemblance to the character who is a warrior of some reputation and an articulate court spokesman in the Old English poem. Yet, ancient and early medieval sources record figures linked to the historical

---

14. Irving, *Rereading Beowulf,* p. 36.

15. Some scholarship seeks to distinguish between the fool and jester, but most often these terms are used interchangeably. While previous scholarship on Hunferth has tended to prefer 'jester', I generally use 'fool' in this study as it is the term most often used in contemporary research on this historical figure.

16. While the artificial or wise fool and its natural or mentally deficient counterpart both appear in early records concerning fools, the latter has no bearing on the character of Hunferth. As John Southworth confirms, records indicate a "basic distinction between two broad categories of fool; between the natural and the artificial; those who were regarded as fools 'by nature' and those who pretended folly to fulfill a professional comedic role. It is a distinction that in Europe was understood and applied from as early as the twelfth century, but, in a wider context, goes back to the earliest recorded beginnings of the fool's history" (*Fools and Jesters,* p. 5).

17. The most important sources for such research include: Billington, *Social History of the Fool*; Doran, *History of Court Fools*; Holcomb, *Mirth Making*; Otto, *Fools Are Everywhere*; Southworth, *Fools and Jesters*; Swain, *Fools and Folly*; and Welsford, *Fool.* Welsford's work is particularly appropos to the present argument, as she specifically identifies Hunferth as a court fool (see pp. 84–87). Interesting psychosocial studies of the fool's function in and impact on society can be found in Willeford, *Fool and His Scepter,* and Zijderveld, *Reality in a Looking-Glass.* Throughout the present study, discussion of the fool's historical and social development is summarized from the sources listed here, unless otherwise noted.

and literary development of the fool who display attributes similar to those of Hunferth. Research further suggests the more familiar performer of mirth, nonsense, and ridicule is probably only the latest and most watered down development of an earlier cultural role. As foreign as it may seem to contemporary audiences, the early precursors of the later court fool are frequently presented, like Hunferth, as persons who were highly regarded; held prestigious court positions; sat often at the king's feet; used verbal wit to test, maintain, and correct the equilibrium of society; had nearly total freedom to say anything and behave in any manner, including what was often judged socially or politically inappropriate; and were sometimes associated with pagan religion. At some point in the development of these primitive, ceremonial, scapegoat figures into the motley-clad, entertaining mascots of later periods, a figure emerged, who is described as a court official of noble lineage, possibly a pagan priest but also frequently a poet, serving the court from a position near the king, whose duty was to verbally test the worthiness of strangers to the hall through a ritualized form of insults and boasts.[18] The *Beowulf* poet's presentation of Hunferth suggests he may be just such a figure.

---

18. Historically, the position of the fool as an accepted member of the court is undisputed. During the early Middle Ages, fools are documented throughout the halls and palaces of Britain, Ireland, Scandinavia, the European continent, the Middle East, and Asia. Extensive examples of fools from many cultures and historical periods appear in Doran, *History of Court Fools*; Otto, *Fools Are Everywhere*; Southworth, *Fools and Jesters*; Welsford, *Fool*. While little is known about the origins of this figure, cultural historians and anthropologists postulate that the fool's roots grow out of the seasonal mock-king ritual of human sacrifice occurring in some primitive societies. Still useful for understanding the background of these primitive cultural figures are early works such as James G. Frazer's *Golden Bough* and René Girard's *Violence and the Sacred*. Even after the rise of Christianity, the social license and authority of the fool, based in such seasonal celebrations, was probably too deeply rooted in practice to dismiss entirely. As a result, the traditional duties of the seasonal figure, whether a pagan priest or community scapegoat, were converted into the purely secular functions of the court fool. Regarding this transfer of the ritual figure's function into secular spheres, Welsford hypothesizes that local lords may have found it advantageous to "employ a permanent scapegoat whose official duty it is to jeer continually at his superiors in order to bear their ill-luck on his own unimportant shoulders" (p. 74). Numerous sources document persons associated with early aristocratic households who possess a wide range of attributes but the fool's performance of his office is most frequently authorized by his ability to use words adeptly, spontaneously, and for pointed effect. For example, in the first century A.D., Quintilian quotes witticisms made by Gabba, one of the imperial fools of Augustus (Welsford, p. 8). In the sixth century, Gregory of Tours mentions another royal fool attached to the house of Miron, king of Galicia (Oglivy, "Mimi, Scurrae, Histriones," p. 606). In addition, Old Irish texts relating legendary-historical tales from the fifth to the ninth centuries, roughly contemporary with the events related in *Beowulf*, also consistently present jester-like figures whose barbed words carry social import and whose office is linked to pagan practices.

While Hunferth's title, *þyle*, is not familiar to modern readers, it refers to an official status requiring specific behavior so familiar to Anglo-Saxon audiences that it warranted no further comment from the poet.[19] Distinct forms of the word *þyle* appear only five times in Old English, twice in Old English glosses[20] and three times in Old English poetry. Of the poetic occurrences, "þyle Rondingum" (line 24) in *Widsith*, is commonly taken as an eponym representing a Norwegian king.[21] The two remaining poetic occurrences are in *Beowulf* (lines 1165 and 1456), both times referring unmistakably to Hunferth. This low frequency of the word in Old English makes a conclusive definition impossible; however, Hunferth's customary seat in the hall and its similarity to regional analogues strongly urges that the profession of *þyle* be associated with the fool's historical development.

Marking the import of the office of *þyle* with a visual cue, the *Beowulf* poet makes clear that Hunferth sits at the king's feet, "æt fotum sæt" (line 500). In the few lines of the poem devoted to Hunferth, the poet emphasizes the importance of his assigned place by noting it in two different scenes. Although the first mention of Hunferth's seat omits his official title, the second specifically links his office with its physical location in the court, "þær [H]unferþ þyle / æt fotum sæt frean Scyldinga" (there Hunferth the *þyle* sat at the feet of the Scyldings' lord, lines 1165–66). One scholar asserts this is a "lowly position fit only for a jester or court entertainer,"[22] while another considers it "an honoured place."[23] Although these

---

19. As Fulk remarks, the poet treats Hunferth as "a man about whom he expects his audience already to know something" ("Unferth and His Name," p. 126).

20. These glosses, "Ductus orator plures sermones paucis uerbis aperit gelæred þyle fela spæca mid feawum wordum geopenað" and "Oratores þylæs," appear in *Complete Corpus of Old English in Electronic Form*, ed. Healey.

21. However, the use of the word here, immediately preceding references to "Breoca Brondingum" (line 25), apparently the same Breca referenced in line 506 of *Beowulf*, suggests the possibility that this may be a reference to Hunferth instead. Given its proximity to the mention of Breca in a poem that records other names occurring in *Beowulf*, such as Hrothgar, Hrothulf, Ongentheow, Geats, Danes, and Wulfings within forty lines of *þyle*, it may be that the word here refers specifically to Hunferth's position, rather than the eponym of a tribe Malone identifies as the Telemark (*Widsith*, p. 205). Such a possibility may be further supported by reading the word *Rondingum* as conceptually related to the term *Scylding*, in that *rond* is an Old English term for 'shield'. In this case, *Rondingum* could denote 'people of the shield', an alternative epithet for Hrothgar's tribe of the Scyldings. If such is the case, then the *Widsith* reference may refer to a story about Hunferth of the Scyldings (or Rondings) that is no longer extant, but which circulated widely enough to need no description and to be included in the scop's repertoire. All references to the text are taken from *Widsith*, ed. Malone.

22. Eliason, "*Þyle* and *Scop*," p. 269.

23. Magennis, "Treatments of Treachery," p. 16.

statements seem irreconcilable, if read as the physical sign of an early fool's social function, Hunferth's appointed seat may accord with the historical fool's traditional right to function as an intermediary between the king and the court.[24] Scholarship on early fool figures suggests that while they are subordinate to the lord, their physical proximity to the lord's authority fostered their right to actively participate in public events and to exert influence over the hall's community.

Klaeber defines *þyle* as simply an "orator, spokesman, official entertainer," possibilities that identify Hunferth's position as one requiring a public audience in much the same manner as a court fool's. The Bosworth-Toller *Dictionary* notes tentatively of Hunferth that "perhaps his function was something like that of the later court jester."[25] Evidence from the Latin glosses further supports such a connection.[26] The semantic field in which *þyle* appears in the Old English glosses includes not only the Latin words *ioculator*, *mimus*, and *pantomimus* but also *musicus*, *cantor*, *histriones*, *orator*, and *parasitis*, as well as the Old English words *gleoman*, *gligman*,

---

24. Doran, Southworth, Otto, Welsford, and Willeford all emphasize that from early periods on, the fool was often positioned at the lord's feet or beside his throne. From this privileged seat near the king, he moved freely about the court as his insights were needed. Later, between the eleventh and fifteenth centuries, Doran (*History of Court Fools*) and Welsford (*Fool*) point out that the fool was still often the only court official to be allowed constant access to the lord and in certain cases even slept in the lord's bedchamber.

25. Bosworth and Toller, *Anglo-Saxon Dictionary*, p. 1084.

26. In "Design for Treachery," Rosier acknowledges that the Old English glossarial evidence connects Hunferth to the fool, but he sees pejorative connotations to the role of *þyle*. To support his reading of Hunferth as treacherous, Rosier interprets the compounds *hofðelum* (hof+þylum), glossing Latin *descurris*, and *fæpelas* (fæ+þylas), glossing Latin *histriones*, as building a case for reading *þyle* as a term fraught with undesirable connotations. He ties the Old Norse cognate *þulr* to villains like Reginn in *Fafnesmol*. However, in "Unferth in the Hermeneutic Circle," Bjork shows Rosier's argument depends on *hofðelum* (which Rosier translates as 'scurrilous jester') and *fæpelas* (which Rosier translates as 'wicked jester'), being synonyms for the more general term *þyle*. Bjork considers this interpretation fallacious since the compounds reduce the term to specific, but not necessarily all, types of *þyle*. Bjork explains that glosses cannot represent a one-to-one correspondence between words of different languages: "the anisomorphism of languages, the tendency of a word in any language to embrace a range of meaning not embraced by its 'equivalent' in another, makes the problems involved with transferring meaning between two languages complex" (p. 136). He also points out what Rosier neglects to discuss, that *scurra* and *histrio*, the same words glossed as *hofþelum* and *fæpelas* in Old English, are more frequently glossed as *ioculator*, *mimus*, and *pantomimus*, words carrying no negative connotations that are linked to figures closely related to the fool. He further notes that because "Reginn is treacherous does not necessarily make *þulr* a term of disapprobation" (p. 138).

and *scop*.[27] Such etymological evidence indicates the *þyle* was one of several professionals who served the court through some verbal interaction or entertainment. In addition, each of these terms commonly appears in documents related to the historical fools of Roman sources as well as to their later medieval counterparts.

The only widely recognized cognate of the term *þyle*, Old Norse *þulr*, may shed additional light on Hunferth's position. Standard definitions for *þulr* include 'wise-man', 'sage', and more rarely 'bard',[28] suggesting that the term denotes a person of keen insight with a recognized authority for his knowledge, who was sometimes also a poet. Other explorations of the relationship between Hunferth's position at Hrothgar's court and that of the *þulr* argue that the role be understood variously as that of a pagan priest or a military advisor.[29] In Scandinavian tradition, both the *þulr* and *skald*[30] enjoyed an official status characterized by unique autonomy, a special relationship with the lord, and the employment of words as a social corrective, all of which establish commonalities between these offices and those of *þyle* and court fool. Several Irish narratives set in the fifth through ninth centuries describe figures similar to the *þulr* or *skald*, who hold office by reason of their verbal aptitude. Labeled as satirists or fools, early Irish *filis* and

---

27. While space does not permit extensive references to these terms in Old English, they appear in glosses as well as in a few other historical records. All references to these terms are taken from *Complete Corpus of Old English in Electronic Form*, ed. Healey. By examining the Latin glosses, Eliason concludes that *þyle* might be associated with both music and comic behavior, encouraging him to suggest Hunferth as a forerunner of the court fool. He further poses that the unnamed *scop*, who appears only twice and always in the same scene with Hunferth, actually may be the *þyle* himself. For Eliason, the "lexical evidence shows that *þyle* and *gleoman* are synonymous: both are glossed alike, as *histrio* and *scurra*. *Gleoman* and *scop* are also synonymous, as the poet's usage shows. Hence if *þyle* = *gleoman* and *gleoman* = *scop*, *þyle* = *scop*" ("*Þyle* and *Scop*," p. 281).

28. Cleasby and Vigfusson, *Icelandic-English Dictionary*.

29. More detailed discussions of the *þulr*'s relationship to Hunferth include: Baird, "Unferth the *Þyle*"; Clarke, "Office of the Thyle"; Enright, "Warband Context"; and Hollowell, "Unferð the *Þyle*." One of the most notable Old Norse examples of a *þulr*, Starkadr, is described as a highly regarded member of his warband, sitting beside his king and acting as his advisor (Ranisch, *Die Gautrekssaga*, p. 27). A useful examination of the issues surrounding this character may found in Ciklamini's "Problem of Starkaðr."

30. In addition to the *þulr*, scholars frequently acknowledge a similarity in function between Old Norse court poets, known as *skalds*, and later court fools. The most important references for such discussions are: Southworth, *Fools and Jesters*; Otto, *Fools Are Everywhere*; and Welsford, *Fool*. Otto even goes so far as to assert that the "jesters of Scandinavia probably originated with the skalds, whose verses often had a double meaning," and that the "skald was closer to the jester than the minstrel in that he shared the license to speak freely" (p. 14).

druths taunt strangers, utter curses, challenge heroes, prophesy the future, recite poetry, and advise the king.[31] Further, Old Irish literature identifies a specific type of fool as a *rigdruth* (king's fool), whose intentionally conceived actions, proximity to his lord, and reliance on verbal wit present him as an early Celtic court fool and encourage comparisons to Hunferth.[32]

Similar to these Irish and Scandinavian counterparts, Hunferth not only holds the position of *þyle* but is also a *secg* (warrior [line 980]).[33] Along with his possession of a sword of estimable power and reputation, this descriptor places Hunferth, no less than Beowulf, firmly in the role of the Germanic warrior. Hrunting is a sword of high value and the fact that Hunferth has not wielded it successfully against Grendel need not condemn his ability or Hrunting's worth; instead, it may testify to the extreme nature of Grendel's violent control of Heorot. Further, the term *beadurune* (line 501), a term unique in the Old English corpus meaning something like 'a secret word of battle', employs a martial metaphor to identify Hunferth's verbal challenge to Beowulf. By merging the use of words with martial purpose, the singularity of *beadurune* in a context attached to the sole figure in extant Old English literature recorded as a *þyle* links the professions of *þyle* and *secg* in a way that again evokes resemblances to the Irish *filis* who were recorded as leading troops into battle by reciting secret chants or by shouting a specific verbal act conjectured to be either laughter or a curse.[34] The name of Hunferth's father, Ecglaf, also bears martial connotations that likely identify him as

---

31. Of particular relevance to the present study, Gingher ("Unferth Perplex") discusses the possible relationship between Bricriu, a well-known literary *fili*, and Hunferth. Although the Irish *fili*'s role resembles that of the *skald*, the early Irish *druth* may provide an even closer correspondence to the court fool and, by extension, the Old English *þyle*. Defined as a 'professional jester' or a 'learned man' (*Dictionary of the Irish Language*, ed. Quin, p. 252), the *druth* is described as a satirist and entertainer in official settings in early Irish literature. Another indication that the role of the fool was an acceptable profession for intelligent persons in Irish society appears in the *Senchus Mor*, an Old Irish legal tract which distinguishes between people who were fools because of their mental deficiencies and people whose adept mental abilities allowed them to support themselves as court entertainers (O'Donovan and O'Curry, *Ancient Laws of Ireland*, pp. 137–38). A few of the many Irish figures bearing the title of *druth*, and also sometimes *fili*, are: Mac-da-Cherda (*Liadain and Curithir*, ed. Kuno Meyer); Lomnae Druth and Tulchaine (*Togail Bruidne Da Derga*, ed. Knott); Do Dera (*Cath Maige Mucrama*, ed. O'Daly); and Ua Maigleine (*Cath Almaine* in *Fragmentary Annals of Ireland*, ed. Radner).

32. See, for example, Tamon, King Conchobar's fool (*Táin Bó Cúailnge*, ed. O'Rahilly).

33. Several Old English scholars discuss the significance of Hunferth's warrior status, including: Bonjour, "Unferth: A Return to Orthodoxy"; Enright, "Warband Context"; Geoffrey Hughes, "Beowulf, Unferth and Hrunting"; and Oglivy, "Unferth: Foil to Beowulf?"

34. See, for example, Southworth, *Fools and Jesters*, p. 21, and Welsford, *Fool*, pp. 107–8.

part of the warrior class. Regardless of formulaic or metrical requirements, by recording the name Ecglaf five times in the poem, more occurrences than the name Hunferth, the poet seems to emphasize this aspect of Hunferth's background. While some would use this same evidence to dissociate the *pyle*'s position from that of the fool precisely because Hunferth is identified as a warrior,[35] in fact early court fools were not precluded from exercising martial skill. Wielding swords as well as words for the benefit of the court are not mutually exclusive abilities in the Irish or Scandinavian analogues. In fact, some evidence suggests the roles of *pulr* and *fili* actually required military training and active participation in a warband.[36] Thus, Hunferth's *secg* status, combined with his role as *pyle*, connects his character to other early fool figures who commonly served as warriors in the early Middle Ages.[37] While we can never be certain that the roles of *pulr, skald, fili*, and *druth* precisely parallel that of the *pyle*, the recorded affinities between these offices, strengthened by their geographical proximity to each other, suggest the Anglo-Saxon profession preserves a common northern European cultural tradition, typified by individual service through verbal skill in entertainment and criticism as well as martial training.

Apart from such cultural analogies between the roles of *pyle* and *secg*, Hunferth's relationship to the court fool is particularly reflected in the

---

35. Among those who cite Hunferth's warrior status as prohibiting him from resembling a court fool, Geoffrey Hughes asserts that the "basic objection" is that "the Fool is a privileged social parasite, always isolated by convention from the world of action; he is permitted to criticize folly or cowardice in others, but he is not expected to do anything brave or distinguish himself" ("Beowulf, Unferth and Hrunting," p. 386). While such an observation may accurately depict figures from later historical periods, it misrepresents what scholarship on the fool tells us about the martial abilities of fools in early periods.

36. Enright ("Warband Context") argues for a direct relationship between the roles of *pyle, pulr*, and Irish martial figures. For Enright, figures such as the *fili* and *pulr* provide close analogues to Hunferth in that their importance as spokesmen for the *comitatus* derives explicitly from their combination of verbal and martial abilities. He explains that for such figures "status flows from degree of expertise and determines place . . . The speaker must have a powerful voice to be heard by many, be a dominant warrior for the sake of respect and morale, and be an official delegate in order to be obeyed" (p. 304). Southworth explains that the *rigdruth* was "required to combine the gift of eliciting laughter with prowess as a warrior; his aggressive potential was fully absorbed in defence of his lord and the defeat of his enemies" (*Fools and Jesters*, p. 6). In a later example, a Norman *joculatoris* called Taillefer (meaning something like "hewer of iron") is "credited with initiating the decisive charge of the French cavalry at Hastings and decapitating an opponent" (Southworth, p. 6).

37. Southworth includes an extensive chapter on "Warrior Fools" in *Fools and Jesters*. In addition, Doran, *History of Court Fools*; Otto, *Fools Are Everywhere*; and Welsford, *Fool*, also comment on the martial activities of historical fools.

Beowulf poet's emphasis on verbal challenge as his primary action in the hall. The political import of Hunferth's speech is highlighted in John M. Hill's comment that "to draw out Beowulf's thoughts and the quality of his resolve is Hunferth's essential function. His battle-speech has too often struck modern readers as an expression of jealousy, rather than as the highly competitive, albeit contentious counsel-speech it is."[38] Although many scholars consider Hunferth's words in lines 499–528 to be verbal attacks on Beowulf, his challenge of the hero probably has a function more in keeping with that of the court fool. The formality of *mapelode*, introducing Hunferth's speech in line 499, adds to the perception that Hunferth's words have an official purpose by implying a listening, nonparticipating public separate from the person to whom the speech is immediately directed.[39] Used formulaically throughout the poem to introduce formal speeches, *mapelode* carries rhetorical weight. Marking the beginning of Hunferth's speech, the formal, even performative, function of *mapelode* adds credence to the likelihood of the phrase *onband beadurune* (line 501) as denoting a particular type of rhetorical act falling to Hunferth by duty and right of his position.

Following Beowulf's statement before Hrothgar of his intention to battle Grendel, Hunferth's sole speech in the poem is characterized by an expertly constructed series of complex rhetorical devices in which he challenges the hero's bravery through metaphors, allusions, insinuation, twisting of literal meaning, and even outright interrogative confrontation.[40] In particular, the *Beowulf* poet presents Hunferth as highly skilled in verbal forms such as riddles, wordplay, and a type of formalized Old Norse verbal competition commonly called *flyting*. Like the Old Norse *flyting*, the exchange between Hunferth and Beowulf is constructed in a highly stylized pattern of claim, defense, and counterclaim through conventional motifs such as immaturity, failure in deeds, drunkenness, prophetic curses, mar-

---

38. Hill, *Cultural World*, p. 77.

39. Clover ("Germanic Context"), Eliason ("*Pyle* and *Scop*"), Gingher ("Unferth Perplex"), and Silber ("Rhetoric as Prowess") are among those who have argued that Hunferth's remarks to Beowulf are officially sanctioned and expected.

40. Studies that explore Hunferth's verbal ploys in more detail include: Frank, "'Mere' and 'Sund'"; and Silber, "Rhetoric as Prowess." In addition, Church ("Beowulf's '*ane ben*'") argues that the *pyle*'s wordplay is constructed according to the rhetorical exercise of confirmation/refutation specific to the *progymnasmata*, thereby attesting to the poet's familiarity with classical learning.

tial metaphors, and accusations of kin-crimes.[41] By engaging the hero in a duel of such extensive verbal wit, Hunferth may be read not only as publicly posing claims against Beowulf to gauge the hero's mettle by his reaction but also as showing off Hunferth's own intellectual adeptness. With its public display of wordplay and wit, Hunferth's speech parallels the activities of the early court fool through intentional use of carefully crafted words to authorize his power in the public setting of the hall.[42] Like the court fool's banter, Hunferth's supposed insults may be more properly intended as a means of testing the hero's worthiness.

Although Roberta Frank characterizes Hunferth's speech as "dripping with irony, oblique and mocking,"[43] his words may be equally read as indicating no aggressive hostility against Beowulf. As rude as the *pyle*'s words may seem to modern readers, they actually ask for little more than clarification and correction of rumor as well as invite the hero to show off his ability to tell a good story. All of the seemingly harsh retorts in the exchange come from Beowulf, not Hunferth. Even though, as Irving notes, "we do not ever hear [H]unferth bragging,"[44] critics normally accuse the *pyle* of speaking to the hero out of malice, jealousy, and overweening pride.[45] They base such readings on the poet's statement that "wæs him Beowulfes sið, / modges merefaran, micel æfþunca, / forþon þe he ne uþe, þæt ænig oðer man / æfre mærða þon ma middangeardes / gehed[d]e under heofenum þonne he sylfa" (lines 501–5). Despite the complexities of clausal construction and disagreement over the appropriate infinitive for the verb *gehed[d]e* in line 505,[46] most translators render these lines to read something like: "For him [Hunferth], the journey of Beowulf, of the courageous sea-voyager, was a great vexation, because he did not want that any other man under heaven

---

41. Carol J. Clover's groundbreaking study of the exchange as related to the Germanic *flyting* is "Germanic Context." Other important studies of the *flyting* and associated verbal exchanges are: Bax and Padmos, "Two Types of Verbal Dueling"; Joseph Harris, "Eddic Poetry as Oral Poetry"; Joseph Harris, "*Senna*"; and Swenson, *Performing Definitions*. See also Jucker and Taavitsamen, "Diachronic Speech Act Analysis"; and Parks, *Verbal Dueling*.

42. Otto notes, "the jester is usually aware of the effect he can have and frequently uses his talents to help others, cause merriment, give advice, or diffuse a perilous situation" (*Fools Are Everywhere*, p. 41).

43. Frank, "'Mere' and 'Sund,'" p. 161.

44. Irving, *Rereading Beowulf*, p. 39.

45. Most interpret these lines as Hughes does when he writes that Hunferth's "reaction shows the natural jealousy of one who feels threatened by a possible supplanter" ("Beowulf, Unferth and Hrunting," p. 386).

46. For details of the grammatical issues involved in this passage, see Pope, "*Beowulf* 505, 'gehedde.'"

should ever obtain more of the glories of middle-earth than he himself."
Alan A. Lee summarizes the usual view that these lines show Hunferth "as
a man caught deep in self-love or pride to the point of not wanting any
other man in the middle-dwelling to achieve more glory than he has and,
consequently, as being envious of the fine effect the newly arrived Beowulf
is making in Heorot. When the poet wishes to show [H]unferth in the
process of sowing discord by discrediting the hero, he uses the 'battle-
rune' kenning."[47] To read the *þyle*'s words as motivated by his envy that
Beowulf's glory might prove greater than his own, however, jars strangely
with what the text has told us of the state of Hrothgar's hall. After emphasizing so many years of terror and failure in Heorot, it seems unlikely that
the poet would choose to portray Hunferth as so oblivious to the heroic
shortcomings of both himself and his comrades that the *þyle* would think
he deserves more glory than anyone else in the world. The reader is given
no reason that Hunferth might think his achievements superior to those
of Beowulf or anyone else. If we are intended to read Hunferth as envious
and prideful, it is difficult to understand why the poet provides no information about the *þyle*'s glorious deeds to explain what leads him to think
so well of himself, especially as explanatory digressions are not uncommon
elsewhere in the poem.

To reconcile such logical contradictions, an alternative translation
might take line 503's *he*, which previous editors have taken as meaning
Hunferth, as referring to Beowulf instead. No grammatical evidence
requires that the pronoun refer to Hunferth. Since the proper name
appears in close proximity to the pronoun, it is just as possible that *he*
refers to the poem's hero. If so, the meaning of the passage would be that
the hero's journey vexed the *þyle* because Beowulf, not Hunferth, did not
wish anyone else to surpass the hero's own glorious achievements. In this
case, the reference reflects the appropriate pride Beowulf has in his own
accomplishments, rather than the *þyle*'s assumed envy over what neither he
nor anyone else in the court has been able to accomplish. In contrast with
traditional views of Hunferth as jealous, this reading allows the possibility
that, from the vantage of his official responsibility as *þyle*, Hunferth is motivated to unbind his battle-rune *flyting* because only a few minutes earlier
Beowulf was rather boldly proclaiming his own youthful glory in front of
the ancient and formerly renowned court now ravaged with terror. The
use of "mærða" (line 504) by the poet here echoes Beowulf's earlier words,

---

47. Lee, *Gold-Hall and Earth-Dragon*, p. 80.

"hæbbe ic mærða fela / ongunnen on geogoþe" (I have undertaken many glories in youth [lines 408–9]). Of the twelve occurrences of *mærða* in the poem, nine others refer to Beowulf's accomplishments.[48] Such a strong textual relationship between the hero and the term *mærða* further supports a reading that in these lines it is meant to recall directly Beowulf's earlier usage of the word. If so, then the poet may expect us not to read Hunferth as jealous of Beowulf but as disturbed by the seeming hubris of the hero's immediately preceding boast to Hrothgar about his past deeds. In such a reading, the *þyle*'s reaction arises not from personal envy but from Beowulf's previous expression of his desire to vanquish Grendel to enhance his own glory, rather than to preserve lives and restore the court's previous greatness.[49] Placing Hunferth again squarely in the court fool tradition, such an interpretation suggests that his reaction of annoyance may be prompted by the apparent self-pride of an as yet untested stranger, a pride which must be sounded and appropriately addressed for the good of the hall.

If the traditional motive of jealousy is suspect in Hunferth's introductory speech, then other incriminatory evidence against him may also warrant review. Even though laudatory descriptions of the *þyle* appear in the poem as frequently as disapprobations,[50] critical commentary generally focuses on what seem to be indictments of Hunferth's character. Yet, because three condemnatory remarks against him (beer-drinking, fratricide, damnation in hell) appear in Beowulf's response to the *þyle*'s challenge, it is possible the hero's castigations may be made in the purposefully exaggerated competitiveness of the *flyting* exchange, rather than seriously questioning Hunferth's character. For example, Beowulf's description of Hunferth as "beore druncen" (line 531) may be only a typical *flyting*

---

48. The two remaining occurrences of *mærða* are included in a description of the young warriors who accompany Beowulf to fight the dragon (line 2640) and the accomplishments of Wulf and Eofor (line 2996).

49. In keeping with this reading, though arguing for a different conclusion, Nelles suggests Hunferth's "challenge is meant to remind Beowulf that there is more riding on this than his own corpse and armor—as in the Breca fiasco, there are other parties counting on him, and he won't be the only one to pay the price of failure" ("Beowulf's sorhfullne sið," p. 307).

50. The instances of apparent praise for Hunferth are: Beowulf's acknowledgment that the *þyle*'s "wit duge" (wit may be strong, line 589); the narrator's remark that his "ferhþe treowde" (spirit was trusted, line 1166); that he has "mod micel" (great mind or spirit, line 1168); that he has "eafoþes cræftig" (strong skill, line 1466); and his reputation as a "widcuðne man" (widely renowned man, line 1489).

motif.[51] In a Germanic culture in which drinking heavily is common hall practice and part of ritual custom, having drunk alcoholic beverages seems at most an extremely minor offense, an infraction more worthy of light ribbing than serious disapproval.[52]

The accusation of fratricide in Beowulf's response to the *þyle* may seem more incriminatory than beer-drinking, but as Ward Parks and others have shown, the nature of verbal dueling in early heroic literature does not require that such charges to be true. Instead, the central feature of verbal competitions such as *flytings* necessitates that participants be able to counter opponents by outdoing their efforts in any way possible, whether through truth or lies. Beowulf's claim that Hunferth caused the deaths of his brothers ("broðrum to banan" [line 587]) may be simply one of the "whopping lies" Eliason sees as the purview of the exchange.[53] It is certainly one of the most commonly appearing insults in Scandinavian *flytings*.[54] Despite the seriousness of the accusation of kin-crime for a Germanic audience, Hunferth's possible fratricide has not substantially altered his reputation in Hrothgar's court. Whether one goes so far as to speculate that Hunferth's position as *þyle* might have required him to sacrifice his brothers in a ritual pagan ceremony[55] or identifies the crime as possibly leading to his status as a foreign exile,[56] it is important that the only explicit reference to this crime occurs as part of the *flyting* game.[57] While Beowulf's statement fol-

---

51. For discussion of the common *flyting* insults, see Clover, "Germanic Context."

52. Among those who note that cultural conceptions of drinking practices in Anglo-Saxon England differ from our own are: Magennis, "*Beowulf* Poet"; Robinson, *Beowulf and the Appositive Style*; and Shippey, *Beowulf*.

53. Eliason, "*Þyle* and *Scop*," p. 272.

54. Clover discusses the fratricide insult's prominent place in *flyting* practice in "Germanic Context."

55. Hollowell, "Unferð the *Þyle*."

56. In "Hunferth and the Paths of Exile," Silber argues for a reading of Hunferth as a non-Danish exile, a member of the court who knows of Beowulf and who, in turn, is known by the hero. As she summarizes, "Beowulf's charge of fratricide, to be repeated by the poet at line 1167, argues strongly for an identification of Hunferth as an exile in light of the known reasons for involuntary removal from protection of a lord, both detailed in the poem: extinction of a people and its leader, as is the case of the Last Survivor, and homicide, which accounts for Ecgtheow's presence among the Danes" (p. 26).

57. Nagy notes that unlike Hunferth, "who gives specific, if inaccurate, details in his allegations of Beowulf's boyhood folly, Beowulf levels the charge of fratricide at [H]unferð and immediately drops the subject. It is almost as if he does not know the full details of the battle himself, or he desires to cast [H]unferð's actions in the least flattering light that he possibly can in order to win the verbal duel in which he is engaged. Either way, Beowulf's claim seems highly suspect" ("Reassessment," p. 23).

lowing his accusation of fratricide, "in helle scealt / werhðo dreogan" (in hell you will suffer punishment [lines 588–89]), normally has been taken as the hero's strangely impolite curse of Hunferth, it is equally likely that this phrase too is simply a common part of the *flyting* and not intended to be personally damning.[58] It might be argued that, since Hunferth never counters Beowulf's accusation of brother-killing or takes obvious offense at being damned to hell for that crime, his dishonorable act was so well known and heinous that no defense is possible.[59] But, if this is true, then we must wonder why Hrothgar, whom the poet consistently presents as the epitome of a good king, has the poor judgment to keep a kin-killer near him in such an important position. A later passage also commonly linked to Hunferth's supposed fratricide is the poet's assertion that "he his magum nære / arfæst æt ecga gelacum" (he was not to his kinsmen honorable at the edges of swords [lines 1167–68]). Occurring immediately after the poet has commented that "his ferhþe treowde" (his spirit was trusted [line 1166]) and that he possesses "mod micel" (a great spirit or mind [line 1168]), this reference to Hunferth's past is mentioned, as Irving notes, "apparently in a tone of tolerant acceptance."[60] Without the rationale of *flyting* play, this remark about Hunferth's dishonorable swordplay with his kin is more difficult to dismiss. Still, if the poet intends the remark to refer to an actual heinous crime in Hunferth's past, the *þyle*'s apparently high status in an otherwise respected court and his freedom to speak bluntly to guests remain inexplicable contradictions. However, if Beowulf's earlier remark represents a stock motif in a game of words rather than an actual event, the two fratricide passages, the one from Beowulf's perspective and the other from the poet's, may not be related at all. While the poet's comment commonly has been taken as a reference to Hunferth's fratricide, the passage notes only Hunferth's lack of honor in swordplay with kin, which could refer to any number of actions less serious than fratricide.

In the introductory verbal exchange, even such innocuous phrases as Beowulf's appellation for Hunferth, "min wine" (my friend [line 530]),

---

58. Clover explains that telling one's opponent to go to Hel was a standard *flyting* curse. She asserts that the "inclusion of a curse in the context of boasts and insults, the drastic tone, and the specific vocabulary are thus fully consonant with flyting practice" ("Germanic Context," p. 464). Further, Robinson suggests the word usually emended to *helle*, but which actually is missing from the manuscript, may be *healle* instead. In this case, he proposes the line would be better translated as "for that which you must endure condemnation in the hall" ("Elements of the Marvelous," p. 33).

59. See, for example, Nagy, "Reassessment," p. 22.

60. Irving, *Rereading Beowulf*, p. 42.

have been taken as ironic hints of the *pyle*'s ignoble nature.[61] Yet, nowhere else in the poem is irony presented clearly as part of Beowulf's character. As Thomas A. Shippey argues, the poet "never presents as right things known to be wrong."[62] Instead, Beowulf's reference to Hunferth as "min wine," a term he applies to no one else in the poem, somewhat softens his harsh earlier remarks and carries marks of at least joviality and probably familiarity. With these words, Beowulf may allude either to a past relationship with the *pyle* or to his awareness that Hunferth has offered him an opportunity to prove himself at the *pyle*'s expense.[63] In either case, the term *wine* most likely connotes affection, admiration, or respect. Such familiarity between the characters enhances the *flyting*'s game-like nature and supports the notion that Beowulf does not feel especially attacked by Hunferth's challenge. In addition, each character has explicit information about the other's previous history; Hunferth knows about Beowulf's contest with Breca, while Beowulf knows Hunferth's lineage. Even though he has not been told anything about the *pyle* in this scene, Beowulf refers to Hunferth's father by name and implies that he has heard Hunferth talk about past exploits when he says "gif þin hige wære, / sefa swa searogrim, swa þu self talast" (if your mind and heart were as battle-fierce as you yourself tell [lines 593–94]).[64] These references simply may indicate knowledge based on the hearsay common in oral cultures. However, Beowulf's use of "min wine" might just as easily acknowledge a former nonantagonistic relationship. At the least, by underscoring the lack of real hostility between the speakers, the phrase suggests Beowulf recognizes the interaction as a planned and expected part of the official role of the court fool.

Although competition is integral to the nature of the *flyting*, it is worth noting that the Hunferth/Beowulf exchange ends not so much in the victory of a winner whose efforts have dominated his opponent through

---

61. See, e.g., Silber, "Rhetoric as Prowess," p. 478.

62. Shippey, *Beowulf*, p. 35. Irving echoes this view when he writes, "Obviously irony does exist in *Beowulf*, but it is not hidden or subtle where it occurs" (*Rereading Beowulf*, p. 15).

63. Since, as the poem makes clear, Hrothgar knew Beowulf previously, it is also possible that Hunferth knew the hero before these events. In fact, Beowulf's insistence on using the dual pronouns *git* and *incer* in lines 583–84 may imply that Breca and Hunferth also knew each other.

64. As Silber remarks, this "extensive mutual knowledge of one another" is probably "gained from observation or gossip" ("Hunferth and the Paths of Exile," pp. 24–25).

superior one-upmanship but rather a concession that evokes approval or at least acceptance not only from the "loser" but also from everyone in the hall.[65] Such tacit approval is evident in Hunferth's silence following the confrontation and later in his seemingly unprompted loan to the hero of his famous sword Hrunting. When read as a brave response to a renowned court fool's expert, offensive verbal blow, Beowulf's ability to gain the *þyle*'s verbal surrender by successfully countering his challenge establishes him as a viable answer to the problem of Grendel. Considered thus, Hunferth emerges from this verbal combat not as a loser but as a winner for exposing new hope for his court where previously there was none. As Enright explains, Hunferth's speech reflects the *þyle*'s "duty and [is] not motivated by personal enmity, Beowulf's victory is not [H]unferth's defeat. No matter what the result, [H]unferth 'wins' because he has unmasked the qualities of the stranger and this enables his lord and the *seniores* of the retinue to form an initial impression."[66]

Contrary to assumptions that Hunferth's speech represents a rude or malevolent interruption of hall activities, the *þyle*'s words to Beowulf are not presented as disruptive to the hall.[67] The poet never indicates that Hunferth's challenge elicits any disapproval from Hrothgar. Following the exchange, the poet makes it plain that Hrothgar's full, pleased attention is directed toward Beowulf.[68] The absence of a reprimand to Hunferth for his boldness implies his behavior is expected, officially sanctioned, and thus deserves no reproach. This supports the probability that Hunferth's battle-rune fulfills a necessary responsibility and contradicts views of the *þyle* as working behind the scenes to promote treachery and dissent. As Andy Orchard explains, "The notion that [H]unferth's verbal attack on Beowulf serves a formal purpose seems underlined by the delighted response of

---

65. Irving agrees when he remarks that Hunferth "does not seem to be especially humiliated in this scene" (*Rereading Beowulf*, p. 43).

66. Enright, "Warband Context," p. 310.

67. Works that perceive Hunferth as incendiary claim that the poet "depicts [H]unferð as scornful" (Eugene Green, *Anglo-Saxon Audiences*, p. 98), that his words disclose the *þyle*'s "quarrelsome mood" (Pope, "*Beowulf* 505, 'gehedde,'" p. 173), that his challenge of the hero is a "virulent attack" (Nelles, "Beowulf's sorhfullne sið," p. 306), or that his speech represents an "invective" (Brodeur, *Art of Beowulf*, p. 144).

68. The passage at lines 607–10 reads: "Þa wæs on salum sinces brytta / gamolfeax ond guðrof; geoce gelyfde / brego Beorht-Dena; gehyrde on Beowulfe / folces hyrde faestraedne geþoht" (Then it was with happiness the treasure dispenser, gray-haired and battle-brave, chief of the Bright-Danes, the protector of the people, learned from Beowulf of [his] firmly resolved intention).

the Danes, who seem neither perturbed at the apparently harsh treatment meted out to their guest, nor offended at his unfavourable comparison of his own might and that of the Danes."[69]

Further, Heorot's joy increases rather than diminishes after the exchange, an unusual response if Hunferth's speech is meant as an unprovoked discourtesy to a guest.[70] Instead of an uncomfortable silence resulting from Hunferth's supposed impudence, the hall erupts, resounding with the din of laughter ("hleahtor, hlyn swynsode" [line 611]). It is surely significant that the only time the poet describes laughter is at this point in the poem.[71] Such laughter informs the exchange with a positive response more akin to the reactions sought by court fools than an uncomfortable confrontation between antagonistic strangers. Such a well-directed challenge, the hint of teasing from both parties, the lack of reprimand, and Beowulf's willingness to engage the *þyle* in this word-match indicate Hunferth's words are not intended to be a surprise. When taken as the words of a precursor to the court fool, they evoke not only Hunferth's privilege to speak as he wishes to whom he wishes but also his duty to use verbal skill in moments of ceremonial import to disclose the worth of visitors, thus revealing potential dangers such strangers might bring to the hall.

As consequential as his responsibility to use his word skills may be, however, Hunferth need not perform his role entirely seriously. Although until recently few scholars have admitted the possibility of humor in Old English literature,[72] the Hunferth/Beowulf exchange can be read as comic in tone, though likely not in intention. If we allow the possibility that Hunferth's *flyting* is motivated by his office, rather than by malice or jealousy, then his court position may require him verbally to test Beowulf's resolve as an attempt to deflate any excess of pride in the hall and to discern the

---

69. Andy Orchard, *Critical Companion*, p. 214.

70. Eliason recognizes that "as part of the evening's festivities, it [the exchange] contributes to the general merriment . . . No one takes it seriously, of course, nor is it meant to be taken thus" (*"Þyle* and *Scop,"* p. 271).

71. While the word *hleahtor* appears in the poem again at line 3020, this instance describes what has been lost because of Beowulf's death, rather than the act of laughing itself.

72. In "Images of Laughter," Magennis has identified and categorized passages in Old English poetry in which laughter is recorded as a particular response to words and events. Another significant publication on humor in Old English is *Humour in Anglo-Saxon Literature*, ed. Wilcox. Of relevance to the present work are three articles in Wilcox's collection: Risden, "Heroic Humor in *Beowulf*"; Shippey, "'Grim Wordplay'"; and Tripp, "Humor, Wordplay."

truth of the stranger's background and character.[73] Yet, humor can be as viable a method of probing a hero's worth as gravity. Reading the dramatic staging of this scene as humorous may enable Hunferth to use the excuse of drunkenness as a convenient cover for assessing the hero in true court fool fashion. As the evidence for the exchange as *flyting* behavior indicates, Hunferth's supposed inebriation may be nothing more than the humorous performance of a fool seeking to engage the unknown quantity of Beowulf in a nonthreatening, but nonetheless challenging, way. Using his performance to gauge the integrity of Beowulf's previous words to Hrothgar as well as the viability of his success against Grendel, Hunferth's behavior here may represent a comedic game of serious import that is intended to amplify the status and credibility of both men.[74] Further, as stock *flyting* motifs, Beowulf's accusations regarding Hunferth's drunkenness and fratricide may be intended as colorful exaggerations to enlarge the humor latent in the exchange between the two verbal opponents. Emphasizing its implicit humor, Risden writes that through "the would-be flyting between Beowulf and Hunferth, the poet adapts the traditional superiority ploy to set up opportunities for humor. Often insults, self-deprecation, or inequitable comparisons set up humor rather than actual dominance as their intended outcome."[75]

Moving beyond the *flyting* scene, Hunferth's loan of his sword Hrunting to Beowulf, which fails against Grendel's mother, has also been interpreted as a sign of its owner's treacherous nature.[76] Yet, the fact that the sword is praised expansively without apparent irony in lines 1455–68 indicates that the poet means it to be considered an honorable weapon. No other sword in the poem receives as much descriptive treatment. While some view the

---

73. The use of comedy to impart serious information was the main method by which "wise fools" of the Middle Ages and Renaissance promoted their status in the court. As Willeford suggests, the fool insulted and satirized the court and its guests as a means of showing the foolishness of every man. By saying things no polite member of the court would dare say, the fool employed verbal humor particularly as a means by which such foolishness could be revealed and healthily purged.

74. Tripp even suggests that the poet's mischievous use of linguistic wit through the wordplay of his speech to Beowulf gives rise to "an abundance of Chaucerian 'game' [that] resonates in the *Beowulf* poet's 'earnest'" ("Humor, Wordplay," p. 69).

75. Risden, "Heroic Humor in *Beowulf*," p. 71.

76. Works that view Hrunting as a means of highlighting Hunferth's treachery include: Enright, "Warband Context"; Hughes, "Beowulf, Unferth and Hrunting"; and Nicholson, "Hunlafing."

term "atertanum" (venom-striped [line 1459])[77] as reflective of the poet's
desire to indict Hunferth's character, the accumulated effect of other
phrases attached to the sword such as "ealdgesteona" (ancient treasure
[line 1458]), "næfre hit æt hilde ne swac" (it had never failed in battle [line
1461]), "wrætlic wægsweord" (ornamented wave-sword [line 1489]), "leof-
lic iren" (beloved iron [line 1809]), "guðwine godne" (good war-friend
[line 1810]), and "wigcræftigne" (battle-skilled [line 1811]), outweigh the
single ambiguous use of "atertanum." In addition, Beowulf's praise of the
sword and his instructions in lines 1488–91 that it be returned to Hunferth
if he fails in his task makes it clear the hero considers the sword estimable.
Any other reading of the sword's value requires that his remarks be taken
as extraneous to the narrative or as indicating an uncharacteristic lack of
good judgment on Beowulf's part.[78] Further, the note that Hunferth lost
glory ("dom forleas" [line 1470]), either by lending Hrunting to Beowulf
or by being unwilling to wage battle with Grendel's mother in her mere-
hall, need not record the poet's disapproval of the *þyle*. Rather, by aiding
the superior warrior with the sword's loan, Hunferth demonstrates his willingness to sacrifice personal honor for the hope of restoring order to the
hall. In such a reading, the *þyle* generously submits the sword to improve
Beowulf's chances of victory, regardless of the cost to his own reputation,
an act which perhaps again suggests the similar willingness of the fool's
historical antecedents to subordinate himself for the needs of the court.

Finally, Hunferth's name may encourage an identification of his role
in *Beowulf* with that of traditional fool figures. Probably more than any
other aspect of the *þyle*'s depiction, Hunferth's name has inspired much
controversy.[79] The initial compound *hun* or *un* has been interpreted variously as a simple negative prefix, 'base', 'high', 'giant', or someone from

---

77. Interestingly, the early Irish literary figure, Bricriu, whose connections with the
profession of *þyle* and fool were noted above, is typically referred to as venom- or poison-
tongued.

78. Irving makes a similar observation when he states, "I find it quite impossible to
believe that this kind of poet would secretly slip a defective weapon into a sequence describing excellent weapons. We would have our attention called to [H]unferth's base treachery if
the sword Hrunting was its symbol" (*Rereading Beowulf*, p. 44).

79. Because critical examination of this aspect of Hunferth's character has been so
extensive, the present study's discussion of the *þyle*'s name only briefly summarizes mate-
rial from many sources. Among the most important works on Hunferth's name are: Fulk,
"Unferth and His Name"; Nicholson, "Hunlafing"; Osborn, "Some Uses of Ambiguity";
Pope; "*Beowulf* 505, 'gehedde'"; Jane Roberts, "Old English -Un 'Very'"; Robinson, "Personal
Names"; Silber, "Unferth: Another Look"; and Vaughan, "Reconsideration."

the tribe of the Huns. Similarly disputed and diverse critical interpretations of *ferþ* include 'peace', 'spirit', 'mind', 'life', and 'journey'. Traditionally, the *þyle*'s name has been rendered as "mar-peace" or "un-peace" in keeping with the usual perception of him as a troublemaker in the poem. Others have interpreted the name as connoting a high spirit, great wisdom, or even intensified peace.[80] Yet, records prove that Hunferth was an actual historical name and, therefore, need not be relevant to the personality of its bearer.[81] Nevertheless, the presence of many names in *Beowulf* with meanings relevant to those who bear them indicates the associations attached to Hunferth's name probably are not coincidental. As Robinson explains, names in the poem accord with "medieval preoccupations with name-meanings" and possible meanings of Hunferth's name are only part of the "ample evidence that significant names are at work."[82]

Whether one retains the manuscript's initial *H* or not, the fact that Hunferth's name carries multiple connotations applicable to his role in the poem has implications for any reading of him in light of the court fool tradition. Those who served as court fools in medieval and later times were most often known by their "stage names" and records of the birth names of such people are largely nonexistent. Instead, fools took such names as Triboulet (meaning something like 'little trial'), Patch, and Pounce. It was common for fools to assume a name that related to their professional behavior, particularly their wit or verbal expertise. Although the correct meaning of Hunferth's name cannot be stated with any certainty, a name like Hunferth, with its variety of possible references—many of which reflect his court role—closely resembles this portion of the fool's history. Taken by itself, any similarity between the nature of Hunferth's name and that of other early fools could be simple coincidence. However, added to the

---

80. Fred C. Robinson has argued also that the element *ferhþ*, when joined to the prefixed particle, is intended to mean "something like 'un-intelligence' or 'folly,'" a meaning with obvious relevance to the present study ("Personal Names," p. 222).

81. Fulk argues that it "reflects a real Germanic name rather than a symbolic literary coinage [which] should serve to reaffirm the conservatism of the poet's treatment of the legendary material from which he constructed *Beowulf.* The name [H]unferð then reveals not a free invention of character and incident, but faithfulness to genuine tradition" ("Unferth and His Name," p. 126). *Hunferth* is documented as an actual Anglo-Saxon name in historical records. *The Complete Corpus of Old English in Electronic Form*, ed. Healey, confirms a bishop named Hunferth in the entries for the years 744 and 754 in the A, C, and E versions of *The Anglo-Saxon Chronicle*.

82. Robinson, "Personal Names," p. 220.

evidence discussed earlier, this aspect of his character further supports identification of Hunferth as a precursor of the early court fool.

The main obstacle to a definitive identification of Hunferth as a court fool is the paucity of reliable historical documents for such figures in early periods. Nonetheless, fools are recorded in English or Norman circles within a short time of the composition of the *Beowulf* manuscript. Along with the evidence suggested by analogous figures in Old Irish and Old Norse literature and history, the fact that such records mention court fools without additional comment shows the office was so well known during the late Anglo-Saxon period it warranted remark only by title. For example, a fool called Nithard served the Anglo-Saxon king Edmund Ironside, who ruled briefly before Cnut in 1016.[83] While we know nothing about his behavior in the court, Nithard is labeled *joculator*, a term used for 'fool' in continental courts and in association with compounds of *þyle*. In addition, his name may be related to the Old English word *niðheard*, meaning either 'battle brave' or 'hard strife', which suggests a name assumed in order to represent his court role as a warrior of both words and weapons. Further, at least two fools are associated with William of Normandy. One of these, Taillefer, is recorded as a *ioglere*, another term for court fool associated with *þyle* in the Old English glosses. Taillefer is recorded in some sources as a member of William's retinue who sang a heroic song before he initiated the first blow at the battle of Hastings.[84] Another of William's recorded fools is Golet, said to have played the role of an informant whose warning of an impending assassination attempt saved William's life prior to his conquest of England.[85] In the *Domesday Book* of 1086, a *joculator regis* (king's fool), named Berdic is listed as holding property in the Welsh marches.[86] While no record identifies whether Berdic served an Anglo-Saxon or Norman king, John Southworth explains that this entry is significant for the history of fools in England because it shows that "From the very beginning of the Norman domination of England, the office of the joculator regis was already established, known to the Domesday surveyors, and duly recorded

---

83. A 1051 charter (Sawyer, *Anglo-Saxon Charters*, S 1647) records that Nithard donated to Christ Church, Canterbury, the town of Walworth in Surrey, a considerable property that had been awarded to him earlier by Edmund Ironside. See Southworth, *Fools and Jesters*, p. 23.

84. Although records of Taillefer's role in the battle occur only in later texts, Southworth makes a strong case for the probable historicity of the joculator (*Fools and Jesters*, pp. 25–28).

85. Southworth, *Fools and Jesters*, pp. 30–31.

86. John Morris, *Domesday Book: Gloucestershire*, p. 162.

as one of those services to the person of the king on which all future claims to the possession of land were to depend."[87] The evidence from these historical fools indicates that figures similar to what has been proposed here for Hunferth were known to audiences in English and Norman courts at a time not far removed from the composition of the *Beowulf* manuscript.

The history of the court fool gives ample support for viewing this figure as a noble, rather than ignoble, character and as a warrior of both words and swords, rather than as a simple entertainer with little social impact. When viewed as an early literary example of the wise fool, Hunferth resembles no allegory or evil counselor. From this perspective, the evidence cannot support readings of him as a "blustering, mean-spirited coward who does not enjoy the respect of his comrades and who seeks to bolster his self-esteem by decrying Beowulf's past performance and present qualifications."[88] He holds a high-ranking social position, wields verbal wit for the good of his court, and lends unexpected aid to the hero. Certainly, given the evidence presented here, the poet means Hunferth to be compared and contrasted to Beowulf, but as a worthy complement to the status of both characters, not as an antithesis or foil who diminishes one in order to elevate the other. Interpretations of the poem that insist on a binary opposition of Hunferth as treacherously evil in order to balance a completely honorable and good Beowulf offer a much too simplistic view that is out of place in the poet's otherwise artistic treatment of purpose and motive. For dramatic purposes, if a villain must exist, we need look no further than Grendel, Grendel's mother, and the dragon, all of whom pose greater narrative potential for heroic threat than any human official of Hrothgar's retinue. A more appropriate reading recognizes the *þyle* as fitting the poem's subtle depictions of heroic responsibility, social obligation, and personal integrity. Within the context of figures from cultures comparable to that of Anglo-Saxon England, the court fool role affords Hunferth a complexity of motives and functions matching the narrative's efforts to address critical issues and offers a resolution for those aspects of Hunferth's character that have been viewed previously as enigmatic and conflicting.

---

87. Southworth, *Fools and Jesters*, p. 28.
88. Robinson, "Elements of the Marvelous," p. 33.

THE *NATHWYLC* SCRIBE AND
THE *NATHWYLC* TEXT OF *BEOWULF*

KEVIN KIERNAN

In 1882 Julius Zupitza succinctly stated as a matter of fact, rather than as a hypothesis, that "all that is distinct in the FS. in fol. 179 has been freshened up by a later hand in the MS."[1] Considering how little it explains, it is surprising that this hypothesis has implicitly prevailed, if only in corrections of supposed freshening-up errors, in editions of *Beowulf* over the past century and a quarter. Zupitza never described the features of the hand that convinced him it belonged to a later scribe. He did not give any indication of how much later the later hand was than that of the principal scribe who copied the folios before and after fol. 179. Zupitza did not even hazard to guess why or how the original text disappeared in the first place; nor why some areas contain overlapping traces of letters and even lines of text; nor why the later hand was so selective in choosing what to freshen up and what to leave untouched, especially when all editors agree that many faint readings are still legible today. Finally, Zupitza did not describe in support of his hypothesis the unique condition of the surface of the vellum, which appears scoured overall, with napped stains over the most illegible passages, perhaps because it was not as obvious in his autotypes facsimile as it was in the manuscript itself. With the advent of digital technology, and superior digital images of the manuscript evidence, we are now able as a scholarly community, rather than as an individual scholar with special access to a rare manuscript, to reevaluate the evidence and to offer and assess other hypotheses to explain it.[2]

My own understanding of what seems to have happened to fol. 179 has evolved over the past twenty-five years as digital images, digital image processing, and digital tools for analysis changed the way I was able to

---

1. In 1882, Julius Zupitza published *Beowulf: Autotypes of the Unique Manuscript Cotton MS. Cotton Vitellius A.XV in the British Museum* (EETS 77). A revised edition was published in 1959, with a new reproduction of the manuscript and an introductory note by Norman Davis (see the bibliography). The first edition will be cited as Zupitza, *Beowulf* (1882). The revised edition will be cited as Zupitza, *Beowulf* (1959). Quotation at Zupitza, *Beowulf* (1959), p. 102.

2. Helen Damico offers a new hypothesis on the historical context of the poem within the dating range of the script in "*Beowulf*'s Foreign Queen and the Politics of Eleventh-Century England."

evaluate the evidence. In an effort to arrive at a comprehensive explanation, I have had to abandon some of my earlier views about this folio and to refine others. There are, I believe, four major stages that account for fol. 179 as it now exists. In stage one the original text was completely removed from both sides of the folio by an overall scouring. As there is no sign of collateral damage to either fol. 178v or fol. 180r, the person who made this palimpsest must have worked with the gathering that begins with fol. 179 detached from the preceding gathering. In stage two an Anglo-Saxon scribe (perhaps the same person), working with the two other *Beowulf* scribes, replaced the original text with a new and different one that bears some convincing signs of a draft still in progress.[3] I call this person the *nathwylc* scribe, for the repeated use of the rare word *nathwylc* ("I know not who" and "I know not what") three times in the space of sixteen lines on this folio.[4] The *nathwylc* scribe has a very similar *ductus* to scribe two, but uses some later letterforms more characteristic of scribe one, which presumably led Zupitza to see the script as a later hand than that of scribe two. The *nathwylc* scribe leaves other paleographical markers, too, such as the unique occurrence of an "oc" form of *a* in *brade* in the first line;[5] an unusually fat bowl for the wynn in *weard* two lines later; the use throughout of a rounded, more three-sided *a* rather than square insular *a*; a more frequent use of caroline instead of insular *s*; and some unexpected spelling and usage variants, which further distinguish the new hand from that of the second scribe.

The other two stages affecting fol. 179 happened, appropriately enough, some indeterminate time "later." In stage three, parts of the *nathwylc* scribe's

---

3. The result of these two stages is a palimpsest, in its primary sense of "writing-material written upon twice, the original writing having been erased or rubbed out to make place for the second" (OED). In addition to a few uncorrected mistakes, its draft status is most evident from the retention of the catch-word, *sceapen*, the unerased remnants of what appears to be an extensive dittographic passage, at the end of the recto and start of the verso.

4. When it first appears on the palimpsest, the word *nathwylc* refers to the thief (*niða nathwylc*, "I know not who of men," 2218); the second time it apparently refers to the theft (*þeof nathwylces*, "thief of I know not what," 2226); and the third time it refers to the person who originally hid the treasure (*gumena nathwylc*, "I know not who of men," 2234). *Nathwylc* is first used as a substantive in the second scribe's section at line 2056: *Nu her þara banena byre nathwylces*, "Here now a son of I know not who of those slayers." The word is also used once as an adjective in the first scribe's part of the manuscript: *þæt he niðsele nathwylcum wæs* ("that he was in I know not what hostile hall") line 1515.

5. I previously resisted this interpretation of the letter, considering it instead a defective *æ* in *Beowulf and the Beowulf Manuscript*, p. 233. Now that a conservator has trimmed away the opaque tape on the top of this letter, I agree with Malone's identification of a unique occurrence in the *Beowulf* manuscript of the so-called "oc-*a*" (*Nowell Codex*).

new text on fol. 179 failed to adhere to the scoured vellum, obliterating parts of words and letters and leaving behind fragments, which Zupitza in many cases described, and editors have for the most part accepted, as incorrectly freshened-up text. It is impossible to know when this fading occurred, but it was plausibly caused by the 1731 fire, by the water used to put it out, or by a combination of the two, probably abetted by whatever concoction was used to dissolve the ink of the original text. We know the fading happened before Thorkelin and his scribe copied the manuscript around 1787, because both transcripts show that the text was illegible in the same places by then.[6] In stage four someone dabbed and rubbed chemical reagents over the most illegible readings to try to resuscitate the ink in these places. Under ultraviolet these areas appear as dark stains, making it almost impossible to identify any letterforms beneath them.[7] Circumstantial evidence that is discussed below suggests that staff at the British Museum applied these reagents to aid in the preparation of Zupitza's facsimile.

Whether or not they have expressed doubts, nearly all editors in their readings have tacitly accepted Zupitza's freshening-up theory. Embracing the theory when it was still relatively new, Frederick Klaeber categorically stated that fol. 179 "has been freshened up by a later hand, but not always correctly," and referred readers to Zupitza's notes for details.[8] It is not surprising to find Zupitza's theory still holding forth in the latest revision of Klaeber's edition, in view of R. D. Fulk's strenuous endorsements in two recent articles.[9] Appealing to an unspecified consensus in the first article, Fulk says that "most of those who have examined the folio believe that the text was at some point retouched by a scribe who traced such letter forms as he could make out (sometimes badly) and left the rest untouched." Fulk

---

6. Kiernan, *Thorkelin Transcripts*, pp. 80–81, 113–14, 144. See also Kiernan, *Electronic Beowulf*, for images and collations of the Thorkelin transcripts.

7. See the note on fol. 179 in Kiernan, *Electronic Beowulf* 2.0 *Help* section under Electronic Edition: "my latest opinion of this folio, a palimpsest, is that it exhibits the handwriting of a third scribe, contemporary with the two main scribes, and that the text on 179 reflects a late revision-in-progress of the poem. Much of this new text failed to adhere to the poorly prepared vellum. I now believe that C.L. Wrenn was right when he proposed that someone in modern times applied a reagent to these faded areas (the reagent fluoresces strongly under ultraviolet)."

8. Klaeber, *Beowulf*, p. 82, textual note.

9. Fulk, "On Argumentation," pp. 15–16; and following examinations of the manuscript, "Some Contested Readings." The fourth edition of Klaeber's *Beowulf and the Fight at Finnsburg*, edited by Fulk, Robert E. Bjork, and John D. Niles, bases its readings on the theory without critically examining it (p. xxix). This edition appeared in 2008, after I had written this essay.

believes that "This [i.e., partial, sometimes inaccurate, retouching theory] explains the stark contrast between dark and faint text as well as the surprising readings, which may be attributed to the later scribe's misapprehension of the faint letter forms he traced." He concludes that, "given how much [this analysis] explains about the damaged folio, alternative analyses must account for a great deal if they are to rival it" ("On Argumentation," p. 15). In the second article, Fulk again summons a mystery consensus, when he claims that "most observers believe that the rewritten letters are intended merely to trace the original ones," but giving as examples only A. E. A. Werner and Zupitza himself.[10] Norman Davis and Kemp Malone, who both spent a great deal of time studying the manuscript in preparing their respective facsimiles, were not members of this seemingly bogus consensus. Davis says that "it is remarkable that the ultra-violet photographs in the present edition do little to support the readings which Zupitza thought he could see in the 'first hand' underneath the 'freshening up'" (Zupitza, *Beowulf* [1959], p. vi). Malone leaves it up to the reader to decide "how much touching up (if any) there has been" and advises the reader to consult Davis "for further discussion of the matter" (*Nowell Codex*, p. 83).

In fact, editors who accept Zupitza's hypothesis (with or without examining the manuscript) have shown no curiosity about what his theory fails to notice, much less analyze. If one believes that some *nathwylc* or other freshened up all of the text that survives, one must accept the corollary that the original text somehow disappeared. Why was the original text removed? How does one account for the unusual appearance of the overall surface of the vellum? What might have caused the stains over completely illegible sections? Why would a brilliant forger not completely restore at least the faded text that anyone can easily see today? Why would someone tracing what was still relatively clear consistently create letterforms for which there were no models on the folio? Why do faded parts of the text show features of this later hand? What happened to disfigure the replacement text? Why are the missing sections particularly discolored, leaving a

---

10. Fulk, "Some Contested Readings," p. 209. Werner, from the British Museum Research Laboratory, was drafted by Norman Davis to "judge of the mere physical appearance of the vellum." He does not presume to verify that a later hand freshened up everything that is distinct on the folio. In a brief statement he says only that "it would appear that attempts have been made in the past to revive the ink in certain areas which appeared to have been damaged. There would also appear to be definite signs of subsequent intensification of certain letters, which now appear darker and have a characteristic sheen; the most obvious example is the initial N on line 14" (Zupitza, *Beowulf* [1959], pp. vi–vii).

gray residue on some letters bordering the gaps? Editors must try to answer such textual questions concerning the transmission of the text if they hope to establish an acceptable modern edition of the poem.

Tilman Westphalen first asked many of these questions.[11] Addressing Zupitza's assertion nearly a century after it was made, Westphalen suggested that someone looking for vellum deliberately erased all of fol. 179, recto and verso, before the second scribe fortuitously rescued his former work and did the best he could to restore it. After a meticulous paleographical comparison of all letterforms on fol. 179 with those of other folios, Westphalen identified the later hand as the second scribe, who tried to restore the erased text about twenty years later. The second scribe's later hand, Westphalen argued, shows some modernizing moves toward insular caroline script as well as some signs of aging in the declining control of his pen strokes. In 1981 in *Beowulf and the Beowulf Manuscript* I accepted Westphalen's identification of the hand and its relative dating, but formulated a new hypothesis. Marshaling previously unnoticed codicological evidence, I argued that the second scribe was participating in a revision that first brought together two poems about Beowulf, one recounting his youthful exploits and the other his troubled reign as an old man and his heroic death.[12] It will be useful to review briefly the wealth of circumstantial codicological support for this revision, as editors have never taken it into account in their implicit theories of transmission of the text. Any reasoned consideration of whether or not fol. 179 is a palimpsest in the context of other textual changes will be incomplete outside of this wider context.

---

11. Westphalen, *Beowulf 3150–55*, pp. 58–69.

12. Kiernan, "Palimpsest." Fulk falsely asserts, "The 'revised edition' . . . is actually a reprint with two new prefaces and a reprint of a 1983 article" ("On Argumentation," p. 9, note 19). My text includes revisions (see, for example, note 46 below) and my preface, "Re-Visions" (i.e., revisions), even briefly discusses Fulk's theories (pp. xxiv–xxvii). The appendix to the revised edition, "The State of the *Beowulf* Manuscript, 1882–1983," adds important textual evidence, not available when the book first appeared, on hundreds of covered readings along the damaged edges of the restoration binding. "Until the advent of digital technology," I explain in "Re-Visions," "there was no practical way to reproduce the hundreds of backlit readings. With the aid of a digital camera and digital image-processing, however, I am now preparing digital facsimiles of all of these covered readings as part of the Electronic Beowulf project" (p. xxviii). The project won an international award for innovation in information technology for developing this method. In fact, Fulk uses the method I developed for disclosing covered readings with fiber-optic backlighting in his article on readings he contests. However, rather than providing visual evidence for his readings for other scholars to examine, as I do in *Electronic Beowulf*, Fulk merely asserts that he saw something else when he looked at the manuscript.

All of the codicological support for a revision converges around fol. 179. Beginning with this folio, the physical format of the manuscript changes in the number of sheets to a gathering (five instead of four), in the sheet arrangement (hair outside all sheets instead of alternating hair and flesh sides), and in the number of rulings of the sheets (from twenty to twenty-one lines). The distinct change in format raises the possibility that these last two gatherings about an elderly king Beowulf might have once existed as part of a different collection. The motivation for a revision might have been to bring the two different stories together. On the folios preceding the palimpsest, a missing fitt-number XXIIII indicates that a revision of this section, beginning in the first scribe's stint, might have involved the removal of at least the beginning of an original fitt XXIIII.[13] The evidence is somewhat obscured by a clumsy postmedieval alteration of number XXV to XXIIII, and by the erasure, presumably by the same person, of the final I in numbers XXVI–XXVIIII in an abortive effort to correct the faulty sequence. This section begins with a gathering (fols. 163–70) anomalously ruled for twenty-two lines, rather than the otherwise unvarying twenty lines in the first scribe's stint, suggesting that the first scribe, with more text than usual to copy, might have prepared a gathering with thirty-two more rulings than usual to hold this part of the revision.

The second scribe takes over copying in the next gathering, fols. 171–78, in an unplanned transition three lines into fol. 172v. One might expect professional scribes to conceal the change of hands by starting the transition at the top of a verso, not three lines down. This careless transition in hand might suggest that the scribes knew the untidy mix would later be concealed in a formal, final copy. In any case, there is compelling evidence that the second scribe took over copying this gathering after he had already completed the last two gatherings, which begin with the palimpsest. The order of copying is evident because, in the gathering he completed for the first scribe, the second scribe deftly and surreptitiously compressed twenty-one lines of text on folios ruled for only twenty lines on four consecutive facing pages (fols. 174v–176r). In other words, the second scribe knew exactly how much extra text he had to fit into the gathering preceding fol. 179. The only obvious reason why the scribe would have added these extra

---

13. Both scribes continue to copy the following fitt-numbers as if XXIIII still existed. For a full discussion, see Kiernan, *Beowulf and the Beowulf Manuscript*, pp. 264–70. For a different accounting of the numbering, see Conner, "Section Numbers in the *Beowulf* Manuscript." His argument also suggests that the two scribes were following different exemplars.

lines in defiance of the rulings was if the following gathering had already been copied.[14] A theory of the text of *Beowulf* should not ignore these paleographical and codicological anomalies, which among other things effectively disprove the unexamined but frequently adduced assumption that two scribes were simply copying from a well-established exemplar that had gone through a long transmission.[15] However one interprets it, the extremely unsettled state of the physical makeup of the manuscript surrounding and including the palimpsest does not support the notion that the scribes were copying a settled text under normal conditions.

It seems no coincidence, then, that textual anomalies also converge on fol. 179. The first line copied by the *nathwylc* scribe (fol. 179r1) abruptly announces, in what sounds like a non sequitur, the fifty-year reign of Beowulf.[16] This sudden and surprising revelation comes in the middle of what is arguably the most convoluted sentence in the poem. When we last saw him, on the preceding folio, a young Beowulf was recounting his recent successes in Heorot and doling out to Hygelac and Hygd the gifts that Hroðgar had just given him. Hygelac in turn gave to Beowulf Hre-

---

14. If the scribe were simply ending a stint, there would be no reason not to stop in the middle of another gathering, as the first scribe did on fol. 172v3. There is an extensive discussion in *Beowulf and the Beowulf Manuscript*, pp. 133–50, and an extracted argument in my "Eleventh-Century Origin of *Beowulf*."

15. For an unduly influential example see Lapidge, "Archetype of *Beowulf*." In a circular argument, Lapidge uses modern conjectural emendations as his only evidence of scribal error, rather than the many scores of examples of scribal corrections of undoubted mistakes. Moreover, by citing only edition line numbers (e.g. "MS 3154"), Lapidge fails to locate for his readers the supposed errors in the manuscript by folio, folio line, and edition number (e.g., fol. 198v3:3154). In fact, Lapidge confuses matters further through a confused understanding of the multiple foliations of the *Beowulf* manuscript. He first describes the "manuscript of *Beowulf*," by which he must mean the Nowell Codex, as comprising "fols. 94–209" (p. 7), but in a footnote on the same page he refers to "the last page of *Beowulf*" (not *Judith*) as fol. 209. *Beowulf* of course ends on fol. 201v in this foliation, or on 198v of the foliation written on the manuscript. Lapidge later inadvertently uses this manuscript foliation, when he says, "I cite no example from the most illegible leaves, such as 179r (= lines 2207–39) and 198v (lines 3150–82)" (p. 9), although he subsequently uses examples from these leaves, which he again cites by the manuscript foliation (p. 21, note 56). For a comprehensive discussion of scribal corrections, see my "Proofreading of the Scribes," in *Beowulf and the Beowulf Manuscript* (pp. 191–218), which Lapidge does not cite.

16. The spelling Beowulf, instead of Biowulf, is in itself unexpected in this part of the manuscript. The second scribe uses the *io* spelling fourteen of sixteen times in his stint, and the two exceptions, at 173r14 and 185v13, first had *io* spellings, too, but either he or, more likely, the *nathwylc* scribe, later emended them to *eo*. For illustrations of these two scribal corrections, see "Re-Visions" in the second edition of *Beowulf and the Beowulf Manuscript*, pp. xxvi–xxvii.

thel's incomparable sword, a sizeable grant of land,[17] a hall, and a *bregostol*, or princely seat (2190–99). If there once were a separate poem on Beowulf as a young man, here on fol. 178 verso would be an appropriate place to end his story.

Then follows the unruly sentence, introducing in midsentence a seventy- or eighty-year-old Beowulf, who has already ruled for fifty years:

> Eft þæt geiode   ufaran dogrum
> hildehlæmmum,   syððan Hygelac læg,
> ond Hear[dr]ede   hildemeceas
> under bordhreoðan   to bonan wurdon,
> ða hyne gesohtan   on sigeþeode
> hearde hil*d*frecan,   Heaðo-Scilfingas,
> niða genægdan   nefan Hererices — :
> syððan [fol. 179] Beowulfe   brade rice
> on hand ge(hwearf);   he geheold tela
> fiftig wintra   — wæs ða frod cyning,
> eald eþelweard — ,   oð ðæt an ongan
> deorcum nihtum   draca rics[i]an . . .
>   (Klaeber 2200–2211)

> After that it happened in higher days,
> in clashes of conflict, when Higelac lay dead,
> and to Heardred harmful-swords
> under shield-guards became killers,
> when they sought him among his succeeding-folk,
> hardened fighters, Heatho-Scilfings,
> for his hostilities assailed Hereric's nephew — :
> afterwards [fol. 179] to Beowulf the broad realm
> passed into hand; he held it well
> for fifty winters — was then a wise king,
> an old land-warden — , until a certain one began
> on dark nights, a dragon, to reign . . .
>   (*my translation of Klaeber's text*)

Klaeber implicitly acknowledges the awkwardness of this sentence, spanning 178v14–179r7, in his note to the last word on fol. 178v, the first word in line 2207: "*syððan* is used, in a way, correlatively with *syððan* 2201." The

---

17. Higelac here gives Beowulf seven-thousand unspecified units of land (*seofon þusendo*), but he later gives Wulf and Iofor one hundred thousand of land (*hund þusenda landes*, 2994–95) and at the same time gives Iofor his only daughter to wed (2997–98). From these figures it is hard to justify the widespread assumption that Beowulf somehow ended up with more property without the daughter and the dowry.

reader must discover the tenuous way these different parts of speech are supposed to correlate from Klaeber's glossary: the first *syððan* is the conjunction, "since, from the time when, when, after, as soon as (s[ome]t[imes] shading into because)," while the second *syððan* is the adverb, "since, thereupon, afterwards."

Following Klaeber's syntax (but omitting his strong pause after "Hererices"), Mitchell and Robinson in their recent edition more explicitly describe the syntactic problem. According to their note to these lines, "2200–8a *þæt* [demonstrative] anticipates the passage of dependent speech which begins at *syððan* [conjunction] 'after' l. 2201b (correlative with *syððan* [adverb] 'then' l. 2207a) and ends at *gehwearf* l. 2208a. The conj. *þæt* would normally have preceded *syððan* l. 2207a in prose and poetry (*OES* §1978) but must be understood before *syððan* l. 2201b to give an idiomatic translation."[18] In a recent discussion of this syntactically problematic sentence while presenting his own theory for the palimpsest, Carl Berkhout has observed, "some translators of *Beowulf* have simply rendered *syððan* here as 'that' and moved on." Berkhout rightly objects that "nowhere else in *Beowulf* or in the entire corpus of OE poetry and prose does the adverb or the conjunction *syððan*, or any of its variants, introduce as a substitute for *þæt* a clause dependent on an impersonal construction with *(ge)gan(gan)*, *gelimpan*, *(ge)weorðan*, or other such verbs." He concludes that, "even if *þæt* were to be understood before adverbial *syððan* in *Beowulf* 2207a, as Mitchell and Robinson suggest, we would still be left with a syntactic anomaly here."[19]

The complementary arguments of these translators, editors, and grammarians convincingly show that the most direct way to solve the syntactic anomaly and justify the translations is to assume that the second scribe simply omitted a crossed thorn, *þ* ("that"), before *syððan*: "After that it happened . . . when Hygelac lay dead and . . . the Heatho-Scilfings . . . assailed Hereric's nephew, [that] afterwards ([*þ*] *syððan*) to Beowulf the broad realm passed into hand." The scribal solecism is easy to understand, particularly if the *nathwylc* scribe was in the process of revising the following folio. Berkhout uses his analysis of this easily rectified syntactic

---

18. OES §1978 in Mitchell's *Old English Syntax* does not discuss these lines. The unusually elaborate section title, "Part Two: Beowulf the King (lines 2200–3182): The Fight with the Dragon (lines 2200–2751): [The accession of Beowulf. The plundering of the dragon's hoard]," highlights the importance of this passage in their edition (Mitchell and Robinson, *Beowulf*, p. 125). The manuscript fitt-numbers, however, present a different structure, as this turning point actually occurs in the middle of fitt XXXI in the manuscript.

19. Berkhout, "*Beowulf* 2200–08: Mind the Gap," pp. 52–53.

problem to explain why the original text on fol. 179 was entirely erased. He posits that the second scribe "accidentally omitted a full clause after *syððan*, amounting to about two or three poetic lines, plus the word *þæt* or *þætte* before *beowulfe*" and that he or someone else in the scriptorium erased all of fol. 179, recto and verso, to make room for the missing lines in a more compactly rewritten fol. 179 ("*Beowulf* 2200–08: Mind the Gap," p. 54). Following this line of argument, Berkhout must assume, as he says, that the second scribe or his associate "became occupied with or distracted by other tasks, leaving *Beowulf* for the next four and a half centuries in far more depleted textual condition than it had been before" ("*Beowulf* 2200–08: Mind the Gap," p. 56). His theory of a pseudo-palimpsest (a completely erased leaf, ready for a new text) is designed to make room, as well, for Laurence Nowell, the sixteenth-century antiquary who owned what we now call the Nowell Codex (including the *Beowulf* manuscript as its fourth item) and who, according to Berkhout's theory, freshened up as much of the erased text as he could see.

Berkhout first proposed that Nowell was "Scribe C" (the *nathwylc* scribe) in a paper he read in 1986 at the annual meeting of the Medieval Academy of America. The published abstract of this paper lays out the essential argument:

> there are good reasons to suspect that the readable text on the defective fol. 179 (182) of the *Beowulf* manuscript, involving lines 2208[*sic*]–2252, is in the hand of the antiquary Laurence Nowell, who, in or about the year 1563, did his textual and aesthetic best to recover the intentionally erased text on this folio. The pattern of linguistic errors and scribal discrepancies, along with other physical indications, strongly suggests that the final scribe of this folio was not Scribe B or any other Anglo-Saxon. It is not reasonable to suppose that the folio might have been freshened up in the post-Conquest or Middle English period. It is very reasonable, however, to suspect Nowell. It is certain—and provable—that he had the opportunity, the ability, the inclination, and the motive to freshen this page while he was in the service of William Cecil. Although the evidence for this argument remains circumstantial, this evidence is considerable and so far passes all tests of arguments against it. We must seriously consider the possibility that one of the most crucial passages in our most important Old English literary texts comes to us only through a good but imperfect scholar at work in the age of Shakespeare.[20]

---

20. Berkhout, "Anglo-Saxon Studies in the Age of Shakespeare." It is not clear why Berkhout rules out a post-Conquest Anglo-Saxon scribe for his refreshener. The Anglo-Saxons did not abruptly stop speaking and writing Old English the day (or year) that the Normans conquered them.

Although there is no evidence that he ever read *Beowulf,* we can agree that Nowell, who wrote his name on the first folio of the codex in 1563, had the opportunity, and even that he might have had the inclination and motive, to repair the palimpsest. The style in which Nowell wrote his name at the start of the *St. Christopher* fragment provides a quick peek at his own formal penmanship (see Fig. 1). Anyone even casually familiar

Fig. 1: Nowell's signature in Cotton Vitellius A. xv, fol. 91(93)r

with his many transcripts of Old English and other collected materials in British Library manuscripts Add. 43703–43710 must seriously doubt that Nowell had the "aesthetic ability" or basic artistic skill to counterfeit the duct of an Anglo-Saxon scribe, even one with the relatively inelegant style of the second scribe or the *nathwylc* scribe. Berkhout agrees with me that these transcripts do not support his thesis. What, then, is the "considerable" evidence that "so far passes all tests of arguments against it"? In a subsequent talk, "In Search of Laurence Nowell," for the International Society of Anglo-Saxonists (ISAS) in 1987, Berkhout first identified the single manuscript on which he based his theory. There he revealed that Nowell's "display" script occurs in British Library MS Davis 30, Nowell's facing translation of the Laws of King Alfred. Berkhout's confident assertion notwithstanding, this evidence cannot, in fact, pass even gentle tests against it, as a cursory comparison of the two scripts reveals (see Fig. 2). Berkhout himself later characterized the script in BL MS Davis 30 as a "stylized insular hand," but has never published a detailed paleographical explanation of why he believes that the "mess," as he calls it, on fol. 179 "is chiefly the result of Nowell's effort to recover an original text crudely erased not long after it was written."[21] Fortunately, in one of several impassioned attacks on my late dating of *Beowulf,* Johan Gerritsen takes Berkhout's evidence and argues his case in some detail in "Have with You [i.e., me] to Lexington! The *Beowulf* Manuscript and *Beowulf.*"[22] Gerritsen

21. Berkhout, "Laurence Nowell," pp. 12–13.
22. Gerritsen, "Have with You to Lexington!" According to Berkhout, his 1987 remarks at ISAS "are more or less embedded in Gerritsen's 1989 article" (*"Beowulf* 2200–08: Mind the Gap," p. 57, note 1).

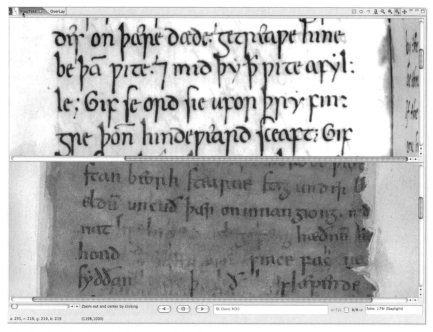

Fig. 2: Nowell's "stylized insular hand" v. the *nathwylc* scribe

in effect undermines Berkhout's case in his fairly thorough description of the features of Nowell's formal script in BL MS Davis M30:

> It is plain that [Nowell] is accustomed to a more rapid script, for he repeatedly lapses into more cursive forms (such as his characteristic ligature long *s+t*), though invariably recollecting himself again. Ascenders are clubbed; descenders are not differentiated as long and short and have no off-strokes, but single and letter-final minims generally have rounded serifs. The cross-strokes of insular *f* are often circle segments; *u* is a one-trace script character, not two minims; *a* is round-headed, its second limb at a variable angle and occasionally straight; the bowl of *g* is always open and low. The most remarkable feature is his tall *e*, both by itself and in combinations: its bowl is mostly a high loop not connected to the stem, and the tongue is frequently absent; the small variety is a vertical bow with a (generally far too small) figure 2 at the top. The pen is cut almost straight and fairly fine, enabling him to write long *s* as a single trace instead of three. (p. 31)

In other words, as Fig. 2 illustrates, Nowell's script in BL MS Davis M30 does not support Berkhout's hypothesis. The *nathwylc* scribe does not use clubbed ascenders; this hand differentiates long descenders (e.g.,

þ, *wynn*, *f*, insular *s*) and short ones (i.e., *r* in proximity to these other
letters), sometimes with off-strokes; single and letter-final minims do
not normally have rounded serifs; the cross-stroke of insular *f* is never
a circle segment; *u* is a two-stroke character of two minims; *a* is indeed
rounded (one of the distinguishing features of the "later" hand), but
unlike Nowell's its top is sometimes a flat, oblique hair-stroke in *æ* (e.g.,
þær r7, *slæpende* r10, *fær* v2) and especially in the *ea*-ligature; the bowl of
g is often closed; the tall *e*-loop is thick and bold, not thin and spindly,
and low *e* (with or without its tongue) always has a pronounced loop,
not a tiny, fastidious one. The pen is cut broad, which accounts for the
bold strokes so unlike Nowell's display hand. Gerritsen does not mention
the double hyphens, semicolons, and marks of abbreviation that bear no
resemblance to the *nathwylc* hand. He admits, however, that "it should be
evident that a comparison of Nowell's work as outlined above with what
we see in his codex [on fol. 179] could not be expected to yield any really
positive result." Yet he concludes, on the basis of "the tall *e*" that the hand
"*could* have been Nowell."[23]

Fulk calls Gerritsen's fallacious logic a "well-reasoned argument" that
points "to a post-medieval freshening" ("Some Contested Readings," p.
201). Neither Berkhout, nor Gerritsen, nor Fulk explains how Nowell or
some other postmedieval forger, if freshening up what was still legible on
fol. 179, consistently managed to "freshen up" letterforms that were uncharacteristic of the second scribe, such as the unique oc-*a* r1, the unusually fat
wynn-bowl r3, or (throughout) the rounder, more triangular *a*, instead of
the second scribe's characteristic flat-topped "square insular" *a*.[24] If one
accepts the freshening-up theory, one is faced with the absurdity of a later
form of *a* as the original reading in *wintra* r2. According to Zupitza, "*wintru*
is owing to the later hand, the *u* standing in the place of an original *a*."
Although I once agreed that *u* was written over *a* (*Beowulf and the Beowulf
Manuscript*, p. 234), the high-resolution images in *Electronic Beowulf* convinced me that the first side of the "*u*" is a minim stroke that does not curve

---

23. Gerritsen, "Have with You to Lexington!" p. 31, his italics.

24. There are accurate illustrations in Westphalen (*Beowulf 3150–55*, pp. 66–67). The
one Michael Lapidge provides of "the square-shaped box-like letter **a** . . . the shibboleth by
which Anglo-Saxon Square minuscule is identified" ("Archetype of *Beowulf*," pp. 12–13) is a
letterform used by neither the second scribe nor the *nathwylc* scribe of *Beowulf*. When they
use a flat-topped *a*, both scribes begin with the left side and bottom of the square *a*, but draw
the top hair-stroke second (not third) and continue its apex downward for the right side and
off-stroke to complete the letter. Because of the oblique hair-stroke, the result for this *a* is
often more triangular than square.

into the bottom of an intentional *u*. The most likely explanation seems to be that the *nathwylc* scribe started to write the wrong letter (perhaps a dittographic *r*), but corrected the mistake by writing the left side of his rounded *a* over it, and completed his *a* normally.

A thorough examination of his most careful attempts at insular script convincingly shows that Nowell lacked the skill of a facsimilist to accomplish what would amount to a brilliant, successful forgery. As A. H. Smith observed in 1938, when the handwriting on fol. 179 was "viewed through a self-illuminating microscope which is powerful enough to show the pen strokes, there did not seem to be that hesitation and lack of coincidence usually associated with freshening up, forgery, and the like."[25] High-resolution digital images corroborate his view. The images of the *Electronic Beowulf*, digitized both in bright light and in response to ultraviolet, have the effect of providing stable views for the microscope readings Smith examined. Zupitza's interpretation that everything legible on the folio was merely "freshened up by a later hand" has paradoxically hampered the analysis of the script on this defective leaf. It is true that the script shows features (the sometimes open *g*-bowl, the preference for tall caroline *s*, and especially the rounder *a*) that are later than the square insular script of the second scribe. However, these later features are not later than the insular caroline script of the first scribe. It would be more accurate to say, therefore, that all that is legible was "written by another hand exhibiting characteristics of both of the two main scribes." The *nathwylc* scribe successfully camouflaged the convergence of features by matching the cut of his pen to the work of the second scribe on the surrounding folios. There is no paleographical reason not to conclude that the three scribes were contemporaries.

In arguing for Nowell, Berkhout expresses disbelief that "the upper text on 179 could possibly be the work of a contemporary Anglo-Saxon scribe with a practiced hand, an idiomatic knowledge of [Old English], and reasonable familiarity with Germanic alliterative versification" ("*Beowulf* 2200–08: Mind the Gap," p. 56). In fact, the *nathwylc* scribe wrote in a practiced enough Anglo-Saxon hand to confound scholarship for over a century. As all writers do, the *nathwylc* scribe made a number of mistakes, but in most cases he corrected them. He normally corrected mistakes immediately, in the course of making them, by overwriting rather than erasing the error, no doubt because of the precarious, perhaps even still damp,

---

25. Smith, "Photography of Manuscripts," p. 200.

condition of the newly scrubbed vellum.[26] These extemporaneous corrections testify to the speed and confidence of his work, and are manifestly
not the tentative signs of a retoucher. As for his supposed lack of familiarity
with Old English verse, no professional metrist has yet assailed the alliteration or meter of these lines. The forty-two lines on this folio display an
accomplished, well-distributed use of the major metrical types according
to the various analyses of Sievers, Bliss, Hutcheson, Hoover, and Russom.[27]
Indeed, in the face of the metrical evidence of competence, I have rejected
two of my own conjectural restorations in *Electronic Beowulf*, because they
present metrical problems.

There is a dittographic error involving alliteration, where the scribe,
repeating an immediately preceding *r*, wrote *rende* for *wende* (179v10), but
otherwise the alliteration in all legible cases is perfectly correct for forty-
two lines of verse.[28] The mistake of *rende* for *wende* is complicated by Zupitza's misreading of the faded *en* for *ih*, a *trompe l'œil* induced by the fading
of the hair-strokes of the *e*-head in *en*, as Sedgefield, Malone, and I have
all explained.[29] The shaft of this supposed *h* is much too short for a real
h, and lacks the onset serif, as a comparison with any of the nearly fifty *h*'s
on the folio will make clear (see *Beowulf and the Beowulf Manuscript*, p. 241).
It should not be surprising that the hair-strokes of the *e*-head have faded,
in view of the general fading of *wine* earlier in the line. To illustrate what
happened to the original *en*, I have in Fig. 3 digitally copied only the hair-
strokes of the *e*-head of *lengest* v9, immediately above "*rihde*" v10 (top), and
pasted them in the space where the hair-strokes faded in *rende* (bottom).

The only grounds for doubting the *nathwylc* scribe's command of idiomatic Old English would be if one accepts nonsensical spellings, such as
rihde, as mistakes in freshening up rather than as subsequent fading, or a

---

26. In addition to *wintra* r2, see *stearne* r6, *innan* r7 (where light erasing was also done),
he (?) r12, *long* v11, *wunode* v12, *mæstan* v17, and *feorh* v19.

27. The results are somewhat biased in that Sievers and Bliss simply accept the traditional editorial restorations, which of course reinforce standard metrical solutions.
Hutcheson, Hoover, and Russom use the same restorations in their metrical data, but openly
mark them as uncertain readings.

28. Fulk erroneously says that I explain *rihde* "as *wende* with portions of *w* and *e* faded"
("On Argumentation," pp. 15–16); in fact I explicitly say, "there is no trace of an original
wynn under the *r*" (*Beowulf and the Beowulf Manuscript*, p. 241).

29. Davis inclines to this view, too: "the form of letters usually read *ih* suggests that they
may have been *en*." He then cites Sedgefield: "MS. *rende*; in the first *e* the fine upstroke is
visible, but the middle horizontal bar is missing; certainly not *rihde*, as Zu. says" (Zupitza,
Beowulf [1959], p. vi). Cf. Malone, *Nowell Codex*, p. 86, and Kiernan, *Beowulf and the Beowulf
Manuscript*, pp. 240–41.

Fig. 3: Conjectural restoration of "*rihde*" to *rende* 179v10

lack of adhesion, of parts of letters that left behind fragments resembling other letters, such as "*ih*" for *en*. To believe the freshening-up hypothesis we must therefore posit an expert forger who also understood the fine details of Old English meter, but who could not recognize simple Old English words and phrases (such as *fea worda cwæð*) because some letters (in this case, *a* in *fea* and *w* in *worda*), though still legible today, were partly faded. No English speaker today would be prone to transcribe incorrectly the comparable modern English phrase, "he spoke few words," because the two *w*'s were faint but visible.

Until Westphalen, no one (including Zupitza) had ever attempted to explain why the original text disappeared from the folio, recto and verso, and why someone had to freshen up everything that is now legible. Yet if someone were simply scavenging vellum, as Westphalen tentatively proposed, one must ask why this person did not cut out the leaf or, if more vellum was needed and the text was considered worthless, pull out the sheet or completely disassemble the quire to ease the task of erasing the text. If, on the other hand, a revision was underway, these questions have uncomplicated answers. To judge by the highly economical use of the preceding two gatherings to accommodate additional text, the scribe either had no available vellum or wished to keep the following gathering, beginning with fol. 179, intact. Scribes would not normally want to use a replacement leaf at the vulnerable start of a gathering. To be sure, the decision to erase the entire original text on fol. 179 while it was bound between fols. 178 and 180 would have made the task quite difficult. Whoever erased the text would have had to protect the rest of the gathering from whatever liquid solution was used to help dissolve the ink before scraping it off. There is no sign of any spillover onto what are now the facing leaves (fol. 178v and fol. 180r) to fol. 179. Scouring fol. 179 would not have been as difficult as it might seem, however, if the *nathwylc* scribe had not yet attached (or could still easily detach) the last two quires, which as we have seen the second scribe must have already copied. Considering the codicological proof that the last two gatherings were copied before the immediately preceding one, the scribe would have been able to scour fol. 179 without harming the folios on either side of it.

Everyone who has described the physical construction of the codex has found that fols. 179–88 formed the outside cover of the penultimate gathering of *Beowulf*. There is no doubt, however, that fol. 179 underwent very different treatment from its presumed conjugate. The relatively rough and discolored condition of the entire surface of the vellum on fol. 179, compared to fol. 188 and to all other leaves in its gathering, shows that fol. 179 was not meticulously smoothed with pumice after the text was removed. The scribe may have feared that the rescraped vellum would become too thin by a thorough repumicing. Or he may have known, because of the widespread revisions, that he or someone else would soon recopy the manuscript, thereby concealing all of the paleographical and codicological evidence of work still in progress. There are various ways to account for why the ink failed to adhere to the palimpsest, especially on the smoother hair side of the recto. For instance, some waxy or greasy residue from whatever concoction the *nathwylc* scribe used to remove the previous text may have dissolved from the heat of the 1731 fire. Its dissolution could have left behind the unique fading, indiscriminately including bits of letters as well as larger sections of text, on this specially treated leaf. We know the fading had occurred by the late eighteenth century, because Thorkelin and his hired scribe were unable to read the same areas of the folio that are obliterated today.

Whatever its cause, subsequent dissolution of parts of the new text, rather than partial refreshening of the original text, best explains why bits of still-recognizable letters survive. It is improbable that a refreshener would touch up only *nat* and the tips of the *h* and the *l* in *nathwylc* r8, as Zupitza says ("only part of *hwylc* freshened up"). It strains belief that an Anglo-Saxon scribe (or a postmedieval restorer, for that matter) would freshen up only *nat-* but not the faint but legible *-hwylc* and *-hwylces* in line 8 and again at lines 16–17 on the recto. Because there is no attempt at all to retouch these letters, it is compelling to conclude that something destructive later happened to *hwylc* and *hwylces*. To put it another way, because *nathwylc* is a high-frequency word only on this folio, and is almost nonexistent elsewhere in the Old English corpus, the dark ink of *nat-* beside the faint ink of *-hwylc(es)* adds some circumstantial support for fading of a new text on a palimpsest, rather than partial refreshening of an old, original text that mysteriously disappeared. Even Fulk eventually seems to acknowledge that the folio is in effect a palimpsest, as the OED defines the term. The folio, he says, "seems, for some reason, to have been washed clean of its original text and rewritten, either by the second scribe or by another with considerable skill in imitating that scribe's hand" ("Some Contested Readings," pp. 208–9). I cannot argue with this description, which I have advocated for over a quarter of a century. Later in this article Fulk suggests that the reason for erasing the original text was to write a corrected one: "Perhaps then the scribe's initial error was simply to begin writing on the second line of the verso rather than the first, and it was the bungled measures subsequently taken to correct this problem (and other errors on the leaf) that led ultimately to the folio's present condition" ("Some Contested Readings," p. 219). One hopes that a more detailed explanation will be forthcoming in the revised edition of Klaeber.

In the meantime, Fulk confidently dismisses as "certainly mistaken" the theory advanced not only by me, as he implies ("Some Contested Readings," pp. 192–93), but by several other scholars (including Malone, A. H. Smith, and Walter Sedgefield) who have studied the manuscript at first hand, that fading and flaking produced a number of paleographical optical illusions. Fulk considers this commonly held theory extravagantly implausible, "since the missing text must then be assumed to have come off the vellum not randomly but in such a way as to leave only fully intact letters or portions of letters that happen to make sense" ("Some Contested Readings," p. 209). Fulk does not mean that these "letters" make sense in the words in which they occur, but that they look like other real letters. In fact they look like malformations of real letters and make nonsense in their semantic context: there are no Old English words *fés*, *rihde*, *fec*, or *bealc*.[30] There are, however, the real words *fér*, *rende* (and *wende*), *fea*, and *beale* or

---

30. Because both *innan* and *innon* are attested in *Beowulf*, I do not count *innan* v14, where the digital images seem to confirm that the off-stroke of *a* is simply faded. Nor do I count what editors have read as *þana* v20, which I believe is *þame*, another *trompe l'oeil* caused by fading of the top of the last minim of *m* and the *e*-head and *e*-tongue. The second "*a*" is not a true letterform. The issue is whether or not there is a better way to fix the textual problem

bealo, which can account for them if bits of the letters *r*, *en*, *a*, and *e* or *o*, faded or flaked off to create plausible (if only they made sense) versions of *s*, *ih*, and (twice) *c*.[31] These few paleographical optical illusions that resemble malformed insular letters should be considered in the context of the overall appearance of the folio, especially on the recto, where one finds the "mass of meaningless strokes that," as Fulk says, "one would expect to result from the random loss of portions of letters" ("Some Contested Readings," p. 193) as well as of words and passages. General fading and some flaking are surely the simplest explanations for faint, but easily read, and uncontested readings such as *iod* of *ðiod* r12, the final *n* in *bolgen* r13; *inc fæt* in *sinc fæt* v2, *ær* in *ærgestreona* v4 and in *ðær* v9, *-ine* in *wine* v10, the second *l* in *eall* v12, *-eald* in *heald* v16, *s* in *hruse* v17, *y* in *hyt* v18, and *w* in *gehwylcne* v20. It makes more sense that these readings faded than that an otherwise diligent refreshener failed to retouch them. In short, an improperly prepared surface explains the subsequent loss of these letters and bits of letters far better than the still undefended theory that a "later" hand failed to freshen them up.

While an improperly prepared writing surface explains the general fading of the revised text, there are additional reasons for our inability to restore with confidence the faded text in the many gaps on the recto and in the first two lines of the verso. The most destructive damage to the text was done not in Old English times, but in modern times, when someone recklessly applied chemical reagents to these areas.[32] The ultraviolet

---

than the traditional emendation, *para,* properly *þa*[*ra*]. This cascading "solution" depends not only on emending *n* to *r,* but also on interpreting the following strokes as a unique form of *a*; and finally on the additional interpolation of the word *lif* later in the same half-line, an extreme emendation-cluster based on an uncertain reading. If one instead conjecturally restores *þa* [*me*]*ðe þis ofgeaf* ("then weary left this behind"), there is alliteration on *leoda minra.* Some might prefer to regularize the alliteration and the syntax by emending *leoda minra* to *minra leoda* (cf. *eowra leoda* 633b, *þinra leoda* 1675b, *para leoda* 2036b; *minra* nowhere else comes second in similar constructions in *Beowulf*).

31. Fulk espouses meaningless *bealc* instead of damaged *bealo* or *beale,* a weakened spelling of *bealo* (cf. *bealewa, bealwa,* where one would expect *bealuwa, bealowa*). Here *-beale* is the second element in the compound *feorhbeale* in the formula *feorhbeale frecne.* According to Kaluza's "law," which Fulk attempts to revive as a criterion of early date, this weak syllable is "resolved" (i.e., not pronounced) in certain cases in the meter. Roberta Frank has recently challenged Fulk's dating argument, pointing out that an Anglo-Dane in late Old English times would not pronounce these light final vowels, as well ("Scandal in Toronto," pp. 858–59). I also mention North Germanic, or Anglo-Danish, spoken dialects in eleventh-century England as alternative explanations for early dating arguments in "Re-Visions" (pp. xxv–xxvi).

32. It appears from the ultraviolet images that two different kinds of reagent might have been used on fol. 179r. Compare the ultraviolet effects on *hwylces* r17 with those in the following lines in Kiernan, *Electronic Beowulf.*

images prepared for the *Electronic Beowulf* (see Figs. 4 and 5) show that someone swabbed and drizzled some liquid solution on the faded sections of the text on these lines. C. L. Wrenn first suggested in 1953 that "the discoloration on these pages seems to have been caused by the application of some chemical reagent in the attempt to improve their legibility."[33] In 1981 I mistakenly dismissed this suggestion on the grounds that "the Thorkelin transcripts show that the text was in as bad shape in 1787 as it is today, and no one would have been treating the MS with chemicals before Thorkelin's time" (*Beowulf and the Beowulf Manuscript*, p. 222, note 46). While true, these observations only establish that the fading of the text on fol. 179 predates the Thorkelin transcripts, while the application of reagents postdates them. My implicit assumption, however, was that officials at what was then the British Museum would not have allowed anyone in modern times to use chemicals on its manuscripts. However, the digital ultraviolet images

Fig. 4: 179r5–9 bright light vs. ultraviolet, showing use of reagent

are decisive, revealing swab-like marks and even drips over some of the letters in lines 5 and 8 on the recto, as I have illustrated and discussed briefly in the textual notes to the *Electronic Beowulf*. The blanks in the Thorkelin transcripts reliably identify the areas where the text had faded and where reagent was later applied to try to restore it. While the facsimiles of Zupitza, Davis, and Malone all obscure the stains, the ultraviolet digital images

---

33. Wrenn, "Introduction: 1. The Manuscript," in *Beowulf*, p. 12. Fulk suggests without citing new evidence that A. E. A. Werner, not Wrenn, was the first to note that "a chemical of some sort has been applied to certain portions of the text" ("Some Contested Readings," p. 209). But Werner's brief report to Davis, which does not mention chemicals, was included in a 1957 letter, four years after Wrenn's edition (Zupitza, *Beowulf* [1959], pp. vi–vii).

in the *Electronic Beowulf* show them clearly. The image on the right in Fig. 4 shows beyond doubt that some liquid was liberally swabbed between and around *hea* and *hord* on line 5, as well as above *stearne sti-* on line 6, drizzled between *beorh* and *stearne* and across the *ð* of *uncuð* in line 7, and then into the faded sections in lines 8–10 and beyond, most obviously including the first line and a half of the verso.

When in the mid-1970s I first examined these areas with an ultraviolet lamp in the old British Library, I was surprised to see heavy stains showing up in the cloudy areas of the Malone and Davis facsimiles of the *Beowulf* manuscript, where I most hoped to recover the illegible text. Neither Malone nor Davis mentions the stains, which may mean that neither used ultraviolet themselves, but instead relied on the photographer. Davis refers only to the "ultra-violet photographs," not to direct examination himself (Zupitza, *Beowulf* [1959], p. vi), and Malone says he used the same photographs.[34] Whether or not they themselves used the ultraviolet lamp, however, the ultraviolet photographs made for their facsimiles fail to show ultraviolet fluorescent effects, in particular the dark discoloration in the gaps in lines 5, 8–10, and 18–21 on the recto, and lines 1–2 on the verso. At the old British Library in the 1970s one had to examine ultraviolet effects on manuscripts in a tiny closet with a huge World War II–era ultraviolet lamp humming ominously overhead. To protect the manuscript and the user, who would fluoresce along with the text, there were strict (and welcome) rules to confine these viewings, including any necessarily hasty notes, to seven minutes at a time. Today, with excellent digital images, which permanently preserve ultraviolet effects, it is possible for anyone to study at leisure these transitory effects brought out by ultraviolet rays, and to reach new conclusions, and reevaluate old ones, about the manuscript evidence. When I first encountered them, I interpreted these areas, which had been rubbed when wet, leaving a napped and grayish appearance in bright light, as evidence of a second stage of revision. I now realize that these stained areas are not revisions-in-progress, but rather modern efforts to resuscitate faded ink with the use of chemical reagents, as Wrenn surmised.

The evidence from ultraviolet fluorescence is equally decisive in the other areas of the folio that were swabbed with reagent where the writing

---

34. Malone explains in his "Note to the Photographs" that the official photographer of the British Museum photographed the *Beowulf* manuscript in 1957 for the second edition of Zupitza's facsimile, and that he used the same negatives for his facsimile. Thus he and Davis list fol. 179 (182 in their numbering) among those photographed by ultraviolet. See Malone, *Nowell Codex*, p. 120; and Davis, "Note to the Second Edition," in Zupitza, *Beowulf* (1959), p. v.

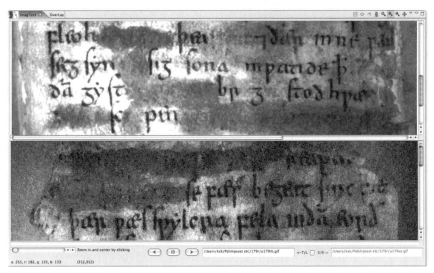

Fig. 5: UV showing use of reagent on 179r18–21 and 179v1–2

was gone (Fig. 5). There would be no reason, after all, to use reagent in these areas unless the writing was in fact illegible, as it must have been at least by the time that Thorkelin and his scribe copied the manuscript. What is surprising are the many records showing that readers at the British Museum in the second half of the nineteenth century (and perhaps later) were allowed to use chemicals on manuscripts. P. R. Harris reports that "permission was granted by the Trustees on a number of occasions to apply chemicals to manuscripts to attempt to make faded writing legible. When C. T. Martin of the Public Records Office wished to treat some Cotton manuscripts in this way in 1870, [the Keeper of Manuscripts, Edward Augustus] Bond was of the opinion that no damage would thus be caused to the documents." Harris also notes that "Professor William Wright of Cambridge (formerly Assistant Keeper of Manuscripts) was allowed to apply chemicals to various Syriac manuscripts in 1871 and 1872, and in 1873 William Stubbs was permitted to use a similar process on Cotton Tiberius G. xv."[35]

After 1873, it appears that special permission from the Trustees was no longer required for the use of reagents. Andrew Prescott, who has searched both catalogued and uncatalogued archives in the Department of Manuscripts, has not found any references to the use of reagents on any man-

---

35. P. R. Harris, *History of the British Museum Library*, p. 276.

uscripts, including *Beowulf,* after this time. Yet Bond, who believed their use was harmless to manuscripts, continued on as Keeper for another five years, and his successor, Edward Maunde Thompson, was still endorsing their use twenty years later in his *Handbook of Greek and Latin Palæography.*[36] In fact, as late as 1912, Thompson repeats his endorsements in his discussion of palimpsests in *An Introduction to Greek and Latin Palæography.* In both works he says, "even if, to all appearance, the vellum was restored to its original condition of an unwritten surface, yet slight traces of the text might remain which chemical reagents . . . might again intensify and make legible." He advises that, "of modern chemical reagents used in the restoration of such texts the most harmless is probably hydro-sulphuret of ammonia."[37] In view of Bond's and Thompson's advocacy of reagents as well as the clear ultraviolet evidence of their unrecorded use on fol. 179 of the *Beowulf* manuscript, it seems safe to assume, as Prescott suggests, that the requirement for the Trustees' approval was dropped after 1873.

Prescott has advanced in personal correspondence the persuasive theory that the Keeper himself, Edward Maunde Thompson, must have authorized, and may have supervised or even undertaken, the use of reagents on the palimpsest, when the facsimile was prepared for Zupitza by Praetorius (Zupitza, *Beowulf* [1882], p. xviii). Prescott believes that it would be entirely consonant with the attitudes of a Victorian curator, who was confident that at least some reagents were harmless to manuscripts, to apply the chemicals, photograph the results for a permanent record, and not worry too much about possible degradation afterwards. In his acknowledgments Zupitza, who did not participate in the photographing of the manuscript, says that his "warmest thanks are due . . . especially to my friend Mr. E. Maunde Thompson, the Keeper of the Manuscripts in the British Museum."[38] The "autotypes" prepared by Praetorius for Zupitza offer some support for this theory. In a few places they seem to show a bit more ink

---

36. Edward Maunde Thompson, *Handbook of Greek and Latin Palæography,* p. 76.

37. Edward Maunde Thompson, *Introduction to Greek and Latin Palaeography,* p. 65. It is possible that Raman microscopy ("a non-destructive, non-invasive and extremely specific technique," according to David Jacobs, senior conservation officer in the British Library) can safely and definitively identify the chemical reagent used on the *Beowulf* palimpsest. See Jacobs's contribution, "An Introduction to The British Library and University College London Raman Microscopy Project" in Michelle P. Brown, *Lindisfarne Gospels,* pp. 430–33.

38. There may well have been additional pressure to try reagents around this time, as Eugen Kölbing in 1876 and Alfred Holder in 1882 both published results from collations with the manuscript, which Zupitza duly lists on the same page as "books referred to" in his notes (Zupitza, *Beowulf* [1959], p. xx).

traces than modern photographs, and in one case a careful comparison of the high-resolution digital image with Zupitza's autotype has convinced me that Zupitza was right about a restored reading that nearly everyone, including me, has rejected as impossible.

Where Zupitza says for the illegible section on 179r5 that "what is left of the two letters after *hea-* justifies us in reading them *ðo*," almost all editors have read *um* and confidently restored *heaum*. And while they are less confident about the following word, and variously restore it as *hæþe, heþe, hofe,* and *hope,* the editors are united in rejecting Zupitza's *hlæwe.* According to Zupitza, "very little of *hlæwe* [was] freshened up; the *h* indistinct, *læwe* pretty certain, but the *w* may be easily mistaken for *þ* in consequence of the *h* of [*nat*]*hwylc* on fol. 179v being visible through the parchment." Klaeber's comments on Zupitza's readings are representative. He says that all the letters are "very indistinct," and that "*ðo* seems too short and *hlæwe* too long for the space in the manuscript." Agreeing with these observations, I once thought that Zupitza's "*h* indistinct" must be an error for "*h* is distinct," because like Klaeber I interpreted the lone surviving dark ascender as the top of an *h*.

As we have seen, digital imaging and image processing programs open new possibilities for editors intending to conserve manuscript readings (as Zupitza, Klaeber, and I all intend in this case) to analyze this kind of evidence more accurately. Digital imagery makes it easy to compare the extreme differences between an image of the palimpsest acquired in bright light and one acquired using ultraviolet. Textual scholars can now use programs like Adobe Photoshop to cut and paste scribal letterforms to test conjectural restorations through its Layers function. John Pope used photocopies in the late 1970s to undertake a similar restoration of a damaged passage in the Exeter Book by physically cutting and pasting letters from other parts of the photocopy of the manuscript.[39] Following his lead, I developed under the *Electronic Boethius* project an OverLay tool to assist editors to make digital facsimile editions including conjectural restorations, in order to show the paleographical justification for conjectural restorations in print editions.[40] OverLay also facilitates the comparison and descriptive tagging of multiple sets of digital images, one set captured using bright light and the other using any number of other techniques,

39. Pope, "Paleography and Poetry." See my discussion of this article in "Old Manuscripts / New Technologies," pp. 44–48.

40. "The *Electronic Boethius*: Alfred the Great's Old English translation of Boethius's *Consolation of Philosophy*" was funded by the National Endowment for the Humanities and the

such as fiber-optic backlighting and ultraviolet fluorescence. An editor can also use OverLay to help isolate and digitally remove manuscript offsets and shine-through.

This flexible tool lets editors overlay one image with another and then minutely examine the differences between digital images. One can use it, for example, to analyze in detail letterforms written by the second scribe or Nowell with the *nathwylc* scribe. With its help I was able to superimpose Zupitza's 1882 autotype of fol. 179 on top of a high-resolution image of the same page illuminated with bright light and captured with a powerful digital camera. The process does not in any way affect the original image but instead generates an independent digital file combining the original image and an overlay incorporating conjectural restorations. To acquire an overlay file of these two images, one first selects two corresponding points ✛ on each image (in this case I chose the tips of the *h*-ascenders in *hea* and *hord*), and then clicks the OverLay icon 🗅. By means of a slider ◀▐░░░▶ that slowly increases and decreases, as desired, the transparency of the superimposed image, one can closely observe the differences between Zupitza's autotype and the modern image. A selection feature ⌶ allows the user to isolate the section from *hea* through *hord* for special examination. When associated with a corresponding transcription, one can then use a tagging feature to encode the selection with descriptive markup (including a textual note with automatically recorded coordinates of the place in the image) for later searching or display.

With the aid of these tools I found that the 1882 autotype in this case shows clearer ink traces than the digital image does today. Using the "transparency" slider in the lower left of Fig. 6, I could minutely compare the two images letter-by-letter, trace-by-trace. As a result of this investigation I now realize that Zupitza meant that the clearly visible ascender belongs to the *l*, not the *h*, which itself is faintly visible (or "indistinct," as Zupitza said) to the left of *l* in the autotype. The *h*-ascender begins slightly to the left of the *r*-descender of *deorcū* in the line above. Because it failed to adhere,

Andrew W. Mellon Foundation, with the cooperation of the British Library and the Bodleian Library, Oxford. When the editing project was overtaken by "The Alfredian Boethius Project: Anglo-Saxon adaptations of the *De Consolatione Philosophiae*," directed by Malcolm Godden and Susan Irvine, I redirected the resources of the *Electronic Boethius* project to develop the editing software. In recent years Ionut Emil Iacob and I, with the support of the Andrew W. Mellon Foundation, have extended this software as the generic, open source, image-based XML suite of tools called EPPT (Edition Production & Presentation Technology), which is now developed as IBX (Image-Based XML). For a discussion of the early stages, see Kiernan, "Remodeling Alfred's *Boethius*."

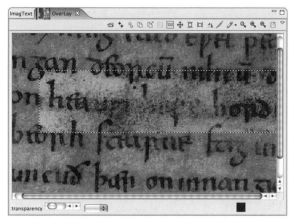

Fig. 6: Highlight of OverLay of Autotype for 179r5

the lower half of the *h*-shaft appears to be the last minim of an *m*. Though faint, its ascender is clearly visible in the autotype, as is the top and most of the right side of the *h*-bow. The rest of *hlæwe* is clearer in the autotype than it is today in the manuscript. These results indicate that the autotype preserves an example of how a reagent can improve a reading, and then destroy the evidence, the very reason we now deplore the widespread practice of using chemicals on manuscripts during the nineteenth century.

Although most editors have considered the reading *heaum* here as virtually certain, there were in retrospect always reasons to doubt it. In the first place, the usual form of *heah* in the dative singular is weak *hean* (used four times) not *heaum*; strong *heaum* occurs nowhere else in *Beowulf*. Moreover, there are ten other words on this folio that end in −*um*, and in every case the scribe uses a macron over *u* as the abbreviation for *m* (*deorcū* r4, *nihtū* r4, *eldū* r7, *hæðnū* r8, *geweoldū* r14, *willū* r15, *-gū* AB v5, *mæū* v8, *wæteryðū* v13, *cræftū* v14). It is difficult to make a convincing case that the one exception occurs in a badly damaged, illegible part of the folio, especially after close scrutiny of the tops of the supposed minims. Klaeber's expressed view that there was not enough room in the manuscript for Zupitza's readings is, moreover, demonstrably unfounded. By cutting and pasting the *nathwylc* scribe's letterforms from elsewhere on the folio, I tested Zupitza's conjectural restoration. Before the advent of image-processing programs, editors could only make conjectural restorations in printed editions without having to show whether or not the reading actually fit the space or otherwise satisfied the paleographical circumstances. Now one can see in a virtual restoration of the scribe's own hand that there is in fact sufficient space for

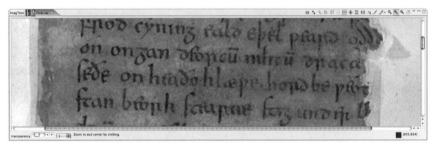

Fig. 7: Digital restoration of *heaðohlæwe*, 179r5

heaðohlæwe with all restored letters coinciding with the remaining ink traces (see Fig. 7). The conjectural restoration of *heaðohlæwe*, "battle-barrow, battle-burial-mound," seems far superior to all previous restorations (*heaum hæpe* or *hepe*, "high heath," *heaum hofe*, "high dwelling or court," *heaum hope*, "high plateau"). Poetic compounds with *heaðo-* are among the most common in the poem, very frequently occurring in *hapax* compounds, as in this case. The second element, *hlæw*, is also a common word in the second part of *Beowulf*. This collocation is particularly appropriate for the barrow where Beowulf holds his last battle. The verse type, *se ðe on heaðohlæwe*, is described in various ways by different metrists in comparable instances: *Ac ic ðær heaðufyres* 2523(2522)a and *nemne him heaðobyrne* 1554(1552)a are Sievers C, Bliss d2c, Hutcheson 3C7I, Hoover nAn, and Russom x/Ssx.[41]

The same image-processing software that helps provide paleographical support for the conjectural restoration of *heaðohlæwe* makes it possible for editors to attempt to justify by means of a restored facsimile any conjectural restorations that purport to represent readings supported by the surviving ink traces.[42] In this case I restricted my choices to letters from this single folio, as they are the only ones written by the *nathwylc* scribe. The OverLay tool can further enhance this process, as well. By overlaying the restored folio (the facsimile edition) on the original unrestored one

41. Despite the bewildering array of codes for describing metrical types, metrical aficionadios are fond of saying that they essentially agree with one another's metrical analyses. It would be a fascinating and salutary advance in metrical studies of Old English poetry in general, and of *Beowulf* in particular, if a member of the guild of metrists would organize comprehensive metrical statistics for the leading metrical theories, with each type (including "hypermeter") linked to its specific instance.

42. The best software for this purpose is, in my experience, Adobe Photoshop, which provides a range of sophisticated image-processing tools for creating conjecturally restored facsimiles that an editor can then use as an OverLay image with the unrestored manuscript image. While generously acknowledging many of the advantages of *Electronic Beowulf*, J. R.

(the original facsimile), scholars, using the slidebar in the lower left corner of the tool, can minutely examine any restored reading compared to the ink traces. As we have seen, by this means editors of electronic editions are able to provide paleographical support for conjectural restorations. Because the restored readings are digital, editors and textual scholars can and should continue to propose new restorations or defend old ones.[43]

The OverLay tool is an analytical resource easily adaptable to other manuscript problems, both on the palimpsest and throughout the manuscript.

Fig. 8: OverLay of covered edge with backlit *g*, 179v19

For example, the tool is especially useful on almost every folio for resituating along the damaged edges the hundreds of covered letters and bits of

---

Hall complains that one cannot alter the lighting of the color images in the main frames nor even magnify the ultraviolet images in the side frames ("Three Studies on the Manuscript Text of *Beowulf*," p. 457). In fact, one can use Photoshop to magnify, or change the lighting or the contrast, or otherwise process any of the images in *Electronic Beowulf*.

43. After spending some time with *Electronic Beowulf* at the British Library, Frederick Biggs remained agnostic over whether a *þegn* or a *þeof* stole from the dragon's hoard in "*Beowulf* and Some Fictions of the Geatish Succession," p. 61, note 29. Both words fit the space, but the vestiges of ink do not serve both readings equally well. Digital tools like Photoshop and EPPT's OverLay can help adjudicate such disputes by providing evidence for everyone to examine.

letters, restored by fiber-optic backlighting, on the versos. In the *Electronic Beowulf* these restored readings are currently available in browser frames as illustrated textual notes, supplementing and correcting Zupitza's 1882 observations on covered readings. Often only slight traces or fragments of letters survive beneath the paper frames, and while fiber-optic backlighting reveals what remains, it is not always easy for a reader to see exactly where the backlit image belongs on the covered edge. By correctly matching two points on the edge of the paper frame, as illustrated in Fig. 8, an editor can use the OverLay tool to restore covered readings wherever they belong. As

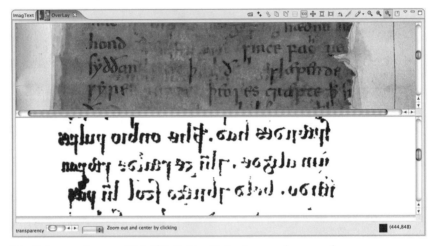

Fig. 9: Inverse image of fol. 178v9–11 with background removed

illustrated in Figs. 9 and 10, the OverLay tool can also help address more difficult editorial problems. Offsets (caused by ink transferring from a facing page) and shine-through (caused by text showing through from the opposite side of a page) are common in medieval manuscripts, both creating obstructive reverse or mirror images. Between lines 8 and 13 of the palimpsest there are many continuous offset letters from the facing folio, 178v, which make it almost impossible to isolate the remaining legitimate ink traces from the faded text on 179r.[44] Because they coincide with the areas where reagent was applied, these offsets were plausibly caused when the manuscript was closed while the vellum was still damp with reagent.

---

44. In *Electronic Beowulf* I used Photoshop's Layers to disclose the offset image from fol. 178v. OverLay is now specifically adapted for editors using EPPT for this and many other purposes.

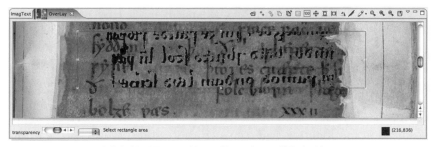

Fig. 10: OverLay of 179r10–12 revealing offsets from 178v9–11

The digital medium makes it relatively easy to discover and display how an offset from the text on fol. 178v further obscures the damaged readings between lines 8 and 13 on fol. 179r of the palimpsest. The OverLay tool has access to its own mini-image processor, which allows the editor to reverse an image, intensify the writing, and render the background vellum transparent. Using these features, I first created an inverse image of fol. 178v; then highlighted the text on the folio and removed the lightened background; next, after locating points where offsets correspond to places on the inverse image of 178v, I overlaid this reversed text onto fol. 179r (see Fig. 10). The overlay shows that the inverse of the text on 178v10, [*þu*]*sendo. bold 7brego stol hī wæs*, is offset on 179r10. The inverse *dl-* of *bold* immediately precedes *slæpende*, and much of the rest of the inverse line shows up as spurious ink traces within and beneath 179r10. After identifying the spurious

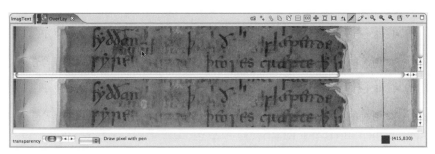

Fig. 11: Removing offsets from 179r10

offset ink traces, the editor can use another feature of the OverLay tool, as shown in Fig. 11, to remove the offset of inverted *hī wæs* below *syððan* in order to focus on the legitimate ink traces from fol. 179. With the offsets removed, an editor can more easily evaluate the ink traces that remain on the palimpsest and offer more plausible conjectural restorations for the faded text.

Editors of print editions have customarily made conjectural restorations while paying attention to sense and meter, but often without sufficient regard to the manuscript evidence. In a recent example, Mitchell and Robinson acknowledge in their note to these lines that "before *syððan* [i.e., where the vellum has crumbled away at the end of 179r9] Thorkelin A has *þ*, Thorkelin B *þæt*," but they still remove "that" from their text on the grounds that it "would make no sense" (*Beowulf*, p.126). They give no justification for doubting that a crossed thorn still survived on the burnt edge of the manuscript, which Thorkelin typically expanded to *þæt*, but which his scribe would accurately transcribe as a crossed thorn. The reason the demonstrative *þæt* seems to make no sense for Mitchell and Robinson is that, following it, they have proposed a conjectural restoration that renders it meaningless (i.e., "þah] *MS illegible*"). Klaeber's conjectural restoration, *bemað*, which according to Fulk "seems the best guess on paleographical grounds," rather surprisingly does not fit in the space between *syððan* and the isolated *þ*, as the digital restoration in Fig. 12 illustrates. Although *bemað* is only five letters long, the letters *m* and *ð* are both wider than all other letters. Taken together, they add in effect the width of an

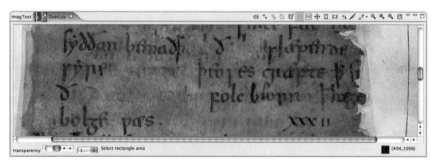

Fig. 12: Conjectural restoration of *bemað* 179r10

additional letter. In Fig. 12 I have digitally cut and pasted letters from other parts of the folio to test Klaeber's restoration. As the reconstruction makes clear, *bemað* is too wide to fit the space, and the cross-stroke of *ð* interferes with the *þ*-ascender. In this hand the cross-stroke of *ð* always extends beyond the bowl (see the two extant examples in this line in Fig. 12), and the cross-stroke would interfere with the *þ*-ascender if the last letter were indeed an *ð* (cf. *cuð þær* 179r7, three lines above). Even an unusually stunted cross-stroke would not provide enough room for *bemað*. In an edition that purports to be based on the manuscript, paleographical evidence should of course carry weight.

My own restoration, *bohte* ("paid for"), in the *Electronic Beowulf* fills the space, does not conflict with the remaining traces of ink, and makes sense in the context. However, while it is metrical in an on-verse, the type does not occur with anacrusis in an off-verse, as Fulk has pointed out. Models of normal meter in *Beowulf* should carry weight when a manuscript reading is not certain. I have accordingly abandoned *bohte* as an acceptable conjectural restoration, and offer instead *beget*, third singular preterite of

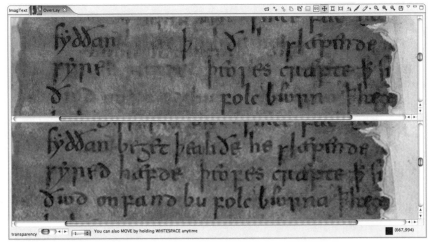

Fig. 13: Conjectural restoration of 179r10–13

begytan, in the sense of "to get, obtain, acquire; to take hold, seize." In Fig. 13 I have followed the same process to test my own conjectural restorations of 179r10–13.

> (He þ) syððan [*beget*]
> þ[*eah*] ð[*e*] [*he*] slæpende   (be)syre[*d*] [*hæf*]de
> þeo[*ſ*]es cræfte;   þ si(e) ðiod [*onſand*],
> b[*u*]folc beorn[*a*],   þ he gebolge[*n*] wæs.

"He [i.e., *niða nathwylc*, "I know not who of men"] afterwards got that [i.e., the stolen item], though he had swindled the sleeping one [the dragon] by a thief's craft; so that his countrymen found out, a nearby-folk of fighters, that it was infuriated."[45] A digital restoration provides paleographical justifica-

---

45. Kiernan, *Electronic Beowulf*, lines 2220b–23; Klaeber, *Beowulf*, 2217b–20. In my edition of these lines Thorkelin readings are in round brackets in roman, while my virtual conjectural restorations are in square brackets with italics.

tion for a conjectural restoration in an edition. The restoration *beget* fills the space, does not conflict with the few remaining traces, makes sense in the context, and also provides unobjectionable meter across many systems (e.g., Sievers B, Bliss 3B*1b, Hutcheson 2B2b, Hoover nAn, Russom x/Sxxs).

In 1981 I argued that a "new edition of the text on the palimpsest is desperately needed, but must await further attempts, by modern techno-logical methods, to decipher all of the extant ink traces."[46] My view then as now was that a "conservative edition," one that intends to conserve the manuscript text, "will strive to retain all of the readings that are clear in the MS, and will try to make sense of the text by emending conjectural res-torations (for which there is little or no MS support), Thorkelin readings,[47] and then doubtful MS readings" (p. 243).[48] Over the past twenty-five years I have had many opportunities to explore these paths, first with a digital camera creating grayscale images for medical image-processing, and then in 1993, with the start of the *Electronic Beowulf* project, with an all-purpose camera that the British Library purchased for the project to prepare high-resolution 24-bit color images.[49] Each stage of exploration has led me to refine, and sometimes recant, aspects of earlier arguments. I believe it is not a scholarly virtue to be inflexible or dogmatic in the face of new, or for that matter, uncertain evidence.

---

46. Kiernan, *Beowulf and the Beowulf Manuscript*, p. 243. Fulk surprisingly comes to a similar conclusion after discussing the last line on this folio: "It is my belief," he confesses, "that improved technologies will make it possible in the future to retrieve some readings in the MS that are currently in part or in whole indecipherable, and particularly on this leaf" ("Some Contested Readings," p. 223).

47. There are still discoveries to be made from the Thorkelin transcripts. A recent example in the *Electronic Beowulf* is the new reading *eorðsele* on fol. 179v3–4, which editors have always restored as *eorðhuse* (see for example Mitchell and Robinson, *Beowulf*, "2232 eorðhuse] eorð..."), following Zupitza. Thorkelin A does not give a reading, but Thorkelin B has "*se*.", not "*..se*". Thus B supports the restoration of *eorðsele*, not *eorðhuse*, which is used in prose, but nowhere else in Old English poetry; *eorðsele*, on the other hand, is used twice again in *Beowulf*. After requesting and reviewing my evidence, the *Dictionary of Old English* duly added this occurrence to its list. Fulk has recently adopted *eorðsele* without attributing it to the *Electronic Beowulf* ("Some Contested Readings," p. 220). In his history of this recalci-trant reading, Hall observes that I corrected the Thorkelin B reading in my text in the 1996 revised (pace Fulk) edition of *Beowulf and the Beowulf Manuscript* ("Three Studies on the Manuscript Text of *Beowulf*," p. 466).

48. A conservative editor will not emend the manuscript solely on the basis of meter, but will reasonably use standard meter as a guide for conjectural restorations where manu-script readings are not certain.

49. For a chronology of my use of a digital camera with the *Beowulf* manuscript from 1982 to the *Electronic Beowulf* project, see "Digital Image-processing and the *Beowulf* Manuscript."

As I have tried to epitomize in various ways in this essay, I am also convinced that image-based electronic editions of a text like *Beowulf* have some clear advantages over traditional print editions such as Klaeber's. With a high-resolution facsimile, there is no reason not to have every textual note linked to its source in the manuscript for all to examine and assess. Print has fostered the idea of an established text, whereas digital editions are now free to present texts in a less-settled state, the way they exist in manuscripts. As I have explained under Edition in the Help facility of the *Electronic Beowulf*: "The new editorial emendations and conjectural restorations are not meant to replace, but rather to supplement or challenge previous editorial changes that have become ingrained in modern editions. Anglo-Saxon readers of this manuscript did not have access to any modern changes and perhaps devised different solutions each time they encountered problems that demanded emendations. The conjectural restorations are informed guesses that try to fill gaps in paleographically and linguistically plausible ways." The great value of digital technology is that it encourages continuing research of textual issues and obviates the need, required of print editions, to establish a text. The manuscript record left by the three *Beowulf* scribes, in particular the *nathwylc* scribe of fol. 179, continually reminds us that there was no established text in Anglo-Saxon times. There is no definitive edition of *Beowulf* today, just as there never was one in Anglo-Saxon times. Electronic editions will help us understand the pleasures of a constantly moving text more than printed editions. The high-frequency occurrence on the palimpsest of the otherwise low-frequency word, *nathwylc,* can perhaps help focus attention on some important theoretical and practical issues surrounding the editing of *Beowulf.*[50]

---

50. I am indebted to Andrew Prescott, in particular for his contributions to the section on the reagent and his preparation of high-resolution images of Zupitza's autotype of fol. 179r.

ÆÐELDREDA IN THE *OLD ENGLISH BEDE*

PAUL E. SZARMACH

As Gordon Whatley has so correctly reminded Anglo-Saxonists, Bede's *Historia ecclesiastica* is a collective hagiography or a compendium of early Anglo-Saxon saints, whatever else scholars may wish it to be.[1] As such, the *Historia ecclesiastica* has been the focus of various and many studies of the saints who appear therein through methodologies traditional and historical in nature to those featuring newer theoretical premises. When comparative in whole or in part, these studies do not generally see the *Old English Bede* as relevant or important for their purposes. Bede and Ælfric, e.g., are a better pair for discussion, as Peter Jackson has recently taught us, particu-

---

In the mid-1980s when I was about to slide into the abyss of higher administration, Helen Damico threw me a lifeline by inviting me to participate in two of her programs. One of the invitations rekindled interest in an old project, while the other opened up a new area of research for me. The essay in this volume continues this second line of inquiry. I am glad that it has always been hard to say "no" to Helen's energy and dynamism. A first version of this paper was read at the Annual Meeting of the Medieval Association of the Pacific, March 22, 2002, held at the University of San Diego.

1. Whatley, "Introduction to the Study of Old English Prose Hagiography," pp. 3, 20. This introduction surveys some of the principal research tools necessary to study the corpus of Old English lives. For further background on Old English-Latin relations, see now Whatley's compendious treatment of "Acta Sanctorum," comprising most of volume 1 of *Sources of Anglo-Saxon Literary Culture.*

Michael Lapidge and Rosalind C. Love survey hagiography in England and Wales in "Latin Hagiography," calling Bede "the greatest hagiographer of the Anglo-Saxon period: not simply for the quantity of his own surviving saints' lives, but for his sophisticated awareness of the hagiographer's duty and his exhaustive control of earlier hagiographical sources" (p. 213). See also Whatley, "Hagiography in England," and Cross, "English Vernacular Saints' Lives."

For an overview of the iconography of Æðeldreda see Blanton-Whetsell, "Imagines Ætheldredae." One may also note here the famous portrait of Æðeldreda; see Deshman, *Benedictional of Æthelwold,* pp. 121–24 and pl. 28, and also pl. 3. These images, as Deshman notes, are the "the only extant representations of [Æðeldreda] before the thirteenth century" (p. 121). As the Blanton-Whetsell article makes clear, the bibliography on Æðeldreda, already immense, is growing apace. See, e.g., P. Thompson and Stevens, "Gregory of Ely's Verse Life," an edition of the text with introduction based on the twelfth-century unique manuscript, Cambridge, Corpus Christi College 393. P. Thompson also offers "St. Æthelthryth"; Otter, "Temptation of St. Æthelthryth," describes Æðeldreda as a "vestal presence," the threats against whose virginity become "not merely a statically remembered fact but a continually re-enacted story" (pp. 162, 163). See also note 9 below.

larly given Ælfric's discussion of chaste marriage at the end of his rendering, which is a clear and somewhat problematic departure from Bede.[2] Jocelyn Wogan-Browne presents a brilliant picture of vernacular saints in English and French beyond the Conquest, and Bede and Æðeldreda play their roles in deep background, but rightly Wogan-Browne has so much good work to do in the Anglo-Norman period that consideration of the *Old English Bede* as an early hagiographic bridge to the vernacular would become a distraction to her main purpose.[3] No doubt, Thomas Miller's edition does not easily support contemporary research agendas, and for more traditionalist scholars the vernacular witness to Bede would appear to be no better than a secondary or marginal text.[4] The anonymous translator, presumably a Mercian trailing Alfredian associations, sometimes receives plaudits for a "poetic turn of mind," but at the same time there is a case to be made for a certain disregard or even perhaps a disrespect of Bede's original.[5] In this essay I would like to open up the question of the *Old English Bede* and its relation to the original with special reference to the treatment of Æðeldreda. The consideration has to be horizontal and vertical: i.e., a point-to-point source comparison is most meaningful when the broad ends and means of both works play a role in the discussion, not just a simple investigation of whether a rendering is faithful. A more descriptive reassessment of the *Old English Bede*, incipient as it can only be here, is the final goal well beyond this paper, while yet a review of the work

---

2. Jackson, "Ælfric and the Purpose of Christian Marriage."

3. Wogan-Browne, *Saints' Lives*, makes a successful case for the importance of Æðeldreda and her cult, especially in the twelfth through the fourteenth centuries; see pp. 204–12, among other places.

4. *Old English Version of Bede's Ecclesiastical History*, ed. and trans. Miller. The Old English equivalent to Bede's Æðeldreda appears in o.s. 96 [=Part 1, 2 (1997)] as 4.21, pp. 316–24. The *Old English Version of Bede's Ecclesiastical History* is another important text in the field of Old English prose that needs a new edition.

5. Stanley B. Greenfield and Daniel Calder give an "in bono et in malo" description and evaluation of the translator's work, noting, among other things, that one-quarter of the Latin original is missing; see their *New Critical History*, pp. 57–59. It is well known that Ælfric erringly attributes a translation of "historia anglorum" to Alfred (always assumed to be a reference to the extant translation) in his homily on Gregory, *Catholic Homilies* 2.9: see Ælfric, *Ælfric's Catholic Homilies, the Second Series: Text*, ed. Godden, p. 72. William of Malmesbury joins Ælfric in this attribution in his *Gesta Regum Anglorum*, 2.123, 1:193.

See now the important overview by Bately, "Old English Prose," and specific consideration of the *Old English Version of Bede's Ecclesiastical History*, ed. and trans. Miller, pp. 103–4, 123–24. The Mercian question runs throughout Prof. Bately's discussion. See also Waite, "Vocabulary." Waite offers a bibliographical survey in his *Old English Prose Translations*, pp. 42–46, and 321–53.

and its relation to the *Historia ecclesiastica* must be part of the baseline for discussion. Along the way female sanctity and its portrayal will necessarily become a major theme, at least in the present, abbreviated treatment, and the function of the *Old English Bede* as a heuristic device should become apparent.

Bede presents his account of Æðeldreda in the *Historia ecclesiastica* 4.19–20.[6] The first of the two chapters is a prose *vita*, treating Æðeldreda and her life from young adulthood through death and some sixteen years thereafter, while the second is substantially an astonishing 54-line poem, the longest in the *Historia ecclesiastica*, which, having written it many years before, Bede finds *oportunum* to insert at this point in the narrative. The insertion comes with an alibi or apologia, for Bede prefaces his poem by citing biblical precedent no less: "imitari morem sacrae scripturae, cuius historiae carmina plurima indita et haec metro ac versibus constat esse conposita" (imitating the practice of Holy Scripture, into the story of which many songs are inserted, and it is well known that these are composed in meter and in verse).[7] His self-consciousness also makes him identify the meter as elegiac, further assisting the understanding of his readers lest, perhaps, they miss the special significance of the insertion. But the content and the form of the poem offer more still. Secular and sacred history, Bede sings, creates the context for Æðeldreda and her moral achievement: Troy, Rome, the Incarnation, and a gallery of virgin martyrs establish the frame of reference after the brief invocation to the Trinity. The themes of grand secular poetry are devalued in contrasts; thus, "Bella Maro resonet; nos pacis dona canamus, / munera nos Christi" (Virgil reechoes of wars; we sing of the gifts of peace, the presents of Christ [lines 3–4]) and "Carmina casta mihi, fedae non raptus Helenae; / luxus erit lubricis" (Mine are chaste songs, not the rape of wanton Helen; debauchery will be for the debauched [lines 5–6]). The foundation myth of the West cannot equal the celebration of the life of Æðeldreda and the *dona superna* that are the poet's theme. The idea of celestial gifts is the link to the theme of the Incarnation, which here is less about Christ as man-God than about his Virgin Mother. In some four couplets on the theme Bede cites "virginity" or some form of the word six times (lines 9–16), and it is a fecund virginity that he emphasizes: "Huius honor genuit casto de germine plures, /

---

6. *HE*, pp. 390–401, Latin and English translation *en face*. The poem occupies pp. 396–401, here cited by line with the Colgrave-Mynors translation.

7. *HE*, p. 396; trans. p. 397.

uirgineos flores huius honor genuit" (Her honor gave birth to many virgin flowers from her chaste bud, her honor gave birth [lines 15–16]).

These virgin flowers are metamorphosed into three pairs of virgin martyrs, Agatha and Eulalia, Thecla and Euphemia,[8] Agnes and Cecilia, each pair linked by the means of torture or death common to the pair in an intricacy that the serpentine couplets allow, respectively "furnace," "lions," or "sword":

> Ignibus usta feris uirgo non cessit Agathe,
> Eulalia et perfert ignibus usta feris,
> Kasta feras superat mentis pro culmine Tecla,
> Eufemia sacras kasta feras superat,
> Laeta ridet gladios ferro robustior Agnes,
> Cecilia infestos laeta ridet gladios. (lines 17–22)

(In furnace fierce stood virgin Agatha, Eulalia stands firm in furnace fierce. Keen lions yield to Thecla's spirit high, To chaste Euphemia keen lions yield. Laughs at the sword [of finer temper she] Agnes, and Cecily laughs at the sword.)

In addition to the wraparound linking where the beginning of the couplet is as the ending, Bede creates an added rhetorical effect when the name of one saint ends the line, and the name of another begins the next line.

At line 25 (the thirteenth couplet) or nearly halfway through the poem Bede at last turns to Æðeldreda, having created a remarkable rhetorical introduction for her. "Nostra quoque egregia iam tempora uirgo beauit" (A distinguished virgin has also enriched our times) becomes the cue for a thematic treatment of her life that while it touches on major biographical details such as royal birth line, monastic life, the sixteen-year interment and miraculous disinterment, and her miraculous healing powers, allows no earthly man to cast any shadow on her holy life. As J. M. Wallace-Hadrill aptly observes, Æðeldreda becomes "a new link between the Early Church and Bede's Church."[9] The poet's question, "Quid petis, alma,[10] uirum, sponso iam dedita summo?" (For what reason do you seek, nourishing one, a man, dedicated now to the highest Spouse? [line 30]) introduces the major image cluster or metaphor that works through the Æðeldreda part

---

8. Bede, *Venerabilis Baedae opera historica*, ed. Plummer, 2:241, suggests that Eufemia should yield to Eugenia, *causa metri*. Thecla is a virgin but not a martyr.

9. Wallace-Hadrill, *Bede's Ecclesiastical History*, p. 160.

10. Lewis and Short's *Latin Dictionary* notes that "alma" is a poetic epithet for Ceres and Venus, among other deities.

of the poem, viz., Æðeldreda as Bride of Christ.[11] The heavenly marriage becomes in effect the perfect marriage where Æðeldreda enjoys queenly status, a heavenly maternity, gifts, while playing the harp with new songs and remaining unseparated from the Lamb's *comitatus* [*sic*, line 53]. The allusion to gifts taken while torches blaze would seem to be a particularly effective evocation of a real marriage ceremony. In this section Bede changes his voice. Whereas in the first section Bede addresses an audience to whom he relates poetic matter in the third person, here he addresses Æðeldreda directly not only with the question above but also in this couplet, also in the second person singular: "Regis ut aetheri matrem iam, credo, sequaris, / tu quoque sis mater regis ut aetherei" (I believe that you (sing.) follow the mother of the heavenly king, you also may be as a mother of the heavenly king [lines 33–34]). The celebration of Æðeldreda's heavenly triumph comes with overt mention of the earthly steps she took to get there, for she was *sponsa dicata deo* (bride dedicated to God [line 35]) and with citation of her miraculous preservation of her body. It is on the heavenly-earthly contrast that the poem ends in a couplet on faithful virginity.

The elevated content of the poem, notably the cosmic and universal context for Æðeldreda's virginity, has its counterpart in the metrical form, which merits further comment. Plummer's classic note conveys the rich texture and resonance of Bede's choice.[12] While, as noted above, Bede cites the meter and biblical precedent to hint at his poetic stance, Plummer identifies the form of elegiac verses, where the last quarter of the couplet repeats the first, as *echoici* or *serpentini* or *reciproci*. The form is medieval, appearing later among the Carolingians, but it also has classical precedent in Ovid. Bede's hymn to Æðeldreda is, moreover, an alphabetic (epanaleptic) or acrostic poem: the first twenty-three couplets begin with the letters of the alphabet in serial order, while the final four couplets spell out "AMEN." Such alphabetic poems were also Carolingian favorites. Alcuin was so impressed with Bede's tour de force as to comment:

---

11. Cf. Morrison, "Figure of *Christus Sponsus*."

12. Bede, *Venerabilis Baedae opera historica*, ed. Plummer, 2:241. Plummer's notes on 4.20 inform the literary history in this paragraph. In the "Leningrad Bede" (now St. Petersburg, Russian National Library, Q.v.I.18) the double-column format (fols. 100v2–101v1) is not hospitable to Bede's elegiacs. Capital letters mark verses, which occupy three lines, with the second and third lines indented under the capital letter. See Arngart, *Leningrad Bede*. In the *Moore Bede* (fols. 86v–87r) the verse is run margin to margin with capitals marking the beginning of lines. See Hunter Blair, *Moore Bede*.

Istius ergo sacrae praedictus Beda puellae
in laudem fecit praeclaris versibus hymnum;
quapropter tetigi parcis haec puella libellis,
utpote commorans veteris proverbia dicti:
"Tu ne forte feras in silvam ligna, viator."[13]

(Bede, of whom I have spoken, wrote in splendid verse a hymn in honour
of that holy maid, and so I have only touched on this subject in sparing
style, remembering the words of the old proverb: "Don't carry wood into
the forest.")

Bede, generally celebrated for his clean and clear prose style, has clearly
outdone himself in this hymn of praise for Æðeldreda. Against the prose
background of the whole of the *Historia ecclesiastica* he has emphasized in
no uncertain rhetorical terms Æðeldreda as a model of moral excellence.
Wallace-Hadrill puts it simply: "Bede is very proud of Æðeldreda. . . . He
is not urging all royal ladies to take the veil . . . but he is insisting that this
is the highest calling for the elect minority and a credit to any Christian
people."[14]

In the face of this remarkable rhetorical display the anonymous Old
English translator does even less than Alcuin could get away with. There
is no indication that in the Old English *Historia ecclesiastica* 4.21, which is
the equivalent of Bede's 4.20, there is a Bedan hymn in the offing in the
next section (Bede gives no forewarning either, of course) and there is no
indication in the Old English *Historia ecclesiastica* 4.22 that the translator
has gone by the Latin. Since Bede's insertion of the poem in his chronological flow is gratuitous, there could be no way to infer from the opening
of 4.21, with its regnal reference, that anything might be amiss. Now it is a
hallowed Alfredian practice to omit the difficult and the problematical in
translation, as consultation with Boethius's *De Consolatione Philosophiae* and
the *Old English Boethius* would quickly establish.[15] What can be said of the
Old English Bede translator's omission of a rendition of Bede's *serpentini* in
honor of Æðeldreda?

---

13. Godman, *Alcuin*, p. 66, with his trans. *en face* (p. 67). In his translation of *Bede: A History of the English Church and People*, Sherley-Price observes that Alcuin "does not attempt to
imitate [Bede's] elaborate device of repetitive half-lines, which makes the hymn remarkable
rather for ingenuity than for any claim to poetic excellence" (p. 242). Accordingly, Sherley-
Price delivers a twenty-seven-line translation. Stevens, as revised by J. A. Giles, offers fifty-two
lines in rhymed couplets, in *Bede's Ecclesiastical History*, pp. 197–98.

14. Wallace-Hadrill, *Bede's Ecclesiastical History*, p. 160.

15. Cf. Bolton, "How Boethian Is Alfred's *Boethius?*" pp. 153–54.

Perhaps the most significant observation is that the Old English translator does not, with one exception, give translations for the Latin poetry
that Bede offers in the *Historia ecclesiastica*. There are some four poetic
epitaphs, viz., Gregory the Great, King Cædwalla, Theodore, and Wilfrid,
and also one poem from Prosper on Pelagius, in addition to the hymn in
praise of Æðeldreda. Æðeldreda is certainly in fast company in Bede, for
there are few churchmen more significant than Gregory, Theodore, and
Wilfrid for Bede's time, but this association, impressive as it is, is only part
of the story. The fifty-four lines on Æðeldreda remain the most extensive
poetry in the *Historia ecclesiastica*. Bede notes that Theodore's epitaph contains thirty-four heroic verses, but he gives only the first four lines and the
last four.[16] Bede incorporates the epitaph written by Crispus of Milan for
Cædwalla, who gave up kingship to travel to Rome where Pope Sergius
baptized him.[17] If Werner Jaager's suggestion is correct, Bede himself may
have written Wilfrid's epitaph.[18] These three epitaphs join the hymn to
Æðeldreda in disappearing from the translation in the *Old English Bede*.
Prosper's six-line poem on Pelagius and the entire section *Historia ecclesiastica* 1.10, which is a very abbreviated account of the spread of Pelagianism,
including the mention of Bede's adversary Julian of Campania/Eclanum,
and for that reason the Old English translator might have chosen to avoid
doctrinal trouble by not mentioning it. But the overall tendency is clear: the
Old English translator has chosen to avoid Latin poetry, even if the poetry
contains praise and honor of Christian saints of great merit. The exception
to this pattern of exclusion is the epitaph of Gregory the Great.[19] One way
to understand this exception is the heavy weight of *pietas*. *Historia ecclesiastica* 2.1, "De Obitu beati papae Gregorii," begins with an explanation of
the signal importance of Gregory to the English: "recte nostrum appellare
possumus et debemus apostolum quia . . . nostram gentem eatenus idoliis
mancipatam Christi fecit ecclesiam" (rightly can we and ought we call him
our apostle because . . . he made our nation, up to then enslaved by idols,
a church of Christ).[20] This section gives a detailed biographical account of
Gregory that ends with the epitaph. In the sixteen lines that summarize

---

16. *HE*, 5.8, p. 474.
17. *HE*, 5.7, pp. 470, 472.
18. *HE*, 5.19, pp. 528, 530; see Bede, *Bedas metrische vita sancti Cuthberti*, ed. Jaager, pp.
50–51.
19. *HE*, 2.1, p. 132.
20. *HE*, p. 122; trans., p. 123.

Gregory's life English affairs occupy much attention, recapitulating in part Bede's first paragraph of this section. Thus, Gregory receives praise again for converting the English and for acting as the shepherd who increases his master's flock. The *Old English Bede* translator renders the epitaph rather closely in a relatively faithful, if not merely straightforward, prose. The Gregorian epitaph does not furthermore pose the same stylistic problems as the *serpentini* verses of the hymn to Æðeldreda. As it is the first bit of intercalated poetry, and indeed as the verses honor the apostle of the English, the translator may have felt ready to offer a rendition.[21]

The Old English translator also misses the structural point, viz., Bede's two chapters on Æðeldreda form an *opus geminatum* of sorts. To be sure it is a "poor man's" *opus geminatum*, even in Bede. Bede may invoke biblical precedents about verse in a prose context, but this self-consciousness in *Historia ecclesiastica* 4.20 does not seem to be of the same order as that found in the prefaces to the *opera geminata* for the lives of Felix and Cuthbert.[22] For the former Bede wrote a prose vita as a pair with Paulinus of Nola's verse life; for the latter Bede wrote a prose life as a pair with his verse life of Cuthbert. In both cases verse is prior, prose later in composition; in both cases prose offers clarity, and in the *vita Cuthberti* more detail. From the prefatory remarks in *Historia ecclesiastica* 4.20 it is clear that the hymn preceded the prose account, a step in the composition process of an *opus geminatum* as one can observe, but it is hard to believe that *Historia ecclesiastica* 4.20, coming first in the narrative order, is a function of the hymn; rather the hymn is a poetic gloss on the prose, and almost as if an afterthought. The force of Bedan precedent, even if the two sections are more collocative than geminate, clearly did not compel the Old English translator to translate "word for word, or sense for sense." The later *Liber Eliensis*, deriving much of its early account of the foundation of Ely from Bede, makes much of Bede's poem and the felt need to add it to the account.[23] The Old English translator felt no such need. In or by *Historia ecclesiastica* 4 perhaps it had become programmatic not to translate poetry.[24]

---

21. See my discussion of the Old English translator and his rendering of the poems found in *Old English Version of Bede's Ecclesiastical History*: "'The Poetic Turn of Mind' of the Translator of the *OE Bede*."

22. For a survey of the *opus geminatum* as a form see Godman, *Alcuin*, pp. lxxviii–lxxxvii, and esp. pp. lxxxiv–lxxxv for Bede on Felix and Cuthbert.

23. *Liber Eliensis*, ed. Blake, pp. 48–50.

24. In discussing the translation of Latin poetry to Old English it is surely not possible to avoid considering in an aside the rendering of embedded poetry in Latin back to

What the Old English translator did not do with *Historia ecclesiastica* 4.20 along with the ramifications of the absence of the hymn describes his "art of translation" in part, and so what the Old English translator did do to *Historia ecclesiastica* 4.19 must offer a positive complement to his treatment of the Life of Æðeldreda. Bede's main narrative line in *Historia ecclesiastica* 4.19 is by and large straight enough, moving with an aside here and there in chronological order from a brief mention of Æðeldreda's family and first marriage, through her relations with her second husband, and then on to her life with the veil until she became abbess at Ely and died. Æðeldreda's life after death, so to speak, continues to a flash-forward sixteen years later when her sister Seaxburh, successor to her as abbess, seeks a proper coffin for Æðeldreda. The second burial allows for a retrospective to her death when the doctor Cynefrith relates the fatal surgery and gives witness to Æðeldreda's miraculous incorruption. Presumably Bede adds another testimony, introduced by the simple "Ferunt autem quia," which, as Colgrave and Mynors punctuate, does not come from Cynefrith, unless somehow indirectly. This testimony is Æðeldreda's self-impeachment that her tumor is punishment for the days when she wore jewelry around the neck. The clothes and first coffin are the occasions for cures, while the second marble coffin proves to be a miraculous fit.[25] *Historia ecclesiastica* 4.19 ends with a brief description of Ely and its East Anglian connection to Æðeldreda. To this broad outline the Old English translator remains true, leaving no major narrative point uncovered. When Ælfric retells the story of Æðeldreda in his Lives of Saints, he straightens out all the incidents, eliminating the retrospection provided by the second burial and creating a full linear narrative.[26] The *Old English Bede* translator was wise to follow Bede closely because he retains the rhetorical emphasis that the retrospection to Æðeldreda's last days and words gives to the Life. In a sense Bede has Æðeldreda die twice: once for historical record and once for moral meaning. The *Old English Bede* translator was equally wise to follow

---

Old English, viz. the relevance of *Cædmon's Hymn* to the Old English translator's methods. Effectively, the matter is one of linguistic colors reversed: in Bede's account of Cædmon, Latin paraphrases an Old English poem; in the *Old English Version of Bede's Ecclesiastical History*, the Old English poem substitutes for the Latin paraphrase. One can argue for some thoughtfulness in rescuing Old English poetry in this instance. See my "'Poetic Turn of Mind' of the Translator of the *OE Bede*."

25. *HE*, p. 396; trans. p. 397. See Fry, "Bede Fortunate in His Translator," for a study of the imagery of light and confinement.

26. Ælfric, *Ælfric's Lives of Saints*, 2:432–41.

Bede in ending *Historia ecclesiastica* 4.19 with a description of Ely. Earlier in the narrative Bede indicates that Ely is an island surrounded by water and marsh and without large stones for burial. The concluding description of Ely seems, at first glance, excrescent and ill-placed exposition, but the emphasis in the description on apartness makes the description serve as an emblem or image of Æðeldreda's chastity and the real and metaphorical dimension of enclosure.[27]

The *Old English Bede* translator, however, shows here and there that he has some difficulties or at least different takes on the level of word-rendering and in thematics. At the outset of *Historia ecclesiastica* 4.19 Bede relates that King Ecgfrith married Æðeldreda:

> Accepit autem rex Ecgfrid coniugem nomine Aedilthrydam, filiam Anna regis Orientalium Anglorum, cuius saepius mentionem fecimus, uiri bene religiosi ac per omnia mente et opere egregii; quam et alter ante illum uir habuerat uxorem, princeps uidelicet Australium Gyruirorum uocabulo Tondbercht. Sed illo post modicum temporis ex quo eam accepit, defuncto, data est regi praefato.[28]

> (King Ecgfrith married a wife named Æthelthryth, the daughter of Anna, king of the East Angles, who has been referred to, a very religious man and noble both in mind and deed. She had previously been married to an ealdorman of the South Gyrwe, named Tondberht. But he died shortly after the marriage and on his death she was given to King Ecgfrith.)

Who is who is a matter that Bede keeps under clear syntactical control. But does the *Old English Bede* translator succeed with

> Onfeng Ecgfrið se cyning gemæccan 7 wif, þære noma wæs Æðeldryð, Anna dohtor Eastengla cyninges, þæs we oft ær gemyndgodon. Wæs se mon god 7 æfest, 7 þurh eal ge on mode ge on dædum æðele. Brohte heo ær oðer wer him to wife Suðgyrwa aldormon. þæs noma wæs Tondberht; ac æfter medmiclum fæce, þæs þe he hy to wife onfeng, he forðferde. Þa wæs heo seald 7 forgifen þæm foresprecenan cyninge[29]

> (King Ecgfrith had received, as his wife and consort, a daughter of Anna, king of the East Angles, already often mentioned, whose name was Ethel-

---

27. Horner, *Discourse of Enclosure*, "seeks to understand how the discourse of enclosure constructs an Anglo-Saxon notion of the feminine within a variety of culturally significant texts" (p. 21). Horner begins with a discussion of Æðeldreda, pp. 1–6.

28. *HE*, p. 390; trans. p. 391.

29. *Old English Version of Bede's Ecclesiastical History*, ed. and trans. Miller, p. 316; trans. p. 317.

dreda. He was a good and pious man, and thoroughly noble both in mind and conduct. She had been previously married to another, a prince among the South Gyrwas, whose name was Tondberht; but he died shortly after the marriage. Then she was given and contracted to the aforesaid king.)

Who is the man "good and pious" in the Old English, Ecgfrith or Anna? When the *Old English Bede* translator moves from the genitives that keep the Latin in control, breaks the sentence structure, and begins a new sentence with the nominative demonstrative, it is possible to read Ecgfrith as the man "good and pious," just as one would do to keep sentence subjects in parallel and pronoun reference effective. This rendering could be simply a flat-out error or perhaps possible anticipation of the difficulties involved in Æðeldreda's second marriage. As a character statement about Ecgfrith the sentence serves as an attempted smokescreen for, as we learn somewhat later, Ecgfrith tries to bribe Bishop Wilfrid to get Æðeldreda to consummate their marriage. To have an authoritative statement about Ecgfrith's probity at the beginning at least modulates Ecgfrith's approach to Wilfrid. The deep structure of Æðeldreda's marriage is also an unusual variation on the "virgin-martyr" genre where a female Christian virgin is promised to marry or is about to marry or does marry a pagan husband who proceeds to torture her to death (thus the virgins mentioned in the hymn to Æðeldreda). Æðeldreda's husband is no pagan torturer to be sure, but the *Old English Bede* translator may be suffering from generic interference and a concern that the story of virginity may go off in a direction not in Bede, but rather in the hagiography that his audience might know all too well. Bede does ask his audience to believe in perhaps the miracle of his time, which no doubt was without parallel in Anglo-Saxon England except for the "composite virgin" Osith of Chich and Aylesbury.[30] Bede does maintain a tension of reality in his account, while the translator may be hinting some discomfort with that reality and some search for the comfort of a pattern. Alcuin anticipates the apparent attempt to exonerate Ecgfrith by dropping all mention of Ecgfrith's impatience.[31] Æðeldreda's second marriage is one of the paradoxes of her story, but the paradox is also Ecgfrith's.

The rendering at the beginning of the Old English chapter may be less stumble than choice, if other renderings in the chapter are sugges-

---

30. See Wogan-Browne, *Saints' Lives*, for a treatment of Osith; the phrase "composite virgin" is Wogan-Browne's, p. 63.

31. Godman, *Alcuin*, line 760, p. 64: "regis patientia mira" is Alcuin's admiring comment as he celebrates their faith, prayers, and the love of God!

tive of active and positive engagement with the Latin, for the Old English translator offers small, quiet touches here and there that may ultimately serve as "his hand" when a full description of his translator's point of view gets written. In Bede this is the description of Æðeldreda's tumor: "illa infirmata habuerit tumorem maximum sub maxilla" (she in her sickness had a great tumor under the jaw).[32] The Old English translator carries over the alliteration of the key elements *maximum* and *maxilla* in his "heo hæfde micelne swile on hire sweoran" where two alliterating nouns in oblique cases in the Old English pick up the echo of Latin alliteration of adjective and noun.[33] The tumor, one may note, moves from "under the jaw" to "on her neck," which, for diagnostic purposes, is not as sharp a description as Bede's.[34] A proximity search in the Dictionary of Old English Corpus finds only two other instances of a close pairing in this spelling, both in *Leechdoms* where tumors on the neck are conditions under discussion.[35] In Old English it would seem a truism that if one is to mention a tumor on the neck, then two *sw-* words will perforce appear. There are two other occasions, however, when *sw-* alliteration may be seen to be less forced. For Bede's "cum praefato tumore ac dolore maxillae siue colli premeretur" (when she was afflicted with this tumour and by the pain in her neck or jaw) the Old English translator offers a triple, "þa heo þrycced wæs 7 swenced mid swile 7 sare hire swiran" (when she was afflicted and suffering with the tumour and the pain in her neck).[36] Somewhat later in the passage, Æðeldreda observes that the red tumor on the neck is proper punishment, given her wearing gold and pearls in former days: "dum mihi nunc pro auro et margaretis de collo rubor tumoris ardorque promineat" (so instead of gold and pearls, a fiery red tumour now stands out on my neck).[37] The Old English translator offers: "me nu for golde 7 for gimmum of swiran forðhlifað seo readnis 7 bryne þæs swiles 7 wærces" (I now for

---

32. *HE*, p. 394; trans. p. 395.

33. *Old English Version of Bede's Ecclesiastical History*, ed. and trans. Miller, p. 320, lines 19–20.

34. See my "Ælfric and the Problem of Women," p. 576 n. 14, for the diagnosis of Dr. James W. Carter, MD FAPC, who determines that Æðeldreda suffered from *actinomycosis*, i.e., an enlargement of the cervical lymph nodes.

35. The Dictionary of Old English Corpus is available online through license at <http://ets.umdl.umich.edu/cgi/o/oec/oec>.

36. *HE*, p. 396; trans. p. 397. *Old English Version of Bede's Eccesiastical History*, ed. and trans. Miller, p. 322; trans. p. 323.

37. *HE*, p. 396; trans. p. 397.

gold and gems have this redness and burning of the tumour and pain standing out from my neck).[38] Even more significant is the rendering "for golde 7 for gimmum" for "pro auro et margaretis," which the Dictionary of Old English Corpus cites as a formula of nine occurrences (one of which reverses the elements).

While the alliterative echo may be de rigueur or induced by a formula, other translation choices are more elective. Bede, as is his custom, is cool and matter-of-fact when he tells of Æðeldreda's personal miraculous powers, relating how her clothing cured the possessed and the variously infirm. The Old English seems to offer the interjection *Hwæt* at the start of the account, which Miller misses in his presentation of Old English text and translation. Later on Bede says that the "uirgines" washed Æðeldreda's body, introducing the statement with "Laverunt igitur," but the Old English translator offers "Ono hwæt heo þa þwogon," which Miller renders as "Well, then, they washed," where the comparatively rare *ono*, a signature word for the *Old English Bede*, could be an error for *ond* introducing another occurrence of the interjection *hwæt*.[39] The use of interjections to heighten emotion or reaction would be in line with a certain strand of hagiography. In many places the Old English translator uses doublets to render single words, a general feature in the inventory of Old English prose often linked later to Wulfstan and his tradition.[40] When the Old English translator renders Bede's *coniugem* by *gemæccan and wif*, one wonders whether, obvious emphasis aside, there is some legal or sexual or thematic point being made here about Ecgfrith's and Æðeldreda's marriage. A proximity search for these words in the Dictionary of Old English Corpus does not clarify any issues. Only here in the *Old English Bede* are the two words paired quite this way in conjunction; in the Boethius Gloss they are a disjunctive pair (*wifes oððe gemæccan*). Antwerp Glosses 6 gives *gemæccan* as the sole gloss for *coniuges*. A doublet here may mean to say that the marriage between Ecgfrith and Æðeldreda began as one between two sexually capable people who were ready and willing to assume the sexual burden at the time, i.e., theirs was a licit marriage. There is one doublet that renders specification to an action. Whereas Bede writes that some of the brothers were

---

38. *Old English Version of Bede's Eccesiastical History*, ed. and trans. Miller, p. 322; trans. p. 323.

39. As suggested s.v. in Bosworth-Toller, *Anglo-Saxon Dictionary*, and the Toller Supplement.

40. See Wulfstan, *Homilies*, ed. Bethurum, pp. 90–91.

ordered to look for stone from which they "locellum . . . facere possent" (they could make a coffin/shrine),[41] the Old English translator chooses a more descriptive possibility with an indefinite pronoun: "mon meahte þa ðruh . . . geheawan and gewyrcan" (out of which a coffin might be hewn and wrought)[42] and thus seems to do Bede one better in knowledge of stone working technique. Other doublets seem no better than ornamental or rhythmical, such as *gespanan 7 gelæran* for *persuadere*, *cyðað and secgað* for *narrant*, *cyðdon 7 sægdon* for *testantur*.

Here and there the Old English translator emphasizes, clarifies, or fills in with minor details not found in the Latin. Bede and his translator both note that Seaxburg was Æðeldreda's sister, but the translator reemphasizes the relationship when in the next sentence unit he calls Seaxburg Æðeldreda's *mægan*. When Cynefrith recounts how he finds Æðeldreda under the tent, he notes in Bede that she was "quasi dormientis simile." In the Old English Cynefrith makes the simile complete: "7 wæs slæpendum men gelicra þonne deadu" (she was more like one asleep than dead).[43] Bede relates that the abbess Seaxburg with a few others went into the tent to wash and raise the bones, but the translator adds the detail that they were going to do so "æfter monna gewuna." These minor additions suggest a certain attention to clarifying details.

Comparative analysis suggests that Bede places all his art and craft at the service of the cult of Æðeldreda to show that miraculous sainthood is manifest and present in his own time, linked to the early church and its tradition of virginity. With her fecund virginity Æðeldreda is the glory of the English church and nation. The Old English translator, who is also the first known vernacular interpreter of Bede and only the second apparent interpreter after Alcuin, does not implicitly see himself up to the task of (poetic) translator when he faces the tour de force that is the hymn to Æðeldreda. He takes fewer liberties than Ælfric did in reshaping the narrative to be sure, but his *translatio* anticipates some audience reception in minor details of style, structure, and specific renderings. However differently he produced a vernacular Bede, the translator did not impede the

---

41. *HE*, p. 396; trans. p. 397.
42. *Old English Version of Bede's Ecclesiastical History*, ed. and trans. Miller, p. 32; trans. p. 32. Miller's choice of the passive instead of the indefinite pronoun is a missed minor subtlety.
43. *Old English Version of Bede's Ecclesiastical History*, ed. and trans. Miller, p. 322; trans. p. 323.

cult of Æðeldreda who, Reginald of Durham tells us, was one of the three major saints of the twelfth century along with Cuthbert and Edmund of East Anglia.[44]

More importantly, however, Bede's treatment of Æðeldreda and the lead he gave to the Old English translator help establish a context of understanding for Bede's treatment of women. It is a context adverse to recent literary discussions of Bede and women that, trailing presentist concerns as they often do, take a generally dim view of Bede's alleged patriarchalism and his downgrading of female figures.[45] Given Bede's fifty-four line tour de force, where virgins and their triumphs are preferred to the foundation myth of the West, it seems unsustainable to make a claim for Bede's patriarchalism—unless, of course, one chooses to devalue the values that Bede clearly espouses. These presentist perceptions tend to cluster around the figure of Hild who because she was "merely" present at the birth of vernacular poetry gets no respect. Before focusing on a few specific points in the presentist analysis, whose complexity is too much for this closing application of the foregoing analysis, let me just sketch briefly a meta-phenomenon that overrides most scholarly positions. In general Anglo-Saxonists who study the *Historia ecclesiastica* believe that Bede wrote it "and a few other things," while Anglo-Saxonists who pursue the vernacular and study the *Historia ecclesiastica* believe that in this particular text Bede wrote about *Cædmon's Hymn* "and a few other things." The former position would challenge Bede's medieval readers who would have valued the body of his work well beyond the *Historia ecclesiastica*, while the latter position reflects the skewed vision of those who take the Hild-Cædmon episode out of the context that is the whole of the *Historia ecclesiastica*. Both perspectives are narrow in ignoring either Bede's total corpus or the range of the masterwork that is the *Historia ecclesiastica*.[46] The discussion of Æðeldreda above should convince (I hope) that for Bede Æðeldreda is the best of women in his time. In her fecund virginity Æðeldreda maintains control over her

---

44. See the story of the noble leper in Reginald of Durham, *Reginaldi Monachi dunelmensis*, pp. 37–41, wherein Æðeldreda is named, along with Cuthbert and Edmund, as one of the three saints *excellentiores*.

45. Cf. Lees and Overing, "Birthing Bishops." This article reappears with changes as chapter 1 in their *Double Agents*, pp, 15–39. Stephanie Hollis also sees "constraints" on Bede's portrait of Hild, citing, e.g., church politics as a factor. See her *Anglo-Saxon Women*, esp. pp. 180–81, 246–48. For an alternative view see Karkov, "Whitby."

46. From their perspective Lees and Overing likewise offer a critique of "received knowledge" regarding Bede with which I am in essential agreement.

body and within a monastic context achieves power and status, ruling over both men and women in her house through the paradoxical power of personal or social abasement acquired by deprivation or humiliation.[47] The powerful Æðeldreda cannot be denied.[48] Susan J. Ridyard gives another way of looking at these chapters in Book 4 when she stresses that Bede recounts the achievements of the "daughters of Anna" or the "'dynasty' of royal ladies"—of whom Æðeldreda is the most prominent.[49] This characterization or subtitling is an accurate depiction of Bede's pro-feminist stance, which is part of a generally favorable, Christian history of East Anglia.

The story of Æðeldreda establishes a context of structure and theme that sheds light on the story of Hild. As an *opus geminatum* the story of Æðeldreda is surely different from the story of Hild, but both accounts are bipartite in this sense: the first chapter is a prose biography or hagiography of the figure under discussion while the second, immediately following chapter is a gloss or "take" on the first. For the story of Hild the structure is a hagiographical one: *vita* first, *miraculum* thereafter.[50] In this reading of the structure of the *Historia ecclesiastica* the story of Cædmon is really about Hild and the monastery she ruled, though the narrative matter is Christian verse and its beginnings. Structurally, there could be no Cædmon without Hild, for there is no easy way to place Cædmon into the overall plan of the *Historia ecclesiastica* except as an aside or a digression. (Operationally or functionally, literary scholars treat the story of Cædmon as a digression implicitly, if not explicitly.) Cædmon fits into the *Historia ecclesiastica* where he only can, just as the hymn to Æðeldreda does. Vernacular purists who base their entire literary history on this chapter in Bede will be very unhappy over this structural reading. The story of Cædmon is primarily a story about a monastery and a special, holy place, not about literature. Bede does not structure the story of Hild so as to inspire literary history

---

47. See my "Ælfric and the Problem of Women," pp. 574, 580.

48. Lees and Overing, "Birthing Bishops," p. 46, observe, relative to Hild's fostering of learning at Whitby, that the "'real woman' [their emphasis] is nowhere to be found." It is not clear to me what the phrase might mean and whether in a constructed, literary work such a pursuit, if possible, would be relevant or desirable.

49. Ridyard, *Royal Saints*, pp. 50–51 and also 176–81.

50. Lees and Overing note, "Birthing Bishops," p. 43, "her life ends as his begins; her obituary precedes his story." While they are literally correct in description, perhaps, Lees and Overing miss the overriding structural feature.

to forget Hild or to omit her, as Lees and Overing would have it.[51] Bede
is interested in the moral history of the English nation and its miracles—
which he seeks to verify—and vernacular verse is but one of these.

Of the many themes common to the stories of Hild and Æðeldreda,
sexuality, power, and politics join with miracle and sacred history to create reflexive and comparative commonalities. The trope of mothering
spiritual children and its related trope "fecund virginity" may startle and
disturb some scholars and critics in its play of paradox and its manifest
challenge to a presentist reading of the medieval past. To a great extent
Bede's story of Æðeldreda operates on sexual paradoxes, and the phrase
mater uirgo says it all, paradoxically: "ubi constructo monasterio uirginum
Deo deuotarum perplurium mater uirgo et exemplis uitae caelestis esse
coepit et monitis" (where she built a monastery and became by the example of her heavenly life and teaching, the virgin mother of many virgins
dedicated to God).[52] The *Old English Bede* makes the point rather more
direct by streamlining the sentence and jettisoning the absolute construction regarding the building of a monastery: "7 heo fæmne monigra modor
ongon beon, ge mid bysenum heofonlices lifes ge eac mid monungum"
(And this virgin began to be the mother of many, both by example of heavenly life and also by her admonitions).[53] The emphasis on process—"she
began to be"—may imply some self-consciousness of metaphor. The mothering metaphor applied in Hild's case makes no mention of virginity: "Non
solum ergo praefata Christi ancella et abbatissa Hild, quam omnes qui
noverant ob insigne pietatis et gratiae matrem uocare consuerant" (And
all who knew Hild, the handmaiden of Christ and abbess, used to call her
mother because of her outstanding devotion and grace).[54] The *Old English
Bede* loses the thread—or Miller does—by allowing for a floating nominative: "Ono seo foresprecene Cristes þeowe Hild abbudisse—ealle, þa þe hy
cuþon, fore arfæstnisse tacne 7 Godes gife gewunedan heo modor cegean

---

51. Lees and Overing, "Birthing Bishops," p. 46, observe remarkably: "Conspicuously
absent from Bede's 'Life of Hild' is any trace of what we may assume with good reason to
be the forceful physical and verbal presence of this politically prominent woman," and p. 47
"Hild deserves to be rescued from Bede and afforded her own place in history." Such readings conveniently ignore the evidentiary base.

52. *HE*, p. 392; trans. p. 393.

53. *Old English Version of Bede's Ecclesiastical History*, ed. and trans. Miller, p. 318; trans. p.
319. Note that Miller renders *fæmne* as 'virgin'.

54. *HE*, p. 410; trans. p. 411.

7 nemnan" (Now the aforesaid servant of Christ, the abbess Hild, by all who knew her, in token of her piety and God's favour, was generally called by the name of mother).[55] Here too there is a quiet acknowledgment of trope when both texts say "all who knew her were *accustomed* to call her mother." If one grants that for an abbess to be called "mother" is a seventh-century Christian compliment, Æðeldreda and Hild are two different kinds: Æðeldreda is a mother of the body, whereas Hild is a mother of learning, be it ecclesiastical affairs or poetry or grace. As we have seen, the story of Ætheldreda is about her bodily integrity and her virginity despite two marriages. The story of Hild stresses rather another aspect of feminine potential: leadership in the church. Bishop Aidan and other devout men, Bede tells us, visited her because of her *sapientia* and, in a pointed summary of Hild's career, Bede writes: "Tantae autem erit ipsa prudentiae, ut non solum mediocres quique in necessitatibus suis sed etiam reges ac principes nonnumquam ab ea consilium quaererent et inuenirent" (So great was her prudence that not only ordinary people but also kings and princes sometimes sought and received her counsel when in difficulties).[56] Though their respective *vitae* touch similar themes, this different emphasis helps suggest the range of positive meaning of the trope within Bede's *Historia ecclesiastica.* Kristeva's complaint that virginity and spiritual maternity conceals and devalues the value and reality of physical maternity is a presentist perspective.[57] The argument over virginity, one might readily grant, becomes a point that differentiates Bede's time from ours, and helps define the differences, but the interpretation of one epoch through another leads to distortion and a devaluation of the past, now mute for a rejoinder or even, perhaps, a rebuttal.

In summary, then, Bede and his translator are in a dialogue over the ecclesiastical history of the English nation that can serve to illuminate their respective purposes not only in the close relation they have in rendering of the story of Æðeldreda, which has been the major example here, but also in similar other common accounts and treatments. As the first vernacular interpreter of Bede, the Old English translator becomes a means to ground a historical interpretation of Bede and to imply the beginning of a

---

55. *Old English Version of Bede's Ecclesiastical History,* ed. and trans. Miller, p. 336; trans. p. 337.

56. *HE,* trans. pp. 407, 409.

57. Lees and Overing, "Birthing Bishops," p. 62 n. 55, cite (Julia) Kristeva generally for her classic "Stabat Mater," which is available in *Kristeva Reader,* ed. Moi, pp. 160–86.

Nachleben of the *Historia ecclesiastica.* His small choices and his great refusal to render the *Hymn* highlight aspects of Bede's art, skill, and achievement in the story of Æðeldreda. This interaction in turn creates a perspective on other accounts, the account of Hild being chosen here for illustration. The overall matter of how to read Bede in present scholarship has its special complications, but Bede and his Old English translator are still at the center of the discussion, not the margins.

Goscelin, the *Liber confortatorius,* and the Library of Peterborough

Katherine O'Brien O'Keeffe

The *Liber confortatorius,* a highly personal work of consolation and instruction, records Goscelin of Saint-Bertin's complex and conflicted relationship with Eve of Wilton, the daughter of a Danish father and a Lotharingian mother. The early pages of the *Liber confortatorius* are filled with tantalizing references to the years of their contact as Goscelin alludes to his persistent (if initially unwelcome) efforts to persuade Eve to adopt the religious life, her eventual consecration as a nun of Wilton, their continuing contacts and letters, and her departure for the Continent. The events surrounding Eve's departure for reclusion in Angers, ca. 1080, prompted a personal and perhaps professional crisis for Goscelin. At some point before her departure, Goscelin, in England as a member of the *familia* of Bishop Herman, was forced to leave his position as chaplain to the nuns of Wilton, when Herman's successor, Bishop Osmund, sent him away. Goscelin does not identify where he went to from the Wilton area, simply stating that he was forced to wander far. Returning after an unspecified time, Goscelin expected to meet Eve and was shocked to learn that she was gone, never to return. Goscelin's response to his bereavement took material form as the *Liber confortatorius,* the overt didactic content of which supported and masked his concomitant emotional outpouring to the nun he referred to as his child and his soul. Eve's departure doubled Goscelin's loss—to his first loss of *familia* and home in England was added the permanent departure of his former pupil. But her withdrawal into reclusion (whether voluntary or not) drew from Goscelin the *Liber confortatorius,* as he struggled to fill the unbearable void created by her departure. That lengthy work of consolation—part letter, part treatise—attempted to continue the relationship he had had with Eve over the years of her life at Wilton. It is a pleasure to offer this essay, which attends to a small part of the relationship between Eve and Goscelin, to Helen Damico, whose work over the course of her career in Anglo-Saxon studies has moved the field to attend to women in the literature of Anglo-Saxon England.

Goscelin has left us in the dark about his wanderings, although some of the places he visited between 1086 and 1091, when he finally reached

St. Augustine's Canterbury, can be inferred from his hagiographical commissions: he was perhaps at Barking (ca. 1087), Ramsey (between 1087
and 1091), London (during the episcopacy of Maurice, bishop of London,
1086–1107), and Ely (1087 or 1088).[1] In the *Liber confortatorius*, written
between 1080 and 1082, Goscelin's reaction to his dismissal and period of
wandering surfaces in some plangent observations about having a place.

> "O quotiens suspirabam simile tuo hospitiolum . . . ubi orare, lectitare,
> scriptitare, dictitare meruissem, ubi cor meum diripientem turbam eua-
> derem, ubi propria mensula uentri legem ponerem, ut in loco pascue
> libris pro epulis incumberem, morientemque scintillulam ingenioli mei
> resuscitarem, ut qui nequeo benefaciendo, quantulumcumque fructifica-
> rem in domo Domini scribendo."[2]

> (O, how often I sighed for a little dwelling like yours, where I might
> deserve to pray, to read, write and dictate frequently, where I might avoid
> the crowd that distresses my heart, where I might make a law for my stom-
> ach at my own little table, where I might recline in a place of pasture with
> books rather than banquets and revive the dying little spark of my small
> talent, so that I, who cannot achieve by doing well, might bear fruit by
> writing something, however small, in the house of the Lord.)

Later, recalling his first lodging in England at the bishop's estate at Pottern
or Canning, he remembers how loathsome it had seemed to him when
he arrived, but after it had been cleaned, made fragrant with herbs and
branches, given hangings and tapestries, he loved the place: "Quod prius
horrebam dilexi, quod fugiebam ultro incolui"[3] (What earlier I loathed,
what I fled from, I lived in willingly). In encouraging her to love her cell,
rather than to feel hemmed in by it, he tells her "in omni tribulatione
magna requies est anime certum locum et sedem habere"[4] (in every trouble, it is a great relief to have a fixed place and home).

Unfortunately, for Goscelin, during the years of his wanderings, he
had no *certum locum*, but in writing to Eve, he refers to the place he was
writing from as "Burgis, ubi adhuc hospitor" (*Burh*, where up to now I have
been a guest). Two different locations have been proposed for *Burh*: Peterborough and Bury St. Edmunds. C. H. Talbot tentatively identified it as

---

1. Goscelin of Saint-Bertin, *Hagiography of the Female Saints of Ely*, ed. and trans. Love, p.
xxi. See *Life of King Edward*, ed. and trans. Barlow, appendix C.
2. Goscelin of Saint-Bertin, *Liber confortatorius*, ed. Talbot, 34.5–11.
3. Goscelin, *Liber confortatorius*, ed. Talbot, 102.20–21.
4. Goscelin, *Liber confortatorius*, ed. Talbot, 88.32–33.

Peterborough, and Frank Barlow thought Peterborough the more likely of the two alternatives.[5] The most recent translators, in the volume by Stephanie Hollis and her associates, express uncertainty, printing *"Burg"* with a note: "Talbot suggests that *Burg* refers to Peterborough."[6] While Hollis and her associates have moved well beyond Talbot in suggesting sources for Goscelin's writing in the *Liber confortatorius*, work yet remains to be done.[7] However much Goscelin portrays the *Liber confortatorius* as the product of a disconsolate man prostrate with grief ("corrui coram altari") and dissolved in a flood of tears ("in diluuio lacrimarum") it is, for all its rhetorical posturing, substantially a work of scholarship, carefully crafted in the library as well as from texts remembered.[8] Goscelin's citations required a library with considerable holdings. The following essay suggests that Goscelin's pattern of citations may help us to locate him at Peterborough when he writes to Eve in her cell in Angers.

In his edition of the booklists surviving from Anglo-Saxon England, Michael Lapidge argues that the booklist on a bifolium in Oxford, Bodleian Library, MS Bodley 163, fols. 250–51, which he dates to xi/xii, was written at Peterborough.[9] A number of items listed on that bifolium are

---

5. Goscelin, *Liber confortatorius*, ed. Talbot, 49 n. 11a: "Forsan BURH, idest, monasterium Sancti Petri Burgensis"; *Life of King Edward*, ed. and trans. Barlow, p. 140. Lapidge and Love, "Latin Hagiography of England and Wales," p. 228, follow Barlow in placing Goscelin at Peterborough at this time. The E text of the Anglo-Saxon Chronicle, s.a. 963, reports that abbot Aldulf fortified the monastery of Medeshamstede with a wall and renamed it "Burch" (Irvine, *MS E*, p. 58). On the fortification see Mackreth, "Peterborough." Michael Lapidge has pointed out to me (personal communication) that Byrhtferth also refers to Peterborough as "Burh": "ad monasterium Sancti Petri (quod dicitur Burh)" (*Vita S. Oswaldi*, iv in Raine, *Historians of the Church of York*, p. 446).

6. Hollis et al., *Writing the Wilton Women*, 1:127 n. 13. Goscelin of Saint-Bertin, *Book of Encouragement and Consolation*, ed. Otter, p. 52, mistakenly prints "Peterbury," though admitting the possibility of Bury St. Edmunds (n. 10).

7. Hollis et al., *Writing the Wilton Women*, p. 317 n. 57, notes the Bodley list but does nothing further with it.

8. Goscelin, *Liber confortatorius*, ed. Talbot, p. 27, lines 23–25.

9. Lapidge, "Surviving Booklists," p. 76; Lapidge, *Anglo-Saxon Library*, p. 143. In his magisterial study of the Anglo-Saxon library, Michael Lapidge edits the Peterborough booklist (pp. 143–47) but omits, for the purposes of that study, vernacular, biblical, and liturgical items. I refer to the full list printed in his earlier edition. Lapidge also prints two booklists from Bury St. Edmunds ("Surviving Booklists," pp. 57–58 and 74–76). His list VII, found in Oxford, Corpus Christi College, MS 197, which he dates to the second half of the eleventh century on paleographic grounds, is culled from an eleventh-century list of possessions and rents of Bury. All eighteen of the books there listed are liturgical books. Lapidge's list XII, which he dates to s. xi[ex], gives fifteen books also from Bury. Aside from liturgical books, the list includes an unidentifiable chronicle, a book of medical recipes, a

identical to items from Æthelwold's Peterborough donation to that house,[10] and Bodley 163 itself has a Peterborough provenance, though the evidence is fourteenth-century. Approaching the question in the context of the early manuscripts of Norman England, Richard Gameson dates the Bodley booklist to s. xii[in] and regards it as "probably from Peterborough."[11] In both Lapidge's and Gameson's careful formulations, the Bodley list offers a record of an English library at the close of the eleventh century, a record for which there is reasonable evidence to suggest a provenance at Peterborough. By contrast, the most recent editors of the Bodley booklist, Karsten Friis-Jensen and James Willoughby, argue that the list is "confirm[ed]" to have originated at Peterborough, though in their view the list is significantly later than ca. 1100 and written with a different purpose.[12] They would date the booklist to "probably between 1111 and 1119" and would read it as a record of the volumes surviving the Peterborough fire of 1116.[13] Their confidence in assigning the booklist to Peterborough rests primarily on the survival of London, British Library, MS Harley 3097, a manuscript the contents of which they match to their lists BP2.15 (the Bodley booklist) and BP 21.9 (the *Matricularium* of Peterborough).[14]

There is a troubling difficulty, however, with their assumptions about the dates of both the Bodley booklist and Harley 3097. Friis-Jensen and Willoughby offer no supporting evidence for dating the booklist as late as 1111 x 1119, and the specificity of their later dating appears to result from a misprision. Gameson's study dates fols. 228–49 of Bodley 163 ("Nennius," *Historia Brittonum*; Pseudo-Methodius, *Reuelationes*; etc.) to "?*c.* 1111–19" but notes that the bifolium containing the booklist, originally separate, dates to s. xii[in].[15] Such a date puts the writing of the Bodley list at least a decade

---

copy of Donatus (or a miscellaneous grammar book), and an unidentifiable book. Rebecca Rushforth, "Eleventh- and Early Twelfth-Century Manuscripts of Bury St Edmunds Abbey," on the basis of some scribal similarities between Cambridge, Pembroke College MS 301 and Bodley 163 wishes to "muddy the waters" by suggesting "a possible Bury St Edmunds connection for Bodley 163" (1:205), but see her discussion of similarities and differences between the two scripts (1:168–70).

10. Lapidge, "Surviving Booklists," p. 76.

11. Gameson, *Manuscripts of Early Norman England*, p. [45] and item 646.

12. *Peterborough Abbey*, ed. Friis-Jensen and Willoughby, p. 7.

13. *Peterborough Abbey*, ed. Friis-Jensen and Willoughby, p. xxvi.

14. *Peterborough Abbey*, ed. Friis-Jensen and Willoughby, p. 7. (See Lapidge, "Surviving Booklists," XIII, items 8, 15, and 16.)

15. Gameson, *Manuscripts of Early Norman England*, p. 129, item 646. In referring to the Bodley booklist as having been "copied" into Bodley 163, Friis-Jensen and Willoughby, eds., *Peterborough Abbey*, p. xxvi, appear not to have recognized the distinction.

before the fire that destroyed so much of Peterborough abbey. Gameson further dates Harley 3097 to xii^1,[16] that is, at some point in the decade following the writing of the Bodley booklist. If his order is correct, the differential dating of the list and of Harley 3097 presses the inference that Harley 3097 survives as a copy made of an earlier volume whose contents were recorded in the Bodley list. Its probative value connecting the Bodley list to Peterborough is thus weakened.[17] Indeed, on purely paleographical grounds, it is difficult to date the Bodley list with the kind of precision that Friis-Jensen and Willoughby offer. On the basis of her examination, Teresa Webber finds that "palaeographically it was difficult to date it more closely than s. xi/xii or s. xii in."[18]

Is it possible to increase the certainty in identifying the Bodley list as a record of the Anglo-Saxon library of Peterborough? If we can use the pattern of Goscelin's citation practice to connect the *Liber confortatorius* with the books listed on the Bodley bifolium, we may manage, arguably, to increase the certainty of both locations—Goscelin in the library at Peterborough and the bifolium of Bodley 163 as a record of its late eleventh-century collection.

This endeavor must begin with an admission that the smoking manuscript, as it were, that might anchor an identification with Peterborough does not exist, since such smoke has long since faded away. Peterborough was no stranger to misfortune in the later eleventh century. In 1070 it was raided by Hereward the Wake, who burned down the monastic buildings except for the church (which subsequently burned). As part of the raid, the Anglo-Saxon Chronicle MS. E claims Hereward and his men took from the monastery various costly objects, including books, saying (presumably in reaction to the appointment of a Norman abbot) "þet hi hit dyden for ðes mynstres holdscipe" (that they did it out of loyalty to this monastery). Thereafter they transferred what they took to Ely for safekeeping.[19] How many books were in the treasure the raiders took is unknown.[20] The

---

16. Gameson, *Manuscripts of Early Norman England*, p. 108, item 448.

17. Friis-Jensen and Willoughby, eds., *Peterborough Abbey*, p. 9, item 15, date Harley 3097 to s. xii^{in}.

18. Personal communication, 26 October 2005. I am very grateful to Dr. Webber for her kindness in examining the hand of the Bodley list and for her expert opinion.

19. *MS E*, ed. Irvine, s.a. 1070, p. 89. For possible survivals from the Bodley list see Lapidge, "Surviving Booklists," items 8 and 16.

20. Friis-Jensen and Willoughby, eds., *Peterborough Abbey*, p. xxiv, believe that the plunder of books was limited to gospel books with precious bindings.

Chronicle of Hugh Candidus describes the booty as: "quicquid ibi erat in auro et argento et ceteris preciosis rebus"[21] (whatever there was of gold and silver and other precious things), and later mentions further theft of liturgical objects. After the treaty between King William and King Swein, Hereward's Danish allies left Ely, taking with them, the E-text claims, "ealle þa forenspræcena gærsume" (all the aforementioned treasure). But the account at this point only mentions some ritual objects that ended up in a church in Denmark. The Chronicle of Hugh Candidus only says that the agreement between William and Swein was "ut quicquid ipse Sueinus in auro et argento adquisierat suum esset et ad patriam suam secum portaret"[22] (that whatever Swein had acquired of gold and silver would be his, and he would take it back with him to his own land). Hereward the Wake continued to defend Ely until the following year.[23] It is likely that a good number of the books survived, given that among the sixty-five items on the Bodley list, copied ca. xi/xii, are some five items from Æthelwold's tenth-century donation to Peterborough.[24] Unfortunately, a catastrophic fire in 1116 burned all the buildings of the monastery except the chapter house and dormitory; the survival of Peterborough's book collection is a matter of conjecture.[25]

The challenges presented by the putative collections of Bury St. Edmunds and Peterborough are complementary ones. In the case of Peterborough, we appear to have a list for a collection destroyed in the early twelfth century. In the case of Bury St. Edmunds, the two surviving booklists, Lapidge, nos. VII and XII, both dating to the late eleventh century, are primarily lists of service books. In a sense, for Bury St. Edmunds we have surviving books without a proper list: Helmut Gneuss's indispensable *Handlist* gives some thirty-seven manuscripts and fragments with arguable Bury provenances surviving.[26] The argument that follows focuses on the relation between the *Liber confortatorius* and the Bodley list, attending to the probability of identification, and on inference from combinations of texts that were otherwise poorly attested in Anglo-Saxon England. It confines itself to an analysis of the extended citations and quotations in book 2 for two reasons: it is there that Goscelin identifies the monastery in which

---

21. *Chronicle of Hugh Candidus*, ed. Mellows, p. 77.
22. *Chronicle of Hugh Candidus*, ed. Mellows, p. 82.
23. Stenton, *Anglo-Saxon England*, p. 606.
24. See Lapidge, "Surviving Booklists," pp. 54–55.
25. *MS E*, ed. Irvine, s.a. 1116.
26. Gneuss, *Handlist*.

he wrote to Eve, and his extended quotations mean that he had the texts in front of him as he wrote. To complement and support this argument, the Appendix presents an annotated list of Goscelin's citations of other works listed on the Bodley bifolium, citations that can be found throughout the *Liber confortatorius*. Reading the *Liber confortatorius* against the Bodley booklist throws into dramatic relief the degree to which the book is a carefully argued, indeed carefully researched, composition. The evidence presented by the quotations in book 2 together with the additional citations throughout the work suggest, I argue, that Goscelin was working at Peterborough.

The verses Goscelin supplies at the beginning of the Prologue offer a theme for each of the four books:

> Primus agit questus et consolamina thomus.
> Bella cupidinibus mouet euincitque secundus.
> Tertius ignitis pellit fastidia uotis.
> Ex humili sumptis quartus petit astra quadrigis.[27]
>
> (The first book pursues complaints and consolations. The second promotes battles against desires and conquers. The third drives away ennui with kindled vows. And when the four parts have been completed, from the ground the fourth seeks the stars.)

Book 1 is the most earthbound, and the most obviously self-reflexive, as Goscelin returns repeatedly to his loneliness, unworthiness, and anger at what he terms Eve's sin against love. Certainly, in its uneasy balance between "questus" and "consolamina" book 1 is the most emotionally fraught of the four. Although Goscelin alludes to or cites directly a small number of authorities in it, the burden of his citation practice in book 1 rests on scripture. Not surprisingly, the most highly emotional parts of book 1 find Goscelin citing scripture, especially the psalms by memory, weaving allusions or quotations into the expression of his distress in the wake of Eve's departure.

Book 2, the focus of this essay, provides the clearest examples of Goscelin's formal citation process and offers, as well, the clearest evidence of connection to the Bodley list. It is in book 2 that Goscelin refers to "Burh"

---

27. Goscelin, *Liber confortatorius*, ed. Talbot, p. 26. I have corrected Talbot's readings in lines 2 and 4 (where his edition gives "Pella cum demonibus" the manuscript reads "bella cupidinibus"; and for his "Edictis" the manuscript reads "ex humili"). Hollis et al., *Writing the Wilton Women*, pp. 210–12, also give a list of corrections to Talbot's edition.

where he had up to the time of writing been a guest. Book 2 begins with a cento of quotation designed to set the stage for the theme of this book—spiritual warfare. The address, at first, is general, "Stand in faith, act as men, all you who hope in the Lord. Put on the armor of God, the lorica of faith, the breastplate of hope," sentiment pieced together from the epistles of Paul.[28] But then Goscelin departs sharply from his earlier practice of scriptural citation, and book 2 virtually explodes into nonscriptural quotation. First comes Aeneas, encouraging his men after they have landed on the shores of Libya.[29] To balance, Goscelin cites "Boetius noster" using the labors of Hercules to urge strong action "ite nunc fortes . . . superata tellus sidera donat" (Go now, bold men . . . the earth overcome will grant you the stars).[30] Immediately following is a tag from Prudentius, "et ad astra doloribus itur" (the stars are reached through suffering) and an approximation of Horace.[31] These quotations indicate a new approach to the *Liber confortatorius*, a reassertion of confidence, and an eagerness to display Goscelin's considerable knowledge. However, all of these peppered lines are schoolroom tags likely given by memory: none of the works I have identified appears in either of the Peterborough booklists, but they do appear in the booklist of Saint-Bertin.[32]

In marked contrast to book 1 and even to this flurry of citations at the beginning of book 2, Goscelin structures the greatest part of book 2 around lengthy extracts of works that can be fitted to his theme of spiritual battle. The following argument examines four such passages in book 2 for what they can tell us about Goscelin's practice and his likely place of writing: the *passio* of Perpetua, Gregory's Homily 37 on the Gospels, Eusebius's account of the unnamed captive woman of the Hiberes, and

---

28. Cor. 16:13, Eph. 6:11, Thess. 5:8.

29. *Aeneid*, 1.204–6, 3.393.

30. Boethius, *De consolatione Philosophiae*, IV. met. vii. 13. 29–30, 32–35. Ferrante, *Glory of Her Sex*, p. 43, appears to believe that the "noster" indicates "their [i.e., Goscelin's and Eve's] shared interests," but it is more likely that the "noster" simply marks Boethius as a Christian in contrast with the previously cited pagan Vergil.

31. Prudentius, *Cathemerinon*, 10.92, and Horace, *Satires* I.ix.59–60.

32. Becker, *Catalogi bibliothecarum antiqui*, list 77 (pp. 181–85). Derolez, *Catalogues*, p. 24, dates the list to "xi^c–xii^c." The relevant items are: Vergil, *Aeneid* (Becker, list 77, items 296–99); Boethius, *De consolatione Philosophiae* (Becker, list 77, item 58); Prudentius, *Cathemerinon* (Becker, list 77, items 203–4). Items 191–94 of the Saint-Bertin booklist comprise "Oratii libri IIII," and it is possible that the *Satires* were among these. On Goscelin's use of classical authors see now Barnes, "Goscelin's Greeks and Romans," in *Writing the Wilton Women*, ed. Hollis et al., pp. 401–17, esp. Appendix.

Origen's homilies on Joshua. The complex evidence of these lengthy passages must be accounted for to establish a connection between Goscelin's citation practice and the texts of the Bodley bifolium.

Goscelin's practice in recounting Perpetua's heroic martyrdom for Eve is an example of how he generally uses his sources: Perpetua's simple Latin was not sufficiently elegant for Goscelin and he recast it. This habit makes it difficult to know precisely what materials Goscelin was working with at any given time. Goscelin's version of Perpetua's martyrdom is a radically abbreviated epitome of the *passio* in which he conflates a number of events and rearranges the order for dramatic effect. To lend authority to his own account, Goscelin persistently refers to events as being in Perpetua's own words as, for example "ut ipsa describit," "sicut ipsa scribit," "que sua latius retexit pagina,"[33] and this maneuver suggests that he was working from a version of the *passio*, rather than from other accounts, like, for example, Augustine's homilies. Given the details he adduces, he must also have worked from the long version rather than from the abbreviation.[34] Verbal echoes of Perpetua's words in the *passio* point also in that direction: for example, Goscelin's description of her foul prison "mox assuetudine carcerem pro pretorio, ut ipsa describit, habebat"[35] echoes Perpetua's words "et factus est mihi carcer subito praetorium, ut ibi mallem esse quam alicubi."[36]

Making the task of connecting Goscelin's account with a particular text more difficult, the epitome departs from the order of the *passio*, presumably for reasons of concision. Goscelin conflates Perpetua's first vision (of the ladder [cap. 3]) with her later vision of the fight with the Egyptian (cap. 10). He follows this with a much-reduced account of Perpetua's vision of her dead brother, Dinocrates. His account of Perpetua's father too conflates different sections of the *passio* and is dislocated after the vision of Dinocrates, rather than before as in the *passio*. Similarly he simply sketches the removal of Perpetua's son here (treated earlier in the *passio*, cap. 3, returned to her for suckling in cap. 4 but not in cap. 6, where she reports that she felt no distress from the sudden weaning).

Bringing the epitome to a close, he has the two saints, Perpetua and Felicitas, face the beasts in the arena, closing the account with Saturus's

---

33. Goscelin, *Liber confortatorius*, ed. Talbot, 50.3, 50.30, 50.27.
34. *Passio sanctarum Perpetuae et Felicitatis*, ed. Van Beek, provides an edition of both versions.
35. Goscelin, *Liber confortatorius*, ed. Talbot, 50.2–3.
36. *Passio sanctarum Perpetuae et Felicitatis*, ed. Van Beek, 10.12–14.

speech now put in Perpetua's mouth. Goscelin's version, "Notate, inquit, diligenter facies nostras quales simus, ut recognoscatis nos in die iudicii,"[37] is very close to Van Beek's text of the *passio*: "Notate tamen vobis facies nostras diligenter, ut recognoscatis nos in die illo,"[38] and additionally includes a telltale word. His addition of "iudicii" is of interest here, since, according to Van Beek's collation, "iudicii" is characteristic of the English manuscripts of the *passio*, whose oldest surviving witness is London, British Library, MS Cotton Nero E. i.[39] Tantalizing as the connection of Goscelin's version with a member of the Cotton/Corpus family is, his use of the *passio* of Perpetua neither provides evidence of a connection with the Bodley list nor can it rule out a Peterborough provenance. The difficulty is that among the sixty-five books listed on the Bodley bifolium, there is no legendary listed as such, nor does one survive with a provenance from Bury St. Edmunds. Yet the necessity of a legendary for monastic liturgical reading means that both Peterborough and Bury St. Edmunds must be presumed to have had one.[40]

The next citation with ambiguous evidentiary value comes from Homily 37 of Gregory's *Homilae in Evangelia*.[41] In Gregory's collection, this homily on Luke 14:26ff. ("If any man come to me, and hate not his father and mother and wife") is indicated for the feast of St. Sebastian. Goscelin identifies Gregory as his source[42] and proceeds to quote the first section of the homily and a bit from the second.[43] Goscelin's copy of the opening two sections of Homily 37 shows some excision but is generally accurate when collated against Étaix's text. The question that is difficult to answer, however, is in what sort of collection Goscelin might have encountered Gregory's Homily 37. Gregory's homilies circulated widely in the early Middle Ages (Étaix called the collection a "best-seller").[44] But Gregory's homilies also

---

37. Goscelin, *Liber confortatorius*, ed. Talbot, 51.4–5.

38. *Passio sanctarum Perpetuae et Felicitatis*, ed. Van Beek, 40.14–15.

39. Van Beek also notes that "iudicii" is present in Paris, Bibliothèque nationale de France, MS lat. 17626. On London, British Library, MS Cotton Nero E. I, see Jackson and Lapidge, "Contents of the Cotton-Corpus Legendary," p. 133: "To judge solely from its content, the compilation must have taken place in northern France or Flanders, because most of the localizable saints are from that region."

40. See Gneuss, "Liturgical Books," pp. 125–27.

41. Gregory the Great, *Homiliae in Evangelia*, pp. 347–58; *PL* 76.1275–76.

42. "Hinc beatus Gregorius . . . ," Goscelin, *Liber confortatorius*, ed. Talbot, 62.19; 62.22–63.1.

43. Gregory the Great, *Homiliae in Evangelia*, 348.1–349.41. The excerpt from the second section is at 349.36–37, 38–41.

44. Gregory the Great, *Homiliae in Evangelia*, p. xiii.

circulated separately in homiliaries (thirty-two were in the homiliary of Paul the Deacon), and could be found in *libelli* for liturgical use in the Night Office.[45] Thomas N. Hall lists some seven appearances of Homily 37 in homiliaries surviving from Anglo-Saxon England.[46] Goscelin's extended quotation from Gregory's Homily 37 (and a brief quotation from Gregory's Homily 34), both identified by Goscelin as Gregory's work, suggest that his own source identified the homilies under Gregory's name. Unfortunately there is no direct record of Gregory's homilies on the Gospels in the Bodley list, nor is there a surviving copy of that text with a Bury St. Edmunds provenance.[47] There is, however, a tease. The Bodley bifolium's "Haimo In euangeliis" (item 33), that is, "Haymo on the Gospels," seems to suggest, by its title, a commentary, though Haymo of Auxerre is not known to have produced a commentary on the Gospels.[48] In his analysis of Carolingian homiliaries, Henri Barré noted that a tenth-century book list from the cathedral of Cambrai mentions "Haymo super evangelia," a title he accepted as referring to the homiliary.[49] Barré further reports that this title appears in an English manuscript, Cambridge, Trinity College, MS B.5.13 (159).[50] Unfortunately, the late date of the hand (s. xv) makes that identification less compelling for the present case.[51] While it seems likely, then, that the Bodley list's item 33 refers to Haymo's homiliary, given the Cambrai title, it is not clear that the book it described contained Gregory's Homily 37.[52] However, a surviving Bury manuscript, Cambridge, Pembroke

---

45. Thomas Hall, "Early English Manuscripts," pp. 128–29 and n. 56.

46. Hall's items 9, 12, 14, 15, 18, 20, 24, "Early English Manuscripts," pp. 122–26. It appears as item 112 in Cyril Smetana's analysis of the Homiliary of Paulus Diaconus available to Ælfric (Smetana, "Aelfric and the Early Medieval Homiliary," p. 179) and was used "in natale unius martyris." On the use of Paul the Deacon's homiliary in the night office see Gneuss, "Liturgical Books," p. 123.

47. Thomas Hall, "Early English Manuscripts," pp. 119–20, lists five surviving manuscripts before ca. 1125.

48. Lapidge, "Surviving Booklists," p. 80.

49. Barré, *Homéliaires carolingiens*, p. 56. The list of some sixty-three items is in Cambrai, Bibliothèque municipale, MS 685, on fol. 1. See now Muzerelle et al., *Manuscrits*, pp. ix–x, n. 4, who prints the list and connects individual titles with surviving Cambrai manuscripts. The title in question is item 37, "Haimo super Euvangelia" [*sic*].

50. Barré, *Homéliaires carolingiens*, p. 61.

51. James, *Western Manuscripts in the Library of Trinity College, Cambridge*, 1:208–9, dates the inscription to s. xv.

52. I have not been able to find Homily 37 in that version of the augmented homiliary that Migne prints in *PL* 118 (the 1536 edition of Jean Praël). The difficulty, however, is that there are so many witnesses to both the authentic and the augmented versions of the homiliary, that Barré (*Homéliaires carolingiens*, p. 54) was unable to analyze all of them.

College, MS 24, a homiliary of Paul the Deacon for the *sanctorale,* does contain Gregory's Homily 37.[53] Our embarrassment for an item naming Gregory's Homilies on the Gospels in the Bodley list, nonetheless, cannot rule Peterborough out as a venue for Goscelin, given the ubiquity of the relevant homily in homiletic collections and its use in the Office; equally, it cannot rule it in.

The next two examples of textual borrowings in the *Liber confortatorius,* book 2, will allow us to look at Goscelin's connection to Peterborough through the Bodley list with greater confidence. In the first, we see Goscelin very likely becoming familiar with a text at Peterborough itself, and in the second, using a text otherwise not well known in England. The first plays a dual role in the *Liber confortatorius*—Goscelin not only recommends it for Eve's reading, he makes an extended quotation from it.

In the section titled "Mensa scripturarum" in book 3, Goscelin lays out for Eve a program of reading. "Lege expositiones sanctorum patrum Ieronimi, Augustini, Gregorii ceterorumque uirtutis doctorum, et pone cor tuum ad intelligentiam scripturarum, que et ecclesie spiritualiumque bellorum in uariis enigmatibus continent misterium"[54] (Read the expositions of the holy fathers Jerome, Augustine, Gregory and the other doctors of virtue, and incline your heart to the understanding of the scriptures, which contain the mystery of the church and of spiritual battles in various figural representations). But Goscelin encourages her as well to read beyond exegesis. To the lives and writings of the Fathers, he adds Augustine's confessions, and then moves to history:

> Ames etiam librum tripartitum ecclesiastice historie cum historia Eusebii, que tibi et sanctorum certamina, et fidei uictoriam canant in Christo fundate et cunctis tempestatibus inuicte. Respice Augustinum *De Ciuitate Dei,* Orosium *De Ormesta Mundi,* Boetium *De Consolatione Philosophie,* et intelliges nil miserabilius seculi gurgite, nil felicius Christi pace[55]

Thomas Hall, "Early English Manuscripts," p. 120 and n. 26, notes a chaotic manuscript, Durham, Cathedral Library, MS B. III. 11, Part I (s. xi[ex]), containing a number of Gregory's Homilies on the Gospels (including Homily 37 and an incomplete Homily 34) followed by an augmented Homiliary of Haymo of Auxerre.

53. For manuscripts from Bury St. Edmunds see Rebecca Rushforth, "Eleventh- and Early Twelfth-Century Manuscripts from Bury St Edmunds Abbey." On the basis of Bury additions to the manuscript (originally copied in France) Rushforth locates Pembroke 24 at Bury "at the very end of the eleventh century or the beginning of the twelfth" (1: 67).

54. Goscelin, *Liber confortatorius,* ed. Talbot, 80.26–29.

55. Goscelin, *Liber confortatorius,* ed. Talbot, 80.36–81.4.

(May you also love the tripartite book of ecclesiastical history along with Eusebius's history, which will recite for you both the struggles of the saints and the victory of faith grounded in Christ and unconquered by all misfortunes. Turn your attention to Augustine's *City of God*, Orosius's *History*,[56] Boethius's *Consolation of Philosophy*, and you will learn that nothing is more miserable than the abyss of the world, nothing happier than the peace of Christ).

The struggle of saints and victory of faith are what Goscelin attempts to illustrate for Eve in portraying for her lives of exemplary women. In book 2, Goscelin's theme is spiritual battle, and the struggles of the women his text commemorates are meant to illustrate for Eve the strength of women and the heroics of spiritual battle. While Goscelin does not cite in the *Liber confortatorius* all of the texts he recommends to Eve (indeed, I have not found a citation of the Orosius, and his quotation of the Consolation is simply a remembered snatch of verse) Goscelin takes his own advice, making heavy use of Eusebius's history.

In addition to recommending this to Eve for her reading, Goscelin uses Rufinus's translation of Eusebius's history for accounts of three women: Blandina,[57] the "mulier quaedam captiva,"[58] and Potamiana (the latter in book IV).[59] For the accounts of Blandina and Potamiana, Goscelin more or less follows the same procedure as he did with the *passio* of Perpetua. He epitomizes the accounts in Eusebius's history, but in each case he carefully identifies his source as an authorizing maneuver: "ut *Ecclesiastica* Eusebii Cesariensis commendat *Historia*" (64.14–15) (as Eusebius of Cesarea's Ecclesiastical History records). As in the case of Perpetua, the accounts of both martyrs are so closely rewritten that it is impossible to conclude from the account that Goscelin had the text of the history to hand. However, in the case of the unnamed captive woman,[60] Goscelin changes his strategy, and quotes the text directly, with considerable accuracy. He explains his reasoning to Eve: "Hinc te adhuc in exercitationem fidei uelim ex pre-

---

56. On "ormesta" see Sims-Williams, "Some Functions of Origin Stories," pp. 116 and 132, nn. 65–66.

57. Goscelin, *Liber confortatorius*, ed. Talbot, 64.14–34 = *Kirchengeschichte*, ed. Schwartz and Mommsen, V.1.17–19, 41–42, 53–56 (p. 409).

58. Goscelin, *Liber confortatorius*, ed. Talbot, 65.1–66.40 = *Kirchengeschichte*, ed. Schwartz and Mommsen, X.11 (pp. 973–76).

59. Goscelin, *Liber confortatorius*, ed. Talbot, 98.7–20 = *Kirchengeschichte*, ed. Schwartz and Mommsen, VI.5.1–7 (pp. 531, 533).

60. *Kirchengeschichte*, ed. Schwartz and Mommsen, X.11.

dicta hystoria doceri, qualiter Dominus Ihesus . . . per captiuam regnum, quod ipsam tenebat, ceperit. Hic modo ut te faciam certiorem, ipsam historiogra<p>hi non meam insero relationem."[61] (And now I wish to teach you from the aforementioned history in an exercise of faith, how the Lord Jesus . . . claimed through a captive woman the kingdom that held her captive. Here only so that I can inform you, I insert this historian's account, not my own). The following account of the captive woman who converts an entire people to Christianity through her perseverance in prayer and vigils (and a judicious miracle or two), occupies two full printed pages in Talbot's edition, some seventy-nine lines of print.[62] Goscelin quotes the full chapter in Eusebius's history, and with such fidelity that it is impossible to conclude other than that he had the text in front of him.

Rufinus's translation of Eusebius's Ecclesiastical History clearly was not rare in Anglo-Saxon England. Gneuss's *Handlist* gives notice of five manuscripts surviving from Anglo-Saxon England.[63] Of these, Cambridge, Pembroke College, MS 108 is a manuscript from Bury St. Edmunds. However, this ninth-century manuscript from eastern France only contains extracts from the Ecclesiastical History dealing with Arius and the Arian heresy.[64] Item 7 in Lapidge's edition of the Bodley list, "Ecclesiastica historia Eusebii Cesaris" [*sic*], suggests that this text was available in the Peterborough library. Interestingly, this work is not listed in the Saint-Bertin Catalogue; if we can put some tentative pressure on this fact, it would suggest that Goscelin became familiar with the work in England.

---

61. Goscelin, *Liber confortatorius*, ed. Talbot, 64.35–40.

62. Goscelin, *Liber confortatorius*, ed. Talbot, 65–66.

63. Gneuss, *Handlist*, item 57: Cambridge, Corpus Christi College, MS 187 (s. xi/xii, provenance probably Canterbury); item 61: Cambridge, Corpus Christi College, MS 192 (extracts; provenance probably Canterbury); item 137: Cambridge, Pembroke College, MS 108 (extracts; provenance Bury St. Edmunds); item 768: Worcester Cathedral Library, MS Q. 28 (provenance France; in England xi or x² [provenance Worcester]); item 773.5: Wormsley, Wormsley Library (s. vii, fragment).

64. Pembroke College, MS 108, fols. 118v/11–124r/7 (Gneuss, *Handlist*, item 137). Rebecca Rushforth, "Eleventh- and Twelfth-Century Manuscripts of Bury St Edmunds Abbey," p. 103, suggests that the contents of this manuscript fit with the drive to include patristic works in English libraries in the late eleventh century. The excerpts are from *Kirchengeschichte*, ed. Schwartz and Mommsen, pp. 960–961.26, 964.17–965.15, 978.7–980.1. In describing this manuscript, Montague Rhodes James and Ellis H. Minns, *Descriptive Catalogue of the Manuscripts in the Library of Pembroke College, Cambridge*, p. 104, indicate that the excerpts from Eusebius/Rufinus continue to the end of 124r. However, the last eleven lines of 124r are Caelius Sedulius, *Carmen paschale*, I.297–306.

The most compelling of these instances of citation in book 2 is an unusual text with a complex text history. Even for Goscelin's announced theme of book 2, "bella cupidinibus," Origen's homilies on the book of Joshua in Rufinus's translation are a peculiar choice for a self-described work of consolation and encouragement. Origen's commentaries are slowly drawn, copious, particular, and difficult. But they offered Goscelin a rich opportunity for a tropological reading of physical battles. Goscelin's extended quotation of Homily 15 ignores the particulars of Origen's scriptural exegesis in favor of Origen's grand tropological interpretation of the relationship of Old Testament history to Christians' moral development: physical battles are figures of spiritual wars. After quoting the first sentence of Homily 15 (Goscelin passes over a great deal of particular interpretation [the significance of hamstringing horses, e.g.]) to resume his citation of Homily 15 well into cap. 5.[65] His particular interest lies in the spirits responsible for various sins and how each human being has multiple spirits prompting him or her to evil deeds. As a kind of balance, the citations from Homily 20 focus on the power of virtue and scripture to put evil spirits to flight.[66]

While quoting Origen's work copiously, Goscelin is unaware of his identity as author of the homilies. Rather, given his identification that "Ieronimus librum Ihesum Naue in XXVI omelias exponit" (which he repeats in various forms five other times),[67] Goscelin clearly believed that Jerome had written the book. Now this identification is a curious one on two grounds: Rufinus's brief preface to the homilies, addressed to Chromatius, indicates that the work following was a translation from Greek to Latin, and attributes it to "senex Adamantius" (Origen's surname); but the preface doesn't explicitly identify Rufinus as the work's translator. W. A. Baehrens has shown how one strand of the textual transmission of the homilies, his class D, erroneously attributed the text to Jerome.[68] In class D

---

65. Goscelin, *Liber confortatorius*, ed. Talbot, 56.16–18, 57.8–58.16 = *Homilien zum Hexateuch*, ed. Baehrens, 381.14–16, 389.16–391.20, 392.11–15 and 25–26.

66. Goscelin, *Liber confortatorius*, ed. Talbot, 59.24–61.32 = *Homilien zum Hexateuch*, ed. Baehrens, 415/4–420/7, with a number of omissions.

67. Goscelin, *Liber confortatorius*, ed. Talbot, 56.2–3, 56.36, 57.5–7, 59.2–6, 59.20–23, 61.33.

68. See *Homilien zum Hexateuch*, ed Baehrens, pp. xxiv–xxv. Baehrens's class D comprises those manuscripts which attribute the translation to Jerome, e.g., "incipit prohemium b. Hieronymi presbyteri in expositione libri Iesu Nave." See also Baehrens, *Überlieferung und Textgeschichte der lateinisch erhaltenen Origeneshomilien zum Alten Testament*, pp. 108–9 and 122.

several manuscripts have as title to the prologue, "incipit proemium sancti ieronymi," and it seems clear from Goscelin's persistent attribution of the work to Jerome that he had such a book to hand. Item 10 of Lapidge's edition of the Bodley list, lists "Hieronimus Super Iosue," and that can only have been Origen's twenty-six homilies as a single volume attributed to Jerome.

To summarize the argument connecting this quoted text to the Bodley list: Goscelin insistently attributes the Latin translation of Origen's Homilies on Joshua to Jerome, and he quotes at length from Homilies 15 and 20. Although there are passages where Goscelin compresses his material (and here and there occasional garbling appears),[69] the greatest part of his use of the homilies is clear quotation and these indicate that he had the homilies to hand. The Bodley list (Lapidge XIII), item 10, records "Hieronimus Super Iosue," that is, it attributes the homilies on the book of Joshua (or Jesu Nave) to Jerome. Not only does Goscelin quote from this text, he identifies the text as the work of Jerome, and his citations contain a number of variants characteristic of Baehrens's class D manuscripts.[70] His extensive quotations from Origen/Rufinus Homilies 15 and 20 show Goscelin working in the library collection at Peterborough, selecting information for Eve's instruction.

If we look at the surviving books from Bury St. Edmunds, the Bodley list, and the pattern of Goscelin's larger citations, two immediate overlaps become apparent: Goscelin used Augustine on the Gospels of John and Jerome on Isaiah. Both works appear on the Bodley list, and they survive as well as manuscripts with a Bury provenance. Cambridge, Pembroke College, MS 17 contains books 8 through 18 of Jerome's commentary on Isaiah, and Oxford, Bodleian Library, MS e Museo 6 is a copy of Augustine on St. John. Neither work thus helps us decide between the two houses. The absence of a listed (or surviving) legendary cannot be used to rule either house out, given the liturgical necessity of such a book. Similarly, the ubiquity of Gregory's Homily 37 gives no unambiguous help. However, if we look at the extended quotations from Rufinus's translation of Eusebius's

---

69. Hollis et al., *Writing the Wilton Women*, p. 137 n. 60.

70. The only other copy of the Origen/Rufinus Homilies on Joshua surviving from Anglo-Saxon England is Gneuss, *Handlist*, item 239: Durham, Cathedral Library, MS B.III.1, s. xi^ex (before 1096), written in Normandy, with an English provenance in Durham. Durham, B.III.1, fol. 106v, line 1a, gives the following incipit: "Incipit Proemium Expositionis Origenis in i<esu>m Naue."

Ecclesiastical History, and add to that the extended quotation of Rufinus's translation of Origen's homilies on Joshua, particularly with its mistaken attribution to Jerome in both the *Liber confortatorius* and in the Bodley list, and if, finally, we consider them along with the other works Goscelin cites that also appear on the Bodley list, the connection of the *Liber confortatorius* to the collection lying behind the Bodley list and the connection of the Bodley list with the Anglo-Saxon library of Peterborough is, arguably, strengthened.[71]

71. I should like to thank Teresa Webber for her kindness in examining the hand of Bodley 163, fol. 251r, and discussing its implications for the possible state of the Peterborough collection in the 1080s. I am very grateful to Michael Lapidge for reading a draft of the manuscript and for his helpful suggestions. Any errors are my own.

APPENDIX

Goscelin's Citations and the Booklist in Oxford, Bodleian Library,
Bodley 163, fols. 250–51

Bodley Title	*Citation*	*Saint-Bertin List*[72]

Augustinus De ciuitate Dei   LC37.21–22; 81[2]   (R)[73]   SB10
     Lapidge 1[74]; Clavis 313. Augustine, *De Civitate Dei Libri XXII*, ed. Dom-
     bart and Kalb, XV.1 (II:59.6–7).[75]

Augustinus Super Iohannem   LC 55.28–30   SB1
     Lapidge 4; Clavis 278. Augustine, *In Iohannis Euangelium Tractatus
     CXXIV*, ed. R. Willems, p. 261, XXVI.4.13–15.

Ecclesiastica historia Eusebii Cesaris   LC 64–66; 80; 98   (R)   --
     Lapidge 8; *Kirchengeschichte*, ed. Schwartz and Mommsen. Gneuss,
     Handlist, gives the following manuscripts surviving from Anglo-Saxon
     England: item 57: CCCC 187 (s. xi/xii CaCC); item 61: CCCC 192
     (excerpts); item 137: Cambridge, Pembroke College, MS 108, prov.
     Bury St. Edmunds (excerpt); item 768: Worcester Cathedral Library,
     MS Q. 28; item 773.5: Wormsley, Wormsley Library (fragment). In
     addition to recommending this to Eve for her reading, Goscelin uses it
     for his account of Blandina (LC 64.14–34 = Schwartz, p. 409 = V.1.17–
     19; 41–42; 53–56), the "mulier quaedam captiva" (LC 65.1–66.40 =
     Schwartz, pp. 973–76 = X.11), and Potamiana (LC 98.7–20 = Schwartz,
     pp. 531, 533 = VI.5.1–7).

---

72. = "Brevis annotatio librorum sancti Bertini," Becker, *Catalogi bibliothecarum antiqui*,
list 77 (pp. 181–85) = SB. On dating the list see Derolez, *Catalogues*, p. 24, who dates it to "xi–
xii."

73. Goscelin, *Liber confortatorius*, ed. Talbot, p. 80 (=LC). "R" indicates books that Goscelin recommends to Eve for her reading. In this appendix I make no attempt to list every
citation of the works in question.

74. Lapidge, "Surviving Booklists," pp. 33–89, List XIII, item 1 (=Lapidge 1, etc.).

75. Talbot's offered source for LC 37.21–22, "Omnis qui ad supernam pertinet ciuitatem
peregrinus est mundi," *Tractatus in euangelium Iohannis*, XXVIII.9 is approximate at best.
(This identification is followed, with qualification, by Stephanie Hollis in *Writing the Wilton
Women*, p. 113 n. 25.) Closer to LC 37.21–22, given the context of both works, is "peregrinus
in saeculo, et pertinens ad civitatem Dei," *De ciuitate Dei*, XV.1 (Augustine, *De ciuitate Dei*, ed.
Dombart and Kalb, 2:59.6–7; *PL* 41.438), referring to Abel.

Tripartita historia   LC 80.36–37   (R)   SB121
Lapidge 9. "Historia tripartita" is the name given to a highly popular
reworking (and translation into Latin) of the ecclesiastical histories of
Socrates, Sozomen, and Theodoret. *Cassiodori-Epiphanii Historia Ecclesiastica Tripartita*, ed. Jacob and Hanslik.

Hieronimus Super Iosue   LC 57–61   --
Lapidge 10 = Rufinus/Origen, Homilies on Josua. Extensive quotation
from homilies XV and XX. *Homilien zum Hexateuch*, ed. Baehrens, pp.
xxiv–xxv. Baehrens's class D comprises those manuscripts which attribute the translation to Jerome, e.g., "incipit prohemium b. Hieronymi
presbyteri in expositione libri Iesu Nave." Goscelin attributes the collection of 26 homilies to Jerome at: LC 56.2–3, 56.36; 57.5–7; 59.2–6;
59.20–23, 61.33.

Hieronimus Contra Iouinianum   LC 43.21–22; 74.3–4, 9–11 --
Lapidge 11; Clavis 610. Jerome, *Aduersus Iouinianum*, PL 23.298, 304.

Hieronimus Super Isaiam   LC 86.28–29 (and passim)   SB113
Lapidge 12; Clavis 584. Jerome, *Commentariorum in Esaiam Libri*, ed.
Adriaen, XI.12/17 (p. 461.74–75).

——— Vita sanctorum.
Nicolai, Botulfi, Guðlaci   LC 44.38   --
Lapidge 16; BHL 6126. The miracle in question is St Nicholas's rescue
of distressed sailors. On the transmission of the vita of St. Nicholas in
Anglo-Saxon England, and on his cult in England and Normandy see
Old English Life of St Nicholas, ed. Treharne, pp. 28–45. The miracle can
be found in Mombritius, *Sanctuarium seu vitae sanctorum*, II.300.28–51
at 33–34. (London, British Library, MS Harley 3097, Gneuss, *Handlist*,
item 434.5.)

Ambrosius De uirginitate   LC ?63, 98   --
Lapidge 22; Clavis 147. The four Anglo-Saxon manuscripts of Ambrose's treatises on virginity have *De uirginibus* followed by *De uiduis*,
De uirginitate, Exhortatio uirginitatis, and *De lapsu uirginis consecratae*. See
Bankert, Wegmann, and Wright, et al., *Ambrose in Anglo-Saxon England*,
p. 37: "Confusingly, in these manuscripts *De uirginbus* is titled 'de virginitate,' while in the two Oxford manuscripts *De virginitate* is identified

as 'liber IIII' of 'de virginibus' . . . For this reason, the entry 'Ambrosius De virginitate' in the Peterborough booklist may have referred to a manuscript containing *De virginibus*, combined with some or all of these other works."[76]

Gregorii Moralia in Iob   LC 54.8–12, 84.2,   SB 95
                                               89.16–17,[77] 94. 1–4
Lapidge 29; Clavis 1708. Gregory, *Moralia in Job*, ed. Adriaen, 335.8;
335.8; 1525.1–4; 1694.94–98 and 1695.118–19.

Vite patrum   LC 58 72–73, 76, 85, ?106   SB289
Lapidge 31; BHL 6524–47. PL 73.876; 802; 860; 684–85; 380ff; ?764.

?Haimo In euangeliis   [LC 62.22–63.1]   [SB94]
Lapidge 33, who notes that Haimo of Auxerre did not compose a commentary on the Gospels. Goscelin cites Gregory, *Homiliae in Euangelia* (ed. Étaix, pp. 348.1–349.41).

Epistolares Hieronimi .iii.   LC 31.36–32.1, 35.1, 74.6, 81.18 SB117
Lapidge 34; Clavis 620. See *Sancti Eusebii Hieronymi Epistulae*, ed. Hilberg, I.329.1–2, I.329–330.7, I.326.16, I.308.11–14.

Prognosticon futuri secli   LC 109–111   SB128
Lapidge 40; Clavis 1258. Julian of Toledo, *Sancti Juliani Toletanae Sedis Episcopi Opera*, ed. Hillgarth.[78]

---

76. Hollis et al., *Writing the Wilton Women*, p. 317 n. 57, believes that Goscelin's remark on Ambrose, *De uirginibus* ("exsors eius libri") meant that the book was "unavailable at Burg." Goscelin's remark is more likely a trope to cover his own rhetorical elaboration of the *passio*, since his presentation gave the story an emphasis different from that of Ambrose.

77. For the citation in LC 89.17, Hollis et al., *Writing the Wilton Women*, p. 173 n. 80, gives, following Talbot, "compare Eucherius of Lyon, *Liber formularum spiritalis intelligentiae*, PL 50.751d–52a." It is more likely, however, that for his commentary on *onager*, Goscelin is using the *Moralia in Job* XXX.15.1–4, which, by contrast with *PL* 50.751, offered Goscelin the following idea of releasing the mind from troubles (LC 89.18–19). See Gregory the Great, *Moralia in Job*, ed. Adriaen, 1525.1–4.

78. The combination and order of Goscelin's citations at LC 109–11 of Augustine, *Enchiridion (De fide)* and of Gregory, *Moralia in Job*, suggests that he was using these works through Julian of Toledo, *Prognosticon futuri saeculi*, book 3. On the influence of the *Prognosticon* see Hillgarth, "St. Julian of Toledo."

THE LADY AND THE VINE: PUTTING THE HORSEWOMAN ON THE HILTON OF CADBOLL CROSS-SLAB INTO CONTEXT

Kellie S. Meyer

INTRODUCTION

Like many hardworking women in academia, the female figure on the Hilton of Cadboll cross-slab remains anonymous; in honor of Helen Damico, my esteemed supervisor and friend during my studies at the University of New Mexico, I shall attempt to illuminate the significance and importance of this most visible though historically silent of Pictish ladies. Sometimes known as the Pictish Queen, this female horse rider appears on a monument which is one of three upright cross-slabs originally located on the Tarbat peninsula in the county of Easter-Ross, Scotland, an area about thirty miles north of Inverness (fig. 1). This group of monuments is also closely related to numerous carved fragments recovered from the grave-yard and Glebe field of Tarbat Old Church, overlooking the seaboard village of Portmahomack. Archaeological investigations concluded in 2007 uncovered an early medieval settlement at this site with evidence that points to a late sixth-century monastic foundation.[1] Current thinking has proposed that this monastic estate expanded sometime in the eighth century to incorporate the entire peninsula with satellite chapels located at Nigg, Shandwick, and Hilton of Cadboll.[2] Indeed, both the iconographic programs and the stylistic details depicted on the cross-slabs at these locations support this argument, and it is very likely that they were carved by

---

1. See *Tarbat Discovery Programme*, Bulletins 1–6. See also Carver, "Iona of the East" and "Sculpture in Action," for discussion of dating and identification of the site as a monastery. For Carver's latest conclusions on the topic, please see his monograph, *Portmahomack: Monastery of the Picts*. I would like to thank Martin Carver and Jane Hawkes, my supervisors at the University of York, as well as Isabel Henderson, Sally Foster, Rosemary Cramp, Anna Richie, and all the other wonderful women without whom any investigation of Pictish art would be impossible.

2. See Carver, "Iona of the East" and "Sculpture in Action," for a discussion of the probable geographical parameters of the Tarbat monastic estate and its expansion in the eighth century, as well as proposals for archaeological investigation of the sites at Nigg and Shandwick. See also his *Portmahomack: Monastery of the Picts*.

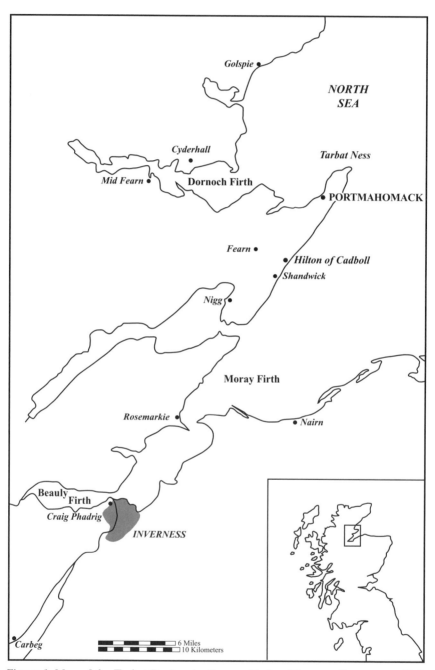

Figure 1. Map of the Tarbat Peninsula. Source: Tarbat Discovery Programme Bulletin 1, reproduced by permission of Martin Carver.

a "school" of stone-carvers that was probably located at the monastery. In addition, I would argue that the iconography and decorative details carved on these stones express a meaning related not only to the function of the monastery in regards to its pastoral and political role on the peninsula but also to the monastic estate's relationship with the rest of the insular world, and indeed, the Continent.[3]

Historical records relating to the Picts are slim, relying primarily upon brief accounts in Bede, Adomnán, and the Irish Annals. Therefore, the images contained on these cross-slabs and the Portmahomack fragments, along with a consideration of the archaeological evidence, may be the best clues we have with which to reconstruct the intellectual, religious, and political climate of this area during the early medieval period in Scotland. For instance, Adomnán reports that St. Columba set out from Iona in 565 on a mission to convert the Picts. Traveling along the Great Glen and by Loch Ness, he eventually met the king of the northern Picts, Bridei, son of Mailchu, somewhere near Inverness. Although Adomnán is only able to provide a few instances of individual conversions at this time, he does state that monasteries were founded which survived until his own day in the early eighth century.[4] Considering the late sixth-century date of the earliest graves excavated in the Old Church at Portmahomack, it is quite likely that this settlement was one of these Columban foundations.[5]

According to Bede, the Picts also received a mission from Northumbria in the early eighth century. In 710 the Pictish king Nechtan sent to Wearmouth-Jarrow for information about the practices of the Northumbrian church in regards to the dating of Easter and mode of tonsure, as well as to the "Roman" method of building in stone.[6] Therefore, the appearance of fully dressed cross-slabs in Pictland has often been claimed to be the result of the Northumbrian's happiness to oblige Nechtan's request. For instance, R. B. K. Stevenson, Sally Foster, and Isabel Henderson have all argued that

---

3. This argument forms the basis of my Ph.D. thesis, "Reading the Stones: The Pictish Class II Monuments on Tarbat Peninsula" (University of York, 2005).

4. See Adomnán, *Adomnán's Life of Columba*, ed. Anderson and Anderson, 1.1, 1.33, 1.37, 2.31, 2.33–35, 2.42, 2.46, 3.14.

5. See Carver, "Sculpture in Action" and "Iona of the East," for discussion of the dating of the burials in Tarbat Old Church. For his latest conclusions see Carver, *Portmahomack: Monastery of the Picts*. See also Simon Taylor, "Place-Names and the Early Church," for a consideration of the linguistic evidence pointing to a sixth- to seventh-century Columban foundation in the Easter-Ross area.

6. *HE*, 3.4.

the high relief characteristics seen on the later Pictish cross-slabs were only possible after the stylistic innovations practiced on the Ruthwell and Bewcastle monuments could be learned by Pictish craftsmen.[7] Douglas Mac Lean further argues that even the earliest Pictish cross-slabs, featuring low relief, could only have been carved after the Ruthwell and Bewcastle monuments since their carving techniques were the direct result of Northumbrian training.[8] Thus the appearance of an extremely popular Northumbrian motif such as the inhabited vine-scroll on Pictish cross-slabs, particularly the sophisticated examples that can be seen on the Hilton of Cadboll stone as well as on a fragment from Tarbat Old Church at Portmahomack (TR1), has been regarded as evidence of a Northumbrian presence in the area. In addition, the fact that the earliest stone building of the Tarbat Old Church has been dated to the eighth century, presumably replacing an older wooden structure, also argues for the success of the Northumbrian mission to teach the Picts to build stone churches in the manner of Rome.[9]

Significant problems with this hypothesis, however, must be addressed. The first is the presumption that only Northumbrians built stone churches in the so-called Roman manner. Though rare, British or Irish churches built in stone did exist, most notably at Whithorn in Scotland and at Kildare and Duleek in Ireland. The second is the presumption that the impetus for carving the vine-scroll ornament on the Tarbat stones must have come from Northumbria, or at least from the Bernician kingdom which included Wearmouth-Jarrow. The third, which results from the first two, is that the stone church and vine-scroll motif signified a religious realignment for the Tarbat Picts from the so-called Celtic or Columban style of their foundation to the "Roman" style practiced by the Bernician kingdom in the eighth century.

It is outside the realm of this study to discuss the differences between the Irish and Roman Christian Church in the early medieval insular world

---

7. See Stevenson, "Chronology and Relationships" and "Sculpture in Scotland," pp. 71–73; Foster, *Picts, Gaels and Scots*, p. 93; Isabel Henderson, "Pictish Art and the *Book of Kells*"; Isabel Henderson, "Shape and Decoration of the Cross," pp. 210, 217 n. 3; Isabel Henderson, "*Book of Kells* and the Snake-Boss Motif"; Isabel Henderson, "Pictish Vine-Scroll Ornament," p. 248.

8. Mac Lean, "Snake-Bosses and Redemption," pp. 247–48.

9. See *Tarbat Discovery Bulletin* (3), pp. 4–7, fig. 3; and Carver, "Iona of the East," "Sculpture in Action," and *Portmahomack: Monastery of the Picts* for discussions of the evidence for an eighth-century stone church.

adequately. However it is important to realize that while the monastic houses at Wearmouth and Jarrow may have been firmly "Roman" in their alignment, "Celtic" or "Columban" elements held sway in other areas of Northumbria and there was ongoing contact between the Irish and Anglo-Saxon kingdoms long after the Synod at Whitby.[10] In addition, the concrete results of Nechtan's request throughout every area of Pictland can only be surmised. Although the *Annals of Ulster* record that Nechtan commanded the expulsion of the Columban monks in 717, it is impossible to determine how well observed it may have been, especially by a Columban foundation located in the far north that most likely enjoyed close relations with Iona.[11] Even if the Columban monks were actually successfully expelled in 717, it didn't take long for them to reappear in Scotland, under the mantle of the Céli Dé in the early ninth century.[12] As will be seen, these concerns must be kept in mind when considering the possible meanings conveyed by both the vine-scroll ornament and the figural composition depicted on the Hilton of Cadboll stone.

Discussion

Carved sometime between the mid-eighth and mid-ninth centuries, the main part of the Hilton of Cadboll cross-slab currently stands in the National Museum of Scotland (fig. 2). The 2001 archaeological investigation of the ruins of St. Mary's chapel, located slightly outside the present-day village of Hilton of Cadboll, shows that the slab stood somewhere in the immediate vicinity of the chapel until 1676 when it was broken down and the front defaced in order to re-create it as a memorial to Alexander Duff and his three wives.[13] The bottom of the stone, which was excavated

---

10. See Michelle Brown, "Echoes: The *Book of Kells*," pp. 341–43; and Kathleen Hughes, "Evidence for Contacts." See also Warren, *Liturgy and Ritual*, p. 53, for the argument that "Celtic" elements persisted in the liturgy practiced at York until the late eighth century. The paschal ritual to which Warren refers, citing Reyner, *Apostolatus benedictinorum in Anglia*, Appendix, p. 87, is also described in the *Regularis Concordia*, the tenth-century document of monastic reform written by Æðelwold. See *Monastic Agreement*, ed. and trans. Symons, p. 39.

11. The relevant entry from the *Annals of Ulster* (ed. Mac Airt and Mac Niocaill; online version ed. Ó Corráin) reads "Expulsio familie Ie trans Dorsum Brittanie a Nectano rege."

12. See Clancy, "Iona, Scotland and the *Céli Dé*"; Patrick Wormald, "Emergence of the *Regnum Scottorum*," pp. 142–44.

13. The excavation was conducted by Historic Scotland and GUARD. The discovery of two parts of the collar stone, the base of the cross-slab, and numerous carved fragments from the defaced front of the slab has led to the hypothesis that the stone was first erected at or near the later chapel site sometime in the eighth to ninth centuries. At some point

Figure 2. Hilton of Cadboll Cross-slab (photo: RCAHMS). Reproduced by permission of the Royal Commission on the Ancient and Historical Monuments of Scotland.

Figure 3. Hilton of Cadboll: Base of the Cross-slab. Photo reproduced by permission of Douglas Scott.

in 2001, underwent conservation and is currently located within the village of Hilton of Cadboll (fig. 3).

As can be seen, in addition to several Pictish symbols located in the top panel and the lower decorative panel of spiral work, the Hilton of Cadboll stone displays an inhabited vine-scroll border and a figural composition that features two trumpeters and several horse riders engaging in a hunt, as well as the centrally located horsewoman. A closer look reveals that this figure is actually superimposed upon a second horse rider who can be identified as male, due to his short beard and large nose, difficult to discern from a photograph, but apparent upon a close inspection of the stone.

In general, the motifs and decorative designs used on the Hilton of Cadboll stone were part of a greater repertoire common to the insular world from the seventh to the ninth centuries. For instance, while ultimately of Mediterranean origin, vine-scroll ornament carved on stone was extremely popular in Northumbria, while its appearance in manuscripts, ivory carving, and metalwork ranged throughout the Anglo-Saxon kingdoms and Ireland as well as on the Continent.[14] The interlace and spiral patterns found on the Hilton of Cadboll stone can likewise be found throughout

---

the slab was broken at its junction with the collar stone and subsequently reerected in the location where the base was found, at the west end of the chapel. The date for reerection is unknown, but the evidence suggests it took place when the stone chapel was built, perhaps in the eleventh to twelfth centuries. Martin Carver (pers. comm., 2001) based on reports from Sally Foster and Heather James of GUARD (Glasgow University Archaeological Research Division). Interim reports can also be found on <www.guard.arts.gla.ac.uk/projects/1078_webpages/default.html>.

14. See Hicks, *Animals in Early Medieval Art*, p. 119; *Durham and Northumberland*, ed. Cramp, vol. 1, p. 24; Cramp, "Early Northumbrian Sculpture," pp. 136–37; Mac Lean, "Northumbrian Vine-Scroll Ornament and the *Book of Kells*."

Figure 4. TR1: fragment found in churchyard of Tarbat Old Church, Portmaho-mack (photo author).

the insular world, while hunting scenes were extremely popular in Caro-lingian and Irish art, as well as on Pictish sculpture, having their origins ultimately in late antique imperial images on mosaics, engraved silver plat-ters, and several different media of Sassanian art.[15] Specific models for the ornament contained on the Hilton of Cadboll stone, therefore, could have come from any number of sources current in the insular world from the seventh to the tenth centuries. Many of these were first considered by Isabel Henderson, and since the search for artistic sources can help to determine lines of communication and trade, as well as the exchange of cultural ideas between two geographical areas, the listing of such parallels is invaluable.[16] In addition, a relationship can be established that speaks of more than just the migration of artistic motifs, when small stylistic details and the specific depiction of iconography are considered. In order to demonstrate this, I will discuss just a few of the most commonly cited parallels to the vine-scroll ornament depicted on the Hilton of Cadboll monument.

The vine-scroll ornament that appears on the TR1 fragment (fig. 4) from the Old Church at Portmahomack is the closest parallel to the Hilton of Cadboll decoration, and it is likely that the same carver worked on both

15. Carrington, "David Imagery."
16. See Isabel Henderson, "Pictish Vine-Scroll Ornament."

stones. However, as the recently excavated bottom of the Hilton of Cadboll stone shows, despite the clear stylistic affinities, such as the light, shallow carving technique, elongated, wiry creatures with tails or hindquarters that extend beyond the scrolls, forelegs that are forced into the "Anglo-Saxon lock" by the passing vine-stem, legs, tails or extended ear-lappets which are entangled with escaping vine-tendrils, and scrolls that pass at least twice around the bodies of each creature, there are several key differences between the two designs that are significant in terms of iconographical interpretation. For instance, the winged quadrupeds on TR1 face a chalice-shaped vessel from which the vine-scrolls spring, while the Hilton of Cadboll creatures are addorsed, even though the right-hand creature does turn its head to face the vine-source. Though significantly damaged, it appears that the left and right sides of the vine-scroll ornament on TR1 mirrored each other, whereas the left and right sides of the Hilton of Cadboll design are quite different from each other. While the right side of the Hilton of Cadboll design parallels that which is carved on TR1, the left side depicts a sharply angular, somewhat denuded vine. The stems of this vine force the creatures into contorted positions, trap them within the scrolls, and prevent them from reaching sustenance. In one case, the berryless stem even chokes one hapless creature. This design is unique to Hilton of Cadboll and has little in common with any other Pictish vine-scrolls or with the Northumbrian designs traditionally regarded as having inspired it, such as those associated with the mid- to late eighth-century Jarrow school of carving.[17]

The inhabited vine-scroll featured on the Ruthwell monument (fig. 5) displays the typical characteristics of the Jarrow style of inhabited vine-scroll: a single-stem vine encloses plump, well-modeled, naturalistically portrayed birds or beasts that are securely perched on a vine stem that passes around the body only once, without forcing the animals into contorted positions. In addition, the execution of the carving on the stone is deep, detailed, and well rounded.

On the other hand, the York school of carvings have much more in common with the Tarbat peninsula vine-scrolls. Those which display the greatest similarities to the Hilton of Cadboll design, such as the cross-

---

17. See Cramp, "Early Northumbrian Sculpture," pp. 148–50; Cramp, "Anglian Sculptures from Jedburgh"; and Collingwood, *Northumbrian Crosses*, pp. 69–81, for a discussion of the sculpture generally included in the Jarrow "school." These include the Ruthwell and Bewcastle monuments, a decorative frieze from Jarrow (Jarrow 19), the Jedburgh panel, and a fragment from a cross-shaft at Rothbury.

Figure 5. Ruthwell Cross Vine-scroll (photo author).

shaft fragments from the Minster and St. Leonard's, both in York, and from Croft-on-Tees in north Yorkshire, are all believed to be the product of the first generation of carvers associated with the York Minster, and are generally dated from the late eighth to the early ninth centuries.[18] These fragments all display a light, shallow style of carving, highlighting thin, denuded stems that entangle the bodies of elongated, stylized animals within the scrolls while their hindquarters slip out below. In particular, the St. Leonard's fragment (fig. 6) displays characteristics very close to the depiction of the inhabited vine-scroll on Hilton of Cadboll, with a vine that passes twice around the elongated beasts forcing their legs into the "Anglo-Saxon lock." In addition, one of the beasts is stretched quite unnaturally in its effort to get at the fruit that dangles just out of reach behind its back.

Additional relevant examples of inhabited vine-scroll are carved on the early ninth-century Mercian friezes that have survived at Breedon-on-Hill, Leicestershire. The vine stems on the various panels of the "broad" frieze pass twice around the animals, and their legs quite frequently display the "Anglo-Saxon lock." Furthermore, the creatures do not actually perch on the vine, but rest their legs on the horizontal frame of the panel, as do the animals in the horizontal section of the Tarbat vine-scroll borders. However, although the Breedon animals are elegant and linear, they are still quite naturalistically depicted with no abnormal extension of limbs or contortion of their bodies.[19] So while I agree with Isabel Henderson's observation that the Mercian inhabited vine-scrolls are much closer to the Tarbat examples than are the Jarrow school depictions, I must respectfully disagree that they are closer than the York examples, in which the elongation and contortion of the animals, as well as the denuded nature of the plant-scrolls, seem particularly close to aspects of the Hilton of Cadboll design.[20]

While the possibility exists that Anglo-Saxon stonemasons had some role to play in the training of the sculptors who carved the Tarbat monuments, thus explaining similarities in the designs, particularly those between the York school and Tarbat, it is more likely that the Tarbat artists

---

18. See *York and Eastern Yorkshire*, ed. Lang, pp. 22–23, 109–10, ill. 1, 369; *Northern Yorkshire*, ed. Lang, pp. 89–91, ill. 147–51; Cramp, "Early Northumbrian Sculpture," pp. 148, 150; and Collingwood, *Northumbrian Crosses*, pp. 42, 54–55, for a discussion of the monuments believed to be part of a school of carving situated in or around York.

19. See Jewell, "Anglo-Saxon Friezes," pls. XLVa, b, d, e, and XLVIIIa; and Cramp, "Schools of Mercian Sculpture," figs. 50–53.

20. Isabel Henderson, *Hilton of Cadboll Chapel Site*, p. 6.

Figure 6. York, St. Leonard's fragment. Reproduced by permission of the
Corpus of Anglo-Saxon Stone Sculpture.

Figure 7. Detail of vine-scroll on *Una Autem* page (folio 285r) from the *Book of Kells*.
Reproduced by permission of the Board of Trinity College Dublin.

had access to portable models. While many sources can be cited, such as
the so-called Ascension Ivory, the Brunswick Casket, or the Ormside Bowl,
it is folio 285r (the *Una Autem* page) in the Book of Kells that contains the
most relevant example of an inhabited vine-scroll in regards to the design
featured on the Tarbat examples.[21] The design on this page (fig. 7) is noteworthy because not only does the vine-scroll form a border around the
central panel of decoration, a feature that is found in stone sculpture only
on Hilton of Cadboll and the TR1 fragment, but the composition features
encircling vines that pass twice around extremely elongated quadrupeds,
as well as escaping tendrils that intertwine with the creature's limbs. In
particular, the central chalice with its facing quadrupeds can be almost
directly paralleled in the design on TR1, though the addorsed creatures
on the Hilton of Cadboll design have no manuscript parallel.

As suggested earlier, the search for parallels is useful in pointing to
connections between the Tarbat peninsula and other areas of the insular
world; and though in no way definitive, the closest of these parallels seem
to be with the carvings found in the late eighth- to early ninth-century
Anglian kingdom of Deira, which included York, and with the location of
the scriptorium that produced the late eighth- to early ninth-century Book
of Kells, which was most likely Iona.[22] As the monastery at Tarbat was most
likely founded by Columba or one of his followers, this latter connection
is to be expected, but the possibility of contact with York points to a wider
range of possibilities. Since by the end of the eighth century the influence

---

21. Book of Kells (Dublin, Trinity College, MS 58 A1.6). See Beckwith, *Ivory Carvings*,
pls. 10–13, 24, for the Ascension Ivory and the Brunswick Ivory. See *Alcuin and Charlemagne*,
ed. Garrison, Nelson, and Tweddle, p. 25, for the Ormside Bowl.
22. Meehan, *Book of Kells*, p. 91.

Figure 8. Detail of vine-scroll on the north side of the Cross of Patrick and Columba (aka South Cross) at Kells. Photo by author.

of the school at York had eclipsed that of Wearmouth-Jarrow, perhaps it is no surprise that if the monastery at Tarbat were looking to Northumbria, it would be looking to Deira rather than Bernicia.[23] Such a connection with York could also provide one possible explanation for continental elements that show up in the iconography of the Tarbat material, as communication between York and the Continent was greatly increased during the tenure of Alcuin's stay at Charlemagne's court.[24] In addition, inhabited vine-scrolls depicted on Irish crosses, such as that carved on the cross-shaft at Kells (fig. 8), also show certain similarities to those depicted on the York stones and on the Mercian friezes. While the Irish inhabited vine-scrolls are unlikely to have had any effect on the Tarbat style of carving, primarily because of their late date, it is interesting to note the affinities between the Mercian, Irish, and York examples, which might be explained by ongoing contacts between the three kingdoms.[25] It is equally possible that the monastery at Tarbat had contact with all three areas as well, and simply reacted differently to the same impetus (such as the *Una Autem* vine-scroll border in the Book of Kells) that inspired their more similar responses. As will be seen, this unique reaction may have been dependent upon literary rather than artistic sources.

In general, the inhabited vine-scroll is a clear reference to John 15:1–10, in which Jesus proclaims "I am the vine, you are the branches." However, other biblical references used the vine as a metaphor for the royal lineage of Christ, which meant that vine-scrolls also conveyed secular and political connotations.[26] At the same time Greek and Latin exegesis equated the vine with the cross, with the blood of Christ and the New Covenant, and with the Church as a whole. While there is no definitive proof that all of the specific exegesis was known in the insular world, writers such as Bede do show a familiarity with many of these ideas which were first explored as

---

23. *Alcuin and Charlemagne*, ed. Garrison, Nelson, and Tweddle, p. 6.

24. Certain "continental" elements can be seen in the iconography depicted on the cross-slabs at Shandwick and Nigg and are fully discussed in Meyer, "Reading the Stones."

25. In addition to previously cited contact between Ireland and Anglo-Saxon England (see note 11 above) a link between York and Ireland could be found at the abbey of Mayo, which, founded by St. Colman after leaving Lindisfarne, came under the influence of the York episcopate by the late eighth to early ninth century. See Hawkes, "Iconography of Identity."

26. Cf. Ez. 17:22–24, Dan. 4:7–14, Hab. 3:17–18, Is. 11:1, 27:2–6, Pss. 1:3, 80:8. See also de Paor, "Some Vine Scrolls," p. 188, where it is argued that the vine-scroll ornament on the fifth- to seventh-century *Spagenhelme* helmets signified royalty since they were worn exclusively by persons of royal or princely rank.

early as the beginning of the second century.[27] This familiarity points to the possibility that those in other monastic environments were conversant with motifs such as those expressed by Bede in his *Homily on the Ascension,* wherein he likens the grapevine to the cross and the chalice to the New Covenant.[28] Likewise, since many of Augustine's works circulated in the insular world, his conflation of the vine and the Holy Church was probably also known within the monastic milieu.[29]

The most prevalent component in the matrix of ideas surrounding the vine-scroll was the conception of the vine as the Tree of Life and, subsequently, the Tree of Virtue.[30] This amalgamation grew out of the conflation of the cross with the Tree of Life, a common literary idea in the early Middle Ages that was most fully expressed by the fourth century in *De Pascha,* a poem mistakenly attributed to Cyprian and copied among his works until the ninth century.[31] The tree in this poem is identical with the Savior and the Church, is located on Golgotha (considered the center of the earth), reaches to the heavens, and provides refuge for all peoples, and nourishment in the form of fruit that is identical to the sacrament of the Eucharist. Three different Carolingian manuscripts dating from the end of the eighth century include the poem, attesting to its popularity on the Continent, and it was likely to have been well known in Britain since

---

27. See, for instance, Clement of Alexandria, *Paedagogus* 2.2.19, translated from the Greek in *Ante-Nicene Fathers,* ed. and trans. Roberts and Donaldson, 4:200, and Cyril of Jerusalem, *Catechesis,* 17.18, translated from the Greek in *Nicene and Post-Nicene Fathers,* ed. and trans. Schaff and Wace, 7:128. Adomnán displays knowledge of at least part of Cyril's *Catechesis* (lecture 13), though it is unclear whether he actually had this text in his possession or simply knew of it through Jerome. See Werner, "Cross-Carpet Page," p. 210 n. 182. There is a slight possibility that Aldhem might also have had knowledge of Clement's work. See *Aldhelm,* ed. and trans. Lapidge and Herren, p. 41 n. 23.

28. Bede, *Homiliae,* 11.15 lines 21–24. Translation in Bede, *Homilies on the Gospels,* ed. and trans. Martin and Hurst, 2.136.

29. See for example, Augustine, *In Iohannis Evangelium,* ed. Williams, 16.16 lines 19–23, and *De catechizandis rudibus,* ed. Bauer, 24.44 lines 1–4, and 25.38 lines 8–11. Both works were known and used by Ælfric, and Bede knew *In Iohannis Evangelium.* See *Bede's Commentary on the Acts of the Apostles,* ed. and trans. Martin, for his use of Augustine. See also *Fontes Anglo-Saxonici* for Anglo-Saxon knowledge of Augustine's works.

30. See O'Reilly, *Studies in the Iconography of the Virtues and Vices* and "Tree of Eden," as well as Greenhill, "Child in the Tree," for excellent surveys of the apocrypha, exegesis, and liturgical sources that contributed to the early medieval literary and artistic conceptions of the Tree of Life.

31. *De Pascha* is included in Cyprian's *Opera,* ed. Hartel, 3:305. Also known as *De ligno crucis,* the poem is available in an English translation in White, *Early Christian Latin Poets,* pp. 136–39.

Bede's *Commentary on St. Luke's Gospel* contains closely related imagery.[32] In addition, the association of the cross with the Tree of Life was asserted in a number of other works read and copied in the insular world such as Bede's hymn on the passion of St. Andrew and his commentary on Psalm 1, the Hiberno-Latin *Commentarius in Evangelium Secundum Marcum XV* by Pseudo-Jerome, and in Amalarius of Metz's *De ecclesiasticis officiis 4.14*.[33] Likewise, early medieval liturgical texts, such as the antiphons in the *Liber responsalis*, used during the *Exaltatio Crucis* ceremony, reinforced the mystical identity of the cross and Tree of Life.[34] Since the *Exaltatio* feast also appears in the Gelasian and Gregorian sacramentaries, it is possible that this feast was observed in the insular world, and indeed, Ó Carragáin has argued that knowledge of the rite inspired the erection of the Ruthwell cross, while knowledge of the *Adoratio Crucis* influenced its iconography.[35] It may be that these rites were also known to the Tarbat community and that the vine-scroll decoration on both Hilton of Cadboll and the TR1 fragment was carved in response to the celebration of these feasts, both of which made use of hymns that stressed the connection between the cross and the Tree of Life.

Within the context of the vine as the Tree of Life, the creatures inhabiting the scrolls quite clearly represent the living community of the Church. At the same time, they might have been meant to depict specific animals that would have conveyed additional layers of meaning to the viewer. For instance, while the winged quadrupeds flanking the source of the vine-

---

32. See Greenhill, "Child in the Tree," pp. 338–39, 351, for a discussion of the Carolingian manuscripts, and Bede, *In Lucam*, ed. Hurst, 23.33 lines 1566–73 for the *De Pascha*–inspired imagery. The influence need not have been direct; Bede may have been using verses from Gregory's Commentary on Matthew 13:31–32 in the *Moralium*, which also contained *De Pascha*–related imagery. See *Commentary on the Seven Catholic Epistles of Bede*, ed. Hurst, and Bede, *Bede's Commentary on the Acts of the Apostles*, ed. Martin, for Bede's use of Gregory's *Moralium*.

33. Pseudo-Jerome, *Expositio quattuor Evangeliorum*, *PL* 30:638B. Amalarius of Metz, *De ecclesiasticis officiis*, *PL* 105:1031B. Bede, *Hymni*, ed. Fraipont, 2.12 lines 1–15. Bede, *De Psalmorum libro exegesis*, *PL* 93:486. See Thomas Hall, "Cross as Green Tree," pp. 299–300, for discussion of the circulation of these works.

34. Thomas Hall, "Cross as Green Tree," p. 303 n. 22. The *Liber responsalis* is a collection of antiphons long associated with Gregory the Great, though according to Hall this attribution is doubtful. However, he believes that they most likely reflect ninth-century French liturgical practices and probably bore some relationship to contemporary English practices.

35. See Ó Carragáin, "Liturgical Innovation"; Ó Carragáin, *City of Rome*; Ó Carragáin, "Necessary Distance"; as well as Werner, "Cross-Carpet Page," for discussion of the various liturgical rites associated with the cult of the cross and the possibility that these rites were practiced in Britain and Ireland. See also Keefer, this volume.

scroll are not confronting a chalice, as they are on the TR1 fragment, if they were intended to represent griffins, they would further the Eucharistic symbolism of the design.[36] Michael Ryan has argued that in addition to suggesting the dual nature of Christ, who was symbolized by both the eagle and the lion, griffins symbolized the dual nature of the Eucharist in the two forms of bread and wine transposed by the words of institution to the body and blood of Christ.[37] Although there does not appear to be any specific biblical exegesis behind this tradition, such an interpretation would certainly explain the prolific use of the griffin and chalice motif in early medieval art.

The birds that inhabit many of the vine-scrolls may be meant to represent peacocks. Since they are established as symbols of immortality in early Christian art and exegesis, Bernard Meehan argues that in the Book of Kells they function to link visually the Eucharist to the Resurrection.[38] Within the context of a vine-scroll, they may very well have the same function. On the other hand, the birds might be meant to be pigeons and turtledoves, which, according to Bede in his *Homily on the Feast of Purification*, represent not only chastity and simplicity but also repentance and the purification of sins, which would certainly fit in with the theme of redemption conveyed by the vine.[39]

The vine-scroll ornament featured on the right side of the Hilton of Cadboll cross-slab could readily express any or all of these various meanings. However, the vine-scroll depicted on the left side, in which the majority of the creatures are trapped by denuded vines, choked by the berries, or contorted into extremely awkward positions, is very different and calls for further analysis. It has been suggested that this unique representation symbolizes a famine that is to be contrasted with the feast depicted on the right side, and both biblical passages and exegesis support this interpretation.[40] Fruitful and barren vines are used throughout the Old Testament

---

36. See the early ninth-century Old Irish treatise on the Mass contained at the end of the Stowe Missal (Dublin, Royal Irish Academy, MS D.11.3) for the metaphor of the chalice as the church. English translation in *Stowe Missal*, ed. Warner, 2, p. 40.

37. Ryan, "Menagerie," p. 160.

38. Meehan, *Book of Kells*, p. 62.

39. Bede, *Homiliae*, ed. Fraipont, 1.18 lines 1–199. English translation in *Homilies on the Gospels*, book 1, ed. and trans. Martin and Hurst, pp. 181–86. The source notes to this work indicate that Bede was using ideas from Augustine's *Tractatus in Evangelium Ioannis*, Jerome's *Adversus Jovinianum*, and Gregory's *Moralia*.

40. I am thankful to Barry Grove for initially pointing this out to me (pers. comm. 2000).

in order to contrast good and evil, while the New Testament and the Early
Church Fathers make it clear that those who do not abide in Christ are like
the withered vine which is cast away and burnt.[41]

Although there are no known early medieval artistic parallels for portraying the contrasting fruitful and barren vines, opposing the Tree of Virtue to the Tree of Vice was a very popular theme in twelfth-century manuscripts, and these pictures bear much in common with the Hilton vine-
scroll design. Often growing from a common source, the Tree of Vice is
always pictured on the left side, while the Tree of Virtue was placed on the
right. The *arbor bona* typically bears the "fruits of the spirit" listed in Gal.
5:22–24 and alludes to the Tree of Life in Rev. 22:2, while the *arbor mala* is
barren of leaves or portrays withered fruits identified as the fruits of the
flesh. A further association of the *arbor mala* with *Synagoga* and the *arbor
bona* with *Ecclesia*, which represent the Old and New Covenants respectively,
is also made explicit in many of the manuscripts.[42] While these twelfth-
century illustrations obviously could not have influenced the design on the
Hilton of Cadboll cross-slab, the ideas that lay behind them could, and it
seems that the impetus for the manuscript illuminations came from the
exegesis of Isidore of Seville and Rabanus Maurus.[43] While the circulation
of Rabanus Maurus's writings began too late in the insular world to have
affected the design of the Hilton of Cadboll cross-slab, Isidore's were well
known in both Ireland and England by the seventh century, and it may very
well be that the two different sides of the Hilton of Cadboll vine-scroll manifest an early insular representation of the two contrasting trees.[44] Further,
Bede's *In Abbacuc* 3.17–18 compares the fig tree, olive tree, and the vine to
the Synagogue of the Jews; observing that while the Jews lived spiritual lives,

41. See Deut. 32:32–33, Jer. 2:21, Hos. 10:1, Joel 1:7, and John 15:5–6. See also St. Basil,
Hexaemeron, 5.6, trans. in *Nicene and Post-Nicene Fathers*, ed. and trans. Schaff and Wace, 8:79,
and St. Cyril *Catechesis*, 1:4 translated in ibid., 7:7. Basil's *Hexaemeron* was known to Bede; see
Lapidge, "Surviving Booklists," pp. 45–50, while at least one of Cyril's catechetical lectures
was known to Adomnán, possibly through Jerome. See note 27 above.

42. See O'Reilly, *Studies in the Iconography of the Virtues and Vices*, particularly pp. 334–36,
340–41; O'Reilly, "Tree of Eden," p. 188.

43. O'Reilly, *Studies in the Iconography of the Virtues and Vices*, p. 336.

44. See Isidore, *Allegoriae quaedem scripturae sacrae*, PL 83:125, and Rabanus Maurus
Allegoriae in sacrum scripturam, PL 112:979. See Aldhelm, ed. and trans. Lapidge and Herren,
pp. 32, 176; *Commentary on the Seven Catholic Epistles of Bede*, ed. Hurst; Hillgarth, "Visigothic
Spain," 83; Hillgarth, "Ireland and Spain"; and McNally, "Isidorian Pseudepigraphia"; for
evidence that Isidore's writings were known as early as the seventh century in Britain and
Ireland.

the fields of the divine scriptures were producing spiritual food for them, but that when they failed to accept the grace of Jesus, the produce on the Lord's vines failed and the fig tree failed to bear the fruits of virtue. This is why, Bede comments, that "when Jesus was thirsty they offered him vinegar rather than wine, when he desired the sweetness of virtues to be shown him they proffered him bitterness; when he longed for their virtues they proffered him vices."[45] This interpretation demonstrates that Bede was very familiar with the conventions of comparing the barren vine (or fig tree) of vice to the fruitful vine of virtues, so it is quite possible that such ideas were also behind the depiction of the two different vines on Hilton of Cadboll.

On the other hand, the peculiar depiction of the vine-scroll on the left side of Hilton of Cadboll may refer to an even earlier idea. In several works available to the insular world, Augustine compared the Church to a sprouting vine which must be pruned of heretics and schismatics who practice the sacraments improperly.[46] Therefore, it may very well be that the denuded vine with its choking inhabitants was an allusion to schismatic practices within the Church. If this is the case then the question of with which sect of Christianity the Tarbat Picts were most closely aligned becomes very important. If the Tarbat peninsula was an outpost of the Northumbrian-based church instigated in the early eighth century by Nechtan, then it could be that the image of the unfruitful vine and starving beasts was a reference to the expelled Columban *familias* and their supposedly schismatic practices of tonsuring and calculating the date of Easter. This would fit in with an early to mid eighth-century date for the erection of the Hilton of Cadboll stone. If, on the other hand, as seems more likely from the artistic parallels with the York group of carvings and with the Book of Kells, the Hilton of Cadboll slab was carved in the very late eighth or early ninth century, then it could very well be that the stone was erected at the instigation of the Céli Dé who, apparently, "portrayed themselves as the irate messengers of Columba's return."[47] In this case, the unfruitful vine and contorted, chok-

---

45. "Propter quod sitienti illi acetum pro uino obtulerunt, id est uirtutum suauitatem in se quaerenti uitiorum acredinem, uirtutes eorum desideranti uita praeferebant"; *In Tobiam*, ed. Hurst and Hudson, 3.17–18 lines 698–99. English translation in Bede, *On Tobit*, trans. Connolly, p. 92.

46. See Augustine, *In Iohannis Evangelium*, ed. Williams, 13.16 lines 19–23, and *De catechizandis rudibus*, ed. Bauer, 24.44 lines 1–4 and 8–11, and 25.48 lines 52–55. Bede used Augustine's commentary on John extensively, though Augustine's doctrinal treatises do not seem to have been well known until Ælfric. See *Commentary on the Seven Catholic Epistles of Bede*, ed. Hurst, and *Fontes Anglo-Saxonici*.

47. Patrick Wormald, "Emergence of the *Regnum Scottorum*," p. 143.

ing beasts would refer to those who had collaborated in the expulsion of the Columban monks. In any case, no matter who the intended recipient of the message was, the warning conveyed by the left side of the vine seems clear and is reinforced by the iconology of the figural composition.

Like the inhabited vine-scroll, the so-called hunt scene on the Hilton of Cadboll cross-slab also displays characteristics that make it unique, even though parallels for the individual components can be found elsewhere. For example, a sort of rudimentary perspective has been used to portray the central pair of horse riders as well as the two trumpeters to their right. While this technique of placing figures in a receding plane is particular to Pictish sculpture, it can be seen on several monuments at Meigle and at Fowlis Wester, all of which feature superimposed horse riders.[48] The Pictish cross-slab Aberlemno 3 also features a pair of trumpeters, though they are not carved in high relief as are the Hilton of Cadboll pair.[49] Stylistically, the flowing drapery of the trumpeters on the Hilton of Cadboll slab bears a close resemblance to that of the figure of David on the St. Andrews Sarcophagus and Isabel Henderson has argued that both the Aberlemno and Hilton of Cadboll trumpeters are "cuts" from a missing panel of the sarcophagus which featured a scene of David and his musicians.[50] This scene in turn is thought to have been inspired by a miniature of the same subject contained on folio 30v of the Vespasian Psalter.[51] The fact that trumpeters are included at all within a configuration of a hunt scene makes the Hilton of Cadboll scene somewhat unusual, though not completely without parallel, as the Aberlemno 3 trumpeters also herald a hunt. What makes the Hilton "hunt-scene" truly singular is the very prominent position of the female rider.

While female figures can be positively identified on five Pictish monuments which also display the Virgin and Child, only four other cross-slabs or carved fragments depict figures which may be women within secular scenes.[52] The most intriguing of these is on Meigle 1, which not only fea-

---

48. See Hicks, *Animals in Early Medieval Art*, p. 153, for a discussion of this carving technique. See Allen and Anderson, *Early Christian Monuments of Scotland*, 2: figs. 306, 311B, 318C and 344, for Meigle 2:10, and 26, and Fowlis Wester 2:1.

49. See Allen and Anderson, *Early Christian Monuments of Scotland*, 2: fig. 228B.

50. Isabel Henderson, "David Cycle," pp. 91–92, 103–5, 107.

51. London, British Library, MS Cotton Vespasian A.1, fol. 30v. See *Insular Manuscripts*, ed. Alexander, pl. 146.

52. See Allen and Anderson, *Early Christian Monuments of Scotland*, 2: fig. 261 (Brechin 1), figs. 397A and 404 (Iona 1 and 10), and fig. 410 (Kildalton), for examples of the Virgin with the Christ child. Kingoldrum 1, (fig. 238) Kirriemuir 1(fig. 239b), and Monfieth 2 (fig. 242B), all feature figures that possibly can be identified as women.

tures a hunt scene and a mirror and comb symbol as does the Hilton of Cadboll composition but also depicts a mounted figure in the lower left-hand corner of the hunt scene who is "enthroned" on a horse in much the same manner as the Hilton of Cadboll lady.[53] Definitive identification of the Meigle figure as a woman is impossible, but the unusual shape of the head hints at an elaborate headdress such as that worn by the Virgin identified on Brechin 3, so it is entirely possible that the Meigle scene also portrays a holy woman, albeit one within a secular context. However, even if this figure is female, she is not portrayed in the central position of the scene as is the Hilton of Cadboll lady. This focus upon the female, as well as the presence of the trumpeters, are integral to the interpretation of the Hilton of Cadboll composition, and it will be seen that these modifications to a standard hunt scene convey a multilayered message that complements the unique depiction of the vine-scroll.

As noted above, the vine was used as a symbol of royalty as well as a religious symbol, and, therefore, integrates well with the most common interpretation assigned to Pictish hunt scenes: that of a realistic portrayal of the secular elite. At the same time, these scenes have been understood as an allegory for the pagan "divine hunt" or as a Christian allegory of the soul, wherein the deer represents either the soul or Christ persecuted by devils in the shape of the hounds and huntsmen, or the deer represents Christ and salvation pursued by the Christian soul.[54] The presence of the woman and the trumpeters on the Hilton of Cadboll stone, however, means that an even more specific and layered interpretation is possible.

To begin with, the presence of a large penannular brooch on the lady's chest almost assuredly guarantees her noble or royal status, if not her precise identity.[55] As it is possible that the Tarbat monastic estate enjoyed noble or even royal patronage, and as the Hilton of Cadboll site was most likely connected in some manner to the Tarbat monastery, it is probable that the Hilton lady is a portrait of a high-status female who donated generously to the church.

---

53. See Allen and Anderson, *Early Christian Monuments of Scotland*, 2: fig. 310B.

54. See Miranda Green, *Animals in Celtic Life and Myth*, pp. 52–65, for a discussion of artistic representations of the "divine hunt." See Alcock, "Image and Icon," pp. 232–33, and Carrington, "David Imagery," pp. 153–57, for the Christian interpretations of hunt scenes.

55. See Nieke, "Penannular and Related Brooches," pp. 132–33, and Foster, *Picts, Gaels and Scots*, pp. 64–66, for the significance, production, and use of brooches in the insular world. Sutherland, *In Search of the Picts*, p. 187, provides a short survey of the various identities assigned to the Hilton of Cadboll lady, the most popular being a Pictish queen who thus "proves" that the Picts traced their royal line through the female side.

The relationship between this royal lady and the monastic estate might be even closer than just mere patronage, however, it may have extended to directorship of the monastic estate at Tarbat, or even to a sister-house for nuns at Hilton of Cadboll. Monastic double houses were a particularly popular institution in Northumbria, and, though not prolific, also existed in Ireland. The majority of these houses were founded and governed by rich and noble ladies who, for various reasons, had abandoned the world, and sometimes even a previous marriage, to become "Brides of Christ."[56] It is therefore possible that the lady on the Hilton of Cadboll stone is a portrait of a new, royal abbess. That this abbess may have been considered a living saint is, perhaps, suggested by the recessed panel carved behind her head which may be meant to represent a square halo. According to early medieval iconography the square halo signified a very holy person who was still alive but had been "sainted" by popular acclaim.[57] Combined with the lady's "enthroned" position on the horse, a feature usually reserved for depictions of the Virgin and Child, as on the Ruthwell monument, it is very likely that this portrait was expressing the local reverence felt for this woman.

The presence of the trumpeters and the shadowy male figure located behind the lady add further layers of meaning to this portrait. Both of these elements suggest a celebratory procession like a marriage ceremony rather than a simple hunt scene. If this is true then several different, though complementary, interpretations can be considered. Although the procession may commemorate an actual historical wedding between two noble secular persons, in view of the prominence of the female, her "enthroned" position, and the possible square halo, it seems more likely that the wedding being celebrated is a spiritual one, such as the "marriage" between an abbess and the Church when she becomes the "Bride of Christ." In either case, the image of a wedding functioned as a religious allegory for the Second Coming and the Day of Judgment, an idea found throughout the Bible and exegesis.[58] In the minds of the early church fathers, marriage

---

56. Godfrey, "Place of the Double-Monastery," pp. 344–50.

57. Fisher, *Square Halo*, p. 93. A square halo can be seen illuminating the head of Theodora Episcopa, the mother of Pope Paschal, portrayed alongside Mary and Saints Prassede and Prudenziana in a ninth-century mosaic from the San Zeno chapel in the Church of Saint Prassede, Rome. A square halo also decorates the head of Pope John VII (705–7) in an early eighth-century mosaic fragment from his oratory in the Vatican.

58. See Luke 12:35–37, 14:16-24, and Matt. 22:2–14, 25:1–13, for the parables of the Wise and Foolish Virgins and the wedding feast thrown by the rich man for his son.

was a powerful symbol, not only of an earthly union but of the sacred covenant between Christ and the community of believers, while the ceremony
itself was equated with entrance into the kingdom of heaven and the Last
Judgment.[59] For instance, Augustine connects the parables of the Wedding
Feast (Luke 14:16–24 and Matt. 22:2–14) and the Wise and Foolish Virgins
(Matt. 25:1–13) to the account of the Marriage of the Lamb (Rev. 19:6–9),
stressing the necessity of preparation and constant vigilance in order to
enter heaven.[60] Likewise, both Augustine and Bede equate the Bride of
Revelation to an ideal Church stripped clean of its heresies and schismatic
practices, and ready for the Holy Union with Christ.[61]

Most important to the interpretation of the trumpeters in the Hilton of
Cadboll scene is Bede's emphasis on the presence of trumpets at the marriage of the Lamb. In his commentary *On the Apocalypse*, Bede provides a
redaction of Rev. 19:6, which describes the heavenly joy at the marriage of
the Lamb. The Vulgate version of this verse reads "Et audiui quasi uocem
turbae magnos et quasi uocem aquarum multarum et sicut uocem toni-
truorum magnorum dicentium: Alleluia." Bede's rendition of this verse
is the same except for one important detail: he substitutes the Vulgate's
turbae (multitude) with *tubae* (trumpets).[62] Thus his version reads "Then
I heard what seemed to be the voice of many trumpets . . ." Bede's use of
trumpets, rather than a multitude of voices raised in praise, may have been
intended to refer back to Rev. 8:2 which states "Et uidi septem Angelos
stantes in conspectu Dei: et datae sunt illi septem tubae." In his commentary on this verse, Bede wrote:

> Et uidi septem Angelos stantes in conspectu Dei: et datae sunt illis septem
> tubae. . . . . cuius prima tuba communem impiorum in igne et grandine
> designat interitum, secunda propulsum de ecclesia diabolum . . . tertia
> hereticos ecclesia decidentes sanctae scripturae flumina corrumpentes,
> quarta falsorum fratrum in sidertum obscuratione defectum, quinta
> maiorem hereticorum infestationem tempus antichristi praecurrentium,
> sexta apertum et suorum contra ecclesium bellum . . . septima diem
> iudicii quo mercedem dominus suis redditurus et exterminaturus est eos
> qui corrupterunt terram.

---

59. See for instance Cyprian, *Testimoniorum libri tres adversus Judaeos*, 3.2.19. *PL* 4:713–14.

60. Augustine, *Sermone* 90.22.1–14, *PL* 38:563, and *Sermone* 95.22.1–9, *PL* 38:583–84.

61. Augustine, *De doctrina christiana*, ed. Martin, 1.16.15 lines 1–8. Bede, *Expositio Apocalypseos*, ed. Gryson, p. 33 lines 76–77, and p. 37 lines 5–18.

62. Bede, *Expositio Apocalypseos*, ed. Gryson, p. 33 lines 67–72; *Explanation of the Apocalypse*, ed. and trans. Marshall, pp. 129, 145 for a discussion of the traditions Bede may have
been following in his choice of *tubae* over *turbae*.

(And then I saw the seven angels standing before God: and seven trumpets
were given to them. . . . The first trumpet denotes the common destruction of the ungodly in the fire and hail, the second, the expulsion of the
devil from the Church . . . ; the third, the falling away of heretics from the
Church and their corruption of the streams of Holy Scripture; the fourth,
the defection of false brethren; the fifth, the greater hostility of heretics,
the precursers of the time of the Antichrist; the sixth, the open war of
the Antichrist and his own against the church . . . ; the seventh, the day of
judgement, in which the Lord is to render to His own their reward, and
to exterminate those who have corrupted the earth.)[63]

Bede does not make the connection between the two passages explicit, but
scenes of Christ with trumpet-blowing angels were standard in representations of the Second Coming dating back to the earliest church, and it
seems reasonable to assume that his decision to include trumpeters at the
celebration of the marriage of the Lamb was a conscious evocation of the
Second Coming and the Day of Judgment.[64]

As a final consideration of the visual allusions contained within the
Hilton of Cadboll cross-slab, Bede's commentary In Abbacuc also draws together the metaphor of the barren vine and the parable of the Wise and
Foolish Virgins to further warn his readers of the coming Day of Judgment.
Immediately after explaining why the fruits of the vine had withered for
the Jews and how Jesus had been given vinegar, rather than the wine that
he had requested, Bede writes: "This is why at the hour of final retribution
it [the general mass of the wicked] is going to bring extinguished lamps
and together with its darkness, is to be precluded from entry into its heavenly homeland."[65]

CONCLUSION

It can be seen, therefore, that if one is to interpret the "hunt scene" on the
Hilton of Cadboll cross-slab as the depiction of a wedding ceremony, then
a whole range of biblical and exegetical references are called to mind. As
the most prominent figure in the composition, the lady can be seen as a

63. Bede, *Expositio Apocalypseos*, ed. Gryson, 11, lines 1–14; Bede, *Explanation of the Apoca-lypse*, ed. and trans. Marshall, p. 56.

64. Veelenturf, *Dia Brátha*, pp. 73–74.

65. "Propter quod tempore ultimae retributionis extinctas ad latura lampades, et cum suis tenebris ab ingressu est patriae caelestis excludenda." Bede, *In Tobiam*, ed. Hurst and Hudson, 3. 17–18 lines 704–6. English translation in Bede, *On Tobit*, ed. and trans. Connolly, p. 92.

Bride; either in terms of dedicating her life to Christ as an anchoress or on a more esoteric level as the Bride of Revelation, signifying the Holy Church purged of its heresies and evil influences and prepared for union with the Bridegroom, Christ. In and of itself, the wedding ceremony evokes the idea of the marriage of the Lamb as well as the Second Coming and the Last Judgment, an allegory made even clearer by the presence of the trumpeters and by the left side of the vine-scroll ornament which features starving, choking beasts and a barren vine.

It should be obvious by now that the images on the Hilton cross-slab work on many levels and can convey several meanings simultaneously. It is impossible to determine at this point which of these meanings might have been intended and who, exactly, the original audience may have been. It is quite likely that the different levels of meaning were accessed by different groups. I would like to suggest, however, that taken as a whole the primary message being conveyed is that of a covenant being made. Whether through the contrast of the left "barren" vine and the right "fruitful" vine and all of their attendant conflations of meaning, or whether through the Eucharistic symbolism of the vine-scroll in general, the reference is to the New Covenant made through Christ. The figural scene, with its prominent display of the female rider, complements this reading. Whether she is a portrait of a secular, possibly royal patroness or a new religious leader, or whether the scene is a depiction of a literal or figural wedding celebration, the message is also one of a new covenant, or a new direction taken, along with a warning of the Last Judgment to dissuade those who persist in the old ways. The question remains as to what, exactly, for the Picts on the Tarbat peninsula, the old and new ways might have been, and with whom this new covenant was being made. At present, the evidence seems to point most strongly to an alliance with the Columban church, but the possibility of a Northumbrian connection, particularly with York, must still be considered and will certainly be investigated further.

Petitionary Poetry in Old English and Early Welsh: *Deor, Widsið, Dadolwch Urien*

David N. Klausner

For at least the last half century, the canonical reading of *Deor* has been that the poem represents a form of Christian consolation, a sort of "bardic Boethius," in which a poet (who may or may not be fictitious) consoles himself for the loss of his position and patronage by rehearsing some of the stories from his stock in which suffering similar to his own has eventually turned to good.[1] A few scholars have, over the years, suggested with some temerity that there may be more to the poem than this. In the late 1960s, Norman Eliason proposed reading *Deor* as a begging poem, a suggestion that has not met with much favor and has been described as "fanciful."[2] More recently, Nicholas Jacobs has raised the possibility of reading *Deor* in the light of the early Welsh poem *Dadolwch Urien*, attributed to Taliesin, though his comparison stopped with the observation that "it is possible to connect its form and function with the *dadolwch* or reconciliation-poem."[3] Frederick Biggs has argued that the Old English poem contains an implicit threat to reveal the name of the patron who has abandoned Deor and should thus be read as a "blame" poem,[4] presumably in the light of traditions of satire. Neil Isaacs notes, not without irony, that given the ambiguity of much of *Deor*'s detail, critics have tended to rely on the interaction of theme and structure to provide useful material. "The consistency of each

---

My most extensive contact with Helen Damico has been through the Medieval Academy of America's Committee on Centers and Regional Associations, where we meet primarily as administrators. I have long been in awe of Helen's administrative skills, and most of my successes at getting blood from a stone have been based on what I have learned from her. Helen, I'm happy to be able to offer this tidbit in grateful thanks for all your advice and help.

1. The principal sources for this interpretation are Markland, "Boethius, Alfred and *Deor*"; Whitbread, "Pattern of Misfortune"; Bolton, "Boethius, Alfred, and *Deor* Again." More recently, Anne Klinck has supported this reading: "If the exact significance of Deor's various *exempla* is obscure, the aim of the poem is clear: it is a consolation" (*Old English Elegies*, p. 45).

2. Eliason, "Two Old English Scop Poems"; Eliason, "Deor—a Begging Poem?"; Jacobs, "Old English Heroic Tradition"; this article first appeared in Welsh as a chapter in *Astudiaethau ar yr Hengerdd*, ed. Bromwich and Jones.

3. Jacobs, "Old English Heroic Tradition," p. 19.

4. Biggs, "Deor's Threatened 'Blame Poem.'"

interpretation supported by the form is striking," he notes, "equally striking is the lack of agreement in interpretation of theme."[5]

None of these alternative readings of *Deor* has found much favor, and
yet I remain struck by the feeling that there is more to the poem than
the canonical reading allows; that a contemporary audience would have
seen without difficulty things that remain opaque to us. While there is no
question that the element of consolation does exist in the poem, such a
bare reading seems to me superficial, for it leaves a number of questions
unanswered. The "consolation" reading is based on the assumption that
the brief "refrain" which appears six times in the poem—"Þæs ofereode,
þisses swa mæg" (That has passed over, so may this)—is central to the
poem's meaning. This reading will frequently ignore the problem that the
precise referents for both *þæs* and *þisses* are not entirely clear in every case,
nor does it explain the curious distribution of narrative material in the
first five sections—two from closely related Germanic legend, one from
International Popular Tale (to use Kenneth Jackson's term), and two from
what seem to be historical sources. Nor does it explain in the final section
whether the word *deor* is a personal name and, if so, whether it is intended
to represent the poet of the poem or a fictional voice. Finally, it is not clear
whether invoking the name of Heorrenda, the name of a poet known from
Germanic legend, is intended to provide sufficient allusive material for the
audience to be able to identify the court of Deor's patron.

In other words, *Deor* remains a problem poem. The alternative readings
of *Deor* that have been proposed over the past thirty-five years or so have
each focused on the possibility of placing the poem in a more or less well-
defined genre (begging, reconciliation, blame) other than consolation. I
will argue that in each of these cases, the generic positioning is unconvinc-
ing because the new genre has been too narrowly defined. In each case,
while some aspects of the poem do fit with the proposed genre, the poem
as a whole does not. I will propose that more sense can be made of *Deor* by
considering it as an example of what I will call "petitionary poetry," a genre
which becomes extremely common in Welsh poetry of the later Middle
Ages, but of which we have relatively few survivors from the period of Old
English and the Welsh *hengerdd* poetry.

I would define petitionary poetry as poetry written with the purpose—
explicit or implicit—of extracting something from a patron. What is being
asked for can be concrete (money, goods, animals) or abstract (friendship,

---

5. Isaacs, *Structural Principles*, p. 108.

safe passage, pardon, a position). Before looking at the way in which several poems from the pre-Norman period might fit into such a classification, I would like to consider briefly the petitionary poem in later Welsh poetry. The type first becomes common in the poetry of the *cywyddwyr* in the later fourteenth and early fifteenth centuries, when it is often call *canu gofyn*, or "request poem." There are many examples: Huw Pennal (mid-fifteenth century) asks for a greyhound from his patron, Dafydd ap Rhys; Rhys Goch Eryri (fl. 1385–1448) requests a dagger from a smith.[6] Tudur Penllyn (ca. 1420–ca.1485) wrote several *cywyddau gofyn*, making requests for a black bull, a cow, a hunting dog, and a horse.[7] Through the fifteenth century these "request" poems become more and more common, and I would see them as a late and somewhat debased aspect of the petitionary poem. By the early sixteenth century, such requests have clearly become a sufficiently common complaint concerning the bardic order that their nuisance value is formally recognized with a regulation in the Statute of Gruffudd ap Cynan. This text (which has nothing to do with the historical Gruffudd ap Cynan, ca. 1050–1137) likely derives from a bardic gathering, or *eisteddfod*, held in Caerwys, Flintshire, in 1523. Its purpose was to reform the bardic order by instituting a minimum series of pedagogical requirements for attaining a set series of bardic levels or degrees, as well as providing regulations for the governance of poets. One of these regulations reads, "Also, it is by this statute commanded . . . that there shall not be a poet who makes a poem to ask for a horse or a greyhound or any such outstanding treasure without the permission of the owner."[8] It is clear from

---

6. Huw Pennal's "Cywydd i ofyn milgi du" is printed in *Cywyddau Dafydd ap Gwilym a'e Gyfoeswyr*, ed. Williams and Roberts, pp. 160–62, where it is attributed to Llywelyn Goch ap Meurig Hen. On the more likely attribution to Huw, see *Gwaith Llywelyn Goch ap Meurig Hen*, ed. Johnston, p. 10. Rhys Goch Eryri's poem "I'r Faslart" is in *Cywyddau Iolo Goch ac Eraill*, ed. Henry Lewis, Roberts, and Williams, pp. 327–29.

7. Tudur Penllyn's poems are in *Gwaith Tudur Penllyn ac Ieuan ap Tudur Penllyn*, ed. Thomas Roberts, pp. 54–60. These examples represent only a few of the large number of surviving poems. The genre of *canu gofyn* has recently been discussed in detail by Huws, *Canu Gofyn*. By Huws's count (pp. 3–6), there are about 187 examples of *canu gofyn* surviving from the period between 1350 and 1500, and about 433 from the period between 1500 and 1630. Huws also provides a list of poets involved in the composition of *canu gofyn*, as well as a list of objects requested (pp. 227–34). See also Bachellery "La poésie de demande." This article, which was found among Prof. Bachellery's papers after his death, indicates that he had planned a comprehensive study of *canu gofyn*.

8. "Hevyd yddydys Trwy yr ystatus honn . . . a wnel kerdd i erchi march nev vilgi nev gyvryw anwyldlws nodedic heb gennad y perchennoc . . . " "Statud Gruffudd ap Cynan," ed. Klausner, lines 110, 114–15 (Welsh text); lines 130, 139–41 (English text).

this regulation that by the early sixteenth century the petitionary poem as a mode of importuning a patron had become sufficiently problematic to require control; in essence, the rule permits petitionary poems only in cases where the patron has already agreed to the gift or boon.

This is, of course, the very end of the tradition, and it is with its earliest examples that I am primarily concerned. Before returning to *Deor,* let us consider two other poems that might fit into such a grouping. The first of these is the early Welsh poem attributed to the late sixth-century poet Taliesin, *Dadolwch Urien.*[9] The poem survives in the early fourteenth-century anthology "The Book of Taliesin" (now Aberystwyth, National Library of Wales, MS Peniarth 2), an extremely miscellaneous collection which, along with religious, prophetic, gnomic, and mythological poetry, includes an elegy for Hercules and a considerable body of poetry connected with Taliesin. Much of this derives from the legendary figure of Taliesin as prophetic shapeshifter, but twelve bardic poems deal with heroes of the sixth century. Nine of these appear to come from the court of Urien Rheged, whose area of influence seems to have covered a considerable part of northwest Britain and southwest Scotland.[10] One of these is described in the manuscript rubric as *Dadolwch Uryen.* The noun *dadolwch* is compounded from *dad* + *golwch,* where the primary element is a verbal noun with the range of meaning 'praise, worship, pray, call, seek, beg, crave, implore' and the prefix is essentially a negative, equivalent to such forms as 'un-', 'dis-', 're-', or 'retro-'.[11] The compound, thus, has a significant range of meaning. It can mean to make amends or provide satisfaction for a wrong; it is often the word used in sacramental contexts for penance or expiation of sins, in which context it can also mean worship, prayer, or supplication. Finally, by extension from the first meaning, it can mean reconciliation. In the context of the relationship between a poet and his patron, the meanings which require a religious context seem unlikely to be productive; we are left then with the related concepts of reconciliation or making amends for a wrong.

---

9. Taliesin's historicity rests primarily on the *Historia Brittonum* in which Ida's foundation of Bernicia around 547 is glossed with the note, "Tunc Talhaern Tataguen in poemate claruit; et Neirin, et Taliessin, et Bluchbard, et Cian, qui vocatur Gueinth Guaut, simul uno tempore in poemate britannico claruerunt." "Nennius," *British History and the Welsh Annals,* ed. and trans. John Morris, p. 78. The poem is no. ix in *Poems of Taliesin,* ed. Ifor Williams, English version by J. E. Caerwyn Williams, p. 11.

10. See *Gododdin of Aneirin,* ed. Koch, esp. pp. xv, xxiii–xxv. Urien is cited in the *Historia Brittonum* as one of four Welsh rulers who fought against Theodric of Bernicia (572–79) (*British History and the Welsh Annals,* ed. John Morris, p. 79).

11. *Geiriadur Prifysgol Cymru,* s.v. "dad-," "dadolwch," "golwch."

These meanings do seem to fit the poem, although the precise wrong for which Taliesin is making amends is not entirely clear. Because the poem is less well known than the Old English poems I will be discussing, I quote the whole of it here:

Lleuuyd echassaf
vryen a gyrchaf.
pan del vygwaessaf.
Ar parth goreuhaf
Nyt mawr ym dawr byth
Nyt af attadunt
Ny chyrchaf i gogled
kyn pei am lawered
Nyt reit im hoffed.
Lloyfenyd tired
Ys meu y gwyled.
ys meu y delideu
med o uualeu
gan teyrn goreu.
Teyrned pop ieith
Ragot yt gwynir
kyt ef mynasswn
Nyt oed well a gerwn.
weithon y gwelaf
Namyn y duw vchaf
Dy teyrn veibon
wy kanan eu hyscyrron

mi nyw dirmygaf.
Jdaw yt ganaf.
kynnwys a gaffaf.
ydan eilassaf.
gweheleith a welaf.
ganthunt ny bydaf.
ar meiteyrned.
y gwnelwn gyghwystled.
Vryen nym gomed.
ys meu eu reufed.
ys meu y llared.
ae gorefrasseu
a da dieisseu
haelaf rygigleu.
it oll yd ynt geith.
ys dir dy oleith.
gweyhelu henwn
kyn ys gwybydwn.
y meint a gaffaf.
nys dioferaf.
haelaf dynedon.
yn tired eu galon.

Ac yny vallwyf i hen
ym dygyn agheu aghen
ny bydaf yn dirwen
na molwyfi vryen.

(I will not abandon the greatest leader, I will go to Urien, I'll sing to him. When my surety comes I'll get a welcome in the very best place, under the chieftain. It doesn't make much difference to me what princes I see; I won't go to them, I won't stay with them, I won't head for the kinglets in the north. Though it would mean much to me to settle things with him, I don't need to boast—Urien won't refuse me. The lands of Llwyfenydd, mine are their riches, mine their bounty, mine their generosity, mine their materials and their luxuries; mead from horns and goods without lack with the best king, the most generous I've heard of. The princes of all peoples are all bound to you; they complain about you and stay out of your way. Although I wanted to jest at the old man, there is no one I love better since I have known him, now I see how much I have received. I will not give him up except to the highest God. Your princely sons, most generous of men, sing their songs in the lands of their enemies. And until I fail from age, in the sore need of death, I will not be happy unless I am praising Urien.)

Taliesin begins by announcing that he will not (never?) abandon the greatest of leaders, he will avoid minor kings and will sing (only?) to Urien, since under him (in his entourage?) is the very best place to be. Taliesin's forthright praise seems somewhat undercut by his admission that he will do all this when his *gwaessaf* comes. This legal term can mean either a guarantor or a guarantee, and seems in this context to indicate that Urien remains, for Taliesin, unapproachable without some kind of safe passage. The poet seems to be involved in a subtle balancing act between self-abasement and self-promotion; claiming that though it would mean a great deal to him to make a settlement (*cynghwystl*), he has no need to boast, since Urien will not deny (or refuse) him.

In a passage that takes the formulaic praise of the patron's generosity to new extremes, Taliesin claims for himself the riches of Urien's lands. The sense of the passage is hyperbolic, even by bardic standards. This is followed by a curious claim that appears to be an implicit apology for jesting at or mocking Urien, an act that was abandoned on the realization that it would cost Taliesin his place. The verbal noun *gweyhelu* seems to be derived from *gwïal* 'twig, rod'; Ifor Williams suggests that it means much the same as the phrase *bwrw llyskyon idaw* 'to throw twigs at' or 'to strike with a rod' in *Peredur*, where the sense of the idiom is "mock" or "jest at."[12] This slightly complicates the reading of the poem: just what has Taliesin done to offend his patron? Lines 5–7 suggest that the offense is composing praise poetry to other princes, the *meiteyrned* in the north of line 6, but the implicit apology of lines 17–19 gives the distinct impression that he has (also?) insulted Urien in some way. The object of the mockery is a *henwn*, an old man, so if this does refer to Urien (as I think it must) his age may well have been the subject of the jest. The poem concludes with the poet claiming that only God will separate him and his patron, and an elegant prophecy of the military success of his sons. The quatrain that follows is a sort of "refrain" that is appended to seven of Taliesin's nine surviving Urien poems. They are rather different from the repeated line in *Deor*, since they occur at the end of each poem, and are immediately clear in their meaning, demonstrating none of the ambiguities encoded in *Deor*'s refrain.

---

12. *Poems of Taliesin*, ed. Ifor Williams, p. 111; *Historia Peredur vab Efrawc*, ed. Goetinck, p. 12, line 24.

The *dadolwch* can best be read as a poem of apology, in which the poet asks for reconciliation and reinstatement to his former position. He also asks, implicitly, for a surety or safe passage which will allow him access to his patron. Although the poem does not make explicit requests or demands of the patron, these are strongly enough set out to make the reading reasonably clear.

As a form, the *dadolwch* appears with some frequency in the poetry of the *gogynfeirdd*, the court poets of the twelfth and thirteenth centuries. Llywelyn Fardd (fl. 1150–1175) apologized to his patron Owain Fychan asking for a return to his favor after having accused him of adultery.[13] Cynddelw Brydydd Mawr (fl. 1155–1200), the greatest of the twelfth-century poets, wrote two *dadolwch* poems to The Lord Rhys, and Einion Wan (fl. 1230–45) wrote one to Dafydd, the son of Llywelyn ap Iorwerth (Llywelyn the Great).[14] In addition, there are a number of *canu gofyn* poems by the court poets. Llywarch ap Llywelyn (known as Prydydd y Moch, fl. 1173–1220) wrote to his patron, Madog ap Gruffudd Maelor, asking for a healing cure, and two poems by Hywel Foel (ca. 1240–1300) to Llywelyn ap Gruffudd ask for the release of Owain Goch ap Gruffudd (Llywelyn's brother) from imprisonment.[15]

There is no question, then, that the genre of petitionary poetry, in which I would include both *dadolwch* and *canu gofyn*, was well established in early Wales. Our sole example among the pre-Conquest poetry is Taliesin's poem to Urien Rheged; there are numerous examples from the court poetry of the twelfth and thirteenth centuries, and the genre becomes increasingly common through the fourteenth and fifteenth centuries by the end of which it has become a sufficient nuisance that the *eisteddfod* of 1523 attempted to institute regulations to control the practice.

What relevance might these Welsh poems have to the surviving Old English materials? The answer is not entirely clear, but I believe this is because the Old English poems tend to be more subtle in their petitioning, quite possibly because the concept of making such requests in the context of a poem to a patron (or potential patron) was less well established in the

---

13. *Gwaith Llywelyn Fardd I ac Eraill*, ed. Owen et al., pp. 44–53.

14. *Gwaith Cynddelw Brydydd Mawr II*, ed. Nerys Ann Jones and Ann Owen; *Gwaith Dafydd Benfras ac Eraill*, ed. Peredur Lynch et al.

15. *Gwaith Llywarch ap Llywelyn*, ed. Elin Jones; *Gwaith Bleddyn Fardd ac Eraill*, ed. Brynley Roberts et al. Llywelyn imprisoned his brother from 1255 to 1277. Édouard Bachellery, not having the advantage of the fine modern editions of the court poets in the *Cyfres Beirdd y Tywysogion*, concluded that for this period, "Si des poèmes de demande ont été chantés alors, ils ne nous ont pas été conservés" ("La poésie de demande," p. 289).

culture. *Widsið* is the first poem I would like to consider for admission to the group. The possibility that *Widsið* might be a "begging poem" was first put forward in 1945 by W. H. French, and was then elaborated some twenty years later by Norman Eliason.[16] This interpretation has more recently been taken up by Ray Brown, and it is principally with his discussion that I wish to engage.[17]

First, it would be well to clarify what we do know about *Widsið*, since so many things in the poem are lacking in clarity. There is, I think, no question that the poem is very highly structured, very likely with the use of elaborate symmetry, centered around the three lists—or *thulas* as Kemp Malone called them—of peoples, places, and kings of which the poet knows or whom he has visited.[18] This structure has been described most convincingly by David Howlett, who outlines a complex and symmetrical structure in which the poem is divided into three fits, each containing one *thula*; fits one and three each open with an exordium and close with two narrative episodes, fit one dealing with Western heroes, fit three with Eastern heroes. The *thula* of fit two is framed by a prelude and postlude on minstrelsy, and the whole poem is framed by a prologue and epilogue which discuss the poet himself and the concept of kingship (with the order reversed in the epilogue). The number of lines in each section is very similar, though not entirely symmetrical; Howlett would also propose omitting the contested lines 79 and 82–84, which deal with British (Picts and Scots) and biblical peoples (Israelites, Assyrians, Hebrews, Egyptians, Medes, Persians, and either Indians or Jews).[19] This elaborate structure implies, I think, a single highly sophisticated author, though much of the material may well have been traditional.

A second important point is that the character/poet Widsið, whose name means either 'far-traveler/journey' or 'vast experience' (a suggestion made by Brown), is without question fictitious.[20] This has been noted frequently, since from both a temporal and spatial point of view attendance at

---

16. French, "*Widsith* and the Scop"; Eliason, "Two Old English Scop Poems"; Eliason, "Deor—a Begging Poem?".

17. Ray Brown, "Begging Scop."

18. The term *þula* derives from Old Norse/Icelandic sources, and is not attested in Old English, though it may perhaps be related to the word *þyle* used in Beowulf (lines 1165b, 1456b) to describe Unferth; Ray Brown, "Begging Scop," p. 281; *Widsith*, ed. Malone, p. 3. See also Donovan, this volume.

19. Howlett, "Form and Genre."

20. On the meaning of the name, see especially Schlauch, "Widsith, Víthförull," p. 969, and Ray Brown, "Begging Scop," p. 289.

all the courts Widsið mentions would be an impossibility. The importance of his fictitious status goes further, however, since it separates the speaker from the author of the poem and indicates that, whatever the apparent purpose of the poem from Widsið's point of view, it need not be the same as the purpose of the real poet. That is, the poem may very well have two purposes, a superficial purpose associated with the fictional speaker, and a deeper purpose—a subtext, perhaps—belonging to the poet.

A third clear fact is that a substantial part of the poem deals with the subject of patronal generosity, and this was the motivating fact behind French's "begging poem" proposal. French presented an outline of the poem, omitting most of the catalogue material of the *thulas*, and Eliason printed this outline in a condensed form.[21] The omission of the lists makes it clear how much of the rest of the poem deals explicitly with the figure of the generous king, listing the things which Widsið has received in much the same way as he lists the courts and peoples he has visited. This praise of patronal generosity is presented both in general terms and as specific examples. The poem is framed with the generalized form: it opens noting of Widsið, "oft he on flette geþah / mynelicne maþþum" (often on the floor of the hall he had received a memorable treasure [lines 3b–4a]) and closes with the observation that Widsið has always been able to find a patron who is "gydda gleawne, geofum unhneawne" (discerning about songs, unmiserly of gifts [line 139]), perhaps emphasizing the importance of the link between poetry and patronage in the rhyme.[22] The body of the poem cites specific examples of such generosity, including Guðhere, who gave the poet a "glædlicne maþþum / songes to leane" (a bright treasure in payment for a song [lines 66b–67a]) and Ælfwine, who had a "heortan unhneaweste hringa gedales" (an unmiserly heart in the giving of rings [line 73]). The climactic example of generosity is Earmanric,

se me beag forgeaf,   burgwarena fruma,
on þam siex hund wæs   smætes goldes,
gescyred sceatta   scillingrime . . . (lines 90–93)

(he, the city-dwellers' lord, gave me a ring in which there was the value of six hundred pieces of pure gold, counted in shillings . . .)

---

21. French, "*Widsith* and the Scop," p. 624; Eliason, "Two Old English Scop Poems," p. 188.

22. All quotations from the poem are taken from *Exeter Book*, ed. Krapp and Dobbie, pp. 149–53.

Again, we must separate the poet from Widsið, the fictional *scop*. Widsið's "begging" is in the past, then, and is exemplary in its purpose. These examples presented of patronal generosity are also useful to the poet, since his purpose is also petitionary. What is he asking for? The answer to this question formed the principal difference between French's and Eliason's readings of the poem, with Eliason suggesting that the descriptions of gift-giving in the poem are purposefully hyperbolic, the poet using "the well-known begging dodge of asking for the moon in the hope of getting a cheeseparing."[23] He has, I think, misunderstood the exemplary nature of these descriptions. Their purpose is not to ask for such things as Widsið has received but to provide a general statement on the pervasive atmosphere of generosity in the courts of kings.

What is the purpose of these statements then, and the lists within which they appear? The fictionality of Widsið and the impossibility of a real poet visiting all the courts he mentions are uncontested, so the purpose of the *thulas* must be something else. They are, I think, the quid pro quo in the poet's petitionary stance. They represent what the poet has to offer in return for a patron's generosity, a list of kings, peoples, and heroes about whom the poet can tell stories; in short, a repertoire list—what Sarah Higley has called "a declaration of poetic prowess."[24] It has frequently been pointed out that *Widsið* is an intensely allusive poem, and that allusive poetry depends on its audience's understanding of the allusions. Such a comment has usually been couched in terms of whether it would be possible for an Anglo-Saxon audience in the tenth century to understand such a wealth of allusion. In the case of *Widsið*, however, the intention of the lists is to tantalize the audience/potential patron with a plethora of possible story-material, and a full understanding of all the allusions can be seen as unnecessary, even counterproductive. What is the poet asking for? Although that is not entirely clear, the most likely answer is a position with the support of a patron. The poem is thus not so much a begging poem, in which the poet asks for gifts, as a resumé in which the poet presents his credentials as a request for a position.

Deor presents us with a similar situation, in which the poem demands to be read on more than one level. On the surface, there is little doubt that the repetition of the line "Þæs ofereode, þisses swa mæg" (lines 7, 13, 17, 20, 27, 42) can be read as consolation, in which the poet rehearses a series

---

23. Eliason, "Two Old English Scop Poems," p. 188.
24. Higley, *Between Languages*, p. 235.

of stories (*þæs*) from a variety of sources as examples of tribulation over-come, leading to his hope that his own present troubles (*þisses*) may simi-larly be overcome.[25] While I think this surface reading is likely intended, it should be noted that it is by no means certain, since it relies on each story dealing with trouble that has passed by, an assumption not entirely war-ranted. The first two sections, dealing with the related stories of Weland and Beadohild, do appear to represent troubles overcome, though in quite different ways—Weland, though hamstrung, escapes from the clutches of Niðhad exacting (on the way) a particularly horrendous revenge. Beado-hild, Niðhad's daughter, weighs two forms of trouble—her brothers' mur-der and her own pregnancy, both thanks to Weland—and finds the latter more problematic.[26] This "trouble" is presumably seen to be overcome in the birth of the hero Wade. The third section is more of a problem, since what evidence we have for the Mæðhild/Geat story does not make it clear that it represents an example of troubles overcome, since one version of the much later surviving story ends tragically.[27] The fourth section, on Ðeo-dric, is even more problematic, since it is neither clear which Theodric is meant, nor whether it is he or the Mærings whom he rules who suffer. With the fifth section we are on rather firmer ground, since most early sources that mention Eormanric (*Widsið* is a notable exception) consider him a tyrant.[28]

One problem that has faced readers of *Deor* is the very range of the nar-rative material to which the poet Deor refers. Interpretations of the poem have been based on the assumption that the stories themselves must repre-sent some structural principle, and that they have been carefully selected

---

25. All quotations from the poem are taken from *Exeter Book*, ed. Krapp and Dobbie, pp. 178–79.

26. This is the usual reading of the first two sections, though Robert Nedoma has pointed out that the range of material referring to Weland in Germanic sources is not clear enough to make it certain in the case of either Weland or Beadohild ("Legend of Way-land").

27. That is, assuming that the two folktale versions of the Magnild/Gauti story collected in the nineteenth century represent the same narrative. These versions are summarized and discussed in *Deor*, ed. Malone, pp. 8–9. A variety of other possibilities have been proposed, and these are outlined and discussed by North, "Jeux d'esprit."

28. The classic example is *Beowulf*, lines 1200–1201, where Hama, who incurred Eor-manric's wrath, "geceas ecne ræd." It is very unlikely that this means (as suggested by Bugge, "Studien über das Beowulfepos," p. 70) that he converted to Christianity and/or entered a monastery, and must essentially mean "he died." On this point, see also Damico, "*Sörlaþáttr* and the Hama Episode," p. 229.

for this purpose.[29] It seems to me far more likely that the primary point of these stories is their very range, and that they represent on the surface examples of trouble overcome, but as a subtext, a display of the poet's range of available material.

This dual reading, as with *Widsið*, assumes that we distinguish clearly between the fictitious poet (Widsið, Deor) in whose voice the poem is presented, and the actual poet, whose motives may be quite different from the fictional motive of the narrator. The fictional characteristics of Deor are enhanced by the first-person presentation of his "present troubles" in the final section. Like Widsið, Deor has a name that is a common noun and is otherwise unattested as a personal name. Like Widsið, it may well be an epithet rather than a name, a possibility which is strengthened by the tense of the verb—"Me *wæs* Deor noma" (Deor *was* my name, line 37b). Deor's place as the *Heodeninga scop* (line 36b) has been taken by Heorrenda, a poet of legendary fame who appears as Hiarrandi in the thirteenth-century Middle High German epic *Kudrun*. On the level of Deor's narrative, both the "refrain" and the overtly Christian musings on the role which God plays in apportioning good and ill become a part of the fictional poet's self-consolation in losing his position to a poet of legendary stature.

On the level of the Anglo-Saxon poet, however, the narrative can be seen quite differently. The broad range of sources for the five narrative "episodes" can be read not as a structural principle—a difficult reading at best, hampered by our ignorance of the details of both the Mæðhild/Geat story and the Ðeodric episode—but as a demonstration of the wide range of the poet's repertoire. The question has frequently been asked whether the poet's audience, that is the audience of the Exeter Book, would themselves have been attuned to the range of allusions in *Deor*. If the narrative references (since they are all far from being full narratives) are intended as a demonstration of repertorial competence—as "teasers"—then this question becomes less important. The poet may well be offering a narrative of which his audience is only dimly or partially aware. But if the primary intent of these allusions is a display of range, then the extent to which they would be within the audience's immediate frame of reference becomes less important than the display itself.

Deor, then, like *Widsið*, can be seen as a petitionary poem. In both cases, the Anglo-Saxon poet presents a dazzling display of narrative material

29. Boren, "Design of the Old English *Deor*."

intended to tantalize a prospective audience or patron. Ray Brown, dealing with *Widsið*, has shown that the poem must be read on two levels. His analysis demonstrates that, while there is certainly a concern with patronal generosity in the poem, the "begging" aspect of the poem must be limited to the fictional Widsið. "Both French and Eliason regard the entire poem as the product of an actual scop, and think that the overall purpose of the poem was to beg, but if this is so, the *Widsith* poet seems a very incompetent beggar."[30] His conclusion is that "[t]here is no reason to assume that, because there is a begging poem *within* the poem, the overall purpose of the poem was to beg."[31] As Brown implies, the poems—both *Widsið* and *Deor*—must be read on two levels. First, on the level of their fictitious narrators, their various purposes seem now well established, *Deor* as a poem of consolation, *Widsið* as a begging poem. It is on the second level, that of the Anglo-Saxon poet, that consensus is lacking. I would suggest that for both of these poems, the purpose is the same and that it involves the demonstration of the poet's competence and of the breadth of his repertoire. In *Widsið* this takes the form of hyperbolic lists of potential narrative material; in *Deor* it is seen in a much more selective list of material drawn from an intentionally wide range of sources. "Begging" is the wrong word for what is happening on this level; the poet does not beg, he presents his credentials in a petitionary stance, hoping only by inference for a position (*Deor*) or remuneration (*Widsið*).

There is no question that there were links between the poetry of the Germanic peoples who settled in England and the Brythonic peoples who preceded them. Centuries of warfare between them had clearly provided the means for some interaction, and the likelihood of "cross-pollination" between Welsh and Old English poetry has been studied by a number of scholars.[32] That there was a mode of poetry in early Britain in which the poet made a request of a patron is also incontestable. By the later fourteenth century such poetry has become common in the form of *canu gofyn*, in which the Welsh poet makes a request for a material object. If we expand the genre to include requests for things immaterial, we can include the

---

30. Ray Brown, "Begging Scop," p. 284.
31. Ray Brown, "Begging Scop," pp. 284–85.
32. Principal among these have been P. L. Henry, *Early English and Celtic Lyric*; Jacobs, "Old English Heroic Tradition"; Sims-Williams, "'Is it fog or smoke or warriors fighting?'"; Higley, *Between Languages*; and various brief articles by Andrew Breeze. See also Klausner, "Topos of the Beasts of Battle"; and Klausner, "Aspects of Time."

earlier *dadolwch*, where the patron is asked for reconciliation or reinstatement to a position of favor. The Anglo-Saxon poems are, for the most part, rather more subtle in their petitionary aspects than are the Welsh poems, and their requests are made implicitly rather than directly. The requests are clearly there, nonetheless, and the linking of these poems in a wider genre of petitionary poetry solves many of the problems in reading them.

Revisiting Anglo-Scandinavian
Settlement and Sculpture

Christopher D. Morris

Introduction

About forty years ago, Rosemary Cramp encouraged me to focus my research interests in Viking studies on questions of the Scandinavian impact on Northumbria. As is sometimes the way of these things, it didn't quite go to plan: some things were completed, others not, and circumstances were such that my research into the Anglo-Scandinavian impact upon northern England occupied less and less of my attention as the years went by. Initially, during the 1970s, I narrowed down onto aspects of settlement as reflected in Anglo-Scandinavian landholding and the study of a particularly important group of stone sculpture in the Tees Valley. Although I traveled part of the way along this road, by the 1980s I had then diverted into aspects of Viking archaeology elsewhere in the British Isles.

In the meantime, Rosemary has published a definitive volume of the *Corpus of Anglo-Saxon Sculpture* for part of this area.[1] The two papers I presented at symposia at Albuquerque and Kalamazoo in 2000 gave me the opportunity to revisit some older themes in my research, by looking at aspects of the Anglo-Scandinavian settlement and sculpture in this important area of northern England. Perhaps this essay—a composite from both symposia—will both repay an old academic debt to Rosemary Cramp and, in part, begin the process of completing some unfinished business! The primary stimulus for my returning to this theme, however, came from Helen Damico, who invited me to contribute both to one of her public symposia at the University of New Mexico's Institute of Medieval Studies and to the sessions at Kalamazoo. This paper, offered to Helen, will firstly revisit some of these older themes at a more general level, and then focus on the relationship of Anglo-Scandinavian sculpture to the evidence for landholding and settlement at estate-centers and vills, ending with a brief look at the remarkable evidence from one particular site in the Tees Valley: Soccaburg or modern-day Sockburn on Tees. It is an inadequate paeon

---

1. Cramp, *Durham and Northumberland.*

of thanks to Helen Damico, doyenne of medieval studies in Albuquerque, whose hospitality to visiting scholars is legendary and much appreciated.

LANDHOLDING AND SETTLEMENT: MONASTIC LANDHOLDING
The starting point for my own study was the realization that the account of the vicissitudes of the Lindisfarne/Chester-le-Street/Durham community estates as recorded in the *Historia de sancto Cuthberto* (hereafter *HSC*), a probable mid-eleventh-century source from within the community, was both an extremely valuable and an underutilized source for our understanding of settlement dynamics in the north of England. Despite nineteenth-century editions,[2] it was not until 1954 that Edmund Craster published an important paper, "The Patrimony of St Cuthbert," detailing the grants.[3] Nevertheless, despite this and the general understanding of the grants of secular (mostly royal) lands to monastic institutions in the Anglo-Saxon period, few people had attempted to visualize what this meant in practice. To my knowledge, at the time only Geoffrey Barrow had even begun to approach this source in such a manner when he mapped the original land grants to Lindisfarne in terms of Norhamshire and Islandshire and reconstructed a further "shire" in Scotland at Yetholm.[4]

My own independent contribution was based upon both a rereading and analysis of the relevant parts of the *HSC* and Craster's previous work; the main object of the exercise was to attempt to map the spatial extent of the Lindisfarne landholdings.[5] As a visual impression of the important role of the monasteries within the overall settlement and economy of Northumbria, this seems to have worked.[6] However, as a health warning now, I

---

2. *Historia de sancto Cuthberto*, ed. Hinde; *Historia de sancto Cuthberto*, ed. Arnold, cited below as *HSC*.

3. Craster, "Patrimony of St Cuthbert."

4. Barrow, "Pre-feudal Scotland," (ch. 1) in his *Kingdom of the Scots*, pp. 7–68, Maps 2 and 5.

5. Christopher Morris, "Northumbria and the Viking Settlement." I should also acknowledge the work of Hart in *Early Charters of Northern England and the Midlands*, who, in editing a range of documents from Northumbria and the northern Danelaw, went over much the same ground. He made a distinction between (a) nineteen "Early Charters of the Northern Counties," of which nine are charters of the Lindisfarne/St. Cuthbert community from the tenth–eleventh centuries preserved in recognizable charter format and (b) records of twenty-eight less formally recorded "Early Northumbrian Monastic Endowments," based essentially upon accounts in the works of Bede, Simeon of Durham, and one or two other sources, of which eighteen referred to the Lindisfarne/St. Cuthbert community.

In the following text, his numbering of the documents will be followed, where possible, cited as Hart no.

6. Christopher Morris, "Northumbria and the Viking Settlement," p. 89; and has been adopted by others, e.g., Higham, *Northern Counties*, fig 7.1, p. 288.

should point out that it is important to note that I was attempting to define spatially and topographically areas of land based upon a particular unit of measure, *terra unius familiae* (OE "hide"), which was never a fixed spatial or topographical unit, but rather a statement of the resource required for utilization and then subsequent support of an idealized group of persons, which could (and did), therefore, vary according to the types of land available and their potential for exploitation. In those terms, all such maps can, to an extent, be legitimately criticized for attempting to define these vague units of measure—even though the boundaries of the exploitation area may well have been defined.[7]

It should be remembered, however, that the context for my own work was an attempt to take discussion of the nature of Viking settlement in Northumbria onto a new base as it was currently mired in a slanging-match between Peter Sawyer and Kenneth Cameron about the interpretation of place-names of Scandinavian origin in England.[8] It never was my intention to study in detail the nature of the Lindisfarne estates per se. In this latter respect, then, it was fortunate that, in the mid-1980s, a very good graduate student, Theodore (Ted) Johnson South, came to Durham and developed this particular area of study under my supervision.[9] As his work gives a clearer chronological analysis of the development of the Lindisfarne landholdings, I shall illustrate this development by referring to his maps for the Viking period (but using document numbers as defined in Hart's volume from 1975).[10]

I am very pleased also to acknowledge that we now also have the benefit of a completely new edition and translation of the *HSC* by Johnson South.[11]

---

7. See Austin, "Late Anglo-Saxon Settlement," p. 202.

8. Cameron, "Scandinavians in Derbyshire"; Cameron, "Scandinavian Place-Names"(ch. 6) in his *English Place-Names*; Cameron, *Scandinavian Settlement*; Cameron, "Scandinavian Settlement . . . Five Boroughs. Part II"; Cameron, "Scandinavian Settlement . . . Five Boroughs, Part III"; Cameron, "Significance of English Place-names," esp. pp. 147–54; Sawyer, "Density of Danish Settlement"; Sawyer, "Danish Settlements" (ch. 7) in his *Age of the Vikings*, pp. 148–76; Sawyer et al., "Two Viking Ages"; Sawyer, "Baldersby, Borup and Bruges"; Sawyer, "Making of the Landscape," (chap. 3) in his *Roman Britain to Norman England*, pp. 132–67; Sawyer, "Medieval English Settlement"; Sawyer, "Conquest and Colonization"; Sawyer, "Conquests and Settlements" (ch. 7) in his *Kings and Vikings*, pp. 98–112, esp. pp. 102–8. See also Fellows-Jensen, "Place-Names Research," esp. pp. 15–18; Fellows-Jensen, "Vikings in England"; Fellows-Jensen, "Place-Names and Settlement History," esp. pp. 4–8.

9. Johnson South, "Toward a Model of Landholdings."

10. Hart, *Early Charters of Northern England and the North Midlands.*

11. Johnson South, "'Historia de Sancto Cuthberto.'" Since this paper was presented, this has been published as *Historia de Sancto Cuthberto: A History of Saint Cuthbert and a Record of His Patrimony.* References to the latter have consequently been added here (cited below as *Historia 2002*).

In this, he has analyzed afresh the primary manuscript sources and come to the conclusion, *contra* Craster, that all three derive from a common exemplar, descending independently (rather than the two from the Bodleian Library and Lincoln's Inn deriving from the third manuscript source— from Cambridge University Library). He also concluded that the archetype was composed from both narrative and cartulary material at Durham, necessarily post-995 and probably sometime between 1031 and ca. 1050.

Amongst the early grants to the Lindisfarne community (essentially in northern Bernicia), is one relating to Cartmel and Gilling:[12] "Hart no. 147. A.D. 685. King Ecgfrith granted lands to St. Cuthbert both at Cartmel 'with all the Britons belonging to it' and also of the vill of *Suth gedluit/Suthgedling* 'with its appurtenances.'"[13]

The only other significant grant outside northern Bernicia before the Viking period was of Gainford (including Wycliffe and Cliffe) and Billingham:[14] "Hart no. 154. A.D. 830 x 845. Bishop Ecgred of Lindisfarne to the church of St. Cuthbert 'in perpetuity' a number of places, including Gainford, the church he had built there, and 'all that pertains to it,' which was then described as being 'from the River Tees to the River Wear, and from the road called "Dere Street" to the hill towards the west, and the land on the other side of the River Tees, 3 miles towards the south, and 6 miles towards the west'; together with the vills of Wycliffe and Cliffe on the Tees; together with Billingham in 'Hartness.'"[15]

However, before any record of alienation of land to the incoming Scandinavians, we have an interesting insight into the internal politics of Northum-

---

12. See Johnson South, "Toward a Model of Landholdings," map I: map of chronological development: 800.

13. This site has been identified as most probably Gilling in the North Riding of Yorkshire [or less possibly Yealand in Cumbria]. Johnson South regards it as "possible, . . . [but] far from certain" (*Historia 2002*, p. 81).

14. See Johnson South, "Toward a Model of Landholdings," Map II: map of chronological development: 850, between pp. 28–29.

15. In this acccount, the named vills were noted by Cyril Hart as later being recorded as part of the "sokeland" of Gilling (*Early Charters of Northern England and the North Midlands*); while Johnson South has suggested (*Historia 2002*, p. 84) that, as Wycliffe and Cliffe lie within the area of Gainford described, the author of the account was putting together two separate sources here. It is also worth noting that an abbot (Edwine or Eda) was apparently buried here in 801 (attributed to Symeon of Durham, *Historia Regum*, ed. Arnold, p. 65, cited below as *HR*), thus suggesting that Gainford already had an ecclesiastical existence prior to Ecgred's church-building. In addition, Austin ("Fieldwork and Excavation at Hart") has suggested that Billingham was originally part of the Hartlepool monastery territory (but offers no explanation as to why it should now have been alienated to Lindisfarne).

bria and the indication that—as in Ireland[16]—monastic estates were subject to alienation by the secular powers: *HSC* § 10 for A.D. 867 records that King Aelle of Northumbria seized Wycliffe, Cliffe, and Billingham from the community of St. Cuthbert. But, thereafter, we get a considerable accrual of lands in Co. Durham and the Tees Valley area over the next century, including a group that relates to territories along the eastern coast south of the River Wear.[17] In this case (as in some other places), we see the entrepreneurial (if not real estate!) facets of the incoming Scandinavians in selling church lands that had been taken by them from other ecclesiastical groups:

> Hart no. 155. ca. A.D. 883. King Guthred (or Guthfrith) gave "in perpetuity" to St. Cuthbert: all the land between the Rivers Tyne and Wear with right of sanctuary, and all customs.[18]

> Hart no. 156. ca. A.D. 883. Abbot Eadred of Carlisle granted to St. Cuthbert estates at Heselden, Horden, two at Eden, Hulam, Hutton [Henry], and *Twinlingatun* "which he had bought from King Guthfrith and the Danish army."[19]

> Hart no. 157. A.D. 900 x 915. Berrard, priest gave to St. Cuthbert his vill of *Twinlingatun*.[20]

> Hart no. 158. A.D. 900 x 915. Tilred, Abbot of Heversham, purchased E. Eden and granted half to St. Cuthbert, and half to Norham, in return for his election as Abbot there.[21]

---

16. I have discussed this in my article "Vikings and Irish Monasteries."

17. See Johnson South, "Toward a Model of Landholdings," Map III: map of chronological development: 950, between pp. 28–29.

18. This is clearly the erstwhile Jarrow-Wearmouth holding, presumably taken by the followers of Halfdan, the Danish king in York from 876, of whom the *Anglo-Saxon Chronicle* specifically tells us that his followers "shared out the lands of the Northumbrians; and they proceeded to plough and to support themselves" (*Anglo-Saxon Chronicle*, ed. Whitelock, Douglas, and Tucker, s.a. 876 [877 C]), p. 48; *Anglo-Saxon Chronicle*, ed. and trans. Swanton, s.a. 876 Winchester (A) and Peterborough (E) Manuscripts, pp. 74–75. However, it appears from this record that, within a few years, it was regranted by the new *Christian* Viking king of Northumbria to the successors of the Lindisfarne community.

19. This too appears to relate to the Wearmouth holding, as previously recorded in Hart no. 148: A.D. 686. King Aldfrith granted the land of three "familiae" lying to the south of the River Wear (i.e., modern Sunderland) to Abbot Benedict Biscop in exchange for two silk altar cloths brought back from Rome; and in Hart no. 150. A.D. 704 x 716, a grant by Wihtmaer of the land of ten "familiae" to Abbot Ceolfrith of Wearmouth at Dalton-le-Dale (which had previously been given to him by King Aldfrith). Also, as Johnson South has said, although this is not recorded in any other source, there is no reason to doubt this claim because of their later leasing to Aelfred (*Historia 2002*, p. 95: see below).

20. This seems to indicate that, notwithstanding its grant in ca. 883, it was again alienated, but ended up in the hands of a priest.

21. This, too, seems to indicate that the grant of ca. 883 had been alienated, and that this is recording its subsequent purchase and regranting to the Cuthbertine community.

Landholding and Settlement: The Viking Impact

Of more particular interest to me was the fate of the estates in this southerly region in the late ninth through tenth centuries, during the main periods of Viking activity in Northumbria. My illustration prepared for a presentation to the Eighth Viking Congress in 1977 shows clearly the close relationship between the lands granted to Aelfred fleeing from the *piratas* in the west and the lands regranted by Raegnald, the Scandinavian victor, after the Battle of Corbridge in 918 to his two followers, Scula (Skúli) and Onlafbal (Óláfr Ballr):[22]

> Hart no. 162. A.D. 901 x 915. Cutheard leased to Alfred, son of Brihtwulf, a number of vills in return for homage and service: Easington, Heselden, Thorpe, Horden, Eden, two at Shotton, E. Eden, Hulam, Hutton [Henry], *Twinlingatun*, Billingham "with its appendages," and Sheraton.[23]
>
> Hart no. 164. A.D. 913 x 915. Raegnald shared out the eastern lands of St. Cuthbert: the southern half from Eden to Billingham is given to Scula; that from Eden to the River Wear to Onlafbal.[24]

Although the *HSC* records Onlafbal as having died when profaning the church at Chester-le-Street, presumably the lands remained in royal hands—as this seems to have led to the reversion again some years later of this estate to the community, as recorded in Hart no. 120: A.D. June 934. King Æthelstan's *testamentum* granting Bishop Wearmouth "with its appendages" to St. Cuthbert: these are then listed southwards from Westoe to Hesleden.

However, as I showed in a paper in honor of Glanville Jones,[25] Raegnald also seems to have seized the lands formerly leased by the community

---

22. Christopher D. Morris, "Viking and Native," p. 224 (late ninth- and early tenth-century land grants in Durham).

23. Hart (*Early Charters of Northern England and the North Midlands*, p. 141) notes that, according to the *HSC*, Alfred died at the second Battle of Corbridge in 918. Although the *HSC* § 10 for 867 records that King Aelle of Northumbria seized Wycliffe, Cliffe, and Billingham from the Cuthbertine community, this entry shows that, despite the likelihood that the Scandinavian rulers Ubba and Halfdan then presumably took them over as part of the settlement and cultivation of Northumbrian land, Billingham at least had made its way back into the hands of the community by the end of the ninth century, so that it was available for leasing out in the early tenth century.

24. Scula probably gave his name to School Aycliffe: Watts, "Place-Names," p. 260; Watts, "Scandinavian Settlement-Names," pp. 33, 35. Also, the northern area is essentially a regranting of the early endowment of Bede's monastery (e.g., Hart nos. 148 and 150 above), now broken up under the impact of the Vikings.

25. Christopher Morris, "Aspects of Scandinavian Settlement."

to Eadred in western and southern Co. Durham (i.e., Chester-le-Street and Gainford estates) after Eadred's death at Corbridge, but then he regranted them to Eadred's two sons: Hart no. 163. A.D. 900 x 915. Cutheard leased to Eadred, son of Ricsige (king of Northumbria 873–76), the land defined as being from Chester-le-Street to the River Derwent, then south to the River Wear, then to "Dere Street to the west and south"; also the vill of Gainford "and all that belongs to it."[26] *HSC* § 23 for A.D. 918. Raegnald seized Eadred's lands (after his death at the Battle of Corbridge) but then gave them to Esbriht, son of Eadred and his brother Aelstan "who were staunch warriors on the fight."[27]

It is also worth noting here that the place-name Sadberge (and presumably the area around it) in southern Co. Durham was recorded later as having been the focus of the only example north of the Tees of the Scandinavian institution of the "wapentake," prevalent in Deira to the south.[28] Thus we can see a picture of Anglo-Scandinavian estates across much of the Wear-Tees area of modern Co. Durham, whether run by men of Scandinavian or English origins, but managed now under the Viking overlords.

LANDHOLDING AND SETTLEMENT: THE ST. CUTHBERT
LANDHOLDINGS IN THE LATER TENTH AND ELEVENTH CENTURIES

As we move into the last century, 950–1050, it will be noted that, whereas the picture had been essentially of a Bernician (i.e., Northumberland and southern Scotland) grouping during the pre-Viking period, from the Viking period on there was a diversification further south.[29] This is hardly surprising, since it reflects the period when the community of St. Cuthbert abandoned their traditional base on Lindisfarne for places further south at Chester-le-Street and then at Durham.[30] Especially notable now

---

26. Hart (*Early Charters of Northern England and the North Midlands*, p. 141) notes that this is the grant of the western properties of the see, just as that to Alfred (Hart no. 162) was of the eastern. Like Alfred, Eadred was killed at Corbridge in 918.

27. As Johnson South has pointed out (*Historia 2002*, pp. 106–7), there is no justification for Hart's assumption (*Early Charters of Northern England and the North Midlands*, p. 141) that Eadred's sons were on Raegnald's side, and his own suggestion is that the community brought pressure to bear upon Raegnald to allow the kin to inherit and thus avoid alienation from its stock of territory. It seems to me just as likely that the proceeds from the estate were now going to Raegnald rather than to the community.

28. Fraser and Emsley, "Durham and the Wapentake of Sadberge," pp. 71–72; Watts "Place-Names," pp. 258–59; Watts "Scandinavian Settlement-Names," pp. 27, 30, 50.

29. See Johnson South, "Toward a Model of Landholdings," Map IV: map of chronological development: 1050, between pp. 28–29.

30. Also see Johnson South, *Historia 2002*, p. 96.

are the holdings in the south of modern Co. Durham and the north of the North Riding of Yorkshire, e.g., South Eden, Hartness, Billingham, Norton, Sedgefield, Darlington, Brompton, Gainford, Staindrop, Auckland.

Despite these alienations, we can chart the survival if not expansion of the territorial holding of the erstwhile Lindisfarne community through the tenth and eleventh centuries.[31] We may note, in the first place, that there is no record of Raegnald seizing the Jarrow-Wearmouth holdings to the north of the River Wear, which therefore presumably remained with the community, along with the Chester-le-Street estate upon which they were now based.[32] And— perhaps surprisingly—there are records of the community increasing its stock of land. Two new places (Sedgefield and Aycliffe) were presumably the centers of community estates since they are mentioned as having "appurtenances" or "dependencies," although unfortunately the bounds were not described:

> Hart no. 159. A.D. 900 x 915. Cutheard, Bishop of Chester-le-Street, purchased the vill of Sedgefield "with its appurtenances."[33]

> Hart no. 165. ca. A.D. 930. Scott, son of Alstan, gave Aycliffe "together with its dependencies" to St. Cuthbert.[34]

Even the gaps between recorded estates may well imply their former existence, as has been suggested at least for the area to the west of Dere Street.[35]

Later in the tenth and early eleventh centuries, significant numbers of further grants came to the community, for instance both in the southern part of Co. Durham and in the North Riding of Yorkshire:

> Hart no. 126. A.D. 979 x 992. Grant by Earl Thored of 2 hides at Great Smeaton (NRY), 2 at Crayke (NRY) and 1 at Sutton-in-the-Forest (NRY) to St. Cuthbert.

> Hart no. 127. ca. A.D. 994. Earl Northman's grant of Escomb and "the fourth acre" at Ferryhill to St. Cuthbert.

---

31. See Johnson South, "Toward a Model of Landholdings," Map V: map of pre-Norman vills and shires, between pp. 28–29.

32. Johnson South, *Historia 2002*, pp. 106–7.

33. Except for some lands held by three named people, over whose lands he nevertheless had "sake and soke."

34. This is presumably the son of the Aelstan recorded above in relation to the Chester-le-Street and Gainford holdings.

35. Clack and Gill, "Land-Divisions," p. 31.

Hart no. 128. ca. A.D. 994. Ulfketel, son of Osulf granted Norton "with sake and soke" to St. Cuthbert.

Hart no. 129. A.D. 995 x 1006. Bishop Ealdhum granted three leases of land from the St. Cuthbert holdings to Earls Northman, Aeth[el]raed and Uhtred: these included Gainford, Quarrington, Sledwitch (near Gainford), Barforth in Cleveland (NRY), *Stretford*, Lartington (NRY), Marwood, Staunton (near Barnard Castle), Streatlam, Cleatham, Langton (near Staindrop), Morton Tinmouth, Piercebridge, two at Auckland, Copeland (near Bishop Auckland), Warsull (near Yarm), Binchester, Cotherstone (in Teesdale), Thickley (near Bishop Auckland), Escomb, Witton-le-Wear, Hunwick, Newton Cap, and Helmington.[36]

Hart no. 130. A.D. 1003 x 1016. Styr, son of Ulf grant of Darlington "with its appendages with sake and soke" to St. Cuthbert; plus other lands purchased by him: 4 *carucates* at High Coniscliffe, 4 in Cockerton, 4 in Haughton-le-Skerne, 3 in *Northmannebi*, 2 in Ketton, "with sake and soke"; and 2 in Lumley.[37]

Hart no. 131. A.D. 1003 x 1016. Snaculf, son of Cytel, grant of Bradbury and Morden (near Sedgefield), plus Sockburn and Girsby (NRY), "with sake and soke" to St. Cuthbert.[38]

Hart no. 132. A.D. 1031. King Cnut granted Staindrop "with sake and soke, just as he himself had held it, with its appendages" (listed, including Auckland) to St. Cuthbert.[39] Also he granted Brompton (NRY) "with sake and soke," as well as confirming several territories held in Yorkshire "by the ancient gifts of kings and princes": these included churches at Great Smeaton (NRY) and Girsby (NRY) and 24 *carucates* of land at Brompton.[40]

Hart no. 135. A.D. 1042 x 1056. Earl Copsi granted "in perpetuity" to St. Cuthbert the church at Marske "with its endowment" (listed).

---

36. All of the places named are located within the area of the original ninth-century Gainford estate, although now this might perhaps reflect the future breakup of the estate into three separate smaller estates based on Auckland, Staindrop, and Gainford (also see Johnson South, *Historia 2002*, p. 113).

37. The first five places are presumably the "appendages" of Darlington, whereas Lumley is a quite separate place near Chester-le-Street (also see Johnson South, *Historia 2002*, p. 111).

38. Sockburn and Girsby, on opposite sides of the River Tees, formed a single parish through the post-Conquest period, and Girsby was listed in the Yorkshire *Domesday Book* as belonging to the bishop of Durham (also see Johnson South, *Historia 2002*, p. 112).

39. This indicates that by now this part of the Gainford estate had been split up, and it may even indicate that it had been alienated at some stage during the tenth century: if so, then the logical assumption would be that it was claimed by some unnamed follower of King Raegnald after 918, but that the event was not recorded (Johnson South, *Historia 2002*, pp. 114–15).

40. Johnson South has pointed out (*Historia 2002*, p. 115) that elsewhere Brompton is described as belonging to the church of Girsby (see below).

However, as I said in 1983: "It would be naive to imagine that all estates recorded by the eleventh century were necessarily the same in extent as those of earlier centuries."[41] For instance, it seems clear that some of these represent a later splitting-up of what had earlier been part of one large estate: e.g., Auckland (and/or Escomb) and Staindrop split off from Gainford, etc. Also, the possibility of continuing Anglo-Scandinavian influence in the running of the estates *may* be indicated by three of these estate-center names that demonstrate evidence of Scandinavianization: Gainford, Staindrop, and Auckland.[42]

LANDHOLDING AND SETTLEMENT: RECENT ANALYSES

Apart from my own restricted analyses, there has been a more general development of forms of topographical analysis in works by Brian Roberts, Peter Clack and Brian Gill, and David Austin on the nature of these upland estates in this area in the tenth and eleventh centuries. In their work, Clack and Gill have emphasized that, although documentary evidence can be cited for four estates in the upland zone of Co. Durham, "The precise limits of the estates are not always easy to establish using these sources."[43] Consequently, their approach was to emphasize the importance of "topographically defined exploitation units, corelands, encroachments, and woodlands, to which the place-names belonged . . . [and] the way in which the estates spread from the corelands into the surrounding areas of less favourable land."[44] They believe the "corelands" to have been settled in the seventh and eighth centuries, with the "encroachments" taking place in the following two centuries.

One of these four upland estates, that of Auckland, has been the subject of some detailed study from sources later in the medieval period, and the extent of what then was called "Aucklandshire" has been delineated by Brian Roberts.[45] Roberts has emphasized that "we are seeing evidence for a deep-seated territorial and economic reciprocity with villages in the lowlands having lands in the hills, the lowlands producing grain, the uplands supporting stock and providing a hunting ground for the lord of

---

41. Christopher Morris, "Aspects of Scandinavian Settlement," p. 7.
42. Watts, "Place-Names," pp. 259–61; Watts, "Place-Name Evidence," p. 224; Watts, "Scandinavian Settlement-Names," pp. 33–35.
43. Clack and Gill, "Land Divisions," p. 30.
44. Clack and Gill, "Land Divisions," p. 33.
45. Brian Roberts, *Making of the English Village*, "9.5: Aucklandshire, County Durham" = pp. 178–81. (An earlier version can be found in *Green Villages*.)

the estate."[46] It is clear that some of the evidence for this is derived from the later picture of this area in Boldon Book, the bishop of Durham's equivalent in the twelfth century of the eleventh-century Domesday Book for areas to the south.

While plotting the late Anglo-Saxon estates in Teesdale and Weardale,[47] David Austin has, from his work on Boldon Book emphasized the nature of tenure and services reflected in the relationship of *villae* to the estate-centers. He also stated the necessity of viewing these *villae* as "fundamentally economic, social and legal units involving both extensive space . . . and exploitable population" and therefore to be equated with "townships" rather than with "villages" or "single discrete locations."[48] He emphasized the "gaps between and within the *villae*" in order to make the point that "it is not possible to draw a line around [the *villa*] and say that all territory within it belonged to the estate."[49] Of particular significance also is the fact that our one securely dated settlement of this period in the area (Simy Folds) is within the bounds of the original Gainford estate,[50] but in an area from which no *villae* have come down to us from the documentary sources.

In his later work on the *HSC*, Ted Johnson South has developed a more sophisticated approach to the analysis of the tenurial and landholding information in this particular source.[51] This is not the place to go into either the details or the implications of his argument, but he does seem to have got around some of David Austin's objections to mapping shires in relation to the *villae* by relating them both to later parish boundaries and to the 200 m. contour: indeed, in relation to the latter, he observes that none of the over one hundred place-names in the *HSC* is to be associated with a site above this line. He is then able to reconstruct the shires or estates in the western parts of the region, and the eastern area shires can also be

---

46. Brian Roberts, "Man and Land," p. 146.

47. Austin, "Late Anglo-Saxon Settlement," fig. 1, p. 201: Late Anglo-Saxon estates in Teesdale and Weardale.

48. Austin, "Late Anglo-Saxon Settlement," p. 202; also see *Domesday Book. Boldon Book*, ed. Austin, p. 8.

49. Austin, "Late Anglo-Saxon Settlement," p. 202.

50. Coggins, Fairless, and Batey, "Simy Folds."

51. He distinguishes between the different terms used: *villa, villa 'cum suis appendiciis', villa 'et quicquid ad eam pertinet', villa 'cum saca et socna', civitas,* and *terra.* He also analyses the size of vills, and groups of vills which go to make up the "shire," and in turn the groups of these into larger territories (Johnson South, "Historia de Sancto Cuthberto," pp. 188–92). See also Johnson South, *Historia 2002,* Appendix II, pp. 124–29.

reconstructed on this basis.[52] As all of these then demonstrate a significant regularity of size (at around 7,000–7,500 hectares), he suggests that this contradicts Austin's objection to mapping such land- or assessment-units on the basis that they are conceptual rather than real.[53]

LINGUISTIC EVIDENCE

Previously, I have also attempted to relate the nature of the landholdings to the evidence of place-names, by looking at both the analyses of the Yorkshire evidence by Gillian Fellows-Jensen[54] and the preliminary work undertaken in Co. Durham by Victor Watts.[55] Much of this was against the backdrop of the debates already alluded to in the 1960s and 1970s between Sawyer and Cameron.[56]

In Yorkshire, Gillian Fellows-Jensen's explanation of Cameron's primary group of Scandinavianized names, the "Grimston hybrids" (i.e., English village names modified with the name of a Scandinavian overlord), related them to the activities of the "invading Scandinavians" as "English settlements . . . taken over by the Danes" (i.e., post-876).[57] This might also have seemed a reasonable explanation for those in southeastern Co. Durham; however, Victor Watts and I tended to favor an association with the Hiberno-Norse takeover post A.D. 918.[58] This would then relate to Raegnald's reshaping of the territorial arrangements at that time, and lead to an explanation of such names in terms of "infilling" rather than settlement on primary sites.[59] However, only in the upper reaches of Teesdale did Watts's analysis seem to give unequivocal evidence of West Norse names, which perhaps were to be interpreted in terms of settlers of Norse-Irish extraction coming over the Pennines from Cumbria.[60]

---

52. Johnson South, "Historia de Sancto Cuthberto," figs. 7–14, pp. 206–17; Johnson South, *Historia 2002*, figs. 2 and 3 (between pp. 118 and 119).

53. Johnson South, *Historia 2002*, pp. 126–27.

54. Fellows-Jensen, *Scandinavian Settlement-Names*; Fellows-Jensen, "Place-Names and Settlement History"; Fellows-Jensen, "Place-Names and Settlement in the North Riding of Yorkshire"; Fellows-Jensen, "Lancashire and Yorkshire Names."

55. Watts, "Place-Names of County Durham"; Watts, "Place-Names"; Watts, "Comment on 'The Evidence of Place-Names'" (reprinted as "The Evidence of Place-Names II"); Watts, "Place-Names of the Darlington Area"; Watts, "Place-Name Evidence," pp. 223–33.

56. See note 8 above.

57. Fellows-Jensen, *Scandinavian Settlement-Names*, pp. 206, 250.

58. Watts, "Place-Names," p. 260; Watts, "Place-Name Evidence," p. 126; Christopher Morris, "Viking and Native," p. 227.

59. Watts, "Scandinavian Settlement-Names," p. 57; Christopher Morris, "Viking and Native," p. 228.

60. Watts, "Place-Names," p. 261; Watts, "Place-Name Evidence," fig. 10.2, p. 126.

More recently, Watts has published a more definitive analysis, with several significantly clustered groupings being evident, some of which may well be as reflective of Scandinavian settlement post A.D. 876 as post A.D. 914/918. Moreover, he now interprets his earlier map of English habitation names, such as those in *hām*, *worth*, *wīc*, *burh*, and *tūn*, as indicating that "at the time of the Viking arrival all the available land resources of eastern Durham were already exhaustively exploited."[61] This then has an implication for the interpretation of other place-names of Scandinavian origin, such as the Grimston hybrids.[62] The Grimston hybrids as a group appear to be largely in the southeast of the area, to be in inferior areas of wet heavy clays, and to be located fairly randomly among the English habitative names: "the pattern fits either a situation of English vills taken over by Scandinavian overlords, or of infilling between existing settlements." The latter explanation is favored because of their high failure rate as continuing settlements.[63]

The second group of names is names ending in -*by*. This cluster of names is largely in the middle Tees Valley area and appears to represent an extension of settlement from North Yorkshire. Six or seven of the ten names include Scandinavian personal names.[64]

The third group is that of other Scandinavian names. Of particular significance here are habitative names such as the five *thorp* names and one associated *toft*, which clearly relate to the southeast of the county where estates came into the hands of Scandinavians in the tenth century.[65]

A fourth group is of topographical habitative names. There are few of these, as many are of Middle English formation, but they include both Sadberge as the name of the only Wapentake in the county corresponding to such administrative and legal units in Yorkshire (ON *set-berg* = 'flat-topped hill')[66] and Copeland (ON *kaupa-land* = 'purchased land'),[67] which presumably relates to a purchase of land for the Auckland estate before ca. A.D. 995 (when it was first attested); most of the remainder appear to relate to westward expansion of settlement by Scandinavians into the upper reaches of Teesdale and Weardale.[68]

---

61. Watts, "Scandinavian Settlement-Names," p. 37.
62. Watts, "Scandinavian Settlement-Names," Map I, pp. 19–22.
63. Watts, "Scandinavian Settlement-Names," p. 38.
64. Watts, "Scandinavian Settlement-Names," Map II, pp. 22–24, 39.
65. Watts, "Scandinavian Settlement-Names," Map III, pp. 24–26, 39.
66. Watts, "Scandinavian Settlement-Names," p. 30.
67. Watts, "Scandinavian Settlement-Names," p. 28.
68. Watts, "Scandinavian Settlement-Names," Map IV, pp. 27–30, 40.

A fifth group is of Scandinavianized names. This group includes two river names (Gaunless and Skerne), the names of three estate-centers (Auckland, changed from Pr W *Alt-clut* [hill overlooking the River Clyde] to ON *auka-land* [additional land];[69] Staindrop, using ON *steinn*,[70] and Gainford, OE *gegn*, *ford* [direct ford] but replacing [j] with [g]),[71] and quite a number of other names both along the Tees Valley and to the northwest of Chester-le-Street.[72]

Overall, the indications from this latest analysis are of "an arc of settlement in some density extending two to three miles north of the river from Yorkshire" and probably reflecting the events of A.D. 876, whereas the Grimston hybrids towards the coast appear to be distinct from these and possibly relate to post A.D. 914/918 events. Those in the upper reaches of the Dales possibly reflected the movements of settlers of Norse-Irish origin from Cumbria. Scandinavian overlordship is reflected in the names of three estate-centers, the Scandinavianized river names (notably Gaunless and Skerne), and the name reflecting land-purchase (Copeland). To Watts, the indications beyond the middle Tees Valley area are more of "infilling of Scandinavians between and around the native population in English-named vills." As he goes on to say, "the two processes, Scandinavian overlordship of the estate organisations and settlement both in and around pre-existing villages, must have led to the cultural and political mixing reflected in the Anglo-Scandinavian art throughout the deep south of the county."[73]

ARCHAEOLOGICAL AND POLLEN EVIDENCE FOR SETTLEMENT

Early Anglo-Saxon settlement is indicated by major finds such as the Darlington (Greenbank) pagan Anglo-Saxon cemetery[74] and the Castle Eden claw beaker;[75] indeed, it is interesting that these were in the areas of two of the estates given over to the church. The thoroughgoing nature of Anglo-Saxon settlement in part of the middle Tees Valley is perhaps reflected in the virtual absence of Scandinavian place-names in the Darlington estate area (except for that of the River Skerne).[76]

---

69. Watts, "Scandinavian Settlement-Names," p. 33.

70. Watts, "Scandinavian Settlement-Names," p. 35.

71. Watts, "Scandinavian Settlement-Names," pp. 32, 34; Watts, "Place-Name Evidence," p. 126.

72. Watts, "Scandinavian Settlement-Names," Map V, p. 31.

73. Watts, "Scandinavian Settlement-Names," pp. 57–58.

74. Miket and Pocock, "Anglo-Saxon Cemetery."

75. Cramp, "Anglo-Saxon Period," p. 200.

76. Watts, "Place-Names of the Darlington Area," p. 42.

As I have discussed previously, there is however very little archaeo-logical evidence for distinctive Viking-age settlements: the best candidates in upper Teesdale (i.e., Simy Folds) appear to relate to the forms of the accepted Viking-age settlement of Ribblehead. But how could we define these as Scandinavian or even Anglo-Scandinavian? Is there an equally good argument for them being native Anglo-Saxon? And are these per-manent or seasonal, shieling settlements? The radiocarbon dates would seem to indicate a late eighth-century reoccupation of a Bronze-age field system. In any case, they appear to represent an upland settlement type, found within the original bounds of the Gainford estate, albeit on very high ground.[77]

In my summary of the pollen evidence, based on information from Alison Donaldson,[78] and comments by Denis Coggins,[79] it has become clear that variety is to be expected, although there is evidence for clearances in various places. But to what extent may they be related to the Scandinavian arrival? How much of this simply related to the needs of estates once they were established? And need we expect much direct impact by Scandina-vians as such, as they took over estates as "going concerns"?

Other evidence is thin but interesting, the find of silver at Gainford-on-Tees, for instance. Brooks and Graham-Campbell have suggested that, while there is nothing distinctively "Viking" about the contents of the Gainford hoard, it may represent—as do others—a Viking hoard associ-ated with the army of Halfdan.[80] Pagan Viking grave material from the area is rare, as is clear from maps of the Viking graves in northern En-gland.[81] The Kildale Viking graves in North Yorkshire are interesting. They have never received the attention they deserve.[82] An interesting single find is the ornamented disc brooch from Cleveland with derived Borre-style knot-pattern.[83]

---

77. Christopher Morris, "Aspects of Scandinavian Settlement," pp. 14–15; Coggins, Fairless, and Batey, "Simy Folds"; cf. King, "Gauber High Pasture." See also Dickinson, "Bry-ant's Gill."

78. Christopher Morris, "Viking and Native," pp. 228–29; Morris, "Aspects of Scandina-vian Settlement," pp. 13–15.

79. Coggins, *Upper Teesdale*, pp. 19, 53, 62–64, figs 7, 8.

80. Brooks and Graham-Campbell, "Reflections on the Viking-Age Silver Hoard," p. 106.

81. David Wilson, "Scandinavians in England," p. 394, fig. 10.1; Graham-Campbell, "Archaeology of the Danelaw," p. 71, fig 2.

82. I have published a preliminary discussion of this material: "Viking and Native," pp. 234–35.

83. Graham-Campbell, "Archaeology of the Danelaw," p. 73, fig 6.

ANGLO-SCANDINAVIAN SCULPTURE
AND THE TEES VALLEY ESTATES

Earlier in this paper, I referred to estates in the Tees Valley area at Gainford, Staindrop, Aycliffe, Sedgefield, Norton, and Billingham. In addition, we have the Wapentake administrative center at Sadberge, and in the eleventh century we get the grants of the estates at Darlington "with its appendages" and Lumley, Bradbury, and Morden, together with Sockburn and Girsby. Overall, on the wider front of the modern Co. Durham, by the eleventh century there were perhaps as many as sixteen or seventeen putative estates.[84] Anglo-Saxon churches survive at five of these.[85]

Sculpture of the Anglo-Saxon period survives at a significant number of sites over and beyond those where church architecture of the period can be recognized. Many years ago, I produced a map showing the distribution of sculpture in the Tees Valley area on the basis of a belief that we needed to move the study of sculpture away from a purely art-historical or typological study to one that considered its contribution to an understanding of broader settlement dynamics.[86] Of course the map of Tees Valley sculpture can provide only an incomplete picture, since it is dependent upon the vicissitudes of survival of the material; indeed it may to that extent be a misleading picture. It does make one very simple point, however, and that is that sculptural evidence is more plentiful than almost any other form of evidence for this period in this area.[87] This must be considered seriously in any discussion of settlement, as it often dovetails, or provides an intriguing contrast with, the evidence from either documentary or linguistic sources. I concluded in 1976 that "the identification of the existence of pre-Conquest sculpture has added twenty-six religious sites to the eleven already known from the area from documentary or architectural evidence."[88] We may also add that chronological analysis of the sculpture indicates that the number of sites involved increased significantly in the Viking period.

One of the earliest estates mentioned above was Gilling in North Yorkshire, but virtually all the sculpture from the site is distinctively Anglo-Scandinavian in character. As there are no later references to the estate, the simple presence of a hogback and other pieces is sufficient to demon-

84. Clack and Gill, "Land-Divisions," p. xx.
85. H. Taylor and J. Taylor, *Anglo-Saxon Architecture*, pp. 34–35, 66–70, 465–70, 555–56, 564–67.
86. Christopher Morris, "Pre-Conquest Sculpture," fig. 47, p. 141.
87. Compare Austin, "Late Anglo-Saxon Settlement," pp. 197–98.
88. Christopher Morris, "Pre-Conquest Sculpture," p. 145.

strate the continuing importance of the estate into a much later period, although one would venture to suggest that it became a secular estate. As Jim Lang and I concluded in our short study of this material: "Clearly Gilling had an important phase of existence in this period, hardly to be inferred from the extant literary sources."[89]

When we go on to look at the evidence from some of the estate-centers in southern Co. Durham some interesting aspects emerge. The grant in 934 of Aycliffe is referred to above, and my own account of the Aycliffe sculpture has emphasized both the need to take a detailed, localized, and holistic view of the sculpture and also its predominantly ecclesiastical nature.[90] However, the carving here of ribbon animals of a form recognizably related to Jellinge-style animals betokens some degree of Scandinavian cultural influence at a mainstream level here. Although the level of influence was relatively small within the corpus from the site, to my mind this is Anglo-Scandinavian sculptural art, even if it may not have been created by a Scandinavian.[91]

Sculptural themes and motifs similar to those at Aycliffe are to be found at the Gainford estate-center, and it should be noted that there were probable family links between Aycliffe and Gainford,[92] and that the Gainford estate area has a number of place-names of Scandinavian origin.[93] There is also a mixture of art styles here, which betokens a slightly different Anglo-Scandinavian influence from that evident further south with the "Great beast" designs, but also ribbon animals of a Jellinge-type style and hogback-fragments.[94]

In contrast, Victor Watts has determined that the place-names of the Darlington estate area demonstrate no direct Scandinavian influence,[95] but it would be too simple to conclude that there was therefore no Scandinavian presence in the area.[96] One dependent *villa*, Haughton-le-Skerne, is a back-formation from the Scandinavianized form of the river name.[97]

---

89. Lang and Morris, "Recent Finds," p. 130.
90. Christopher Morris, "Aycliffe."
91. Christopher Morris, "Aycliffe," pp. 103–4; Christopher Morris, "Viking and Native," pp. 231–33; *Durham and Northumberland*, ed. Cramp, p. 29.
92. Christopher Morris, "Aycliffe," pp. 99, 104.
93. Watts, "Scandinavian Settlement-Names," pp. 48, 57.
94. Christopher Morris, "Viking and Native," p. 233; Lang, "Hogback," pp. 132–33; Cramp, *Durham and Northumberland*, pp. 29–30.
95. Watts, "Place-Names of the Darlington Area," p. 43.
96. Christopher Morris, "Pre-Norman Sculpture of the Darlington Area," pp. 47–48.
97. Watts, "Place-Names," p. 259.

We may also get a hint from the sculpture of the social and cultural influences at work in the area, as there is one fairly well known example of a Jellinge-style animal at this site, as well as a second, but much more battered, version of the Jellinge animal design.[98] Further south, at Darlington itself, although the name is purely Anglo-Saxon and we know of the early Saxon cemetery at Greenbank,[99] the church site has produced an Anglo-Scandinavian hogback, which is of a standard form.[100]

If we now stretch our gaze a few miles to the southeast, probably beyond the bounds of the Darlington estate, we find an interesting similar group of sculptured stones, including another hogback at Low Dinsdale within one of the "gaps" in the estate picture.[101] Of course, this may mean simply that it was within a secular estate that never came within the purview of the erstwhile Lindisfarne community. Presumably, then, the sculpture from Low Dinsdale (as at Haughton-le-Skerne and Darlington) betokens a significant Anglo-Scandinavian influence in the area, even though there is no hint in the historical record of such and even though there are no place-names demonstrating distinctively Scandinavian settlements here.[102]

It could be argued that this influence may be purely cultural (the transmission of artistic "style") and need not be related to any individual of Scandinavian origin. It may be debated further whether it was the "style" of the patron or that of the artist that dominated to create the final artistic amalgam of stylistic influences. Even so, for myself, I find it rather difficult to conceive that the distinctive form of the hogbacks at Darlington and Low Dinsdale would have been commissioned by, or then stood over the bones of, anyone other than a member of an Anglo-Scandinavian family, if not a member of the minor aristocracy of the area. By extension, I think that this would also be true of those monuments with elements of decoration that were in very recognizable mainstream Scandinavian styles, such as the Jellinge-style ribbon animals at Haughton-le-Skerne.

---

98. Christopher Morris, "Viking and Native," pp. 230–31; Cramp, *Durham and Northumberland*, p. 29.

99. Miket and Pocock, "Anglo-Saxon Cemetery."

100. Lang, "Hogback," pp. 128–29; *Durham and Northumberland*, ed. Cramp, pp. 31, 62–63.

101. Christopher Morris, "Pre-Norman Sculpture of the Darlington Area," sculpture map = fig. between pp. 47 and 48.

102. Lang, "Hogback," pp. 130–31; Cramp, *Durham and Northumberland*, pp. 63–66.

Sockburn: Site and Sculpture

It is at Sockburn, the most southerly site in Co. Durham, that we face the most obvious discontinuity of evidence.[103] As noted above, the *HSC* records grants of lands at Sockburn, Girsby, Great Smeaton, and Brompton in the eleventh century. Clearly, although the first three of these are near to Darlington, it would not appear that this group was ever part of that estate, or any other of the previously mentioned St. Cuthbert landholdings of the Tees Valley. The relationship of Sockburn to Girsby and Brompton might well suggest that it could it have been a detached part of a secular estate to the south, i.e., in Allertonshire.

What was its status in the earlier period? There is a reference in the Anglo-Saxon Chronicle sub anno 780 to the consecration of Bishop Higbald of Lindisfarne "aet Soccabyrig," which is usually related to this site,[104] and a further reference in the *Historia Regum* (*HR*) to the appointment of Archbishop Eanbald at a monastery "quod dicitur Sochasburg" in 796.[105] However, no primary source validates Knowles's claim that in 883 King Guthred presented the place to St. Cuthbert.[106] Clearly this was an important location for the business of the pre-Viking church of Deira, and this has perhaps overinfluenced Taylor and Taylor in their assignation of a "possible period A" label to the ruined and abandoned (after 1838) church building here. While there is obviously evidence for a later medieval church, one may well raise considerable doubts about its authenticity as an early, pre-Norman building.[107] However, Sockburn also has a history

---

103. Both Jim Lang and I visited this site on many occasions and we had long planned a collaborative article on it; indeed the second set of aerial photographs by the late Peter Scott was taken specifically at my request in relation to our plans. It should be noted in this regard, that there are a number of references to a "Lang and Morris forthcoming" article! Jim and I particularly enjoyed opening our visitors' eyes to the riches of this site during the Collingwood symposium in 1978, and we originally intended to include the paper in that volume (*Anglo-Saxon and Viking Age Sculpture*, ed. Lang). Unfortunately this did not happen. This is particularly ironic since we both at various times lived nearby in Darlington. Our diverging academic pathways during the 1980s—I seeking out the Vikings in the earldom of Orkney and Jim looking to Viking Dublin and Ireland more generally (not to mention his move to English Heritage and my later move to the University of Glasgow)—meant that, despite our original good intentions and quite a lot of discussion and preliminary work, we never made it. His untimely death has robbed me of an academic colleague, a critical collaborator with high standards, and a personal friend.

104. *Anglo-Saxon Chronicle*, ed. Whitelock, Douglas, and Tucker, s.a. 780 MS. D (E), p. 34; *Anglo-Saxon Chronicle*, ed. Swanton, s.a. 780 Peterborough Manuscript (E), p. 53.

105. *HR* § 58, p. 58.

106. Knowles, "Sockburn Church," p. 99.

107. Taylor and Taylor, *Anglo-Saxon Architecture*, 2:555–56.

and importance in relation to the presentation of later Palatinate bishops to their see, through the formal handing over up to the nineteenth century of the so-called Conyers falchion to the bishop on his arrival at the Tees crossing. The Conyers go back to the time of William the Conqueror, for whom Roger was supposedly constable of Durham Castle. This falchion is, in folk memory, the sword with which Sir John Conyers is said to have slain "ye monstrous venoms and poysons viverms Ask or worme which overthrew and Devourd many people in fight, for the scent of the poyson was so strong." It is one of several medieval dragon-slaying folk stories from the northeast of England.[108]

The church was retained as an episcopal property, despite the alienation of the surrounding land in the post-Reformation period to secular holding. There is clear evidence from the aerial photographs of a later medieval settlement to the south of the chapel, and it is also clear that originally there was a churchyard, although its extent is not immediately obvious. Presumably also in this area, if anywhere, would have been the buildings of the putative Anglo-Saxon monastery, although there are no surface indications of them. More recently, there was a grand hall on the site. In recent years, however, the whole area was given over to dog-breeding by the Misses Gatherall, and the impact of this activity has been catastrophic upon the building and surrounding areas, and the hall is now essentially a ruin.

There can be little doubt that the difficulties of access have obscured the original importance of the site, although the results of rudimentary excavations at the beginning of the last century unearthed a remarkable collection of over twenty crosses and grave-covers in a distinctive Anglo-Scandinavian style, the locations for at least some of which lay in the foundations of the later church.[109] These sculptures are of a predominantly secular nature. The first point to note is that, despite the references to pre-Viking ecclesiastical activity and a monastery, not a single piece of sculpture is pre-Viking! The second point is that one might speculate that the use of the stones as foundations might be associated with the eleventh century (i.e., the time of the documentary reference to it in relation to the St. Cuthbert community), and it would certainly be paralleled elsewhere (e.g., Kirkdale and Middleton, both North Riding of Yorkshire).[110] This

---

108. Hodges, "Conyers Falchion"; Wall, "Conyers Falchion."

109. Knowles, "Sockburn Church," pp. 100–104 and plan of church, p. 100.

110. Taylor and Taylor, *Anglo-Saxon Architecture*, 1:357–61, 419–24; Lang, *York and Eastern Yorkshire*, pp. 156–66, 181–87.

is not the place to go into the minutiae of sculptural analysis; there have been quite a number of references in the specialist literature on sculpture to particular pieces from this site,[111] and Rosemary Cramp's first volume of the *Corpus of Anglo-Saxon Stone Sculpture* has systematized the various accounts of them.[112] But a brief overview of the range of sculpture will give an indication of the clear importance of Sockburn within the Anglo-Scandinavian cultural milieu of the pre-Conquest period. Knowles recovered a total of twenty-five stones that can be divided into subgroupings.

To begin with, there is the remarkable collection of hogbacks, and Jim Lang has pointed out that "it is possible to see almost the complete stylistic development of this class of monument exemplified in microcosm at this single site."[113] As is well known, the monument type is especially common in Yorkshire to the south,[114] but these (along with those at Brompton) are amongst some of the earliest of the group.[115] There are examples at Sockburn of both the house-shaped form and the end-beast forms, and within them, examples of niche-type, extended niche-type, panel-type, illustrative-type, and so on, many of which can be directly paralleled at Brompton, and some of which are apparently identical.[116] Of particular note are the "illustrative" or "narrative" hogbacks.[117] At Sockburn, two are especially interesting because of their direct links to Scandinavian mythology. There is little doubt that one has a fragmentary representation of a Valkyrie-type female figure (which has been compared with Swedish depictions), and the other is of the god Tyr and the Fenris wolf, although there may well be Christian overtones of "Salvation," at least for the latter.[118] Another hogback, with mounted warriors on horses, also appears best considered in a Scandinavian context, if without specific mythological reference.[119]

---

111. Lang, "Illustrative Carvings"; Christopher Morris, "Pre-Conquest Sculpture"; Bailey, *Viking Age Sculpture*; Lang, "Hogback," pp. 162–67.

112. Cramp, *Durham and Northumberland*, pp. 135–44.

113. Lang, pers. comm.

114. Lang, "Hogback," pp. 87, 89, fig. 3; Lang, *Northern Yorkshire*, pp. 21–24.

115. Lang, "Hogback," p. 97.

116. Lang, "Hogback," p. 90.

117. Lang, "Hogback," type VII, pp. 99–100, 109–10; Cramp, *Durham and Northumberland*, pp. xx–xxi, fig. 6.

118. Lang, "Illustrative Carvings"; Bailey, *Viking Age Sculpture*, pp. 134–36; Lang, "Hogback," Sockburn 5, pp. 164–65; Sockburn 6, pp. 166–67; *Durham and Northumberland*, ed. Cramp, Sockburn 15, p. 141; Sockburn 21, pp. 143–44.

119. Lang, "Hogback," Sockburn 9, pp. 166–67; Bailey, *Viking Age Sculpture*, pp. 234–35; Cramp, *Durham and Northumberland*, Sockburn 14, pp. 140–41; also see Gainford 4, pp. 81–82 and Hart 1, p. 93.

These stones on their own indicate that this was a site in the mainstream of Anglo-Scandinavian artistic traditions in the north of England.

This is no less true of the Sockburn cross-shafts which, although bringing together features and motifs from a variety of sources, point to a very distinctive repertoire. Some of these are again in the mainstream of Anglo-Scandinavian artistic production. For example, the large cross-shaft clearly has a mixture of both Jellinge-style animal ornament and native Anglo-Saxon traditions, which has parallels on, for example, the Great Stainton shaft.[120] Other shafts show a paneled layout including individual animals and warriors, the latter in a well-known tradition of such "portraits" in the Anglo-Scandinavian north.[121] Yet others show an eclectic mixture of both traditional Scandinavian and Christian subjects: a mounted figure, who may well be Odin, with a bird, above a Valkyrie scene,[122] and a second with a scene of David the harpist.[123]

It is also quite clear that there are a number of decorative details, such as the "S-twist" or "Como" braid, as well as similarities of form, which link the stones from this site with those from neighboring ones to the south, such as Kirkleavington and Brompton, to provide evidence for the functioning of what Jim Lang described as "the Allertonshire workshop."[124] These stones show some immediately obvious visual parallels, as well as similarities in some of the techniques used to produce them. The latter are now well understood thanks to the work of Richard Bailey on mechanical aids and templates[125] and Jim Lang on "gridding" and units of measurement.[126]

---

120. Christopher Morris, "Viking and Native," pp. 230–31; Bailey, *Viking Age Sculpture,* pp. 185–87; Cramp, *Durham and Northumberland,* Sockburn 8, pp. 138–39.

121. Christopher Morris, "Viking and Native," pp. 231–32; Bailey, *Viking Age Sculpture,* pp. 185–87; Cramp, *Durham and Northumberland,* Sockburn 5, p. 137; Sockburn 7, p. 138. Also see Cramp, "Viking Image."

122. Lang, "Illustrative Carvings," pp. 244–45; Cramp, *Durham and Northumberland,* Sockburn 3, pp. 136–37.

123. Bailey, *Viking Age Sculpture,* p. 155; Cramp, *Durham and Northumberland,* Sockburn 6, pp. 137–38.

124. Cramp, *Durham and Northumberland,* p. 30; Lang, *Northern Yorkshire,* pp. 44–47.

125. Bailey, "Chronology of Viking Age Sculpture"; Bailey, *Durham Cassiodorus;* Bailey, *Viking Age Sculpture,* pp. 238–56; Bailey, *England's Earliest Sculptors,* pp. 111–15.

126. Lang, "Recent Studies in the Pre-Conquest Sculpture of Northumbria"; Lang, "Fine Measurement Analysis"; Lang, "Compilation of Design"; Lang, "Distinctiveness of Viking Colonial Art"; Lang, "Principles of Design"; Lang, "Some Units of Linear Measurement."

Much more could be said about this remarkable group of carvings from Sockburn; however, I would simply conclude that here, at an apparently important eighth-century ecclesiastical site, later recorded in the eleventh century as reverting to the St. Cuthbert community, it would appear that we have clear evidence in between those times of the presence of high-status secular patrons undoubtedly of Scandinavian origin or extraction. The obvious conclusion is that it relates to one of the two periods of Scandinavian control in this area (i.e., post-876 and post-918), and I would favor that of Raegnald and the tenth century; Sockburn probably functioned as a secular estate for an aristocratic follower of the Scandinavian ruler. It perhaps, therefore, reflects a further stage removed from the situation represented by the grant of the Gainford estate; for although we have no surviving primary documentary record, it is in another "gap" area on the map. In my opinion it must have been an estate taken (however briefly) under the control of the ruler and run by unnamed and unknown individuals of Scandinavian or Anglo-Scandinavian extraction, who then left their imprint—if not perhaps even their portraits—in the remarkable collection of sculpture we can still (with difficulty) see today. These works typify par excellence the wider contribution of sculpture to our understanding of the mechanisms of settlement and landholding in the Anglo-Scandinavian north of England, which I have attempted to address here.[127]

---

127. Finally, it has to be said that, despite the catalogue of the sculpture in the *Corpus* volume there is still a need for a comprehensive overview of the site, history, church, and sculpture, such as Jim Lang and I planned many years ago now. The occasion of the Kalamazoo and Albuquerque symposia have now provided the opportunity for me at last to reopen this particular file and, I hope, to bring it forward—if very belatedly—towards publication in the future.

The *Málsháttakvæði* or "Proverb Poem" Englished

Roberta Frank

The craggy island of Chios that claims Homer as son more certainly launched our own Helen Damico, whose multiple contributions to medieval studies are celebrated in this volume. "What any one person says can be denied," begins *Málsháttakvæði*; but when a dozen or more admirers strew praises in Helen's path, deniability is not an option. Although Orkney is far from the tideless Aegean, skalds from these northern isles sailed past Chios (perhaps even stopping for wine, mastic, and song) three centuries before the young Columbus sojourned there. Greece may have nurtured Helen, America may have embraced her, but it was the North and its poetry, pounding with the surge of the Atlantic behind it, that won her heart.

The composition here translated into English in its entirety was almost certainly composed in Orkney, probably in the first quarter of the thirteenth century.[1] The text of *Málsháttakvæði* is found, along with that of *Jómsvíkingadrápa*, on the final folios of the Codex Regius (GkS 2367 4to) of Snorri's *Edda*, a manuscript from ca. 1325 written in one hand.[2] The poem is a *drápa*, the preeminent skaldic genre. Its thirty stanzas are organized into three panels of identical length: an *upphaf* or 'exordium' of ten stanzas, a *stefjabálkr* or 'refrain section' of another ten, and a ten-stanza *slœmr* or 'conclusion'—the smooth beginning-middle-and-end arc that Aristotle drew on the Athenian sand. The refrain, forming the second half of

---

1. For a synopsis of current opinion on authorship, see Fidjestøl, "Bjarni Kolbeinsson." On dating and dialect, see Finnur Jónsson, *Den oldnorske og oldislandske litteraturs historie*, 2:47–48. The only previous English paraphrase, that of Guðbrandur Vigfússon and F. York Powell in *Corpus Poeticum Boreale*, 2:363–69, is loose, with odd gaps and odder "restorations" (see n. 5 below).

2. *Málsháttakvæði*, untitled in the manuscript, has had many names in modern scholarship. Sveinbjörn Egilsson, *Lexicon*, chose *Amatorium Carmen* or *Mansaungsdrápa*; Fritzner, *Ordbog*, preferred *Mansöngskvæði*. In 1874 both Theodor Möbius in his edition of the poem (*Zeitschrift für deutsche Philologie*) and Guðbrandur Vigfússon in his *Icelandic-English Dictionary* called it *Málsháttakvæði*. In the 1880s Konráð Gíslason championed *Fornyrðadrápa*, a name briefly used by Eiríkr Magnússon, "Anmærkninger til I, 'Fornyrðadrápa' . . . ," and Finnur Jónsson, "Fornyrðadrápa (Málsháttakvæði)." A century later Hermann Pálsson plumped for *Griplur* 'pickings, gleanings' but it was too late ("Florilegium," p. 260).

stanzas 11, 14, 17, and 20, alludes to King Harald Fairhair's legendary passion for a Finnish enchantress, the most famous Norse exemplum of what happens if you let a strange woman wrap you in her arms.[3] *Málsháttakvæði* is a gallimaufry of proverbs and maxims, old and new, interspersed with allusions to Norse gods, heroes, and myths, the whole framed by an unhinged speaker's bitter first-person account of his betrayal in love. The poem is unparalleled, unforgettable, and worth sampling, even in warmed-over translation.[4]

Málsháttakvæði is composed in four-stressed, alliterating, end-rhyming verses. Each line contains seven or eight syllables and usually forms a complete sentence. Some of the sound effects must have startled and amused, as in this stanza, which portrays the death of Baldr as a kind of domestic tragedy, not the beginning of the end of the world:

> 9. Friggjar þótti svipr at syni,
> sá var taldr ór miklu kyni,
> Hermóðr vildi auka aldr,
> Éljúðnir vann sólginn Baldr,
> ǫll grétu þau eptir hann,
> aukit var þeim hlátrar bann,
> heyrinkunn er frá hǫnum saga,
> hvat þarf ek of slíkt at jaga.

> (That was a shock about Frigg's son.
> He was reckoned from a great family.[5]
> Hermóðr wanted to extend his life.
> Éljúðnir (=Hell's hall) had swallowed up Baldr.

---

3. The story of Harald's infatuation with the beautiful Saami, Snjófríðr, is most fully told in the late twelfth-century *Ágrip af Nóregs konunga sǫgum*, chs. 3–4. Snorri quotes the anecdote in *Heimskringla* (pp. 125–27). The legend appears again, briefly, in *Flateyjarbók*, *Þáttr Haralds hárfagra* (I, 582), which includes a love stanza ascribed to the king himself. On the five fragmentary stanzas in the same unusual meter preserved in Snorri's *Edda*, and assigned to an otherwise unknown skald, see Russell Poole, "Ormr Steinþórsson and the *Snjófríðardrápa*," who compares Ormr's poem to *Jómsvíkingadrápa* and *Málsháttakvæði*.

4. I discuss its structure and affiliations in "Sex, Lies, and *Málsháttakvæði*." I would like to thank Judith Jesch and the Centre for the Study of the Viking Age for permission to reproduce a revised translation here. I am grateful as ever to Ian C. McDougall for suggestions incorporated in that essay and this translation.

5. Vigfússon and Powell's *Corpus Poeticum Boreale*, p. 365, first alters this couplet to "Friggjar þótti svipr at sveini: / sá var tældr af Mistilteini" and then translates it as 'Frigg's boy was snatched away, he was done to death by Mistletoe.'

They all wept for him.
Their laughter-ban (=grief) grew.
The story about him is very well known.
No need for me to harp on it.)

In the closing couplet of this stanza, Old Norse *saga* 'history, tale' rhymes
incongruously with colloquial *jaga* 'to move to and fro, like a door on a
hinge; to jabber on about something', a touch of light relief. The translation of the poem that follows is based on Finnur Jónsson's emended text,
itself based on his transcript of 1889.[6] Brief notes identify names, allusions
to Norse myth, lexical cruces, and the occasional new reading.

Málsháttakvæði

1. - - - - - - - - - - þegir;
   dylja má þess, er einn hverr segir;
   - - - - - - - - - - - -
   - - - eitt bregzk hóti síðr;
   fœra ætlum forn orð saman
   (flestir henda at nøkkvi gaman,
   gleði minnar veit geipun sjá),
   griplur er sem hendi þá.

2. Ekki hefk með flimtun farit,
   fullvel ættak til þess varit,
   (yrkja kann ek vǫnu verr)
   vita þykkisk þat maðrinn hverr;
   stolit væri mér ekki ór ætt,
   jafnan þótt ek kvæða slétt;
   róa verðr fyrst til ens næsta ness,
   nǫkkut ættak kyn til þess.

3. Þjóð spyrr alt þat's þrír menn vitu,
   þeir hafa verr, er tryggðum slitu,
   ekki er því til eins manns skotit,

---

6. *Den norsk-islandske skjaldedigtning*, ed. Finnur Jónsson, B 2:138–45; Finnur Jónsson,
"*Málsháttakvæði* eller *Fornyrðadrápa*," pp. 283–88 (transcript).

ýmsir hafa þau dœmi hlotit;
hermðar orð munu hittask í,
heimult ák at glaupsa of því,
(nǫkkut varð hon sýsla of sik)
svinneyg drós hvé hon fór við mik.

4. Ró skyldu menn reiði gefa,
raunlítit kømsk opt á þrefa,
gagarr er skaptr, því geyja skal,
gera ætlak mér létt of tal;
verit hafði mér verra í hug,
var þat nær sem kveisu flug,
jafnan fagnar kvikr maðr kú,
kennir hins, at gleðjumk nú.

5. Alllítit er ungs manns gaman,
einum þykkir daufligt saman,
annars barn er sem úlf at frjá,
óðfúss myndi blindr at sjá;
dýrt láta menn dróttins orð,
drekarnir rísa opt á sporð,
ǫðlingr skyldi einkar rǫskr,
œpa kann í mœrum frǫskr.

6. Fylki skal til frægðar hafa,
fregna eigum langt til gafa,
oddar gerva jarli megin,
útsker verða af bǫrum þvegin;
ýmsir bjóða ǫðrum fár,
(ormar skríða ór hamsi á vár)
vel hefr sás þat líða lætr,
langar eigu þeir bersi nætr.

7. Bjarki átti hugarkorn hart,
herlið feldi Stǫrkuðr mart,
(ekki var hann í hvíldum hœgr),
Hrómundr þótti garpr ok slœgr;
ókat þeim né einn á bug,
Eljárnir var trúr at hug,

fílinn gat hann í fylking sótt,
fullstrǫng hefr sú mannraun þótt.

8. Bana þóttusk þeir bíða vel,
    Brandingi svaf loks í hel,
    Mardallar var glysligr grátr,
    gleðr sá mann er opt er kátr;
    Ásmundr tamði Gnóð við gjálfr,
    gulli mælti Þjazi sjálfr,
    Niðjungr skóf af haugi horn;
    hølzti eru nú minni forn.

9. Friggjar þótti svipr at syni,
    sá var taldr ór miklu kyni,
    Hermóðr vildi auka aldr,
    Éljúðnir vann sólginn Baldr,
    ǫll grétu þau eptir hann,
    aukit var þeim hlátrar bann,
    heyrinkunn er frá hǫnum saga,
    hvat þarf ek of slíkt at jaga.

10. Sitt mein þykkir sárast hveim,
    sáttargǫrð er ætluð tveim,
    oddamaðr fæsk opt enn þriði,
    jafntrúr skal sá hvárra liði;
    engi of dœmir sjálfan sik
    (slíkt ætlak nú henda mik),
    ýta lið þótt alt fari byrst,
    engi læzk því valda fyrst.

11. Stefjum verðr at stæla brag,
    stuttligt hefk á kvæði lag,
    ella mun þat þykkja þula,
    þannig nær sem ek henda mula.
    Ekki var þat forðum farald,
    Finnan gat þó œrðan Harald,
    hǫnum þótti sólbjǫrt sú,
    slíks dœmi verðr mǫrgum nú.

12. Skips láta menn skammar rár,
    skatna þykkir hugrinn grár,
    tungan leikr við tanna sár,
    trauðla er gengt á ís of vár;
    mjǫk fár er sér œrinn einn,
    eyvit týr, þótt skyndi seinn,
    gǫfgask mætti af gengi hverr,
    gǫrva þekkik sumt hvé ferr.

13. Afli of deilir sízt við sjǫ́,
    Sǫrli sprakk af gildri þrǫ́,
    stundum þýtr í logni lǫ́,
    litlu verr, at ráðak fǫ́;
    mǫrgum þykkir fullgott fé,
    frænuskammr er enn deigi lé,
    kvæðit skal með kynjum alt,
    konungs morginn er langr ávalt.

14. Bráðsét láta bragnar opt,
    bregðr at þeim, er heldr á lopt,
    allmargr er til seinn at sefask,
    svá kǫllum vér rǫ́ð sem gefask.
    Ekki var þat forðum farald,
    Finnan gat þó œrðan Harald,
    hǫ́num þótti sólbjǫrt sú,
    slíks dœmi verðr mǫrgum nú.

15. Auðigr þykkir einn sér hvar,
    annars rœðir margr of far,
    ørgranns erum vér lengst á leit,
    lundvær þykkir bezta sveit;
    skammæ þykkja ófin ǫll,
    ekki mart er verra en trǫll,
    eigi spillir hyggins hjali,
    hefkat ek spurt at bersa kali.

16. Engi þarf at hræðask hót,
    heldr kømr opt við sáran fót,

hlutgjarn ferr með annars sǫk;
nøkkvi ríkstr er heima hverr,
- - - - - - - - - - -
øngu tala ek umb at síðr,
orðin fara þegar munninn líðr.

17. Varla sýnisk alt sem er
    ýtum þeim, er bægir drer,
    eigi at eins er í fǫgru fengr,
    fundit mun þat er reynt er lengr.
    Ekki var þat forðum farald,
    Finnan gat þó œrðan Harald,
    hǫnum þótti sólbjǫrt sú,
    slíks dœmi verðr mǫrgum nú.

18. Efnum þykkir bezt at búa,
    brǫgðótt reyndisk gemlu fúa,
    margar kunni hon slœgðir sér,
    svá nǫkkvi gafsk Rannveig mér;
    illa hefr sás annan sýkr,
    eigi veit áðr hefndum lýkr,
    bráðfengr þykkir brullaups frami,
    brigða lengi er hverr enn sami.

19. Lýtin þykkja skammæ skarar,
    skrautligt kǫllum nafnit farar,
    trautt kallak þann valda er varar,
    verða menn þeir er uppi fjarar,
    ógipt verðr í umbúð skjót,
    élin þykkja mǫrgum ljót,
    engi of sér við ǫllum rokum,
    jafnan spyrja menn at lokum.

20. Ástblindir 'ro seggir svá
    sumir, at þykkja mjǫk fás gá,
    (þannig verðr of mansǫng mælt)
    marga hefr þat hyggna tælt.
    Ekki var þat forðum farald,
    Finnan gat þó œrðan Harald,

hǫnum þótti sólbjǫrt sú,
slíks dœmi verðr mǫrgum nú.

21. Ynðit láta engir falt,
allopt verðr í hreggi svalt,
andaðs drúpa minjar mest,
magran skyldi kaupa hest;
œrit þykkir viðkvæm vǫ,
vinfengin eru misjǫfn þá,
fasthaldr varð á Fenri lagðr,
fíkjum var mér ramligr sagðr.

22. Grandvarr skyldi enn góði maðr,
Gizurr varð at rógi saðr,
etja vildi jǫfrum saman,
ekki er mér at stúru gaman;
kunna vildak sjá við snǫrum,
sjaldan hygg at gyggvi vǫrum,
vel hefr hinn, er sitr of sitt,
svartflekkótt er kvæði mitt.

23. Jafnan segir enn ríkri rǫ́ð,
rǫskvir menn gefa ǫrnum brǫ́ð,
upp at eins er ungum vegar,
engi maðr er roskinn þegar;
falls er vǫ́n af fornu tré,
fleira þykkir gott en sé,
auðsénna er annars vamm,
engi kømsk of skapadœgr framm.

24. Engi knettr of annars mein,
(aldri lætk at munni sein)
heimi heyrik sagt at snúi,
sumir einir hygg at mér trúi;
erfitt verðr þeims illa kann,
engan þarf at hjúfra mann,
þannig hefr mér lagzk í lund,
langviðrum skal eyða grund.

25. Sjaldan hittisk feigs vǫk frørin,
    fljóðin verða at ǫldrum kørin,
    lengi hefr þat lýst fyr mér,
    lítinn kost á margr und sér;
    sagt er frá, hvé neflauss narir,
    nú verðr sumt þats mangi varir,
    (væri betr at þegðak þokks)
    þat hefr hverr er verðr er loks.

26. Þrýtra þann er verr hefr valt,
    verða kann á ýmsa halt,
    misjafnir 'ro blinds manns bitar,
    bǫlit kǫllum vér ilt til litar;
    eik hefr þats af ǫðrum skefr,
    ekki mart er slœgra en refr,
    jafnan verðr at áflóð stakar,
    auðfengnar 'ro gelti sakar.

27. Gullormr á sér brennheitt ból,
    bjartast skínn í heiði sól,
    undrum þykkir gagnsætt gler,
    glymjandi fellr hrǫnn of sker;
    allar girnask ár í sjá,
    ekki er manni verra en þrá,
    fýsa munk ens fyrra vara,
    flestr mun sik til nǫkkurs spara.

28. Geta má þess er gengit hefr,
    gerir sá betr er annan svefr,
    veitkat víst hvat verða kann,
    villa er dælst of heimskan mann,
    fláróðum má trautt of trúa,
    til sín skyldi enu betra snúa,
    hugga skal þanns harm hefr beðit,
    hølzti mjǫk er at flestu kveðit.

29. Orða er leitat mér í munn,
    mælgin verðr oss heyrinkunn,
    (Yggjar bjór hverr eiga myni

ósýnt þykkir lýða kyni);
eyvit mun sjá atfrétt stoða,
allmjǫk er mér lund til hroða,
þeygi var sjá aflausn ill,
eiga skal nú hverr er vill.

30. Stjórnlausu hefk slungit saman,
svá vildak [mér hitta gaman].

1. . . . . is silent.
what any one person says can be denied.
. . . .
. . . . only deceives somewhat less.
I intend to bring old sayings together.
Most people take pleasure in something.
This nonsense shows my good cheer.
It is then as if one gathers pickings.

2. I have not gone in for lampoons.
Full well would I have had excuse for that.
I can compose more rudely than you'd expect.
Everyone seems to know it.
I would not be robbed of my patrimony,
even if I should always speak bluntly.[7]
One has to row first toward the nearest ness.
I would have some pedigree for that.

3. The world learns all that three people know.
They behave worse who break sworn pledges.
I'm not aiming that at any one person.
Many in turn have experienced its truth.
Angry words shall be found here.
I have the right to speak mouthfuls about that—
she rather managed to look after herself,
the wise-eyed woman—how she treated me.

---

7. ON *slætt* 'bluntly' (rhyming with *ætt*); the manuscript reads *slétt* 'smoothly, plainly'.

4. Men should give rest to their wrath.
   Often a very little thing occasions strife.
   A dog is shaped for barking.
   I intend to make my speech lighthearted.
   Something worse had been in my mind.
   It was almost like the pain of a boil.
   The living man always rejoices in a cow.
   It is clear that I am cheering up now.

5. It takes very little to amuse the young.
   Life seems dreary to one alone.
   To love another's child is to cherish a wolf.
   Desperately would the blind wish to see.
   People say a lord's word is precious.
   Dragons often rise up on their tail.
   A prince should be especially brave.
   A frog can croak in the marshes.

6. One shall have a prince for glory.
   We ought to hear of a bird of prey from far off.[8]
   Spears give strength to a jarl.
   Outer skerries are washed by waves.
   Many offer harm to another.
   Snakes crawl from their slough in spring.
   He behaves well who lets it pass by.
   A bear and his kind have long nights.

7. Bjarki[9] had a fierce corn of courage [=heart].
   Starkaðr[10] felled a great troop.
   (He was not gentle in repose.)
   Hrómundr[11] seemed bold and cunning.

---

8. *gafi* '?bird of prey'. This may be the word used once for 'carrion bird' in *Stjórn* 316/20 paraphrasing Leviticus 11:13; or it may be an otherwise unknown term meaning 'fool': cf. Scottish dialectal *gaff* 'loud, rude talk', OE *gegafspræc* 'foolish speech'.

9. Bǫðvarr bjarki 'little bear', hero named in *Hrólfs saga kraka* and *Bjarkamál in fornu*.

10. Hero featured in Saxo's Danish history, in *Gautreks saga*, and elsewhere.

11. Champion in *Hrómundar saga Gripssonar*, seventeenth-century saga, probably based on late medieval *rímur*, themselves preceded by a now-lost saga like that famously mentioned in *Þorgils saga ok Hafliða* (after 1237).

(No one made him give way.)
Eljárnir[12] was loyal and brave.
He conquered the elephant in the phalanx.
That test of manhood seemed very tough.

8. They determined to face death well.
Brandingi[13] slept at last in hell.
Mardǫll's[14] weeping was glittering.
That person gladdens who is often happy.
Ásmundr[15] accustomed Gnóð to the sea.
Þjazi's[16] own speech was gold.
Niðjungr[17] scraped a horn from the mound.
This is exceedingly old lore now.

9. That was a shock about Frigg's son.
He was reckoned from a great family.
Hermóðr[18] wanted to extend his life.
Éljúðnir[19] had swallowed up Baldr.
They all wept for him.
Their laughter-ban [=grief] grew.
The story about him is very well known.
No need for me to harp on it.

10. To each his own pain seems the sorest.
It takes two to arrange a reconciliation.
Often a mediator is brought in as a third.
Equally trustworthy must he be to both sides.
No one passes sentence on himself.
(I suppose such will happen to me now.)
Though all the troop of men go bristling,
No one allows that he caused it first.

---

12. Eleazar in 1 Maccabees 6:43–47.
13. Unknown; giant-name in Snorri's *Edda*.
14. The tears of Mardǫll (=Freyja) are gold.
15. Hero of the popular *Egils saga einhenda ok Ásmundar berserkjabana*; his ship, Gnoð, is said to have been "the largest . . . north of the Aegean Sea."
16. The word or mouthful of a giant (Þjazi) is gold.
17. Unknown; *niðjungr* 'kinsman, descendant'.
18. Brother of Baldr, according to Snorri.
19. 'Rain-damp', Hel's hall.

11. Poetry has to be fitted with refrains
    (I have an abrupt manner in this verse)
    else it shall seem a rigmarole,
    almost as if I were grabbing at crumbs.
    It wasn't a plague in the old days.
    Still, the Lappish girl drove Haraldr out of his mind.
    To him she seemed bright as the sun.
    An example of such comes to many now.[20]

12. Men say the ship's sailyards are short.
    The heart of magnates seems grey.
    The tongue plays with the aching tooth.
    One scarcely walks on ice in spring.
    Very few are sufficient in themselves.
    It helps not though the slow hasten.
    Each man could gain stature from his company.
    I recognize fully how sorrow goes.

13. One vies in strength least against the sea.
    Sǫrli[21] burst from great longing.
    At times coastal waters resound in a calm.
    It hardly matters that I prevail but little.
    To many a man wealth seems good enough.
    Of short sharpness is the soft scythe.
    The whole poem shall be really weird.
    A king's morning is always long.

14. Men often let things be hastily seen.
    He whose hand is generous prospers.
    Very many a man is too slow to calm down.
    We judge counsels as they turn out.
    It wasn't a plague in the old days.
    Still, the Lappish girl drove Haraldr out of his mind.

---

20. This refrain (lines 5–8) is also found in the late fourteenth-century *Flateyjarbók*, *Þáttr Hauks hábrókar* (I, 577–83, at 583).

21. Identified by Reiðar Th. Christiansen as Seurlus, son of the king of Bergen in a Gaelic ballad, whose heart and ribs broke when he swam out to sea after his mermaid-lover (*Vikings and the Viking Wars*, pp. 413–16).

To him she seemed bright as the sun.
An example of such comes to many now.

15. A single man seems to himself rich everywhere.
     Many a one speaks about the conduct of another.
     We seek longest after the flawless.
     Peaceable company seems the best.
     Everything beyond the mean seems short-lived.
     Not much is worse than a troll.
     Nothing spoils the talk of a wise man.
     I have not heard that [a polar bear freezes].

16. No one needs to fear threats.
     Rather often does something touch a sore foot.
     . . . .
     A busybody conducts another's suit.
     At home each man is something of a king.
     . . . .
     In no way do I speak about it the less.
     Words travel as soon as they leave the mouth.

17. All seems hardly as it is
     to those men afflicted by eye-disease.[22]
     Not only in the beautiful is there gain.
     That shall be found the longer it is tested.
     It wasn't a plague in the old days.
     Still, the Lappish girl drove Haraldr out of his mind.
     To him she seemed bright as the sun.
     An example of such comes to many now.

18. It seems best to live with resources.
     The vixen proved cunning to the old ewe.
     Many tricks she knew for herself.
     So indeed Rannveig showed herself to me.
     He behaves badly who betrays another.
     One's lot is not known until vengeance ends.

---

22. ON *drer* 'cataract, eye ailment': see Konráð Gíslason, *Efterladte Skrifter*, pp. 140–41.

The glory of the wedding feast seems quickly won.
Exceedingly long is every man the same.

19. Hair's flaws [from a poor cut] seem of short duration.
We call the name of an expedition 'glorious'.
I scarcely declare the one who warns to be at fault.
Men there are who end up high and dry.
Misfortune is quick in its preparations.
Snowstorms seem ugly to many.
No one avoids all sudden gusts.
People always ask about conclusions.

20. Some men are so blinded by love
that they seem to heed very little.
So it is said in a love-song:
it has deceived many wise men.
It wasn't a plague in the old days.
Still, the Lappish girl drove Haraldr out of his mind.
To him she seemed bright as the sun.
An example of such comes to many now.

21. None puts his love up for sale.
Very often sleet makes for cold weather.
Memories of the dead fade fast.
One should buy a lean horse.
Woe seems tangible enough.
Friendships are unequal then.
A fetter was laid on Fenrir.[23]
I was told it was hugely strong.

22. The good man should be guileless.
Gizurr[24] proved guilty of slander.
He wanted to incite kings against each other.
I have no delight in gloom.
I would like to be able to avoid snares.

---

23. Wolf fettered by the gods until the end of the world.
24. Name for Óðinn.

I think the wary man seldom stumbles.
He behaves well who tends his own.
Black-flecked is my poem.

23. The more powerful always offers advice.
Valiant men give raw meat to eagles.
Only up is the young man's path.
No person is at once fully grown.
There is expectation of a fall from an old tree.
More seems good than may be.
The blemish of another is more easily seen.
No one goes beyond his fated day.

24. No one bemoans another's misfortune.
(I never rein in my mouth.)
I hear tell that the world is turning.
Only some, I think, will believe me.
Life is difficult for him who poorly understands.
One need not lament anyone.
The thought has thus lodged itself in my mind:
With long-lasting storms shall the earth be laid waste.

25. Seldom is a doomed man's ice-hole found frozen.
Women are chosen at drinking parties.[25]
That has been clear to me for a long time.
Many a one has little in his power.
It is related how a noseless[26] person languishes.
Now comes something that no one expects.
It were far better that I should be silent.
Each gets what he deserves in the end.

26. The badly behaved never loses his touch.
First one, then another, gets the short stick.
Unequal are the mouthfuls of a blind man.
We call grief bad for the complexion.

---

25. *at ǫldrum* 'at drinking parties'; Finnur Jónsson read: 'according to their ages'.
26. MS *neflauss* 'noseless' is sometimes read as *nefalauss* 'without kinsmen'.

An oak has what is scraped from others.
Not much is slyer than a fox.
A torrent always up-ends things.
Readily devised are grievances against a hog.[27]

27. The gold-serpent has for itself a burning-hot den.[28]
The sun shines brightest in a cloudless sky.
Glass seems wondrously transparent.
The wave falls roaring over the skerry.
All rivers yearn to run to the sea.
Nothing is worse for a person than longing.
I strongly advise prior caution.
Most will spare themselves something.

28. What has passed can be related.
He does better who soothes another.
I know not for certain what can happen.
It is easiest to lead astray a foolish man.
One can scarcely trust the deceitful.
One should turn the better toward oneself.
One shall console the man who has suffered sorrow.
Exceedingly much is decreed about most.

29. They search in my mouth for words.
The chatter is well known to me.
Who shall possess Óðinn's mead [= the poem]
seems unclear to the race of men.

---

27. The Old Norse word for 'hog' is now almost illegible in the manuscript. The word read by Jón Sigurdsson and Theodor Möbius as *gelti* (dative of *goltr* 'hog'), and by Finnur Jónsson as *gellti*, appears in Valgerður Erna Þorvaldsdóttir's new transcription of the poem as *gesti* (dative of *gestr* 'guest'): 'easily devised are grievances against a guest.' The earlier reading (followed here), which suggests that one easily condemns to death what one wants to eat, is perhaps supported by the Greek and Latin proverb cited by Erasmus (III.iii.99): "canis peccatum sus dependit" 'the dog offended, the sow paid the penalty.' Erasmus is puzzled by this adage, saying only that it is "used when one person has done wrong, and someone quite different pays the penalty. The occurrence which gave rise to it is not clear; nor does it matter very much, for it smacks of the common herd." See Erasmus, *Collected Works*, vol. 34: *Adages II.vii.i to III.iii.100*, p. 315.

28. Dwelling-place of dragon = gold (in skaldic diction).

That inquiry will be of no use.
I very much have a mind for 'refuse'.
Not at all was this 'release' poor.
Now anyone who wants it shall have it.[29]

30. I have thrown together without rudder
as I wished . . .

---

29. This entire stanza seems to me to allude, sometimes indelicately, to the story told by
Snorri in his *Edda* about the origin of poetry. In his fright (a giant in eagle-costume was right
on his tail), Óðinn voided some of the mead backwards (i.e., he shat): "that part," Snorri concludes, "was the fool-poet's share, and *anyone who wanted could have it*." ON *aflausn* 'release,
compensation' but also 'diarrhea'; ON *hroði* 'refuse, coarseness' but also 'excretion'.

From the Wound in Christ's Side to the Wound in His Heart: Progression from Male Exegesis to Female Mysticism

George Hardin Brown

The development and changes in the devotion to the wounds and instruments of Christ's Passion provide a fascinating study in religious, literary, and iconographic history. It is especially instructive to chart devotion to the wound in the side of Christ as it evolves from typological exegesis to fervid piety. This devotional mutation occurred during the massive cultural shift in the West between the early Middle Ages and the later Middle Ages, with the great watershed of the eleventh and twelfth centuries dividing them.[1] Devotional practices underwent an alteration from thoughtful rumination to powerfully emotive mysticism. No devotion was more fraught with such a dynamic than that to the wound in Christ's side that later became the wound in his heart.

The key scriptural text that forms the basis of the devotion is the gospel of John, 19:33–34. The Revised Standard Version translates the Greek as "But when they [the Roman soldiers] came to Jesus and saw that he was already dead, they did not break his legs. Instead, one of the soldiers pierced his side with a spear, and at once blood and water came out." In that verse rather than the verb ἔνυξεν ("enyxen"), 'pierced, stabbed' attested in most of the Greek versions, there are a few variant readings with the verb

I offer this essay as a tribute to Helen Damico, a dear friend and admired scholar-teacher, who has done so much in her career for medieval studies and for medievalists. Her interests in Bede and in feminist literature inspired this paper. I also want to thank Catherine Karkov for a number of references and suggestions, Jeffrey Hamburger for his generous help with iconography and bibliography, and my wife Phyllis for her sage editorial assistance.

1. The shift in devotional sensibility from the early to the late Middle Ages has been remarked on variously by historians in the past. For a recent sensitive synthesis see Fulton, *From Judgment to Passion*. Her book, which begins with an appreciation of the *Heliand* as a culturally accommodating text, emphasizes the early medieval Christ as Judge in contrast to the later suffering Jesus who elicits compassion. My essay, which begins with an even earlier period, does not treat Christ as Judge but as the Savior whose side wound evokes a different devotional response in the early commentators from that of the later mystics, a movement from a sober and symbolic interpretation to an intensely personal and amatory involvement.

(probably formed by itacism) as ἤνοιξεν ("ēnoixen"), 'opened'. Hence the Vulgate Latin translates the verb as "aperuit" 'opened'.[2] The Latin version facilitated Augustine's interpretation: "Vigilanti uerbo euangelista usus est, ut non diceret: Latus eius percussit, aut uulnerauit, aut quid alius; sed aperuit; ut illic quodammodo uitae ostium panderetur, unde sacramenta ecclesiae manauerunt, sine quibus ad uitam quae uera uita est, non intratur" (The evangelist has used the word with care, so that he does not say "He struck his side," or "wounded it," or anything else, but "he opened it," that there somehow the gate of life was opened, whence the sacraments of the church poured forth, without which there is no entry into the life which is the true life).[3] Bede and later exegetes embraced this interpretation.[4]

In the patristic and early medieval period, of which Bede is representative, the wound described in this Vulgate text proved a rich source of metaphoric and allegorical exegetical interpretation and formed the basis of a complex devotional ensemble. Only later, however, from the twelfth century to our modern era, was the text understood to mean that the spear thrust opened Jesus' heart. What had been considered a wound that opened the interior of Christ's body so that fountains of sacramental grace welled up from it became a wound in his heart so that that organ as a source of life and of love poured forth its vital power on man and woman.

Of course the symbolic power of the heart has always been prominent in Western culture. The heart is ubiquitous in both classical and medieval secular and sacred texts.[5] The Bible, in both the Old and New Testaments, is full of references to the heart as the center of both human and divine compassion.[6] But it is after the eleventh century that Christ's heart, purportedly opened by Longinus's lance, becomes the focus of his Passion and

---

2. See *Nestle-Aland Novum Testamentum Graece et Latine*, ed. Nestle, Nestle and Aland, note to John 19:34.

3. *Anchor Bible*, ed. Raymond E. Brown, p. 935, calls attention to this passage in Augustine. The text is here taken from *Sancti Aurelii Augustini in Iohannis Evangelium tractatus CXXIV*, CCSL 36, Tractatus 120.2, p. 61; followed by my translation.

4. Bede, following Augustine, insists on the reading *aperuit*: "The Holy Church believes his right side was opened by the soldier. Here too the evangelist used the appropriate word when instead of saying he struck or wounded his side, said *opened*, that is to say, as it were, the door of the middle side through which a path to heavenly things might be thrown open to us," *On the Temple*, ed. and trans. Connolly, p. 29. On Augustine's reading of John 19:34, see Houghton, *Augustine's Text of John*, p. 349.

5. On this vast subject see, for instance, Anonymous, *Das Herz*, vol. 1: *Das Herz im Umkreis des Glaubens*; vol. 2: *Das Herz im Umkreis der Kunst*; vol. 3: *Im Umkreis des Denkens*; also Jager, *Book of the Heart*.

6. See *Theological Dictionary of the New Testament*, ed. Kittle, 3:605–13, καρδία.

the emblem of intense love and union with the disciple.[7] It may come as a surprise that the exegetical and iconographic topos of the Sacred Heart is historically late. The reason for this delayed development is threefold, physiological, semantic, and affective. First, the widespread patristic and noncanonical tradition that the lance pierced Christ's *right* side makes an entry of the lance into Christ's heart on his left side physiologically unlikely, although one physician has declared it feasible.[8] The idea that the lance pierced the right side finds support in the Ethiopic version of John's Gospel and is nearly universal in the iconography of the Crucifixion.[9] But the physiological impediment was eventually ignored for the symbolic rectitude of right over left, and for typological analogies favoring the right side, such as water flowing from the right side of the temple in Ezekiel's vision (47:2, Vulgate). Second, the semantic problem: neither in the text, John 19:33–34, nor in a supporting text, John 7:37–38, does "heart" occur. In the latter, John quotes Jesus at the Feast of the Tabernacles, "If anyone thirst, let him come [to me]; and let him drink who believes in me. As the Scripture says, 'From within him shall flow rivers of living waters.'"[10] "From within him" translates the Greek ἐκ τῆς κοιλίας 'from the belly', not, despite some modern translations, 'from the heart'.[11] Third, the delay in concentration on Christ's heart as the seat of love: Origen, Ambrose, and especially Augustine treat the heart as the moral and spiritual core of the human being, and Bede and other exegetes often cite Christ's words, "Learn of me

---

7. The name Longinus is derived from the instrument the soldier used, Greek λόγχη 'lance'.

8. Barbet, *Doctor at Calvary*, ch. 7, "The Wound in the Heart," pp. 113–27. On p. 115, Barbet quotes a sentence from Augustine's *De civitate Dei* 15.26 but includes the word "dextro" after "in latere," for which there is no textual justification from any scholarly edition of the work. Whatever his source, this indicates how insistent writers and copyists were to augment "side" with "right."

9. *Anchor Bible*, ed. Raymond E. Brown, p. 935: "The Ethiopic specifies that it was the right side, a specification that appears also in the apocryphal works (*Acts of Pilate*) and has guided artistic reproduction of the scene." However, I have been unable to find such a specification in any edition of the *Acts of Pilate* (also known as *The Gospel of Nicodemus*), either in the Greek versions or any of the translations.

10. Trans. *Anchor Bible*, ed. Raymond E. Brown. The grammatical problems of these lines have generated an enormous literature and protracted discussion among exegetes, well summarized in ibid., pp. 320–23. The RSV translates verse 38 as "Out of the believer's heart shall flow rivers of living water," thus siding with those interpreters, ancient and modern, who understand the waters as welling from the believer's, not from Jesus's, heart, and translating κοιλία 'innards' as 'heart', but with a note, "Gk 'out of the belly'."

11. See Raymond E. Brown's informative note, *Anchor Bible*, pp. 323–24.

for I am meek and humble of heart" (Matt. 11:29); however, the concentration on the Savior's heart as a seat of all-consuming love for mankind is a mark of the Cistercian movement and then of the religious orders of men and women from the twelfth century onwards.[12] So the exegesis of the Johannine texts by the Fathers and early medieval commentators such as Bede remains on the wound in Christ's side and the cavity that the spear thrust made in his interior, considered as a well from which poured forth his redeeming blood and sacral water. Only later do devotional writers, following the Cistercians, locate the wound actually in Christ's heart.

Adopting the interpretations by Ambrose, Augustine, Quodvultdeus, and Jerome and retextualizing them, Bede sees the birth of the Church in Christ's sending forth his Spirit on the cross and the pouring out of blood and water from the wound in his side. By Christ's offering and death the sacramental water of baptism purifies, and the blood of the Eucharist redeems and nourishes.[13] Drawing upon a common patristic comparison, Bede says that just as from Adam's side Eve, "the mother of all the living," was formed during Adam's sleep, so from the second Adam's side the Church, the mother of all the spiritually living, was formed during Christ's sleep of death.[14] This he expresses in verse as well:

De carne Christo propria
Et sanguinis mysterio

---

12. That is not to say that love for the suffering Christ and union with him in his Passion first emerged in the twelfth century. The nun Baudonivia in her Life of Queen Radegunde, who died in 587, stressed Radegunde's fervent devotion to the crucified Christ in her heart, where she felt he dwelt. See *La Vida Radegundis di Baudonivia*, ed. Santorilli, ch. 5, lines 110–14, ch. 20, and ch. 21, line 538, and commentary, pp. 122 and 151. There is a translation of Baudonivia's Life in *Sainted Women of the Dark Ages*, ed. and trans. McNamara and Halborg with Whatley, pp. 86–105. But even though Radegunde's intense devotion to Christ's passion motivated her acquisition of the relic of the Cross for her convent at Poitiers, it was not until the twelfth century that religious concentrated that devotion on the wound in Christ's heart.

13. Ambrose, *Explanatio super Psalmos XII*, Ps. 45, ch. 12, CCSL 64, p. 337; *Expositio Evangelii secundum Lucam*, CCSL 14, lib. 10, line 473; *Epistulae*, lib. 1, epist. 2, par.10, CSEL 82, p.19; Augustine, *Tractatus in Evangelium Iohannis*, 120.2, PL 35, 1953; *Sermones de scripturis*, Sermo 5, *PL* 38.55; Sermo 311, *PL* 38.1415. Bede, *In Genesim, liber primus, PL* 91. col. 38; CCSL 118A, p. 38; *De Templo*, ch. 8, "Aqua scilicet, qua abluimur in baptismo, et sanguis quo consecramur in calice sancto," *PL* 91, col. 735; CCSL 119A, lines 744–84 at 767, pp. 165–66.

14. Augustine, Sermo 5 (*PL* 38, 55): "Et quando exivit sanguis et aqua de latere? Cum jam dormiret Christus in cruce: quia Adam in Paradiso somnum accepit, et sic illi de latere Eva producta est." See Bede, *In Genesim* 1,2, CCSL 118A, p. 38, lines 1175–91. For an extensive list of other patristic sources for this concept, see Tromp, "De Nativitate Ecclesiae," p. 503.

Iam sponsa nata est in cruce
Obdormiente splendida.

(From Christ's own flesh and the mystery of his blood, the spouse has
been born on the resplendent cross, during his sleep.)[15]

By such a birth the Church is at once daughter and spouse, troping the
text of the Song of Songs, "my sister, my bride" (4:9). In a homily for Holy
Week Bede writes that the Church "has been produced from the side of
her Redeemer, that is, imbued with the water of cleansing and the blood
of sanctification which came forth from his side when he was dying for her
sake."[16] Bede also points out in his commentary to the First Letter of John
that the living water and blood poured from the dead body of the Lord
gave us life.[17] In these he is of course emphasizing a theme inherent in the
Johannine texts.

In the homily on Luke 24:36–47, for a Sunday after Easter, Bede explains the meaning of the resurrected Lord's showing the wound in his
side to his disciples:

> It was not without cause that he ordered them to see and recognize his
> hands and feet instead of his countenance, which they knew equally well.
> He ordered it so that, when they saw the signs of the nails with which he
> had been fastened to the cross, they would be able to understand that it
> was not only a body which they saw, but the very body of their Lord, which
> they knew had been crucified. Hence John, when he mentions the appear-
> ance of the Lord, does well to testify that he also showed his disciples his
> side, which had been wounded by the soldier, so that as they recognized
> many indications of the passion they knew so well and the death he had
> undergone, they might rejoice with more certain faith in the resurrection
> and the destruction of death he had accomplished.[18]

Bede then gives four reasons why Christ kept the scars of his wounds after
his Resurrection, namely, "that he was not a spirit without a body but a
spiritual body," that by keeping the scars of his wounds he shows forever
what he has done for humanity, that the elect will in seeing the signs of his
Passion "never stop thanking him," and that even the damned at the final
judgment "will see him whom they have pierced" (John 19:37).[19]

---

15. Bede, *Hymni et preces* I. st. 16, CCSL 122, p. 409.
16. Bede, *Homilies on the Gospels*, Homily 2.4, 2.36; CCSL 122, Homilia 2.4, p. 209.
17. Bede, *In epistulas septem catholicas*, In 1 Ioh., 5.7–8, CCSL 121, p. 321.
18. Bede, *Homilies on the Gospels*, Homily 2.9, p. 81; CCSL 122, Homilia 2.9, p. 241.
19. Bede, *Homilies on the Gospels*, Homily 2.9, pp. 82–83; CCSL 122, Homilia 2.9, p. 242.

The Carolingian poet and author of the *Libri Carolini*, Theodulf of Orléans, was so impressed with this passage of Bede that he wrote a poem, "Why Did the Scars of Christ's Passion Remain on His Body after the Resurrection?" Helen Waddell, not recognizing Theodulf's source and accepting it as wholly his, declared that nothing else in Carolingian verse was worthy to stand beside it.[20]

Bede relates other biblical texts to the verse in John's Gospel. For instance, in his Commentary on the Acts of the Apostles, when he comes to the passage (12:7) where the angel struck Peter on the side, he remarks: "The striking of his side was a remembrance of Christ's passion, from whose wound our salvation poured forth."[21] In his Old Testament commentaries Bede finds significant passages that prefigure the wound in the side of Christ. To the modern reader his interpretations may seem extravagant and impressionistic. As we read Bede's scriptural commentaries, we observe that where Bede speaks of Christ's wounds, especially the wound in his side, he deals with the subject in two different ways. In the commentaries on the New Testament (Luke, Mark, Acts, and the Catholic Epistles), Bede discusses the wounds and their significance in a simple fashion, relating them to Old Testament figures and types, pointing out the spiritual significance of the wounds for the Christian, but not venturing far into symbolic interpretation. As a rule, he simply alludes to a pertinent Old Testament figure, such as the spouse in the Song of Songs, or he cites a passage such as Isaiah 53:5, "But he was wounded for our transgressions, crushed for our iniquities; upon him was the punishment that made us whole, and by his bruises we are healed." From that passage he stresses the irony that through Christ's wounding comes our healing, as before he pointed out that in Christ's death is our life.

In his commentaries on the Old Testament (Genesis, Samuel, Ezra, Song of Songs, and On the Temple), Bede enters into an elaborate allegorical mode. He becomes highly allusive and richly poetic; he alludes to Christ's wounds in a complex and figurative manner. This difference of treatment is surely due to what Bede perceived as the function of allegoresis. From St. Paul and Origen through the entire patristic period exegetes

---

20. Waddell, *Poetry in the Dark Ages*, pp. 25–27, cited in Freeman and Meyvaert, "Meaning of Theodulf's Apse Mosaic," pp. 133–34. See also Meyvaert and Davril, "Théodulfe et Bède."

21. Bede, *Bede's Commentary on the Acts of the Apostles*, p. 112; *Expositio Actuum Apostolorum*, 12.7 CCSL 121, p. 58.

interpreted the events, people, and descriptive details of the Old Testament as symbolically pregnant with meaning for the New Dispensation. By divine plan the Old Testament is hermeneutically seeded for the exegete to harvest. Bede's own special patristic mentor, Gregory the Great, in his *Moralia* ingeniously interpreted every verse and thing in the Book of Job. Respecting the patristic precedent, Bede undertook with his own formidable interpretive and editorial talents Old Testament exegesis, extracting its allegorical and typological significance. For Bede as for Gregory, the Old Testament object or event is not as important in itself as what it portends for the New, whereas the object or event in the New Testament is the inherently significant, self-referential reality that fulfils the Old Testament figure. In treating the Old Testament books, the allegorical meaning is superior to the literal meaning. As Bede explains in his introductory remarks on the book of Tobit, "Yet anyone who knows how to interpret the text not just historically, but allegorically, sees that just as fruits surpass their leaves, this book's inner sense surpasses its literal simplicity. For if understood spiritually, it is seen to contain in itself the great mysteries of Christ and the Church."[22] The New Testament and the Church are the actualization in history of what the allegory of the Old Testament presaged. Bede's treatment of the wounds of Christ therefore varies according to whether he speaks of them in the context of an Old Testament verse or event or whether he speaks of them in the historical context of the New Testament and their sacramental meaning in the life of the Church. For him, the former is allegorical, poetic, suggestive, and symbolic of the later reality; the latter, nonrelative and historically realized. The wound in the side of Christ is meaningful in itself, whereas the entry into the ark of Noah and the entry into the Temple are figural representations or types of that wound.

Before we proceed to the symbolic interpretations of the Johannine text in Bede's Old Testament commentaries, I should first quote the verse from John 19:34 as Bede gives it in his commentary on the Book of Kings: "Passo in cruce Domino, 'unus militum lancea latus ejus *dextrum* aperuit, et continuo exivit sanguis et aqua'"[23] (When the Lord suffered on the cross, "one of the soldiers opened his *right* side, and immediately came forth blood and water"). Why did Bede, who rarely tampers with a biblical quotation, insert that word, *dextrum* 'right', into the Gospel text? As I pointed

---

22. Bede, *Bede: A Biblical Miscellany*, p. xxx and 57; Bede, *In librum beati patris Tobiae*, p. 3.
23. Bede, *In Regum XXX quaestiones*, 12 (3 Reg. 6:8), p. 304, lines 24–25.

out above, it is not found in any canonical text of the Gospel, including the Codex Amiatinus written in Bede's own monastery during his lifetime; but it does occur in citations of some Fathers and in two poems by Prudentius (fourth century).[24] By placing the wound on the right side the biblical and patristic favoring of the right over the left is observed.[25] This preference occurs in both the Latin and vernacular texts, such as that moving Old English poem, *The Dream of the Rood*.[26] Early liturgical directions stipulate that the priest break the host at the *fractio* on its right side,[27] and later liturgical interpreters also require that the chalice be placed on the right side of the host to recall that blood and water that emerged from Christ's right side.[28] Such a tradition has guided artistic reproduction of the scene from the Syrian Rabbula Gospels of 586 (Florence, Biblioteca Medicea Laurenziana, MS Laur. Plut.I.56, fol. 13) to the present, even though doing so forces devotees of the Sacred Heart to imagine an anatomically problematic passage of the

---

24. *Anchor Bible*, ed. Raymond E. Brown, 2.935; Gougaud, *Devotional and Ascetic Practices*; *Dévotions et pratiques ascétiques*, p. 97 and n. 84.

25. For biblical examples of such partiality recall Psalm 102 (Vulgate) 110 (RSV), v. 1: "The Lord said to my lord, 'Sit at my right hand until I make your enemies our footstool'"; in the New Testament Christ says that at the Last Judgment the just will be placed on the right, the damned on the left (Matthew 25.33); Bede typifies the patristic tradition, for example, *In Genesim*, 2.6. 13–14, CCSL 118A, p. 103, lines 1071–74, where left is associated with this life and right with the future life.

26. *Dream of the Rood*, ed. Swanton, p. 89, lines 19–20, "þæt hit ærest ongan / swætan on þa swiðran healfe"; and see Swanton's comment on p. 109.

27. The earliest surviving *ordo* (ceremonial) of the papal Mass in Rome, which served as a model for Masses in the Middle Ages, at the *fractio* (breaking of the host) has the rubric: "Tunc pontifex rumpit ex latere dextro et particulam quam ruperit super altare relinquit" (Then the pontiff breaks the host on the right side and leaves the particle that he has broken on the altar), *Ordines Romani*, ed. Andrieu, 2:98, #97. See also Jungmann, *Mass of the Roman Rite*, 2:309–10.

28. Mentioned by Gougaud, "Coeur vulnéré du Sauveur," p. 201. It seems likely that Gougaud derives his information from the *Micrologus de ecclesiasticis observationibus* ascribed to Bernold of Constance (eleventh century): "Cum autem dicit: *Per Dominum nostrum*, rumpit hostiam ex dextro latere juxta Ordinem ad designandam Dominici lateris percussionem. Deinde majorem partem in duo confringit, ut tres portiones de corpore Dominico efficere possit" (*PL* 151, cap. XVII, col. 988C); and "Ita autem juxta Romanum ordinem in altari componenda sunt, ut oblata [i.e., hostia] in corporali posita, calix ad dextrum latus oblatae ponatur, quasi sanguinem Domini suscepturus, quem de latere Dominico profluxisse credimus" (cap. X, col. 983C–D). (I owe this citation of the *Micrologus* to Christopher A. Jones.) The tradition continues in the twelfth century with Pope Innocent III's influential treatise, *De sacro altaris mysterio libri sex*, 2.38 (*PL* 217.833D): "Calix ponitur ad dextrum latus oblatae, quasi sanguinem suscepturus, qui de latere Christi dextro creditur vel cernitur profluisse" (The chalice is placed at the right of the oblation, as if it to receive the blood, which is believed [or perceived] to have flowed from the right side of Christ).

lance from Christ's left side into his right. However, by placing the wound
on the right side the Old Testament typological representations can be conveniently accommodated. Although the side of the entrance into Noah's ark
is not specified in Genesis, the entrance into Solomon's temple in 3 Kings is,
as Bede emphasizes, on the right. The entrance forms the antecedent, *typus*,
for the entry, *ostium*, into the right side of Christ's breast. Bede has liturgical
support from the antiphon chanted during the paschal season for the ceremony of sprinkling, "Vidi aquam egredientem de templo a latere *dextro*,"
inspired by the text of Ezekiel 47:1–2. In later medieval developments, the
nonbiblical but traditional right sidedness is confirmed by the appearance
of the wound in the side of St. Francis at his reception of the stigmata. That
and the devotion of St. Clare to the wound on Christ's right side as well as
the reception of the wound usually in the right side by various stigmatics in
following ages bolstered the generally held belief.[29]

Let us return to Bede's exegesis of the wound. In his Commentary
on Genesis, Bede explores the relationship of the entry into the ark of
Noah as symbolic of the entry into the wound in the side of Christ, which
immediately suggests the entry into the right side of the temple, prefigur-
ing the entry into the "temple" of Christ's body (cf. John 2:19). First, the
ark of Noah symbolically prefigures the cross as vessel of salvation on a sea
of destruction. Its form symbolizes the cross, for the length of the ark was
thirty cubits and the Greek symbol for thirty is the letter Tau, "which is
written in the form of a cross."[30] Moreover, the human body has the same
proportions as the ark, says Bede following Augustine and Isidore, and the
one body is Christ.[31] The text of Genesis 6:16 reads "Ostium autem arcae
pones ex latere deorsum." "You will put the door of the ark down in its
side," which Bede interprets thus:

> This door through which entered both men and all animals that were to
> be saved designates the very unity of faith, without which no one is able
> to enter—"one Lord, one faith, one baptism." One God, for the door is
> aptly placed in the side, because it signifies that very large entry which

---

29. For further references to the artistic positioning of the wound in Christ's side, see
Gurewich, "Observations on the Iconography of the Wound in Christ's Side," and Barb,
"Wound in Christ's Side."

30. Bede, *In Genesim*, CCSL 118A, 2.6,15, p. 106, lines 1183–94; see also 2.5, 23–24, p.
97, lines 868–73.

31. Bede, *In Genesim*, 2.6, 15–16, p, 107, lines 1203–31. Lines 1203–12 are derived from
Isidore, *Quaestiones in Vetus Testamentum*, 7.8–10 (231), *PL* 83, col. 231; lines 1212–31 are from
Augustine, *De civitate Dei*, 15.26, CCSL 48, pp. 493–94.

was opened in the side of our Lord Savior placed on the cross, from which "immediately flowed forth blood and water" (John 19:34). By those mysteries all of the faithful are received into the company of the Holy Church as into the interior of the ark. The entry is to be placed not only in the side but *deorsum*, 'down'. This signifies the humility of the Lord himself through which he died for us, or our own, without which we are unable to be saved. Likewise, the entry of the ark is down and placed near the earth, so that there the men and the animals to be saved would enter, and having entered they soon would ascend to the higher decks into their own places, because the Lord appearing in the depth of this mortality, "was wounded on account of our iniquities," so that he might lead us redeemed through the mysteries of his wounds to the supernal seats of the virtues in the present life and by an invisible ascent to supernal rewards in heaven.[32]

The aperture in Christ's side allows the true disciple to enter into the divine chamber just as Noah and his family found refuge in the ark.

In the *Thirty Questions on the Book of Kings* and then more extensively in the *De Templo* Bede develops the metaphor of the entry into the temple. Christ is the temple (John 2:19), whose side was opened in the Passion, "through which portal we may pass from the present life of the holy church to the eternal rest of souls in the future life."[33] As the temple entrance faced west and had a portal in the right side which led to the upper story, *cenaculum*, so Christ on the cross facing westward has the pierced entry in his side which leads into his divine chamber, where we, having been washed in the baptismal waters from his side and with our thirst slaked by his blood here on earth, can find hospice. After being released from our body we will be with him there but then at the final resurrection we will be united in him with our own reunited bodies.[34]

Bede takes an interpretation from the Commentary on the Song of Songs by the otherwise unknown fifth-century author Apponius that proved attractive to generations of later exegetes and mystics. On the verse "Come my dove into the clefts of the rock, into the crannies of the wall" (Song 2:14) Bede reworks Apponius:[35] "If according to the exposition of

---

32. Bede, *In Genesim*, 2.6, 16, pp. 108–9, lines 1265–85; see also Bede, *In Ezram et Neemiam*, 2, CCSL 119A, pp. 300–301, lines 508–19.

33. Bede, *In Genesim*, 2.6, 16, pp. 109–10, lines 1275–1313.

34. Bede, *In Regum librum XXX quaestiones*, CCSL 119, p. 12, lines 21–31 (my translation); *De templo libri ii*, CCSL 119A, 1, pp. 165–67, lines 744–84.

35. Apponius, *In Canticum Canticorum expositionem*, CCSL 19, p. 107, 4 (2.14), 40–41. The editors explain in the avant-propos, p. v, that the spelling of Apponius's name with two p's has the authority of the earliest manuscripts and tradition.

the Apostle [Paul, in I Cor. 10:4], 'the rock was Christ,' what are the clefts of
the rock except the wounds that Christ received for our salvation? Indeed
in those clefts the dove resides and nests when the meek soul or indeed the
whole church places its sole hope of salvation in the Lord's Passion. In the
mystery of his death it entrusts itself to be protected from the seizure of
the hawk, and it undertakes to procreate offspring of spiritual children or
virtues in that same place."[36]

In England devotion to the wounds of Christ from Anglo-Saxon times
onward was always strong, in liturgy, literature, public and private devotion. The Benedictine Monastic Agreement, *Regularis Concordia*, includes
in the Office for None on Good Friday, besides the traditional adoration of
the cross, a prayer to the wounded Christ.[37] There are frequent allusions in
vernacular literature to the side wound, for instance, in the Vercelli Homilies and Old English poetry like *The Dream of the Rood*.[38] Besides depictions
of Christ's bleeding side in manuscript illustrations and sculpture, the
piercing of Christ's side by the centurion's lance gets specific treatment.[39]
Worthy of special record, however, is the devotion of St. Edith (Eadgyth) of
Wilton (961–84). She commissioned the monk Benno of Trier to decorate
the cruciform porch of the chapel she designed, which housed a relic of
a nail from the Crucifixion. She asked Benno to paint Christ's Passion on
the wall "as she had pictured it in her heart." As André Willmart, the editor of Goscelin's Life of Edith, remarks, Edith's compassion with Christ's
suffering continued to increase until her death.[40]

Moving ahead in time, place, and Zeitgeist, we note that Bernard of
Clairvaux (1090–1153) uses the same text and the same metaphor of the
clefts in the rock signifying Christ's wounds as Bede had done, but Bernard signals a major shift in devotion to those wounds. For him, the converted courtly lover turned fervent exponent of spiritual love, devotion to
Christ has become more amatory, more intimately personal, and more sen-

---

36. Bede, *In Cantica Canticorum*, 2.1 in Cant.2.13–14, CCSL 119B, p. 224, lines 495–503.

37. *Monastic Agreement*, ed. Symons, p. 43; *Regularis Concordia*, ed. Kornexl, p. 92; Gjerløw, *Adoratio Crucis*, p. 17.

38. See *Vercelli Homilies*, ed. Scragg, Homily 1, p. 38, lines 258–62; Homily 2, p. 54, lines
15–18; Homily 8, p. 146, lines 57–62; Homily 15, p. 259, lines 138–40. For *The Dream of the
Rood*, see above, p. 61.

39. See, for instance, Gameson, *Role of Art*, pl. 5b.

40. "Légende de Ste Edith," ed. Wilmart, p. 87 and n. 3. Wilmart includes a testimonial
from a fifteenth-century chronicle in Middle English. See now also *Writing the Wilton Women*,
ed. Hollis et al. Unfortunately this book appeared too late for its arguments to be incorporated in the present essay.

suous. Christ's wounds are the ineffable expression of sacrificial love and the divine effusion of mercy. "There is no lack of clefts by which his mercy is poured out. They pierced his hands and his feet, they gored his side with a lance, and through these fissures I can suck honey from the rock and oil from the flinty stone. . . . The secret of his heart is laid open through the clefts of his body; that mighty mystery of loving is laid open. God has even led us by the open clefts into the holy place."[41]

However, even with Bernard we have not yet arrived at devotion to the heart of Christ as pierced. Bernard does not say directly that the spear entered Christ's heart. Although one translation of Bernard's *On the Song of Songs* has "They pierced His Hands and His Feet and thrust His Heart with a spear," Bernard, combining Psalm 21:17 and John 19:34, actually says, "Foderunt manus eius et pedes, latusque lancea foraverunt" (They pierced his hands and his feet, and they stabbed his side with a lance). A little further on, while paraphrasing Psalm 104:18 and 54:22, he only asserts, "Ferrum transiit animam eius et *appropinquavit* cor illius" (The iron pierced his soul and his heart has drawn near).[42] As Bernard juxtaposed Christ's heart next to his open wound, "Patet Arcanum cordis per foramina corporis" (The secret of his heart is laid open through the clefts of his body),[43] so his friend and brother Cistercian, William of St. Thierry, exclaims: "I want to see and touch the whole of him and—what is more—to approach the most holy wound in his side, the portal of the ark that is there made, and that not only to put my finger or my whole hand into it, but wholly enter into Jesus' very heart, into the holy of holies, the ark of the covenant, the golden urn, the soul of our humanity that holds within itself the manna of the Godhead."[44] Here is not only visual but also tactile penetration. Guerric d'Igny (d. 1157), like William a friend and disciple of Bernard, also uses Song 2:14 to encourage the brethren "to build a nest in the clefts of the rock," Christ's wounds, for these clefts "offer pardon to the guilty and bestow grace on the just."[45] Ailred

41. Bernard of Clairvaux, *On the Song of Songs*, 3.143–45. Even the translation takes the liberty of translating Bernard's "Quidni viscera per vulnera pateant" by translating "viscera" as 'his heart', p. 144.

42. Bernard, *Sermones super Cantica Canticorum*, in *Sancti Bernardi opera*, 2, Sermo 61.4, pp. 150–51. One might be tempted to translate *appropinquavit cor illius* as "it [the iron] drew near his heart," but *appropinquo* is an intransitive verb that takes *ad*+accusative or the dative, even in postclassical latin, so *cor* must be the subject, not *ferrum*.

43. Bernard, Sermo 61.4, pp. 150–51; Sermo 61.4, p. 144.

44. William of St. Thierry, *On Contemplating God*, p. 38. See also pp. 152–53, and "Meditation" 8.4, p. 14; cf. *Contemplation de Dieu*, p. 64.

45. Guerric of Igny, *Liturgical Sermons*, the fourth sermon for Palm Sunday, 2: 77. See also Bynum, *Jesus as Mother*, pp. 121–22.

(1109–67), the "Bernard of the North," preaches that "the blood that flows from the wound in Christ's side is changed into wine to gladden you"—a sort of reverse transubstantiation—"and the water into milk to nourish you."[46] Other visionaries treat the blood itself from Christ's wound as milk for spiritual nourishment. This transfer from blood to milk is eased, as Caroline Bynum has pointed out, by the fact that "in medieval medical theory breast milk is processed blood," and "in medieval devotions like the sacred heart, milk and blood are often interchangeable, as are Christ's breasts and the wound in his side."[47] Rachel Fulton is even more explicit: "Christ himself is here, in an image well known to all medievalists, envisioned as a mother, the blood flowing from his side transmuted into milk to feed his children, his side wound transmuted into a nipple flowing with the 'milk of sweetness.'"[48] To understand also medieval mystics' frequent cross-gendering of both Christ and themselves, another of Bynum's insights is key: "Medieval authors do not seem to have drawn as sharp a line as we do between sexual responses and affective responses or between male and female. Throughout the Middle Ages, authors found it far easier than we seem to find it to apply characteristics stereotyped as male or female to the opposite sex. Moreover, they were clearly not embarrassed to speak of all kinds of ecstasy in language we find physical and sexual and therefore inappropriate to God."[49] Karma Lochrie in her important essay, "Mystical Acts, Queer Tendencies," quotes this passage of Bynum and proceeds to show that mystical sexuality was often ambiguous and in contemporary terms queer.[50] Christ's bleeding side becomes sometimes a lactating breast, sometimes a procreating womb.

Ardent devotion to Christ's wound is a mark of Cistercian spirituality already by the mid-twelfth century. Members of other religious groups and orders, such as the Victorines, the later Benedictines, the Franciscan and Dominican friars and nuns, took up the ever more intense worship.[51]

46. Aelred of Rievaulx, *Works*, vol. 1: *Treatises and Pastoral Prayer*, p. 73, cited in Bynum, *Jesus as Mother*, p. 123.

47. Bynum, *Jesus as Mother*, pp. 132–33, and see esp. n. 78.

48. Fulton, *From Judgment to Passion*, p. 422.

49. Bynum, *Jesus as Mother*, p. 162.

50. Lochrie, "Mystical Acts, Queer Tendencies," p. 182.

51. For a history of the medieval and modern development of the devotion, see Stierli, "Devotion to the Sacred Heart," in *Heart of the Saviour*, ed. Stierli, pp. 59–130; and Richstätter, *Medieval Devotions to the Sacred Heart*. The illustrations in Richstätter from late medieval sources serve as complements to the earlier iconography described in this essay.

Bonaventure (ca. 1217–74) in his treatise, once falsely attributed to Bernard, *Vitis Mystica* (*The Mystical Vine*), and also in his *De Ligno Vitae* (*The Tree of Life*), proposes an ardent devotion to the crucified Lord and to his pierced heart.[52] Extracts from both treatises are incorporated in the present Office of the Feast of the Sacred Heart.[53] In both works Bonaventure vividly expounds the plant metaphor. In *The Mystical Vine*, however, devotion to Christ's wounded heart is especially advocated. After a beautiful poetic passage describing the wound in Christ's heart as a second cause of death after the mortal wound of love, Bonaventure prays: "Your side was pierced so that an entrance might be opened there for us; Your heart was wounded so that, free from all worldly tribulations, we might live in that Vine; but Your heart was also wounded in order that, through the visible wound, we might see the invisible wound of love. For one who ardently loves is wounded by love. How could Christ better show us his ardor than by permitting not only His body but His very heart to be pierced with a lance?"[54]

Among the Dominicans in the fourteenth century, Johannes Tauler (d. 1361) and Henry Suso (Heinrich Seuse, ca. 1295–1366), spiritual disciples of Meister Eckhard (ca. 1260–ca. 1328), were renowned both for their mystical devotion to Christ's Passion and for their direction of nuns. Suso was so enamored of the Sacred Heart and so desirous of union with it that in order to be united with it he slashed his own breast, carving Jesus' name with his blood upon it.[55] "In almost all the images," writes Hamburger of Suso's autobiography, *Exemplar*, "which were integral to Suso's design for the book, the Dominican friar appears in the guise of a bride, crowned with a garland of red and white roses, bearing his other 'attribute' the monogram of Christ, on his chest."[56] Although Suso does not imagine himself pregnant with Christ, as Rupert of Deutz did, he thinks of Christ as embracing his naked soul.[57] In *The Soul's Love-Book*, in a chapter called "A

---

52. Bonaventure, *Works*, trans. de Vinck, 1.95–144, esp. 128, 145–206, esp. 155; Bonaventure, *Opera omnia*: *Lignum vitae*, 8.68–87; *Vitis mystica*, 8.159–89.

53. Three Lessons of the Divine Office (or Breviary) for the Third Nocturn on the Feast of the Sacred Heart.

54. "The Mystical Vine," in Bonaventure, *Works*, trans. de Vinck, p. 155.

55. Suso, *The Exemplar*, trans. Edward, ch. 4: "He Brands the Name of Jesus on His Heart," 1.13–14.

56. Hamburger, *Nuns as Artists*, p. 64. On Suso's alternate gender roles, see Jager, *Book of the Heart*, pp. 97–102.

57. On Rupert of Deutz see Fulton, *From Judgment to Passion*, pp. 310–13; on Suso's portrait of his soul as Christ's lover, see Hamburger, *Nuns as Artists*, pp. 147–48 and figure 89.

Delightful Colloquy of the Soul with Her Spouse Christ, after His Descent from the Cross," he tells his heart, "Behold you have a secure refuge, the deep wound of his heart."[58] In his *Büchlein der ewigen Weisheit* (*The Little Book of Eternal Wisdom*) Suso records the words of Wisdom to him: "You must enter through my open side into my heart wounded by love, where you must shut yourself in. There you will find a dwelling in which you may remain. I will purify you then in the living water and I will color you red with my blood; I would attach myself to you and bond with you forever."[59]

Suso imagines himself the female spouse, but in his addresses he remains very much the male spiritual director. He and his fellow male theologians continue as those responsible for the exegesis, biblical imagery, allegorical treatment, and intense love of the wound in Christ's side.[60] However, even though men predominate as writers on the spiritual life, and there are poetic mystics among them, it is the women, and especially the women mystics, who bring an even more intense fervor and passion to devotion to the wound in Christ's side and to his Sacred Heart. As Caroline Bynum has pointed out and discussed, "For the first time in Christian history we can document that a particular kind of religious experience is more common among women than men. For the first time in Christian history certain major devotional and theological emphases emanate from women and influence the basic development of spirituality."[61] That devotion is exquisitely expressed in the visions granted to Mechthild of Hackeborn (ca. 1240–99) and Gertrude the Great (1256–1302) at the convent of Helfta. Thereafter, the development of the devotion to the Sacred Heart increases especially among later women mystics.

These were all preceded by the extraordinary Hildegard of Bingen (1098–1179), contemporary of Bernard, her advocate to Pope Eugenius III. Many of the symbols, images, and metaphors relating to the wound in

---

58. Suso, "The Soul's Love-Book," in *The Exemplar*, 2.344–49, at 348.

59. Suso, *Büchlein der Weisheit*, in *Deutsche Schriften*, ed. Bihlmeyer, 2.130, cited in Gougaud, p. 95 and n. 79.

60. Historians of the devotion, such as Stierli, Richstätter, and Hugo and Karl Rahner, are all male (and witness all the names in the bibliography by Stierli, *Heart of the Saviour*, pp. 261–62). Although women devotees are named, their unique contributions and the extent of their influence are not adequately acknowledged and described. In recent years, more editions and translations of the women mystics' works have appeared to right the record, and art historians, such as Jeffrey Hamburger, have called attention to the powerful and sometimes lurid illustrations by these women and their followers.

61. Bynum, *Jesus as Mother*, ch. 5: "Women Mystics in the Thirteenth Century: The Case of the Nuns of Helfta," pp. 170–260, at p. 172.

Christ's side found in patristic and medieval writers are exploited in the writings and art of religious women, but Hildegard with brilliant originality modified and augmented the traditional material. In her poetry she expresses the meaning of Christ's wounds and the profusion of his blood. For instance, she apostrophizes Christ's blood:

> O cruor sanguinis
> qui in alto sonuisti,
> cum omnia elementa
> se implicuerunt
> in lamentabilem vocem
> cum timore,
> quia sanguis Creatoris sui
> illa tetigit,
> ungue nos
> de languoribus nostris.

> (O outpoured blood / that resounded on high, / when all the elements/ folded themselves / into a voice of lament / with trembling: / for the blood of their Creator / touched them! / Anoint us, / heal our diseases.)[62]

We have seen that the flood of blood and water coming from Christ's side was recognized as a symbol of the establishment of the Church and her sacraments by Augustine, Bede, and the Cistercians, but in the artistic representation in *Scivias* the image is enhanced: Ecclesia is standing in the attitude of Mary at the right side of the cross catching the blood in a chalice, which she then in the lower register offers in prayer on the altar at Mass.[63] The motif of a female figure or an angel catching the blood from Christ's side occurs elsewhere in the iconography of the period,[64] but the doubling of the figure and coupling of the action of offering the blood on the altar is unique.[65]

The mystics of the Cistercian-inspired convent of Helfta, Mechthild of Magdeburg (ca. 1207–ca. 1282), Mechthild of Hackeborn, and Gertrude the Great, were instrumental in giving devotion to the Sacred Heart its

---

62. Hildegard of Bingen, *Symphonia*, pp. 102–3.

63. The frequently reproduced image from the *Liber Scivias*, a copy of the former Rupertsberg Codex, ca. 1180, can be found in Schipperges, *World of Hildegard of Bingen*, p. 124; Saurma-Jeltsch, *Die Miniaturen im "Liber Scivias"*; and Beer, *Women and Mystical Experience*, p. 53.

64. See Schiller, *Iconography of Christian Art*, 2: #371–73, 432, 442, 446–47, 527–29, 531.

65. In a late painting of ca. 1510 (Schiller, *Iconography of Christian Art*, #530), Christ's blood drops directly into the chalice on the altar while the priest consecrates the host.

explicit form.[66] In book 1 of *Das fliessende Licht der Gottheit* (*The Flowing Light of Divinity*), the elder Mechthild (of Magdeburg) describes *Die Hofreise der Seele* (*The Soul's Trip to Court*), in which God "shows her his divine heart: it is like reddish gold, burning in a large charcoal fire. Then he places her in his ardent heart so that the noble Prince and the little servant girl embrace and are united as water and wine."[67] Gertrude in the *Legatus Divinae Pietatis* (*The Herald of God's Loving Kindness*) constantly refers to the Sacred Heart and her attachment to it.[68] Gertrude reports, "I knew in my spirit that I had received the stigmata of your adorable and venerable wounds interiorly in my heart."[69] Like Mechthild she describes the fire of Christ's molten heart, but she presents many other striking images in her account of her visions of the Sacred Heart. Plants and trees are part of Gertrude's visionary experiences. She sees her soul as a tree planted firmly in Christ's side, which draws the sap of love from his heart, the core-power "of the humanity and divinity of Jesus Christ."[70] She thinks of herself as a plant overwhelmed and flattened by the force of Christ's drenching love but with a promise of gentler rains proportioned to her capacity.[71] One of Gertrude's most exquisite descriptions is that regarding the fluid flowing from Christ's wound (cf. John 19:34 and Rev. 22:1):

> He extended from his left side, as if from the depths of his sacred Heart, a liquid stream of the purity and strength of crystal. As it went forth it covered that adorable breast like a collar; it seemed translucent, tinted with gold and rosy pink, flickering between the two colors. While this was happening the Lord added, "The sickness which causes you distress at present has sanctified your soul with the result that whenever, for my sake, you lower yourself to the thoughts, words and deeds, which are not concerned with me, you will never go further from me than is shown you

---

66. Introduction by Maximilian Marnau to Gertrude of Helfta, *Herald of Divine Love*, p. 34. See also Voaden, "All Girls Together."

67. Mechthild von Magdeburg, *Das fliessende Licht der Gottheit*, p. 14; English translation by Hughes in *Women Mystics*, ed. Brunn and Epiney-Burgard, p. 57.

68. See the numerous references to Christ's heart listed in the indexes of Gertrude of Helfta, *Herald of God's Loving-Kindness*, trans. Barratt, books 1 and 2; book 3, pp. 181 and 246. (There are so many instances that Barratt after listing more than two dozen gives up with an "etc.")

69. Gertrude of Helfta, *Herald of Divine Love*, trans. Winkworth, p. 100. In a note to this passage on p. 139, Winkworth remarks that "it seems that Gertrude's wound would be in the left side. Stigmatics have varied as to the side in which they have received the wound."

70. Gertrude of Helfta, *Herald of Divine Love*, trans. Barratt, book 3, ch. 18, p. 72; see also book 3, ch. 15: "The Tree of Love," pp. 59–61.

71. Gertrude of Helfta, *Herald of Divine Love*, trans. Barratt, book 2, ch. 10, p. 128.

in this stream. Moreover, just as it shines with gold and rosy pink through the purity of crystal, as the co-working of my golden divine nature and the perfect patience of my rosy human nature will be pleasing, suffusing and permeating all that you will."[72]

Gertrude reveals other visions that are similar imagistically but are different in content. For instance in another vision she uses the collar imagery again. She takes delight in a necklace on Christ's breast, a three-pointed one of which the points signify Christ's closeness to her, his delight in her, and her faithfulness to him.[73] Twice more she describes the liquid flowing from Christ's heart, but in those visions she draws the blood into her mouth with a reed (or straw).[74] It is noteworthy that in these as in other visions, Gertrude is an active agent, often a partner, rather than a passive receptacle, as in the imagery of earlier contemplatives. Gertrude's visions, especially in book 3, are replete with images of spears, bloody wounds, and open heart, but also with mutual, heart-to-heart, exchanges.[75] The descriptions are not only visual but also auditory. For instance, Christ's heart is a musical instrument, which she accompanies with chant.[76] Gertrude involves her whole being, body and soul, in her loving and passionate devotion to the Sacred Heart.

Mechthild and Gertrude like other mystics apply to themselves the text of Song of Songs 4:9, "You have wounded my heart, my sister, my spouse," and envision their wounding Christ's heart.[77] Others, however, describe the virtues as Christ's tormentors. Under the influence of exegetical interpretations by Jerome, Augustine, Rabanus Maurus, and especially Bernard, which link the virtues to the Crucifixion, nuns in the thirteenth century portray the virtues as crucifying Christ. This may seem a perverse interpretation, but it links the virtues, especially charity, with Christ's sacrifice. "The Cross appeared to the women mystics in the nunneries as so abso-

---

72. Gertrude of Helfta, *Herald of Divine Love*, trans. Barratt, book 2, ch. 9, pp. 124–25.

73. Gertrude of Helfta, *Herald of Divine Love*, trans. Barratt, book 1, ch. 3, p. 47.

74. Gertrude of Helfta, *Herald of Divine Love*, trans. Barratt, book 3, ch. 26, p. 95, and ch. 30, p. 102.

75. Although Gertrude is fully intimate with Christ as a lover, she also venerates him as Sovereign and Judge. In this she represents a median between the earlier medieval "tough" piety and the gentler piety of fourteenth-century mystics, such as Julian of Norwich. See Bynum, *Jesus as Mother*, pp. 187–90.

76. Gertrude of Helfta, *Herald of Divine Love*, trans., Barratt, book 2, ch. 21, p. 168.

77. For an illustration of the *sponsa* thrusting a lance into her beloved's side, see Camille, *Medieval Art of Love*, p. 58; also Hamburger, *Rothschild Canticles*, color pl. 5.

lutely an event of salvation that it becomes a virtue even to wound the Source of Salvation."[78]

As the nuns of Helfta represent feminine Cistercian spirituality, Angela of Foligno (ca. 1248–1309) exemplifies one mode of feminine Franciscan spirituality, in the spirit of Bonaventure but more intensely sensuous. Of one vision she relates:

> Then Christ called me and said I should put my mouth to the wound in his side. And it seemed to me that I saw and drank his blood flowing freshly from his side. And I was given to understand that by this he would cleanse me. And at this I began to feel great joy, although when I thought about the passion I felt sadness. And I prayed the lord that he would cause me to shed all my blood for his love, just as he had done for me. And I was so disposed myself on account of his love that I wished all my limbs might suffer a death unlike his passion, that is, a more vile death.[79]

Catherine of Siena (?1347–80) has a similar vision, in which the maternal body of Christ provides her with the blood from his side, not as bath but as an aphrodisiac milk, developing the mystical theme of the lactating wound discussed above (p. 264): "With that, he tenderly placed his right hand on her neck, and drew her towards the wound in his side. 'Drink, daughter, from my side,' he said, 'and by that draught your soul shall become enraptured with such delight that your very body, which for my sake you have denied, will be inundated with its overflowing goodness.' Drawn close in this way to the outlet of the Fountain of Life, she fastened her lips upon that sacred wound, and still more eagerly the mouth of her soul, and there she slaked her thirst."[80]

These highly charged and emotive texts find striking contemporary counterparts in paintings and drawings by and for women, many of them simple and even crude but all quite arresting, depicting fervid devotion to Christ's wound. Flora Lewis in the first paragraph of her insightful article, "The Wound in Christ's Side and the Instruments of the Passion," observes:

---

78. Schiller, *Iconography of Christian Art*, 2:138 and figs. 443–58. See also Hamburger, *Rothschild Canticles*, pp. 75–76 and illustrations 142 and 143.

79. Angela of Foligno, *Liber de Vera Fidelium Experientia*, trans. Petroff in her *Medieval Women's Visionary Literature*, p. 257. See also *Angela Foligno*, ed. Lachance, p. 176: "At times it seems to my soul that it enters into Christ's side, and this is a source of great joy and delight; it is indeed such a joyful experience to move into Christ's side that in no way can I express it and put words to it;" and Angela of Foligno, *Le Livre de l'expérience des vraies fidèles*.

80. Raymond of Capua, *Life of Catherine of Siena*, quoted by Bynum, *Holy Feast and Holy Fast*, p. 172, and by Lochrie, "Mystical Acts, Queer Tendencies," p. 188.

"Although in the majority of images the five wounds are shown centred on the wounded heart, the earliest images combine the *arma christi* not with these, but with a single wound: that in Christ's side. Women, particularly nuns, played an important part in the creation of these early images. . . . The wound in Christ's side could be seen as female and yet explored by men, as a site of union between sponsus and sponsa, and also of parturition."[81]

The large red pointed oval-shaped wound in Christ's side, often depicted as life-sized, is reminiscent both of the womb and especially of the female genitals, from which the Church is born and into which the mystic penetrates.[82] The oval image of the wound in Christ's side was transferred to the wound in his heart. As Voaden remarks about devotion to Christ's heart among the mystics of Helfta, "The Sacred Heart became a site of female biological characteristics: it bleeds, it flows, it opens, it encloses. Sometimes it is overwhelmingly fleshly. Medieval illustrations of the Sacred Heart resemble nothing so much as a vagina. The wound was graphically represented as a slit between two gaping edges; sometimes, but not always, drops of blood were shown emerging."[83]

While writers of the patristic and early medieval period associate various flowers, fruits, and spices with the Lord's Passion,[84] women in the later Middle Ages, following the devotional precedent of Bonaventure,[85] gave the honor to the red rose as the Passion flower.[86] Meditation on Jesus covered with blood, as represented by Bernard and by Bonaventure ("Behold how the crimsoned Jesus blossomed forth in the rose") led to some horrific nuns' art, such as the drawing of Bernard and a nun "embracing a cross transformed into a geyser of redeeming blood."[87] Many of these drawings

---

81. Flora Lewis, "Wound in Christ's Side," p. 204.

82. Flora Lewis, "Wound in Christ's Side," pp. 214–16. For the wound, *vulnus*, as vulva, see Lochrie, "Mystical Acts, Queer Tendencies," pp. 189–92 and figs. 9.1 and 9.2.

83. Voaden in "All Girls Together," p. 74; see also p. 85.

84. For instance, Bede, *In Cantica Canticorum*, CCSL 119B, p. 248, associates with Christ's Passion the ruddy pomegranate of Song 4:3, as also, pp. 265–66, the purple cassia and dusky cinnamon of Song 4:4.

85. Bonaventure, *Mystical Vine*, ch. 15, "On the Red and Ardent Rose in General"; ch. 16, "On the Rose of Love"; ch. 17, "On the Rose of the Passion," pp. 186–91; see also p. 200: "Behold how the crimsoned Jesus blossomed forth in the rose."

86. Hamburger, *Nuns as Artists*, pp. 63–100. See also Joret, *La rose*, pp. 231–58, esp. 243–46.

87. Hamburger, *Visual and the Visionary*, p. 139. The gory drawing is shown in full color in Hamburger, *Nuns as Artists*, pl. 1, following p. 134.

are illustrated and commented on by Hamburger in *Nuns as Artists: The Visual Culture of a Medieval Convent.*[88]

One further example of *Nonnenarbeit* will serve to show the vivid extent to which devotion to Christ's wound and his heart developed in art. The disembodied pierced heart became a common image in the later Middle Ages.[89] It was sometimes shown as a chamber in which the devoted spouse embraces her Savior, often depicted as a child.[90] In Hamburger's description of the St. Walburg drawing, *The Heart on the Cross,* "We zoom in on the stunning, even shocking, image of the heart at the center, penetrating the gash to find ourselves—in the person of the nun, identified by her habit—nestled within it, exchanging vows with Christ."[91]

The mystics were enraptured by the Passion of Christ, his wounds, his blood, and especially his Sacred Heart, which express concretely his personal and universal love. Limits of space and intention prohibit a full examination of more writings and art here. Christ's wounds and especially his Sacred Heart elicited the deepest devotion in saints such as Bridget of Sweden (1303–73), Frances of Rome (1384–1440), and in the seventeenth century Margaret Mary Alacoque (1647–90). Let us conclude in summary with some remarkable visions of Julian of Norwich (ca. 1342–after 1416), in her two versions of her *Book of Showings* (also called *Revelations of Divine Love*). The first gift that Julian asked of the Lord was that she experience the Passion of Christ and knowledge of his bodily suffering.[92] She was given the gift, so that she sees his bloody head and face (Showings 1 and 2), and in Showing 4 she sees "the body of Christ bleeding abundantly," so that "the hot blood ran out so abundantly that no skin or wound could be seen, it seemed to be all blood." She understands that this profusion of blood cleanses our sins, "for there is no liquid created which he likes to give us so much; it is as plentiful as it is precious by virtue of his holy Godhead."

---

88. See also Hamburger, *Visual and the Visionary*, ch. 2; and *Rothschild Canticles*, ch. 5 and pls. 142, 143.

89. The gashed heart, usually surrounded by thorns and surmounted by a small cross, was a common emblem painted in prayer books and sewn on clothing. For example, see Hamburger, *Nuns as Artists*, figs. 77 and 78, pp. 118–19.

90. For instance, see Mâle, *L'art religieux*, p. 108.

91. Hamburger, *Nuns as Artists*, p. 116 and the color pl. 10.

92. Julian of Norwich, *Revelations of Divine Love*, ed. Spearing, short text (ST) 1, p. 3, long text (LT) 2, p. 43. The critical edition in the original Middle English is *A Book of Showings to the Anchoress Julian of Norwich*, ed. Colledge and Walsh. Though I have consulted the latter edition, for convenience I have cited Spearing's modern English translation.

Indeed, "the precious plenty of his beloved blood overflows the whole earth and is ready to wash away the sins of all people."[93] In Showing 8 Julian sees Christ suffering bodily death, and in Showing 10 Jesus shows Julian his heart within his wounded side, saying "Look how much I loved you": "Then, with a glad face, our Lord looked into his side, and gazed, rejoicing, and with his dear gaze he led his creature's understanding through the same wound into his side. And then he revealed a beautiful and delightful place which was large enough for all mankind who shall be saved to rest there in peace and love. And with this he brought to mind the precious blood and water which he allowed to pour out completely for love. And in this dear vision he showed his sacred heart quite riven in two."[94]

Such words and pictures manifest a world of interpretational difference between early medieval exegesis and later mystics' visions. Text and iconography from the early medieval period do not hesitate to depict Christ's suffering and his wounded side, but the earlier asceticism views the Savior as sovereign king and judge, and the devotee as penitent subject. In the later medieval period, from the twelfth century on, the suffering Christ is described as intimate friend, desirous lover, and reciprocating spouse. The earlier writers are seriously devout but do not exhibit that same affect, the emotional intensity, the erotic passion, and the personal involvement that the mystics display. Just as the crosses of the early Middle Ages, such as the Ruthwell monument and other insular monuments,[95] are sober and restrained and the crucifixes of the later Middle Ages are realistically bloody and vividly painful, so Bede's wounded Savior is heroically reserved and dignified, while the Jesus of the later Middle Ages is a demonstrative lover and ardent victim. Though the earlier devotees are pious servants of the suffering Lord, the later men and women contemplatives are more active in their relationship with him, and engaged in such acts as drinking the Lord's blood with cup or straw, binding Christ's wounds, soothing his suffering, and assuaging his grief. Many of the scriptural allusions used by the Fathers and early exegetes to describe Christ's side wound, such as entry into the ark, entry into Temple and the holy of holies, and the clefts in the rock, continue to appear in the writings of the mystics, with some embellishments. However, among the later contemplatives other images suited their ardently poetic and graphic experiences. Among these visions,

---

93. Julian of Norwich, *Revelations of Divine Love*, LT 12, pp. 59–60; cf. ST 8, p. 13.
94. Julian of Norwich, *Revelations of Divine Love*, LT 24, p. 76; cf. ST 13, p. 20.
95. See, for example, Kellie Meyer, this volume.

as we have seen, are the tree growing in Christ's wound, the collar and the necklace on his breast, the devotee's wounding his side with her lance, the stream from his side as colored crystal, the red rose of his wound, as well as the wine press and the well into which his blood pours.[96] Prominent too in the later period is the depiction of Christ's members as disembodied parts—the slashed heart surmounted by crown of thorns and cross, the side wound in female guise as the vulva pierced by the lance. These parts are often accompanied by the *arma* of the Passion (the nails, whips, sponge, and lance). Like the fervent writings of the mystics, all of these symbols mark the development and changes in the devotion to the wounds of Christ's Passion, particularly the wound in his side and in his heart.

---

96. For illustrations of the wine-press and the well being filled with Christ's blood, see Mâle, *L'art religieux*, figs. 58–65, pp. 111–22.

TRANSLATING IMAGES:
IMAGE AND POETIC RECEPTION IN FRENCH, ENGLISH, AND LATIN VERSIONS OF GUILLAUME DE DEGUILEVILLE'S *TROIS PÈLERINAGES*

RICHARD K. EMMERSON

In the mid-fourteenth century Guillaume de Deguileville, a monk of the Cistercian Abbey of Chaalis, composed three pilgrimage poems cast as visionary narratives.[1] The first, the *Pèlerinage de vie humaine* written in 1330–32,[2] describes how the narrator falls asleep after reading the *Roman de la rose* and dreams of the Heavenly Jerusalem, which becomes the goal of his allegorical pilgrimage.[3] During this semi-autobiographical pilgrimage, the protagonist is assisted by the Grace of God and other allegorical figures and opposed by a series of personified characters, including the deadly sins described in sharp detail. The introductory framework of the poem is illustrated by the two miniatures decorating the opening folio of London, British Library, Additional MS 22937 (fig. 1), a French manuscript produced ca. 1450.[4] The upper miniature depicts a realistic domestic setting divided by a column into two scenes. On the left Guillaume stands while

I am pleased to contribute to this volume in honor of Helen Damico, who has contributed so selflessly and vigorously to all aspects of medieval studies. In 2003, when I served as Executive Director of the Medieval Academy of America, she received the Award for Outstanding Service to Medieval Studies offered by the Committee on Centers and Regional Associations of the Medieval Academy of America. I am delighted that this volume now recognizes her equally outstanding contributions to scholarship. Earlier versions of this paper were read to the History of the Book Seminar, The Newberry Library, 11 November 2000; and to the Medieval Studies Seminar, Harvard University Humanities Center, 19 March 2003. I am grateful to Raymond Clemens and Beverly Kienzle for inviting me to speak to these seminars and thank the participants for their many helpful suggestions.

1. For Guillaume's life and works see Faral, "Guillaume de Deguileville." On his name, see Boulton, "Digulleville's *Pèlerinage de Jésus Christ*," p. 140 n. 1.

2. Guillaume de Degulleville, *Pèlerinage de la vie humaine* and *Pilgrimage of Human Life*. Scholarship has focused on the poem's genre and literary influence; see, for example, Padelford, "Spenser and *The Pilgrimage of the Life of Man*"; Wenzel, "Pilgrimage of Life"; and Phillips, "Chaucer and Deguileville."

3. On the poem's relationship to the *Roman de la rose*, see Stephen K. Wright, "Deguileville's *Pèlerinage de vie humaine*"; and Huot, *Romance of the Rose*, pp. 207–25.

4. See "Les Trois Pèlerinages," in Ward, *Catalogue of Romances*, 2:558–85.

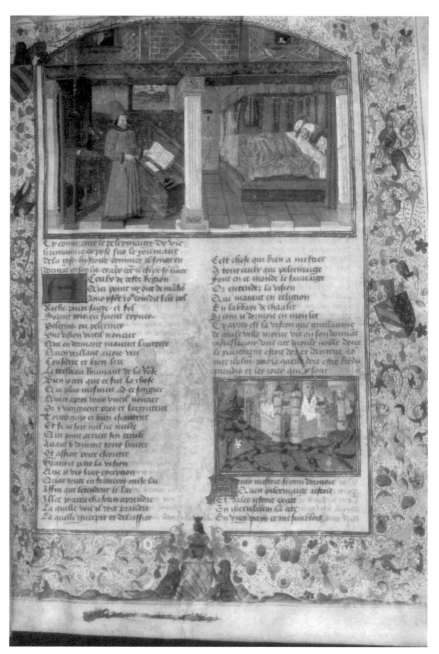

Figure 1. Narrator reading and dreaming and vision of the New Jerusalem. Opening of *Trois Pèlerinages*; London, British Library, Additional MS 22937, fol. 1r. (Photo: By permission of the British Library.)

reading the *Rose*, and on the right he dreams in bed, a scene recalling illustrated *Rose* manuscripts. After the prologue text, the miniature in the lower right illustrates the poem's first narrative scene, which begins with a vision of the New Jerusalem. These images exemplify a rich illustrative tradition beginning in the fourteenth century and continuing throughout the fifteenth, a tradition that both reflected and influenced the reception of Guillaume's three visionary poems in a variety of French, English, and Latin manuscripts.[5]

Even the earliest extant manuscripts of the *Pèlerinage de vie humaine* are illustrated, such as New York, Pierpont Morgan Library, M.1038, which dates from the second quarter of the fourteenth century and originally included 110 small framed miniatures inserted within the columns of the poetic text. Michael Camille suggested that early copies of the poem and their illustrations possibly originated "from Deguileville's own planned programme,"[6] and it is significant that Guillaume describes his reception of the *Roman de la rose* in terms not only of reading and contemplation but also of seeing, as if he had been looking at an illustrated manuscript:

En veillant avoie lëu
Consideré et bien vëü
Le biau roumans de la Rose.

(While I was awake, I had read, studied, and looked closely at the beautiful *Romance of the Rose*.)[7]

These lines not only credit the inspiration of his poem to the famous allegorical dream vision but also suggest that Guillaume may have similarly envisioned the presentation of his dream vision as an illustrated work. It is certainly the case that from the beginning he intended it to be illustrated at least in some fashion, for he refers to pictures that he expects to accompany his text and thus to elucidate his verbal descriptions. One such place is illustrated in London, British Library, Additional MS 38120, a French

5. On the French illustrated manuscripts, see Camille, "Illustrated Manuscripts," to be used with caution: folio citations and transcriptions should especially be double-checked. The best literary study of the images in relation to the *Vie humaine* is Tuve, *Allegorical Imagery*, pp. 145–218. Hagen, *Allegorical Remembrance*, includes numerous images from English manuscripts.

6. Camille, "Illustrated Manuscripts," p. 52.

7. Guillaume de Degulleville, *Pèlerinage de la vie humaine*, 1. 9–11; *Pilgrimage of Human Life*, p. 3.

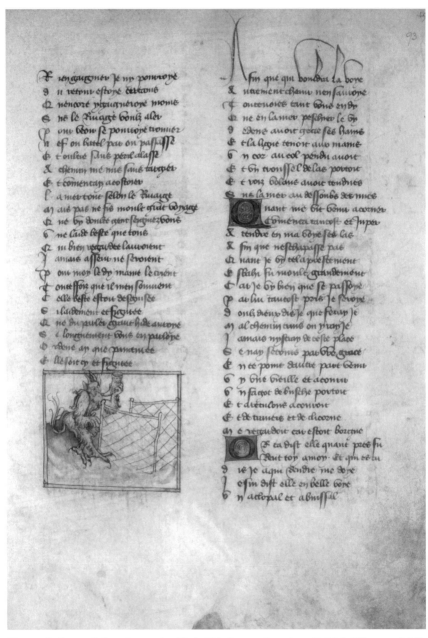

Figure 2. Satan fishes for souls. *Trois Pèlerinages*; London, British Library, Additional MS 38120, fol. 93r. (Photo: By permission of the British Library.)

manuscript produced around 1400 that pictures Satan fishing for souls (fig. 2).[8] This scene illustrates a passage early in book 4 that explains how the pilgrim meets a beast so hideous it cannot be described in words. In order for the monster to be understood, therefore, the poet has ordered it to be pictured for those who wish to see it.[9] In this manuscript, the miniature is placed immediately after this explanation.

Guillaume sought to write a poem that would appeal to a wide audience. His prologue states that he composed in French so that the laity would understand the poem, and he may have conceived of its illustrations as an extension of the vernacular—yet another way to reach a lay audience. He notes that he wishes to reach rich and poor, wise and unlearned, both kings and queens, and male and female pilgrims.[10] His prologue addresses this audience directly and in person, asking them to gather, sit, and listen. Thus, in an early iconographic tradition, Guillaume's opening is illustrated not by the poet reading in his study and then falling asleep, as in Additional MS 22937 (fig. 1), but by a miniature showing the poet speaking to his audience, as in Oxford, Bodleian Library, MS Douce 300, fol. 1r (fig. 3).[11] The representation of the dream's beginning in this manuscript is then delayed until its second miniature, which shows the narrator in bed, receiving his vision of the New Jerusalem in a mirror.[12] This early tradition in which the opening miniature depicts the poet in the pose of a preacher implies the aural reception of the poem, which, as Joyce Coleman has argued, was a common form for the public reception of vernacu-

---

8. For the manuscript see *Catalogue of the Fifty Manuscripts and Printed Books Bequeathed to the British Museum by Alfred H. Huth*, pp. 8–9.

9. I transcribe the lines preceding this miniature on fol. 93r as follows:

> Si laidement et figuree
> Que du parler grant hide auroye
> Se longuement vous en par loye
> Ordene ay que painturee
> Elle soit cy et figuree."

These lines correspond, with some minor variations, to Guillaume de Degulleville, *Pèlerinage de la vie humaine*, 4.475–80.

10. Guillaume's terms are "riche, povre, sage et fol / soient roys, soienet roynes / pelerins et pelerines" (*Pèlerinage de la vie humaine*, 1.4–6).

11. For this manuscript see Pächt and Alexander, *Illuminated Manuscripts in the Bodleian Library*, p. 50, no. 639. For representations of Guillaume as author see Peters, *Das Ich im Bild*, pp. 140–62.

12. On the significance of this poetic image and its representation, see Hagen, *Allegorical Remembrance*, pp. 7–29 and figs. 1, 2, 4–8.

Figure 3. Guillaume addressing audience. *Pèlerinage de vie humaine*; Oxford, Bodle-ian Library, MS Douce 300, fol. 1r. (Photo: The Bodleian Library, University of Oxford.)

lar literature—particularly poetry—in the fourteenth century.[13] Although such reception does not mean the lack of literacy on the part of audience members, it is one way in which Guillaume could reach, as he states, both the "wise and the unlearned."

Despite the poem's popularity, Guillaume revised the *Vie humaine* in 1355, explaining that the first version circulated before it was finished. This second edition elaborates the poem's theological learning, adds another 4,000 lines of French verse and 1,100 lines of Latin, and drops its address to the poet's audience and thus the suggestion of aural reception. A quarter-century after its first edition credited the *Roman de la rose* as motivating the dream vision, the revised version also deletes the opening praise of the *Rose* and later adds a condemnation of the romance in a 200-

---

13. Coleman, *Public Reading*. Coleman does not discuss Guillaume's poems, however.

line conversation between Venus and the pilgrim.[14] These changes suggest a significant shift in the poet's purpose and audience, implying that the poem was now reaching a more learned audience comfortable with Latin who would receive the more didactic poem through silent reading rather than public presentation. These changed circumstances affected the illustrations of second-recension manuscripts, which, as Camille notes, "indicate the changed nature of the text and encourage a more learned client's interest in the Latin and scholastic additions by making the frontispiece a scene of scholastic study."[15] Although the poem's longer, more erudite, second edition was less popular than the original version, it is the revised edition—along with an anonymous prose recasting of the poem made in 1464 for Jeanne de Laval, queen of Sicily and Jerusalem, duchess of Anjou, and countess of Provence—that became the basis of early printed editions of the poem.[16]

The revised edition's greater emphasis on religious moralism and theological didacticism is evident again in Guillaume's second visionary poem, the *Pèlerinage de l'âme*. Composed between 1355 and 1358, about the time the *Vie humaine* was revised, the "Soul," as the poet notes, is a continuation of his earlier poem.[17] In more than 11,000 lines it follows the progress of the pilgrim's soul, from its release from the dreamer's body, to its judgment and consignment in purgatory, to its visit to hell and vision of heaven. Although illustrated manuscripts of this second pilgrimage did not appear until near the end of the fourteenth century, it was particularly popular in the fifteenth, when it was recast in French prose by Jean Gallopes, a scholar at the University of Paris, who is shown writing at his desk in Oxford, Bodleian Library, MS Douce 305, a Flemish manuscript

---

14. On the second recension, see Lofthouse, "'Le Pèlerinage de vie humaine,'" esp. pp. 176–91. On its differing treatment of the *Rose*, see Badel, *Roman de la Rose au XIVe Siècle*, pp. 362–76; and Huot, *Romance of the Rose*, pp. 225–30.

15. Camille, "Illustrated Manuscripts," p. 77. See also Huot, *Romance of the Rose*, p. 226.

16. The French prose version was made by an anonymous clerk of Angers; Hagen is mistaken in citing Gallopes as the author (*Allegorical Remembrance*, p. 218 n. 8). On the issue of authorship, see Faral, "Guillaume de Digulleville." For a comparison of the first poetic and prose versions, see De Wolf, "Pratique de la personification." The first printed edition, based on the French prose redactions, was published by Mathieu Husz as *Le pèlerin de la vie humaine* (Lyons, 1485) and was reprinted three times. Antoine Vérard published the prose version (Paris, 1499) and *Le pèlerinage de l'homme*, the second poetic redaction (Paris, 1511). For the printed editions see Camille, "Reading the Printed Image."

17. See lines 25–32, Guillaume de Degulleville, *Pèlerinage de l'âme*. See also Galpin, "Sources."

produced ca. 1435.[18] This work, like the revised *Vie humaine*, does not imply
aural reception, but suggests a more learned text probably intended for
silent reading.

Such is also the case with Guillaume's third visionary poem, the *Pèlerinage de Jésus Christ* (1358), which in 11,400 lines details the major events
in the life of Christ based on Gospel and apocryphal narratives as well as
poetic license.[19] Although receiving less critical attention than the other
two poems, this third visionary pilgrimage appropriately concludes the trilogy, as Maureen Boulton notes, "presenting the model journey of the ideal
pilgrim, Jesus Christ."[20] Focusing on the life of Christ, it nevertheless covers all salvation history, beginning with the Fall of Adam and concluding
with an image of Guillaume kneeling before an enthroned and crowned
Christ.[21] This image recalls Revelation 21, where the visionary John kneels
before Christ, a scene often represented in illustrated Anglo-French Apoc-
alypses.[22] It suggests that over the course of his visionary narratives Guillaume as pilgrim—who first saw the New Jerusalem in the opening dream
of his *Pèlerinage de vie humaine*—has now reached his heavenly destination.

Interestingly, the *Pèlerinage de Jésus Christ* rarely appears in manuscripts
as a single work. Instead, it is usually joined to the other two pilgrimages in
manuscripts of *Les Trois Pèlerinages*.[23] By the beginning of the fifteenth century, it became increasingly popular to anthologize the three poems in one
codex, as evident in the frontispiece to Paris, Bibliothèque nationale de
France, MS français 823, a manuscript dated 1393. The rubric below this
beautiful four-part miniature states that it introduces all three pilgrimage
poems and implies that the three have here become one book: "Cy commence le liure du pelerinage de vie humaine de ihesucrist et de lame" (fol.

---

18. For this manuscript see Pächt and Alexander, *Illuminated Manuscripts,* 1:24, no. 312,
pl. XXV. On the prose redaction see Faral, "Guillaume de Digulleville," p. 92.

19. Guillaume de Degulleville, *Pèlerinage de Jhésucrist.*

20. Boulton, "Digulleville's *Pèlerinage de Jésus Christ,*" p. 128.

21. For this image, see Amblard, *Vie de Jésus,* p. 194, which reproduces Paris, Bibliothèque Sainte-Geneviève, MS 1130, fol. 229r.

22. On these manuscripts see Emmerson and Suzanne Lewis, "Census and Bibliography of Medieval Manuscripts."

23. For an early example dated 1370, see Paris, Bibliothèque Sainte-Geneviève, MS
1130; Boinet, *Manuscrits a peintures de la Bibliothèque Sainte-Geneviève de Paris,* pp. 96–107, pl.
xxxi. The miniatures from the *Jésus Christ* portion are reproduced in Amblard, *Vie de Jésus;*
the manuscript's miniatures are available on the Liber floridus website: <http://liberflori-
dus.cines.fr>.

1r).[24] This development, in which the three pilgrimages are understood as forming one unified book, is crucial to the reception of the three French poems during the fifteenth century. In fact, twenty-eight of the eighty-six extant manuscripts of the French poems contain the combined *Trois Pèlerinages*. In a study of some woodcuts in early printed versions of the *Pèlerinage de vie humaine*, Michael Camille states that "in the three hundred years of its illustration the most radical shift in this text's visualization occurs not when it is translated from one language or form to another . . . but when it speaks a new presentational 'language' in the medium of print."[25] However, based on analysis of several of the poem's fifteenth-century manuscripts, I must disagree with this statement, because many of the features of the so-called radical shift Camille detected in the woodcuts of the early printed versions of the *Pèlerinage* are already quite evident in earlier manuscripts. Changes in the *ordinatio* of these manuscripts and the design of their illustrated pages, for example, are significantly affected by the fifteenth-century notion that the three poems make up one book. In the remainder of this essay I study various ways in which fifteenth-century manuscripts broaden the audience of Guillaume's pilgrimage poems by tracing their reception in some distinctly differing manuscripts, both vernacular—specifically French and Middle English—and Latin. In so doing, I will argue that the now generally accepted notion that medieval texts "were adapted to different audiences at different periods"[26] can be expanded to show how images—their iconography, design, and layout in relation to their accompanying texts—participated in establishing meaning and constructing audience response.

The design, layout, and iconography of fifteenth-century manuscripts both inform and reflect the tastes and interests of their patrons, readers, and viewers. In contrast to the early printed editions of the *Pèlerinage de vie humaine*, which—based on the poem's second, longer and more learned, edition—elide the *Roman de la rose* and stress instead the moral value of the pilgrimage for a bourgeois audience, deluxe fifteenth-century manuscripts emphasize the poem's connection to the *Roman de la rose*. The opening miniature of the beautiful *Trois Pèlerinages* in British Library, Additional MS 22937 (fig. 1), for example, both pictures the first edition's close link to the *Rose* and emphasizes it by means of an opening rubric. Inscribed in the

---

24. For this miniature see Camille, *Master of Death*, fig. 6.
25. Camille, "Reading the Printed Image," p. 261.
26. See the discussion of audience in Wogan-Browne et al., *Idea of the Vernacular*, p. 110.

Figure 4. Latria, Old Age and Infirmity, and Abstinence presiding in the refectory. *Pèlerinage de vie humaine*; New York, Pierpont Morgan Library, M. 772, fol. 93r. (Photo: The Pierpont Morgan Library, New York.)

upper left column, before the initial *A*, the rubric reads: "Cy commence le pelerinaige de vie humainne expose sus le roumant de la rose" (fol. 1r). This suggests that not only did reading the *Rose* lead to the vision resulting in the original *Pèlerinage* but also Guillaume's new allegorical quest is to be read in this deluxe manuscript in terms of the *Roman de la rose*. Thus, almost a century after Guillaume sought to disconnect his poem from what was becoming an increasingly notorious erotic visionary pilgrimage, this deluxe manuscript underscored the original connection for the mid-fifteenth-century reader. This particular emphasis may well have appealed to the manuscript's patron, Claude de Montaigu, seigneur de Couche and knight of the Golden Fleece (d. 1470), whose arms appear on this opening folio as well as on two other folios in the manuscript.[27] It is certainly the case that deluxe manuscripts of the *Trois Pèlerinages* that may be associated with aristocratic patrons often include the original version of the *Vie humaine*.[28]

Changes in the *ordinatio* of the page and the iconography of the miniatures are also evident in manuscripts of the deluxe *Trois Pèlerinages*. Early manuscripts of the *Vie humaine*, such as New York, Pierpont Morgan Library, M.772, which includes 110 grisaille miniatures, place illustrations within the columns of verse, without a break in the continuity of the text (fig. 4).[29] On folio 93r, for example, the three miniatures appear just before the verses they illustrate and not always at the literary subdivisions of the poem, which are marked by colored capitals, or at changes in speakers, marked by brief rubrics. This arrangement typifies the layout of the poem's fourteenth-century manuscripts. Although these are often heavily illustrated, the poetic text nevertheless dictates the reading process and provides continuity for the visionary narrative. In contrast, French prose rubrics—some quite lengthy and often highlighted in red ink—break the flow of the verse in the deluxe *Trois Pèlerinages* and introduce or summarize the miniatures. This design typifies fifteenth-century deluxe manuscripts, which seem to invite readers to read from rubric to rubric as they examine each miniature. The miniatures are treated less as illustrations of the

---

27. See Ward, *Catalogue of Romances*, 2:558.

28. Boulton, "Digulleville's *Pèlerinage de Jésus Christ*," lists six manuscripts of the *Trois Pèlerinages* that were "in the possession of prominent laymen" (p. 126).

29. M. 772 is the earliest dated manuscript of the *Vie humaine* (1348, colophon fol. 99r). For its miniatures see the Morgan Library's Corsair catalogue, <http://corsair.morganlibrary.org>.

Figure 5. Pilgrim followed by Memory; Pilgrim meets Rude Entendement. *Trois Pèlerinages*; London, British Library, Additional MS 22937, fol. 29v. (Photo: By permission of the British Library.)

poetic text than as narrative pictures in their own right or as continuations
of the rubrics.

For example, in British Library, Additional MS 22937, fol. 29v (fig. 5),
which inscribes the end of book 1 and beginning of book 2 of the *Vie
humaine*, the miniature on the left pictures the narrator walking, followed
by Memory, who has eyes in the back of her head, on which she carries the
Pilgrim's armor. This image serves as a memorial device for the concluding
section of book one, where the Pilgrim discarded the armor provided by
Grace Dieu. Given its own rubric, the miniature is transitional and is thus
set off in the lower left column from the narrative itself, which begins at
the top of the right column, where it is introduced by a three-line initial.
The more specific opening image of this poetic book is then illustrated
by the miniature in the lower right column, which pictures the Pilgrim's
meeting with Rude Entendement. The miniature is introduced by a rubric
that leads directly into the image, breaking its upper frame. This mode of
reading could perhaps on occasion even dispense with the original poetic
text, substituting in its place the image explained by the prose rubric. In
this manuscript we seem to have moved from the aural public reception
imagined by the poet in the mid-fourteenth century to private reception
through silent reading and a corresponding focus on the visual, highlighted by miniatures introduced by blocks of red ink.[30]

Some iconographic changes seem designed to appeal to the fifteenth-
century audience of the deluxe *Trois Pèlerinages*, stressing not only a specific interest in the *Roman de la rose* but also a more general interest in the
romance qualities of Guillaume's visionary quest. One such change is evident in the representation of the pilgrim narrator. In earlier manuscripts
containing only the *Vie humaine*, the pilgrim is presented as a member
of a religious order (for example, fig. 3), an appropriate reminder of the
author's calling. But in the deluxe manuscript of the *Trois Pèlerinages*, the
pilgrim narrator has been transformed into a secular figure and placed in
a romance setting (fig. 5). In the two scenes at the beginning of book 2,

---

30. A similar *mise en page* is evident in New York, Pierpont Morgan Library, M. 126,
a Flemish manuscript of John Gower's *Confessio Amantis* produced ca. 1470 for Elizabeth
Woodville, book-collecting queen of Edward IV. Similarly stressing the illustrations over the
poetic narrative, it sets the miniatures next to Gower's Latin verse and prose commentary
inscribed in red. On this manuscript as well as the reading practices suggested by other
Gower manuscripts, see Emmerson, "Reading Gower." For its miniatures see the Morgan
Library's Corsair catalogue, <http://corsair.morganlibrary.org>.

the pilgrim has become a fashionably dressed and wealthy man, perhaps another way in which he can appeal to, and represent, the noble patron of this manuscript. Class distinctions are thus fully emphasized in this manuscript, as the miniature of the Pilgrim meeting the rude and illiterate rustic in the lower right column makes quite evident. In the original allegorical pilgrimage of life, the Guillaume pilgrim plays the role of Everyman,[31] although admittedly a religious one. That role, however, is narrowed by the illustration in the deluxe fifteenth-century manuscript, which suggests that the narrative is suited particularly to the wealthy patron's own pilgrimage of life. If we take seriously the point made by Miri Rubin, that "people act through narratives, and they remember through narrative,"[32] then such changes in the visualization of the narrative are an important way in which the artist accommodates Guillaume's poem to new readers a century after its original composition.

Changes in the number of illustrations, their design, and their location are also evident in the two Middle English translations of the *Pèlerinage de vie humaine*. The best known is the verse translation made around 1426, probably by John Lydgate at the request of Thomas Montague (d. 1428), fourth earl of Salisbury and the duke of Bedford's deputy in Paris. The translator states that Montague asked for the English translation so that "men schold[e] se, / In ovre tonge, the grete moralyte / Wych in thys book ys seyde & comprehendyd."[33] The great morality is certainly emphasized, for Lydgate managed to extend the already long-winded second edition of the *Pèlerinage*, translating it into more than 24,800 lines of Middle English couplets. C. S. Lewis, usually a sympathetic reader of allegory, describes it as "unpleasant to read, not only because of its monstrous length and imperfect art, but because of the repellent and suffocating nature of its content."[34] But this exasperated response is overly harsh. The poem has received more sympathetic treatment in Susan Hagen's *Allegorical Remembrance*, which reproduces many of the miniatures in the incomplete and

---

31. A point made by Calin, *French Tradition*, p. 194.

32. Rubin, *Gentile Tales*, pp. 2–3.

33. Lydgate, *Pilgrimage of the Life of Man*, ed. Furnivall, lines 135–37. On the issue of Lydgate's authorship, see Walls, "Did Lydgate Translate the *Pèlerinage?*" The frontispiece of London, British Library, MS Harley 4826, probably pictures Lydgate introducing the kneeling pilgrim, who hands the translation to a standing Montague. On this image see Scott, *Later Gothic Manuscripts*, cat. no. 111, illus. 391.

34. C. S. Lewis, *Allegory of Love*, p. 271.

unfortunately quite badly damaged manuscript, London, British Library, MS Cotton Tiberius A. VII. Kathleen L. Scott, who dates it to the second quarter of the fifteenth century, notes that "the original manuscript must have been remarkable. If fifty-three illustrations survive for 5,360-odd lines from the *rear* of the manuscript (where the number of pictures might ordinarily decrease) and if pictures were present in roughly the same proportion in the first 18,300 lines, then the total number of illustrations would have been about 248, a phenomenal amount for any type of 15th-century English book."[35]

Indeed such would be unusual. More typical of late medieval illustrations of English vernacular texts are the manuscripts of the other Middle English translation, the prose *Pilgrimage of the Lyfe of the Manhode* made near the beginning of the fifteenth century.[36] Two of its six extant manuscripts are illustrated.[37] Oxford, Bodleian Library, MS Laud Miscellaneous 740, copied ca. 1430, includes twenty colorful miniatures with gold details decorating rich folios.[38] The radical reduction in the number of illustrations, only twenty in comparison to the 110 miniatures found in the early French manuscripts, is much more representative of English-language manuscripts. This reduction, furthermore, resembles the "paring down" that Camille sees as characterizing the woodcuts in the later printed books.[39] The opening of this manuscript includes the traditional scene emphasizing the aural reception of the poem by showing the poet as preacher. This visual tradition continues despite the fact that the English translation seems designed for the individual reader rather than a social performance, becoming a moral tract written to be studied alone by the serious reader rather than a visionary narrative to be heard during a social gathering. The manuscript

---

35. Scott, *Later Gothic Manuscripts*, 2:252; for this manuscript, see Scott cat. no. 89, illus. 351–54. The miniatures are listed in Ward, *Catalogue of Romances*, 2:578–80. On the artist, see Alexander, "William Abell 'lymnour.'"

36. Avril Henry, *Pilgrimage of the Lyfe of the Manhode*. To my knowledge, there is no manuscript or other evidence for Emily Steiner's claim that by 1368 Deguileville's *Vie humaine* "was already well-known in England, most likely as an anonymous English prose version of the poem's first redaction, the *Pilgrimage of the Lyfe of the Manhode*"; see Steiner, *Documentary Culture*, p. 29.

37. See Avril Henry, "Illuminations in the Two Illustrated Middle English Manuscripts."

38. See Pächt and Alexander, *Illuminated Manuscripts*, 3:81, no. 925, pl. LXXXVIII; and Tuve, *Allegorical Imagery*, figs. 28, 30, 32, 34, 38, 42, 63, 78, 80, 83, 86, 88, 90.

39. Camille, "Reading the Printed Image," p. 264.

Figure 6. Pilgrim meets Grace Dieu. *Pilgrimage of the Lyfe of the Manhode*; Oxford, Bodleian Library, MS Laud misc. 740, fol. 3v. (Photo: The Bodleian Library, University of Oxford.)

introduces Latin rubrics for some of its miniatures, a linguistic feature not found in the French manuscripts. It may seem odd that Latin rubrics were added to a manuscript of a poem that was translated into English because its readers might not understand French, but this new feature may be a way to underscore the bookish packaging of the prose translation, which is evident in the miniature depicting the first meeting between the pilgrim and Grace Dieu (fig. 6). The upper border of the miniature's frame has been indented to accommodate the Latin rubric, set off by a blue paraph. It reads, "hic gratia dei apparens primo homini nato" (fol. 3v).

The other illustrated manuscript of the Middle English *Lyfe of Manhode*, now Melbourne, State Library of Victoria *096/G94, was produced in Yorkshire or Lincolnshire in the 1430s for a member of the lower gentry.[40] It links two originally distinct and anonymous Middle English prose translations of Guillaume's two pilgrimage poems, of the "Life of Man" and of

---

40. See Manion and Vines, *Medieval and Renaissance Illuminated Manuscripts*, pp. 110–12, pl. 28, figs. 96–103.

"the Soul." Through its consistent *ordinatio* and its sequence of seventy-one unframed pen and ink drawings, this stylistically unified manuscript, like the French manuscripts of the *Trois Pèlerinages*, makes originally separate works into a single work, the two distinct English prose translations becoming one unified allegorical book tracing the spiritual progress of "humankind" in life and after death, on earth and in the otherworld. Throughout, the miniatures "serve the allegorical narrative by providing visual clarification of the often dense and difficult text."[41]

Guillaume's second poem, the *Pèlerinage de l'âme*, was translated into Middle English prose in 1413, perhaps for a noblewoman.[42] Also known as *Grace Dieu*, it is extant in ten manuscripts and was published by William Caxton in 1483. Remarkably, all ten manuscripts were designed and prepared to include miniatures and seven are illustrated, which suggests that *The Pilgrimage of the Soul* is a rare example of a Middle English work conceived as an illustrated book from its beginning.[43] The miniatures emphasize the book's structural divisions and introduce new chapters, a feature that characterizes the early printed editions,[44] but evident here a half century earlier. As in the woodcuts illustrating the later books, the illustrations function as introductory summaries. This is evident in New York, Public Library, MS Spencer 19, copied ca. 1430, perhaps in Lincolnshire, and owned by Sir Thomas Cumberworth of Somerby in mid-century.[45] Each of its twenty-six miniatures covers about a third of a folio and each is placed at the head of a chapter.[46] Again, the subjects of the miniatures are identified by rubrics, written sometimes in Latin, sometimes in English.

The shift to silent reading by a studious audience, which Camille sees as affecting the design of the printed books,[47] is already suggested by manuscripts of the Middle English translation. As in the printed books, some manuscripts include a table of contents as an aid to reading, to allow readers to locate material and move back and forth in their study, thus releas-

---

41. Maddocks, "'Me thowhte as I slepte that I was a pilgrime,'" p. 67.

42. For an edition see McGerr, *Pilgrimage of the Soul*.

43. See Lawton, "Text and Image," 1:116.

44. See Camille, "Reading the Printed Image," p. 262.

45. See Paltsits, "Petworth Manuscript"; and Scott, *Later Gothic Manuscripts*, cat. no. 74, 2:217–19.

46. Three color miniatures (for fols. 7r, 48r, 81r) are included in Lucy Freeman Sandler's catalogue entry no. 94 in Alexander, Marrow, and Sandler, *Splendor of the Word*, pp. 400–404.

47. Camille, "Reading the Printed Image," p. 284.

Figure 7. Table of contents. *Grace Dieu*; New York Public Library, Spencer MS 19, fol. 4r. (Photo: Spencer Collection, The New York Public Library, Astor, Lennox and Tilden Foundations.)

ing readers from the necessity of following the linear narrative.[48] Such an
aid to reading is included in Spencer 19 (fig. 7), whose opening "kalender"
is introduced by a three-line rubric: "This is the kalender of þe boke called
Grace dieu which boke is divided into v partes of whiche partes this seide
kalender evidently shewith þe chapiters" (fol. 4r). These chapters and their
numbers are then consistently marked in Latin at the conclusion of the
English rubrics following each chapter-introducing miniature. To quote
Camille's comment on the early printed books, "The [book's] modernized
version, with its internal 'speakers' and its chapter construction outlined in
a new table of contents at the beginning, removes the work from its roots in
oral presentation and sets it securely within the single gaze of the reading
. . . eye."[49] I agree with this conclusion, but note that it applies to fifteenth-
century manuscripts copied long before the earliest printed editions that
Camille is describing and that he sees as representing a "radical" shift in
the poem's reception. Without minimizing the importance of the graphic
changes introduced by printing, I believe that the early printed editions do
not *cause* a shift in the reception of the poem but *confirm* changes evolving
throughout the fifteenth century, developments reflected in the poem's
illustrated manuscripts, both French and English.

Rosemarie Potz McGerr has shown that the Middle English translation
of the *Soul* is not literal but makes several changes to elaborate selected
theological points for the anonymous early fifteenth-century woman for
whom the text was translated. It transforms "Guillaume's courtly poem
into a polemical text offering material in the vernacular that implicitly
answers Lollard attacks on Roman Catholic doctrine."[50] The result is a
conscious attempt to provide vernacular support for orthodox positions
then under attack by Lollards, who questioned both orthodox doctrine
and its visualization in imagery. The *Soul* is thus associated in a late
fifteenth-century manuscript, London, British Library, Additional MS
34193, with other English and Latin visionary texts, moral treatises, hymns,
and hagiographic narratives such as *St. Patrick's Purgatory*, the *Spiritu Guidonis*,

---

48. On this development in later medieval manuscripts, see Andrew Taylor, "Into His
Secret Chamber."

49. Camille, "Reading the Printed Image," p. 284.

50. McGerr, *Pilgrimage of the Soul*, p. xxix. See also McGerr, "Editing the Self-Conscious
Medieval Translator." Michael Camille has suggested that Lydgate's translation of *The Pilgrimage of the Life of Man* was similarly influenced by the need to counter Lollard heresy,
especially its iconoclastic attacks on images; see Camille, "Iconoclast's Desire," pp. 163–70.

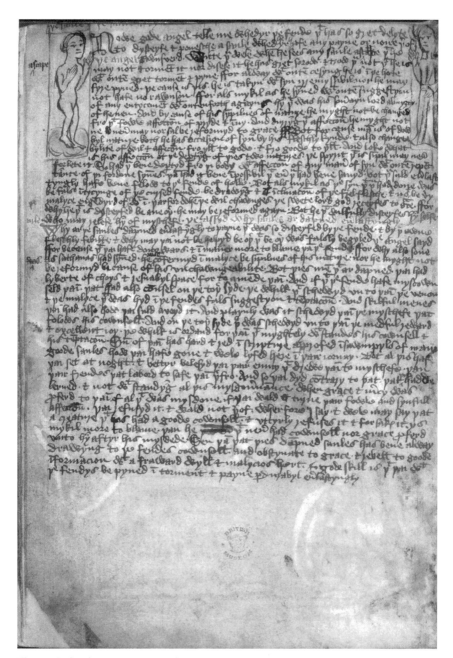

Figure 8. Soul questions Angel. Carthusian Miscellany; London, British Library, Additional MS 37049, fol. 73v. (Photo: By permission of the British Library.)

and the *Golden Legend*.[51] This use of a vernacular translation and imagery to support orthodoxy resembles Nicholas Love's *Mirrour of the Blessed Lyf of Jesu Christ*, written just three years before the translation of the *Soul*. The first book to submit to Archbishop Arundel's Constitutions of 1409 in the orthodox counteroffensive against Lollardy, the *Mirrour* was written by the prior of the Carthusian monastery of Mount Grace in Yorkshire.[52] The Carthusians became a bulwark of orthodoxy for the laity and were particularly fascinated by eschatological topics, as evident in a Carthusian miscellany, London, British Library, Additional MS 37049, copied in northern England ca. 1460–70.[53] It comprises over ninety devotional, historical, mystical, penitential, and eschatological texts, "illustrating," as Douglas Gray has noted, "nearly all the themes of Middle English religious literature."[54] Twelve selections are from the Middle English *Soul*, and these are accompanied by seventeen illustrations.[55] One, for example, shows a passage borrowed from its second book (fig. 8), in which the pilgrim soul questions the angel guide regarding the devil. The visionary characters are portrayed in the upper side margins as if in dialogue, performing the conversation inscribed between them. Such anthologizing is yet another way in which Guillaume's poem, now in English prose, reached a wider audience in fifteenth-century manuscripts, in this case exemplifying "some of the intimate and complex relationships between private reading, visual culture, and spirituality that were dominant during the period."[56]

It is hard to imagine a greater contrast between the Carthusian miscellany, a humble vernacular manuscript from a provincial English charterhouse, and London, Lambeth Palace Library, MS 326, one of two manuscripts of the Latin translation of the *Pilgrimage of the Soul*. Entitled *Liber peregrinacionis anime*, it was translated by Jean Gallopes for John, the duke of Bedford, copied by the scribe Jean Thomas ca. 1426, and decorated

---

51. See *Catalogue of Additions to the Manuscripts in the British Museum in the Years 1888–93*, pp. 225–26.

52. See Watson, "Censorship and Cultural Change."

53. For the manuscript see *Catalogue of Additions to the Manuscripts in the British Museum, 1900–1905*, pp. 324–32; Doyle, "English Carthusian Books"; and Scott, *Later Gothic Manuscripts*, 2:193. For the illustrations see Hogg, *Illustrated Yorkshire Carthusian Religious Miscellany*, and Brantley, *Reading in the Wilderness*. On its eschatological themes, see Hennessy, "Remains of the Royal Dead," and Emmerson, "Imagining and Imaging the End."

54. Douglas Gray, "London, British Library, Additional MS 37049," p. 115.

55. See Lawton, "Text and Image," 1:73–74.

56. Hennessy, "Passion, Devotion, Penitential Reading and the Manuscript Page," p. 216.

by "the Master of the Harvard Hannibal."[57] Like the Spencer *Grace Dieu,* this deluxe manuscript also emphasizes the scholarly nature of the text. But instead of as many as ninety-three illustrations of the original French poem, the Latin prose version contains only four miniatures, an extreme version of the "paring down" that distinguishes the printed editions.[58] More significantly, no miniature illustrates the actual pilgrimage narrative; instead, all four picture either the translator or the author and are designed to frame the Latin text. The miniatures emphasize the scholarly nature of the manuscript, which clearly privileges the Latin text over visual representations of the dream, so that the learned language is never interrupted by visual interpretations. Perhaps the narrative images that are so ubiquitous in earlier French manuscripts are too closely linked to the original French poem, or perhaps the visual was understood as a kind of vernacular in its own right and therefore inappropriate for this learned Latin prose *liber* with all its authorizing gestures.

The first miniature (fol. 1r), introducing the translator's prologue, pictures Jean Gallopes presenting his translation to the duke of Bedford, who is dressed in a golden robe and seated under a canopy of the arms of England and France. Despite what this image implies, the manuscript is not likely to have been a presentation copy, since, as Jenny Stratford has argued, "the arms of the presentation miniature are incorrect."[59] Nevertheless, the miniature does link the translation to Jean Gallopes and to his famous patron. Commenting on a presentation image in another manuscript (Paris, Bibliothèque de l'Arsenal, MS 2319, fol. 1r), a miniature showing Jeanne de Laval accepting the prose translation of the *Vie humaine,* Camille notes that "such an image of production which enhances the prestige of the text is not really of much use to someone who wants to understand the meaning of the work."[60] But this assumes that "meaning" is inherent in the words of the text alone, as if a text carries meaning outside of its context. But if meaning is a product of reading practices produced during a text's reception, the packaging of a text in different ways in different manuscripts at different times and in different places influences reception and therefore meaning. A "prestige" image carries meaning, for

57. See James, *Descriptive Catalogue of the Manuscripts in the Library of Lambeth Palace,* pp. 427–31; and Meiss, *French Painting in the Time of Jean de Berry,* part 3: *The Limbourgs and Their Contemporaries,* 1:390–91.

58. Camille, "Reading the Printed Image," p. 264.

59. Stratford, *Bedford Inventories,* p. 123.

60. Camille, "Reading the Printed Image," p. 288.

example, by underscoring the text's claim as aristocratic, which necessarily affects its reception, just as the meaning of a poem will be affected by its narrative illustration or its translation from the vernacular into Latin or its recomposition into prose.

Similarly, the second miniature (fol. 2v, fig. 9) also affects the reception of the text by emphasizing its scholarly nature. An author portrait of Guillaume seated at his desk with an open book, it introduces the author's prologue and visualizes the authorizing claim for Guillaume as poet that the first miniature claims for Jean as translator. The third miniature (fol. 4v)— picturing the author in bed, surrounded by books, at the beginning of his vision—also emphasizes the scholarly nature of the text while underscoring its visionary origins. The last miniature (fol. 83v) is placed at the end of the text and shows the author kneeling in a landscape, experiencing a vision of the Trinity. Based on the pilgrim's concluding vision, it now models the response appropriate for the reader of this religious text. The body of the visionary narrative itself is not illustrated, probably because the Latin translation essentially ceases to be a narrative and presents itself as a learned "tractatus," a generic shift influencing reception and also affecting meaning.

In contrast to the Lambeth Palace manuscript's emphasis on verbal and Latin textuality are the marginal illustrations in the *Hours of Isabella Stuart* (Cambridge, Fitzwilliam Museum, MS 62).[61] They represent by far the most radical treatment of Guillaume's poems in either manuscript or printed form. This deluxe book of hours was produced in the workshop of the Rohan Master (ca. 1420), perhaps for Yolande of Aragon, duchess of Anjou and mother of King René, whose second wife was Jeanne de Laval.[62] It eventually came into the possession of Isabella Stuart, daughter

---

61. See James, *Descriptive Catalogue of the Manuscripts in the Fitzwilliam Museum*, pp. 156–74; and catalogue entry by James Marrow in Binski and Panayotova, *Cambridge Illuminations*, pp. 202–4. I have unfortunately been unable to make use of the recent study of this manuscript published by Elizabeth L'Estrange, *Holy Motherhood: Gender, Dynasty and Visual Culture in the Later Middle Ages*, pp. 113–51.

62. The provenance and dating of the manuscript remain uncertain. Meiss dates it to ca. 1417–18 (*French Painting in the Time of Jean de Berry*, part 3: *The Limbourgs and Their Contemporaries*, 1:265), as does Harthan (*Book of Hours*, p. 116). Francis Wormald and Phyllis M. Giles also date it early, to ca. 1415 (*Illuminated Manuscripts in the Fitzwilliam Museum*, p. 30, no. 68). More recently, François Avril, who tends to date the mature work of the Rohan workshop later, has suggested that Yolande of Aragon may have commissioned the manuscript for her younger daughter, Yolande of Anjou, for her marriage in 1431 to Francis, the future duke of Brittany; see Avril and Reynaud, *Manuscrits à peintures en France, 1440–1520*, pp. 25–26, 115.

Figure 9. Guillaume at his desk. *Liber peregrinacionis anime*; London, Lambeth Palace Library, MS 326, fol. 2v. (Photo: Lambeth Palace Library.)

of James I of Scotland, upon her marriage in 1442 to Francis I, the duke of Brittany.[63] The manuscript includes four cycles of small scenes illustrating Guillaume's three visionary poems and the romance-like biblical text, the Apocalypse of John.[64] Interestingly, other than brief marginal rubrics identifying the beginning and end of each cycle, the manuscript's 341 miniatures depicting Guillaume's three poems are not accompanied by the poetic texts or even by brief explanatory captions. Presumably, like the Apocalypse, the three poems are now so well known that the reader needs no verbal text to follow their visual narratives. The poems are instead illustrated by the small scenes placed within lozenge-shaped or rectangular frames within the lush decorated borders of the book of hours.[65] Sometimes these accompany the central images of the hours, and sometimes they accompany only its Latin text.

The manuscript's designer must have known a cycle of Guillaume illustrations as well as illustrations of the Apocalypse found in many Anglo-French manuscripts popular from the mid-thirteenth through the mid-fifteenth century.[66] Yet the layout suggests the illustrations were selected and reorganized to fit the specific needs of a book of hours.[67] For example, unlike most manuscripts of the *Trois Pèlerinages*, the Fitzwilliam hours inverts the order of Guillaume's three poems, so that the first illustrations are not from the first and most popular poem, the *Vie humaine*, but from the *Jésus Christ*.[68] Significantly, the illustrative cycle is delayed to folio 13r to correspond to the beginning of the Gospel sequences in the hours. The cycle is introduced by a portrait of John writing at his desk and the

---

63. The manuscript includes a portrait of Isabella, probably painted over an original portrait of Yolande of Aragon; see Harthan, *Book of Hours*, p. 114, with border miniature depicting a scene from the *Pèlerinage de Jésus Christ*.

64. Northrop Frye has described the Apocalypse as having "a fairytale atmosphere of gallant angels fighting dragons, a wicked witch, and a wonderful gingerbread city glittering with gold and jewels" (*Secular Scripture*, p. 30).

65. For illustrations see Binksi and Panayotova, *Cambridge Illuminations*, p. 203 (with border miniature depicting Guillaume dreaming at the beginning of the *Pèlerinage de vie humaine* sequence); Emmerson and McGinn, *Apocalypse in the Middle Ages*, fig. 52, with border miniature depicting Apocalypse 7:10; and Emmerson "'A Large Order of the Whole,'" with illustrations of twenty-six images.

66. See Camille, "Visionary Perception and Images of the Apocalypse."

67. The argument of this and the next paragraph is expanded in Emmerson, "'A Large Order of the Whole,'" pp. 64–88.

68. The vast majority of *Trois Pèlerinage* manuscripts begin with the *Vie humaine*, followed by *Ame* and *Jésus Christ*, but three manuscripts shift the order to begin with *Jésus Christ*. See Boulton, "Digulleville's *Pèlerinage de Jésus Christ*," pp. 127 and 141 n. 11.

Latin text opening his Gospel, "In principio erat verbum."[69] The smaller image in the right border shows Guillaume asleep leaning on his book while receiving his vision of Christ. The juxtaposed images thus link the following Gospel images as well as their "authors" Guillaume and John, which is appropriate since John's vision is called the Revelation of Jesus Christ and medieval exegetes identified John the Revelator with John the Evangelist. Interestingly, the poet is depicted in a manner that recalls representations of John receiving his apocalyptic vision on the isle of Patmos.[70] It is therefore not surprising that after the sequence of images illustrating the *Pèlerinage Jésus Christ*, instead of a cycle of pictures illustrating the other pilgrimage poems, the Apocalypse of John follows. The 139 pictures illustrating the biblical text begin with a French rubric, but otherwise they are accompanied by no caption or other explanation. The apocalyptic imagery and creatures are so well known the images need no identifying texts.[71]

At the conclusion of this Apocalypse cycle, the *Hours of Isabella Stuart* includes a *Vie humaine* drawing on elements of the poem's second recension. Its placement after the scenes picturing the life of Christ and the Apocalypse suggests that humankind is understood to be living in the Last Days. The *Vie humaine* cycle ends with Death approaching the pilgrim, but the images depicting Guillaume's third visionary poem, the *Pèlerinage de l'âme*, do not follow immediately. They are instead delayed for ten folios so that the cycle can begin appropriately at the point where the book of hours introduces the Office of the Dead, linking once again the hours and Guillaume's poems, now both focusing on eschatological matters. Throughout, the three cycles of images based on Guillaume's *Trois Pèlerinages* are carefully apportioned, distributed, and designed not only to link to the biblical Apocalypse but also to correspond to the Latin text and to the central images of this deluxe book of hours. Without accompanying texts, the *Pèlerinage* images function something like a vernacular gloss on the book's sacred text. Now, furthermore, the gloss is completely visualized in what must have been a well-known picture language for the aristocratic female owners of this deluxe book of hours, a series of images illustrating all three

---

69. See Emmerson, "'A Large Order of the Whole,'" fig. 5.

70. See Suzanne Lewis, *Reading Images*, pp. 19–39.

71. This differs from the Bedford Book of Hours (ca. 1422), which includes 310 marginal images of the Apocalypse paired to illustrate the biblical text and its interpretation, with explanatory captions inscribed at the foot of the page. On this manuscript see Emmerson, "Apocalypse Cycle"; and König, *Bedford Hours*.

of Guillaume's extremely popular poems as well as the Apocalypse, which was also popular with female readers during the later Middle Ages.[72]

This essay, part of a long-term project studying the intersection of linguistic and visual signs in late medieval manuscripts to understand the reception of literary texts by various interpretive communities, analyzes the effect of linguistic and generic translation during the fifteenth century on the visual images of a popular fourteenth-century poetic trilogy. Its goal is to examine some ways in which the language, genre, layout, and iconography of medieval texts were designed and reshaped for various audiences. Guillaume's pilgrimage poems, probably originally intended in the fourteenth century to be received aurally, and by the sixteenth century appealing to many readers in the new medium of print, were received in the fifteenth century in new linguistic and generic versions and through a wide variety of manuscripts. These ranged from a humble miscellany assembled by Carthusians in Yorkshire to a deluxe Latin book claiming to be designed for the duke of Bedford; from a didactic Middle English translation for an anonymous lady to a textless cycle of pictures in a book of hours produced for a wealthy and powerful duchess. The designers, copiers, and illuminators of these manuscripts modified the texts and the manuscript contexts of Guillaume's poems to meet the needs of their differing audiences, a reworking that was as significant to the needs of the fifteenth century as were the later changes made for readers of printed editions in the sixteenth century.

---

72. On the manuscript's likely reception, see Emmerson, "'A Large Order of the Whole,'" pp. 97–98. For the circulation of Guillaume's poems among members of the House of Anjou, see Legaré, "Reception du *Pèlerinage de Vie humaine.*

Dante's Views on Judaism, Christianity, and Islam: Perspectives from the New (Fourteenth) Century

Christopher Kleinhenz

The advent of the twenty-first century was greeted in a variety of ways: from joyful noises of celebration accompanying glasses raised high to toast the dawn of a new and better age to more subdued sounds of relief (perhaps even groans or muffled cheers) for the passing of what was certainly one of the most savage centuries in human history. One common element in most events of this nature and particularly at this point in history was, and continues to be, the general appeal for greater tolerance and understanding among peoples, nations, and religions. Seven centuries ago the world was a much different place . . . or was it? We may be able to gain some insight on the concerns of our own age by considering how authors in earlier periods dealt *mutatis mutandi* with similar issues. In this essay I would like to focus on the interaction of the three monotheistic religions—Judaism, Christianity, and Islam—in the medieval world and, more specifically, on Dante's appraisal of them in medieval Italy and his presentation of them in the *Divine Comedy*.[1]

The third story of the first day in Boccaccio's *Decameron* is both pertinent to the subject and a good place to begin. In this tale "Melchizedek the Jew, with a story about three rings, avoids a most dangerous trap laid for him by Saladin."[2] Saladin, having "expended the whole of his treasure in various wars and extraordinary acts of munificence," found himself in need of ready cash from the wealthy but miserly Melchizedek. In order to

---

1. As a study of views on religion and religious tolerance in the Middle Ages, this essay examines Dante's particular positions vis-à-vis the three monotheistic religions as they are presented in the *Divine Comedy*. This consideration of a literary text in the light of its historical, social, political, and theological context is, by its very nature, interdisciplinary and quintessentially "medieval." With it I would like to pay tribute to the wide-ranging interests and substantial achievements that Helen Damico has demonstrated both in her scholarly work and in her many and various professional activities on behalf of the Medieval Academy, CARA, and TEAMS. This small contribution can only begin to express my appreciation of and affection for Helen as friend and colleague.

2. The translation follows Boccaccio, *Decameron*, ed. and trans. McWilliam.

obtain the money by smoother channels than force, the wily Saladin presents Melchizedek with the following conundrum: "Which of the three laws, whether the Jewish, the Saracen, or the Christian, [do] you deem to be truly authentic?" "The Jew," so the story continues, "who was indeed a wise man, realized all too well that Saladin was aiming to trip him up with the intention of picking a quarrel with him, and that if he were to praise any of the three more than the others, the Sultan would achieve his object. He therefore had need of a reply that would save him from falling into the trap, and having sharpened his wits, in no time at all he was ready with his answer." Melchizedek tells a story about a "great and wealthy man who . . . possessed a most precious and beautiful ring. Because of its value and beauty, he wanted to do it the honor of leaving it in perpetuity to his descendants, and so he announced that he would bequeath the ring to one of his sons, and that whichever of them should be found to have it in his keeping, this man was to be looked upon as his heir, and the others were to honor and respect him as the head of the family." And so the ring was passed down through many generations, until such time as it "came to rest in the hands of a man who had three most splendid and virtuous sons who were very obedient to their father, and he loved all of them equally. Each of the three young men, being aware of the tradition concerning the ring, was eager to take precedence over the others, and they all did their utmost to persuade the father, who was now an old man, to leave them the ring when he died." The father secretly had two additional rings made that were identical to the original, and "when he was dying, he took each of his sons aside in turn, and gave one ring to each. After their father's death, they all desired to succeed to his title and estate, and each man denied the claims of the others, producing his ring to prove his case. But finding that the rings were so alike that it was impossible to tell them apart, the question of which of the sons was the true and rightful heir remained in abeyance, and has never been settled." "The same applies," Melchizedek concludes, "to the three laws which God the Father granted to His three peoples. . . . Each of them considers itself the legitimate heir to His estate, each believes it possesses His one true law and observes His commandments. But as with the rings, the question as to which of them is right remains in abeyance." Pleased with the wit of Melchizedek's answer, Saladin approaches his creditor openly and receives the desired amount in loan. Not only is Melchizedek repaid, but Saladin makes him a lifelong friend and honored member of his court.

Boccaccio does, to be sure, play on certain cultural stereotypes in his presentation of these characters—the usurious and miserly Jew, the crafty

Arab. Nevertheless, the moral of the tale is that of tolerance, appreciation, and respect for traditions different from one's own. These characters
inhabit an ideal world, one in which largeness of view is the norm, and virtue and integrity of character (at least in a classical sense) are prized. And,
generally, in the *Decameron*, the stories the young men and women tell are
charged with just such a restorative, civilizing function; are charged, even
as their sequestered garden is, amid the horrors and despair of plague-
stricken Florence, with the humor of hope. Boccaccio's "human comedy"
forms in many ways a complement, or response, to Dante's *Divine Comedy*,
which, of course, is the object of this essay.

Dante, we must admit, would probably not have appreciated the lesson
of Boccaccio's story of Saladin and Melchizedek. Convinced of the Truth
of the Christian faith, Dante, had he been one of the three sons in Boccaccio's tale, would no doubt have sworn on a stack of Bibles that his was
the one, original, and true ring. It is precisely this depth and firmness
of belief, however, which prevents him from turning rabid in his views.
Indeed, Dante's constant concern is with justice, with Divine Justice, whose
wonderful operations elude all dull and personal "concerns" with it.

It is an unfortunate misconception on the part of some that Dante put
his enemies in Hell and his friends in Purgatory and Paradise. However, the
Divine Comedy is not a loose game of favorites. Nor is it an allegory on the
plan of Prudentius's *Psychomachia* with its cold but gory combats between
personified vices and virtues. The *Comedy* does not move through an alle-
gorized terrain with "Sloughs of Despair" and the like, nor does it deal in
a "one size fits all" variety of punishment. Rather, in the *Comedy*, Dante
the Poet has his Pilgrim (and us along with him) meet with, speak to, and
learn from real historical personages, who represent themselves, with all
their individual traits, good and bad, pleasures and pains, successes and
failures, aspirations and dashed hopes. We meet, in very fact, their souls,
fixed forever at the sum total of their ontogeny. So formidable are Dante's
powers of narration that we are caught up in the web of his art; we buy into
his "fiction"—and "the fiction of the *Comedy*," to cite the famous formulation by Charles Singleton,[3] "is that it is not fiction"—and we ignore to our
peril its real, inhering moral force. Dante describes for us how the entire
physical, moral, and spiritual universe is structured, and how imperfect
human society might operate after that model of true-ordered perfection.

---

3. Singleton, "Irreducible Dove," p. 129.

The *Comedy* is like a great cosmic chart which can help us to coordinate life with morality, and the spirit with Divine Providence and Justice.

Now, if we must find a quibble in all this, the obvious place to look would seem to be in Dante's Christian "prejudice," which, wholesome though it be, still might argue according to a very narrow logic. We might expect, for example, that the lot of all nonbelievers would be to be cast straight into Hell. But this is not the case. A simple census of the *Divine Comedy* produces, it is true, relatively few souls outside the Christian faith; but these are scattered up and down the three realms of Judgment. And apparently they make the list at all thanks to some eminence of character, whether for good or evil, with which Dante could strengthen the moral weave of his poem's fabric, and at the same time purfle it with something of his pedant's pride. If, then, we find more un-Christian names in Hell, this fact does no more than mirror the ineradicable bias, so-called, of human history, filled up as it is by a host of exemplary sinners: Sinon and Potiphar's wife, the tyrant Dionysius of Syracuse, incestuous Myrrha, the traitors Cassius and Brutus, and Ulysses renowned for his wiles! But Dante has remembered Cato, too, and honors him with the sentinel's post on the Mountain of Purgatory. The emperor Trajan circles in the Heaven of Jupiter, and, with him, the Trojan Ripheus—saved, it would seem, by Virgil's superlative description of him in the second book of the *Aeneid* (vv. 426–27) as most just: "Ripheus, iustissimus unus / qui fuit in Teucris, et servantissimus aequi" (Ripheus . . . foremost in justice among the Trojans, and most zealous for the right).[4] Evidently, Dante allows a very wonderful temper to the steel of Divine Justice. Let us now turn our attention to those relatively few specific examples of Jews and Muslims in the *Comedy*.[5]

There are certain decisive moments in Providential History that guide Dante's placement of souls in the afterlife. One such episode is the Harrowing of Hell, when Christ descended in triumph through the underworld

---

4. Citations and translations from the *Aeneid* follow the edition by H. Rushton Fairclough.

5. For medieval perspectives on Islam see Southern, *Western Views*, and Tolan, *Medieval Christian Perceptions*. For the relationship of Dante to Islam see Asín Palacios, *Escatologia*; Cantor, "Uncanonical Dante"; Cerulli, "*Libro della Scala*"; Conklin Akbari, "Islam and Islamic Culture"; Corti, "La *Commedia*"; D'Ancona, "Leggenda di Maometto"; Gabrieli, "Islam" and "Maometto"; Menocal, *Arabic Role*; Russell, "Dante e l'Islam" and "Dante e l'Islam oggi"; Tatlock, "Mohammed and His Followers"; and Ventura, "Presenze islamiche." Among the relatively few studies on Dante and Judaism see Penna, "Ebrei"; Roth, "New Light"; and Tomasch," Judecca."

and delivered the souls of the Old Testament patriarchs and prophets—Adam, Abraham, Moses, David—and illustrious women—Rachel, Judith, Ruth— from the power of death unto highest Heaven. Thus, in the final cantos of *Paradiso,* Dante sees almost half of the great amphitheater, the celestial rose, taken up by the souls of those virtuous Hebrew men and women who died before Christ's redemption. The other half holds the souls of the Christian blessed, and but a few seats remain empty; this may suggest either that Dante expected an imminent eschatological crisis or that he was thoroughly convinced by the corruption engulfing Christian society that very few additional souls would ever be chosen. The first Jews we find in Dante's *Inferno* are Caiaphas, Annas, and the other Pharisees—among the hypocrites (canto 23). Again, these souls appear where they do because of their role at a crucial moment in Providential History—the Passion of Jesus. One of the Jovial Friars identifies them to the Pilgrim, and comments:[6]

> "Quel confitto che tu miri,
> consigliò i Farisei che convenia
> porre un uom per lo popolo a' martìri.
>   Attraversato è, nudo, ne la via,
> come tu vedi, ed è mestier ch' el senta
> qualunque passa, come pesa, pria.
>   E a tal modo il socero si stenta
> in questa fossa, e li altri dal concilio
> che fu per li Giudei mala sementa." (*Inf.* 23.115–23)

> (That transfixed one you are gazing at counseled the Pharisees that it was expedient to put one man to torture for the people. He is stretched out naked across the way, as you see, and needs must feel the weight of each that passes; and in like fashion is his father-in-law racked in this ditch, and the others of that council which was a seed of evil for the Jews.)

They are specially devoted, thus, to suffer—as properly redounding to them—the entire world's weight of hypocrisy, and in the same attitude as Jesus bore all men's sins. The idea of the "evil seed"—the "mala sementa"—will return as part of a more general discussion of the *vendetta* pronounced on the Jews for Christ's Crucifixion in *Paradiso* 6.

Needless to say, Dante's Providential History does not overlook the Betrayal. Judas (*Giuda*) is heaped with the further miserable distinction of

---

6. Citations and translations from the *Comedy* follow Singleton's edition.

lending his name to the last division of the circle of traitors, the absolute nadir of Hell, "Giudecca." Here, at the very center of the earth and thus of the whole Ptolemaic universe, three-faced Lucifer, the infernal mockery of the Trinity, is fast-imprisoned in ice and torments in his three mouths the souls of the three arch-traitors to Empire and to the Church: Cassius and Brutus, who betrayed Julius Caesar, and Judas, who sold Christ for thirty pieces of silver:

> Da ogne bocca dirompea co' denti
> un peccatore, a guisa di maciulla,
> sì che tre ne facea così dolenti.
>   A quel dinanzi il mordere era nulla
> verso 'l graffiar, che tal volta la schiena
> rimanea de la pelle tutta brulla.
>   "Quell'anima là sù c' ha maggior pena,"
> disse 'l maestro, "è Giuda Scarïotto,
> che 'l capo ha dentro e fuor le gambe mena.
>   De li altri due c' hanno il capo di sotto,
> quel che pende dal nero ceffo è Bruto:
> vedi come si storce, e non fa motto!;
>   e l'altro è Cassio, che par sì membruto." (*Inf.* 34.55–67)

(In each mouth he champed a sinner with his teeth, as with a heckle, and thus he kept three of them woeful. To the one in front the biting was nothing compared to the clawing, for sometimes his back remained all stripped of skin. "The soul up there that has the greatest punishment," said the master, "is Judas Iscariot, who has his head within and plies his legs outside. Of the other two who have their heads below, the one that hangs from the black muzzle is Brutus: see how he writhes and utters not a word; the other is Cassius, who seems so stark of limb.")

It is worthwhile to notice the force here gained by the poem's architectonic quality (namely of symmetry), keeping in mind always that what Dante gives to his art, he takes (and would have us take as well) from the majestic order and outline of Providence. Lucifer presumed on the throne of God, and was cast out of heaven, for bright angel's wings he received those of the loathsome bat, and the wind they fan sends the chill of evil inspiration through the world below; less in contest with, more in perversion of, the divine grace effected by the Holy Spirit. Lucifer is "buried alive" in the deepest deep of the material universe, at the farthest possible remove, appropriately, from God's light—the "light of glory" (*lumen gloriae*)—that emanates from the center of the perfect, immaterial universe. Likewise, Lucifer, "the Emperor of the woeful realm" ("Lo 'mperador del doloroso regno" [*Inf.* 34.28]), is all but overwhelmed by the tributes of sin and sorrow that hail upon his head from the nine circles of Hell that, surrounding him, comprise his kingdom; while God in the Empyrean receives back the joy of nine choirs of angels that circle the Triune Deity endlessly. Canto 34 borrows for its first words the *incipit* of the Easter hymn in honor of the cross by Venantius Fortunatus, "Vexilla regis prodeunt" (The banners of the king advance), only to invert the sense suddenly by the addition of the genitive *inferni* (The banners of the king *of Hell* advance). The procession of the cross, the triumph of Christ over death, the resurrection to eternal life: these are snatched from our fancy and replaced by another reality—also eternal—of death and hellnight. Such is the first impression of the canto. And the terrific vision of Judas head-first in the middle mouth of Satan is the last. To regard this consummate, spiritualized art as mere refined bigotry would be even more vile than it is foolish.

There are only five Muslims in Dante's *Inferno*: three in Limbo (*Inf.* 4)—Averroes, Avicenna, and Saladin—and two among the schismatics—Mohammed and Alì (*Inf.* 28). The presence of the three souls in Limbo suggests Dante's due allowance for their virtues. Virgil describes the condition of the souls in Limbo, which is also his own:

> . . . ei non peccaro; e s' elli hanno mercedi,
> non basta, perché non ebber battesmo,
> ch' è porta de la fede che tu credi;
>   e s' e' furon dinanzi al cristianesmo,
> non adorar debitamente a Dio:
> e di questi cotai son io medesmo.
>   Per tai difetti, non per altro rio,
> semo perduti. (*Inf.* 4.34–41)

> (. . . they did not sin; but if they have merit, that does not suffice, for they did not have baptism, which is the portal of the faith you hold; and if they were before Christianity, they did not worship God aright, and I myself am one of these. Because of these shortcomings, and for no other fault, we are lost.)

Damned through no fault of their own and possessed of enough Reason to apprehend now the Faith denied to them, all the souls in Limbo suffer an acute sadness that Virgil encapsulates in the tragic phrase "sanza speme vivemo in disio" (without hope we live in longing [*Inf.* 4.42]). We would like to believe, for their sakes, that there is some solace in a state so like the Elysiums of old and in the pleasant company of classical poets, philosophers, warrior-heroes, scientists—the richest cream of Antique society. Specious illusion! Limbo indeed is a kind of Christianized Elysian Fields or worse Hades, but none who dwell there ever looked forward to its shadowy nothings as fair sequel to the brilliant substance of life.

The fate of Mohammed and his son-in-law Alì is much more severe. The poet stoops to the lowest linguistic register and coarsest imagery in his description of their punishment. Indeed, it would appear that Dante was following a popular medieval belief according to which Mohammed and Alì were Christians who bore responsibility for the great schism.[7] This legend to which Dante apparently subscribed presented Mohammed as an ambitious prelate, in some accounts a cardinal, who, enraged by his failure to be elected pope, moved to form his own sect and thus succeeded in splitting the Church. Thus, it is as the principal dividers of Christian unity that Dante presents them in canto 28, reserved for the schismatics and sowers of discord:

> Già veggia, per mezzul perdere o lulla,
> com' io vidi un, così non si pertugia,
> rotto dal mento infin dove si trulla.
> Tra le gambe pendevan le minugia;
> la corata pareva e 'l tristo sacco
> che merda fa di quel che si trangugia.
> Mentre che tutto in lui veder m' attacco,
> guardommi e con le man s' aperse il petto,
> dicendo: "Or vedi com' io mi dilacco!
> vedi come storpiato è Mäometto!
> Dinanzi a me sen va piangendo Alì,
> fesso nel volto dal mento al ciuffetto.
> E tutti li altri che tu vedi qui,
> seminator di scandalo e di scisma
> fuor vivi, e però son fessi così.
> Un diavolo è qua dietro che n' accisma
> sì crudelmente, al taglio de la spada
> rimettendo ciascun di questa risma,
> quand' avem volta la dolente strada;
> però che le ferite son richiuse
> prima ch' altri dinanzi li rivada." (*Inf.* 28.22–42)

(Truly a cask, through loss of mid-board or side-piece, gapes not so wide as one I saw, cleft from the chin to the part that breaks wind; his entrails were hanging between his legs, and the vitals could be seen and the foul

---

7. See Gabrieli, "Maometto," and the unsigned entry "Alì" in the *Enciclopedia Dantesca*, as well as Singleton's commentary on v. 31 of *Inferno* 28.

sack that makes ordure of what is swallowed. While I was all absorbed in gazing on him, he looked at me and with his hands pulled open his breast, saying, "Now see how I rend myself, see how mangled is Mohammed! In front of me goes Alì weeping, cleft in the face from chin to forelock; and all the others whom you see here were in their lifetime sowers of scandal and of schism, and therefore are thus cleft. A devil is here behind that fashions us thus cruelly, putting again to the edge of the sword each of this throng when we have circled the doleful road; for the wounds are closed up before any of us pass again before him.")

The complementary nature of their punishment—the fissure that rends Mohammed's body continues upward through his son-in-law's head, so that together they are the emblem of the body of Christendom they divided. The more minor wound suffered by Alì may suggest the lesser degree of his responsibility for the schism, or it may indicate that Dante was aware of Ali's role in the founding of the Shiite sect, dividing thus the "head" of Islam into two parts. In Islamic countries today this passage, so offensive to the prophet, has been removed from Arabic versions of the *Comedy*, and, in some countries, the entire poem has been either confiscated or banned.[8]

What should emerge from this rapid survey is that Dante's *Inferno* is decidedly a Christian-occupied zone. Moreover, while most architectural features of Hell resemble the bastions of fortified castles and towns of medieval Italy, one distinct feature of the City of Dis, the location of the heretics, is that of flaming mosques ("le . . . meschite / . . . vermiglie come se di foco uscite," mosques . . . red as if they had come out of the fire [*Inf.* 8. 70, 72]). This particular zone becomes the infernal counterpart to the city of the infidel, yet its guardians are the fallen angels and the three Furies and its inhabitants the Epicureans, those who denied the immortality of the soul. Among the heretics, we meet or hear about only four, all from the thirteenth century: Farinata degli Uberti, Cavalcante dei Cavalcanti, the emperor Frederick II, and Cardinal Ottaviano degli Ubaldini of Bologna. Even in those places where we might expect to find souls that conform to certain stereotypical attitudes, we do not. The third ring of the seventh circle—the burning desert sands upon which descends a rain of fire—is reserved for those sinners who committed violence against God, God's child Nature, and Nature's offspring Human Industry. Thus, together with the blasphemers and sodomites, we find the usurers, but their ranks are full of Christian families of Florence and Padua. Reginald Scrovegni is here,

---

8. Gabrieli, "Maometto."

whose son Enrico had the Arena Chapel built and decorated by Giotto in an attempt—futile, after all, it would appear—to expiate his father's sin.

One or two very mild references to Jews and Muslims do creep into Dante's text, but these potentially stereotypical characterizations and condemnations, in my view, reflect more the language of the times than any animus on the Florentine poet's part. In *Paradiso* 5, for example, Beatrice discusses the serious nature of holy vows and warns against spiritual capriciousness. In so doing, she holds up examples of the unwise pledges made by Jephthah and Agamemnon:

> Non prendan li mortali il voto a ciancia;
> siate fedeli, e a ciò far non bieci,
> come Ieptè a la sua prima mancia;
>   cui più si convenia dicer "Mal feci,"
> che, servando, far peggio; e così stolto
> ritrovar puoi il gran duca de' Greci,
>   onde pianse Efigènia il suo bel volto,
> e fé pianger di sé i folli e i savi
> ch' udir parlar di così fatto cólto. (*Par.* 5.64–72)

(Let mortals never take the vow in sport. Be faithful, and with that be not perverse, as was Jephthah in his first offering, who ought rather to have said "I did amiss," than, by keeping his vow, to do worse. And you can find the great leader of the Greeks in like manner foolish, wherefore Iphigenia wept that her face was fair, and made weep for her both the simple and the wise who heard the tale of such a rite.)

Beatrice concludes her discussion of vows by urging the Christian flock to avoid idle temptations that would make them the laughingstock of their neighbor, the steady-minded Jew who rigidly follows Mosaic law:

> Siate, Cristiani, a muovervi più gravi:
> non siate come penna ad ogne vento,
> e non crediate ch' ogne acqua vi lavi.
>   Avete il novo e 'l vecchio Testamento,
> e 'l pastor de la Chiesa che vi guida;
> questo vi basti a vostro salvamento.
>   Se mala cupidigia altro vi grida,
> uomini siate, e non pecore matte,
> sì che 'l Giudeo di voi tra voi non rida! (*Par.* 5.73–81)

(Be graver, you Christians, in moving. Be not like a feather to every wind, and think not that every water may cleanse you. You have the New Testament and the Old, and the Shepherd of the Church, to guide you: let this suffice for your salvation. If evil greed cry aught else to you, be you men, and not silly sheep, so that the Jew among you may not laugh at you.)

Similarly, the term *saracino* (aligned with *giudeo* ['Jew'] on a couple of occasions) is put to invidious use. In *Purgatory* 23, Forese Donati contrasts the goodness and modesty of his widow Nella with the more-than-Saracen dissoluteness of contemporary Florentine women:

> Tempo futuro m' è già nel cospetto,
> cui non sarà quest' ora molto antica,
>   nel qual sarà in pergamo interdetto
> a le sfacciate donne fiorentine
> l'andar mostrando con le poppe il petto.
>   Quai barbare fuor mai, quai saracine,
> cui bisognasse, per farle ir coperte,
> o spiritali o altre discipline? (*Purg.* 23.98–105)

(Already in my vision is a future time, to which this hour shall not be very old, when the brazen-faced women of Florence shall be forbidden from the pulpit to go displaying their breasts with the paps. What Barbarian, what Saracen women were there ever, who required either spiritual or other discipline to make them go covered?)

Again, the real object of Dante's attack is vain Christian conceit: even heathen women would be more decorous in their dress and actions. It should be noticed, moreover, that Dante relegates these potential slurs to a *rhetorical* office, where they can spend their passion with the strictest poetical propriety.

In *Paradiso* 15, during his meeting with his great-great-grandfather Cacciaguida, Dante learns about his death as a crusader in the army of Conrad III:

> Poi seguitai lo 'mperador Currado;
> ed el mi cinse de la sua milizia,
> tanto per bene ovrar li venni in grado.
>   Dietro li andai incontro a la nequizia
> di quella legge il cui popolo usurpa,
> per colpa d' i pastor, vostra giustizia.
>   Quivi fu' io da quella gente turpa
> disviluppato dal mondo fallace. (*Par.* 15.139–46)

(Afterward I followed the Emperor Conrad, who girt me with his knighthood, so much did I win his favor by good work. I went, in his train, against the iniquity of that law whose people, through fault of the Pastors, usurp your right. There by that foul folk was I released from the deceitful world.)

Harsh words for the Muslims, no doubt. Much indignation, too, at craven popes. But then who would seriously expect a Christian knight, confirmed in his martyrdom, to speak of such personal events in a "disinterested" manner?

In *Paradiso* 11, Thomas Aquinas, relating the life of St. Francis of Assisi, tells about his voyage with the crusaders to Egypt and his audience there with the Sultan:

> . . . per la sete del martiro,
> ne la presenza del Soldan superba
> predicò Cristo e li altri che 'l seguiro,
>   e per trovare a conversione acerba
> troppo la gente e per non stare indarno,
> redissi al frutto de l'italica erba. (*Par.* 11.100–105

> (. . . in thirst for martyrdom, he, in the proud presence of the Sultan, had preached Christ and them that followed him, and, finding the people too unripe for conversion and in order not to stay in vain, had returned to the harvest of the Italian fields.)

The passage turns on words and concepts that speak of fertility and productivity: Islam, though yet too proud, will someday be ripe for conversion, and unity in the Christian flock will be reestablished. Here, then, we have Dante's deliberate opinion on the matter, and he chooses to express it in language measured, attractive, and hopeful.

It is appropriate here to return to the idea of the "evil seed," the "mala sementa." As a by-product of his belief in Divine Providence, Dante carefully insists on the original motives of things, particularly of things bearing on the moral body. Often he will use physiological metaphors of seeds or semen. For example, the noble seed of the Romans springs from the Fall of Troy: "l'agguato del caval che fé la porta / onde uscì de' Romani il gentil seme" (*Inf.* 26.59–60). The souls awaiting passage across the Acheron in Charon's boat echo in their curses biblical images of moral heredity and dread judgment: "Bestemmiavano Dio e lor parenti, / l'umana spezie e 'l loco e 'l tempo e 'l seme / di lor semenza e di lor nascimenti" (They cursed God, their parents, the human race, the place, the time, the seed of their begetting and of their birth [*Inf.* 3.103–5]). And Dante has Ulysses sow his soul's fate with a very liberal hand indeed, when he spurs on his ship's crew with the stirring conclusion of his speech: "Considerate la vostra semenza: / fatti non foste a viver come bruti, / ma per seguir virtute e canoscenza" (Consider your origin: you were not made to live as brutes, but to pursue virtue and knowledge [*Inf.* 26.118–20]). Thus, the "concilio / che fu per

li Giudei mala sementa" (council which was a seed of evil for the Jews [*Inf.*
23.122–23]), referred to earlier in connection with the punishment of the
Pharisees, exemplifies this same bent of Dante's for back-tracing the arrivals
of Divine Justice. Another issue from this "bad seed" emerges in canto 6 of
Paradiso, where the emperor Justinian is made to share Dante's predilection
for seeing the Fear of God advanced under the aegis of the Roman eagle:

> Ma ciò che 'l segno che parlar mi face
> fatto avea prima e poi era fatturo
> per lo regno mortal ch' a lui soggiace,
>   diventa in apparenza poco e scuro,
> se in mano al terzo Cesare si mira
> con occhio chiaro e con affetto puro;
>   ché la viva giustizia che mi spira,
> li concedette, in mano a quel ch' i' dico,
> gloria di far vendetta a la sua ira.
>   Or qui t' ammira in ciò ch' io ti replìco:
> poscia con Tito a far vendetta corse
> de la vendetta del peccato antico. (*Par.* 6.82–93)

(But what the standard that makes me speak had done before, and
after was to do throughout the mortal realm subject unto it, becomes in
appearance little and obscure if it be looked on in the hand of the third
Caesar with clear eye and pure affection; because the living Justice which
inspires me granted to it, in his hand of whom I speak, the glory of doing
vengeance for Its own wrath. Now marvel here at what I unfold to you:
afterwards it sped with Titus to do vengeance for the vengeance of the
ancient sin.)

Justinian, who codified the laws of the empire, is thus tasked anew with the
vendetta clause of Divine Law, which ordered, in turn, Christ's Crucifixion
as satisfaction for Original Sin, and the destruction of the Temple in A.D.
70 for the horror of Calvary. Dante purposes to brace us Old Testament–
wise, because only on such stern theory can we be brought into accord with
the inscrutable decrees of God's justice toward the world.

The goal of Dante's vision is unity—unity in Florence, in Italy, and in
universal Christendom, the world as a whole. Time and again in the *Divine
Comedy,* disintegrated civil life and degenerate spiritual life are bemoaned.
In canto 16 of *Purgatory* Dante asks Marco Lombardo why it is that things
have gone so wrong on earth and asks where the cause lies:

> Lo mondo è ben così tutto diserto
> d'ogne virtute, come tu mi sone,
> e di malizia gravido e coverto;

> ma priego che m' addite la cagione,
> sì ch' i' la veggia e ch' i' la mostri altrui;
> ché nel cielo uno, e un qua giù la pone. (*Purg.* 16.58–63)

> (The world is indeed as utterly deserted by every virtue as you declare to me, and pregnant and overspread with iniquity, but I beg you to point out to me the cause, so that I may see it and show it to men, for one places it in the heavens and another here below.)

Marco's immediate response focuses on the nature of free will and how if things go wrong on earth, then the cause is to be sought in humankind: "Però, se 'l mondo presente disvia, / in voi è la cagione, in voi si cheggia" (Therefore if the present world goes astray, in you is the cause, in you let it be sought [*Purg.* 16.82, 83]).[9] In the extension of this speech, Marco Lombardo indicates the additional problem of the lack of proper guidance in earthly and spiritual matters and concludes with the wonderful image of the two suns of Rome:

> Soleva Roma, che 'l buon mondo feo,
> due soli aver, che l'una e l'altra strada
> facean vedere, e del mondo e di Deo.
>   L'un l'altro ha spento; ed è giunta la spada
> col pasturale, e l'un con l'altro insieme
> per viva forza mal convien che vada;
>   però che, giunti, l'un l'altro non teme. (*Purg.* 16.106–12)

> (Rome, which made the world good, was wont to have two Suns, which made visible both the one road and the other, that of the world and that of God. The one has quenched the other, and the sword is joined to the crook: and the one together with the other must perforce go ill— since joined, the one does not fear the other.)

To Dante's idealizing imagination, History and Revelation, Reason and Faith, unanimously attest that man's double beatitude—happiness in this life and happiness in the eternal life—rests in the cooperative superintendence—*not* in the contest or conflation—of Emperor and Pope.[10]

---

9. This statement seems to anticipate Walt Kelly's famous formulation in the comic strip *Pogo*: "We have met the enemy and he is us."

10. In his treatise on world government, *Monarchia*, ed. and trans. Kay, 3.15.7, Dante makes the following distinction:

> Duos igitur fines providentia illa inenarrabilis homini proposuit intendendos: beatitudinem scilicet huius vite, que in operatione proprie virtutis consistit et per

Pope Boniface VIII is especially derided for his worldly lusts; Dante even calls him the "Prince of the new Pharisees":

> Lo principe d' i novi Farisei,
> avendo guerra presso a Laterano,
> e non con Saracin né con Giudei,
>   ché ciascun suo nimico era Cristiano
> e nessun era stato a vincer Acri
> né mercatante in terra di Soldano. (*Inf.* 27.85–90)

(The Prince of the new Pharisees, having war near the Lateran—and not with Saracens or with Jews, for his every enemy was Christian, and none had been to conquer Acre, nor had been a merchant in the Soldan's lands.)

In 1297, a short six years after the fall of Acre, Boniface was waging war on Christians—on the Colonna family in particular—and for no good purpose, since none of his so-called enemies had sided with or traded with Islam. Boniface's crusade against his own Christian flock was not informed by religious zeal, not motivated by a desire for vengeance against political or mercantile traitors to the Christian cause. Rather, Boniface's goals were much more immediate, earthly, and local—any larger geopolitical issues were foreign or of little interest to him.

The true, effective direction of Dante's polemic is not at the two other monotheistic religions, but at his own; at the colossal failure of the Church and of her helpmate, Empire. We could say that Dante is so concerned with the problems within Christendom that he does not pay attention to problems outside it. If he embattles his country, it is not in the manner of a new Pharisee, but of a new Prophet. Florence had not yet taken to killing her prophets; she exiled them instead. And this experience—the more that it was undeserved—rendered Dante peculiarly sensible to the position of the world's "strangers"; a position, the difficulty and tenuous nature of

---

terrestrem paradisum figuratur; et beatitudinem vite ecterne, que consistit in fruitione divini aspectus ad quam propria virtus ascendere non potest, nisi lumine divino adiuta, que per paradisum celestem intelligi datur.

(Two goals, therefore, have been set by God's inexplicable providence for man to attain. One is the beatitude of this life, which consists in the exercise of man's own powers, and which is symbolized by the earthly paradise. The other is the beatitude of eternal life, which consists in the enjoyment of the divine vision [to which man's own powers cannot ascend unless aided by divine light], and which is symbolized by the heavenly paradise.)

which are so vividly comprehended in Cacciaguida's prophetic account of the poet's banishment:

> Tu lascerai ogne cosa diletta
> più caramente; e questo è quello strale
> che l'arco de lo essilio pria saetta.
> Tu proverai sì come sa di sale
> lo pane altrui, e come è duro calle
> lo scendere e 'l salir per l'altrui scale.
> E quel che più ti graverà le spalle,
> sarà la compagnia malvagia e scempia
> con la qual tu cadrai in questa valle;
> che tutta ingrata, tutta matta ed empia
> si farà contr' a te; ma, poco appresso,
> ella, non tu, n' avrà rossa la tempia.
> Di sua bestialitate il suo processo
> farà la prova; sì ch' a te fia bello
> averti fatta parte per te stesso. (*Par.* 17.55–69).

(You shall leave everything beloved most dearly; and this is the arrow which the bow of exile shoots first. You shall come to know how salt is the taste of another's bread, and how hard the path to descend and mount by another's stairs. And that which shall most weigh your shoulders down will be the evil and senseless company with which you shall fall into this vale; which shall then become all ungrateful, all mad and malevolent against you, but, soon after, their brows, not yours, shall redden for it. Of their brutish folly their own conduct shall afford the proof, so that it will be for your fair fame to have made you a party by yourself.)

We sense in these poignant words Dante's isolation, perhaps here more so than anywhere else in the poem. But if his outer life was stripped bare and rough, his inner life was full to overflowing by the grace of his great love Beatrice. And to her the world, which itself could make nothing of Dante, and would have let the pilgrim languish in solitude—to Beatrice the world owes the appearance of one of its greatest poets and teachers. In *Purgatory* 32 Beatrice charges Dante with the special mission of his earthly life: "Però, in pro del mondo che mal vive, / al carro tieni or li occhi, e quel che vedi, / ritornato di là, fa che tu scrive" (Therefore, for profit of the world that lives ill, hold your eyes now on the chariot, and what you see, mind that you write it when you have returned yonder [*Purg.* 32.103–5]). What she commands the Pilgrim to witness—and the Poet afterwards to write— is the infamous "pageant of the Church": a moving allegorical tableau representing a thousand years of vicissitudes of the Church, from its early persecutions to its final physical and spiritual debasement in Avignon. In the midst of these tribulations, Dante maintained a degree of equanimity toward Jews and Muslims. He reserved his greatest powers of invective for the decadence and anarchy that he saw everywhere in Christendom; he reserved his greatest powers of oratory to point the way toward salubrious reform. The year 1300 was a major turning point in his life and work as an author: it was the historical year in which he set his journey through the three realms of the afterlife, the year in which the first Papal Jubilee took place, and the first year of the new century. It would also signal, he hoped—or feared—, another charged moment in Providential History, one worthy of being remembered as the new (fourteenth) century.

BIBLIOGRAPHY

Adomnán. *Adomnán's Life of Columba.* Edited by A. O. Anderson and M. O. Anderson. 2nd ed. Oxford: Oxford University Press, 1991.

Ælfric. *Ælfric's Catholic Homilies, the Second Series: Text.* Edited by Malcolm Godden. EETS s.s. 5. London: Oxford University Press, 1979.

———. *Ælfric's Lives of Saints.* Edited and translated by W. W. Skeat. EETS o.s. 76, 82 94, 114. London: Oxford University Press, 1881, 1885. Rpt. in two vols., 1966.

Aelred of Rievaulx. *The Works of Aelred of Rievaulx.* Vol. 1: *Treatises and Pastoral Prayer.* Translated by M. P. McPherson. Spencer, MA: Cistercian Studies, 1971.

Alcock, Leslie. "Image and Icon in Pictish Sculpture." In *The Age of Migrating Ideas: Early Medieval Art in Northern Britain and Ireland,* edited by R. Michael Spearman and John Higgitt, pp. 230–36. Edinburgh: National Museums of Scotland, 1993.

Alexander, J. J. G., ed. *Insular Manuscripts: 6th to 9th Century.* London: Harvey Miller, 1978.

———. "William Abell 'lymnour' and 15th-Century English Illumination." In *Kunsthistorische Forshungen Otto Pächt zu seinem 70. Geburstag,* edited by Artur Rosenauer and Gerold Weber, pp. 166–72. Salzburg: Residenz Verlag, 1972.

Alexander, J. J. G., James H. Marrow, and Lucy Freeman Sandler. *The Splendor of the Word: Medieval and Renaissance Illuminated Manuscripts at the New York Public Library.* New York: New York Public Library, 2005.

"Ali" (unsigned). In *Enciclopedia Dantesca,* 1:124–25. Rome: Istituto della Enciclopedia Italiana, 1984.

Alighieri, Dante. *Dante's "Monarchia."* Edited and translated by Richard Kay. Toronto: Pontifical Institute of Mediaeval Studies, 1998.

———. *The Divine Comedy: Inferno—Purgatorio—Paradiso: Italian Text and Translation; Commentary.* 6 vols. Translated by Charles S. Singleton. Princeton, NJ: Princeton University Press, 1970, 1973, 1975.

Allen, J. Romilly, and Joseph Anderson. *Early Christian Monuments of Scotland.* 2 vols. 1903, rpt. Balgavies, Angus: Pinkfoot Press, 1993.

Amalarius of Metz. *De ecclesiasticis officiis de libri quattuor.* PL 105:985–1242.

Amato, Pietro. *De Vera Effigie Mariae: Antiche Icone Romane.* Milan: A. Mondadori, 1988.

Amblard, Paule. *La vie de Jésus selon Guillaume de Digulleville, moine du XIVe siècle.* Paris: Flammarion, 1999.

Ambrose. *Epistulae.* Edited by O. Faller. CSEL 82. Turnhout: Brepols, 1968.

———. *Explanatio super Psalmos XII.* Edited by M. Adriaen. CCSL 64. Turnhout: Brepols, 1957.

———. *Expositio Evangelii secundum Lucam.* Edited by M. Petsching. CCSL 14. Turnhout: Brepols, 1919.

Andaloro, Maria. "L'Icona della Vergine 'Salus Populi Romani.'" In *Santa Maria Maggiore a Roma,* edited by Carlo Pietrangeli, pp. 124–27. Florence: Nardoni, 1988.

Andaloro, Maria, and Serena Romano. "L'immagine nell'abside." In *Arte e iconografia a Roma dal tardoantico alla fine del Medioevo,* edited by Andalora and Romano, pp. 73–102. Rome: Palombi, 2002.

Andrieu, Michael, ed. *Les Ordines Romani du Haut Moyen Age.* 5 vols. Louvain: Specilegium Sacrum Lovaniense, 1960.

Angela of Foligno. *Le Livre de l'expérience des vraies fidèles.* Edited and translated by M. J. Ferré and L. Baudry. Paris: E. Droz, 1927.

Apponius. *In Canticum Canticorum expositionem.* Edited by B. de Vregille and L. Neyrand. CCSL 19. Turnhout: Brepols, 1986.

Arngart, O., ed. *The Leningrad Bede.* EEMF 2. Copenhagen: Rosenkilde and Bagger, 1952.

Asín Palacios, Miguel. *La escatología musulmana en la Divina Comedía.* Madrid: Estanislao Maestre, 1919.

Aubin, Paul. "Intériorité et extériorité dans les *Moralia in Job* de Saint Grégoire le Grand." *Recherches de science religieuse* 62 (1974), 117–66.

Augustine. *De catechizandis rudibus.* Edited by J. B. Bauer. CCSL 46. Turnhout: Brepols, 1969.

———. *De ciuitate Dei.* Edited by B. Dombart and A. Kalb. 2 vols. Stuttgart: Teubner, 1993.

———. *De doctrina christiana.* Edited by J. Martin. CCSL 32. Turnhout: Brepols, 1962.

———. *De Genesi ad litteram.* Edited by Josef Zycha. CSEL 28.1. Vienna: Tempsky, 1894.

———. *Sancti Aurelii Augustini in Iohannis Evangelium tractatus CXXIV.* Edited by Radbodus Willems. CCSL 36. Brepols: Turnhout, 1954.

———. *Sermones de scripturis.* PL 38–39:23–1638.

———. *Tractatus in Evangelium Iohannis.* PL 35.

Austin, David, ed. *Domesday Book Supplementary Volume. Boldon Book. Northumberland and Durham.* Chichester: Phillimore, 1982.

————, ed. "Fieldwork and Excavation at Hart." *Archaeologia Aeliana*, 5th ser., 4 (1976), 72–75.

————. "Late Anglo-Saxon Settlement in the North-East of England." In *Studies in Late Anglo-Saxon Settlement*, edited by Margaret Faull, pp. 197–207. Oxford: Oxford University Department for External Studies, 1984.

Avril, François, and Nicole Reynaud, eds. *Les Manuscripts à peintures en France, 1440–1520*. Paris: Flammarion, 1993.

Bachellery, Édouard. "La poésie de demande dans la littérature galloise." *Études celtiques* 27 (1990), 285–300.

Backhouse, Janet A., D. H. Turner, and Leslie Webster, eds. *The Golden Age of Anglo-Saxon Art 966–1066*. London: British Museum Publications, 1984.

Badel, Pierre-Yves. *Le Roman de la Rose au XIVe Siècle: Etude de la reception de l'Oeuvre*. Geneva: Droz, 1980.

Baehrens, W. A., ed. *Homilien zum Hexateuch in Rufins Übersetzung, Origenes Werke*. Vol. 7. Leipzig: J. C. Hinrichs'sche Buchhandlung, 1921.

————. *Überlieferung und Textgeschichte der lateinisch erhaltenen Origeneshomilien zum Alten Testament*. Leipzig: H. C. Hinrichs'sche Buchhandlung, 1916.

Bailey, Richard N. "The Chronology of Viking Age Sculpture in Northumbria." In *Anglo-Saxon and Viking Age Sculpture*, edited by James Lang, pp. 173–203. Oxford: British Archaeological Reports, 1978.

————. *The Durham Cassiodorus*. Jarrow Lecture for 1978. Jarrow: St. Paul's Church, 1978.

————. *England's Earliest Sculptors*. Toronto: Pontifical Institute of Mediaeval Studies, 1996.

————. *Viking Age Sculpture in Northern England*. London: Collins, 1980.

Baird, Joseph L. "Unferth the Þyle." *Medium Ævum* 39 (1970), 1–12.

Baker, Peter, and Michael Lapidge, eds. *Byrhtferth's Enchiridion*. EETS s.s. 15. Oxford: Oxford University Press, 1995.

Baldovin, John. *The Urban Character of Christian Worship. The Origins, Development, and Meaning of Stational Liturgy*. Rome: Pontificalis institutio studiorum orientalium, 1987.

Bankert, Dabney Anderson, Jessica Wegmann, Charles Wright et al. *Ambrose in Anglo-Saxon England. OEN Subsidia* 25 (1997).

Banting, H. M. J., ed. *Two Anglo-Saxon Pontificals: The Egbert and Sidney Sussex Pontificals*. Henry Bradshaw Society 104. London: The Boydell Press, 1989.

Barb, A. A. "The Wound in Christ's Side." *Journal of the Warburg and Courtauld Institute* 34 (1971), 320–21.

Barbet, Pierre. *A Doctor at Calvary: The Passion of Our Lord Jesus Christ as Described by a Surgeon*. New York: P. J. Kennedy, 1953.

Barlow, Frank, ed. *The Life of King Edward Who Rests at Westminster*. 2nd ed. Oxford: Clarendon Press, 1992.

Barré, Henri. *Les Homéliaires carolingiens de l'école d'Auxerre*. Studi e Testi 225. Vatican City: Biblioteca Apostolica Vaticana, 1962.

Barrow, Geoffrey W. S. *The Kingdom of the Scots: Government, Church and Society from the Eleventh to the Fourteenth Century*. London: Edward Arnold, 1973.

Bately, Janet M. "Old English Prose before and during the Reign of Alfred." *ASE* 17 (1988), 93–138.

Bax, Marcel, and Tineke Padmos, "Two Types of Verbal Dueling in Old Icelandic." *Scandinavian Studies* 55 (1983), 143–74.

Becker, Gustav. *Catologi bibliothecarum antiqui*. Bonn, 1885; repr. Hildesheim: Georg Olms Verlag, 1973.

Beckwith, John. *Ivory Carvings in Early Medieval England*. New York: Harvey, Miller and Medcalf, 1972.

Bede. *Bedae opera de temporibus*. Edited by Charles W. Jones. Cambridge, Mass: Medieval Academy of America, 1943.

———. *Bedas metrische vita sancti Cuthberti*. Edited by Werner Jaager. Leipzig: Mayer and Müller, g.m.b.h., 1935.

———. *Bede: A Biblical Miscellany*. Translated by W. Trent Foley and Arthur G. Holder. Liverpool: Liverpool University Press, 1999.

———. *Bede's Commentary on the Acts of the Apostles*. Edited and translated by Lawrence T. Martin. Kalamazoo, MI: Cistercian Publications, 1989.

———. *Bede's Ecclesiastical History of the English People*. Edited and translated by Bertram Colgrave and R. A. B. Mynors. Oxford: Clarendon Press, 1969.

———. *De Psalmorum libro exegesis*. *PL* 93:477–1098.

———. *De Templo*. *PL* 91:735.

———. *De Templo*. Edited by David Hurst. CCSL 119A. Turnhout: Brepols, 1969.

———. *The Explanation of the Apocalypse by Venerable Beda*. Edited and translated by Edward Marshall. London: J. Parker and Company, 1878.

———. *Expositio Actuum Apostolorum*. Edited by M. L. W. Laistner. CCSL 121. Turnhout: Brepols, 1983.

———. *Expositio Apocalypseos*. Edited by Roger Gryson. CCSL 121A. Turnhout: Brepols, 2001.

———. *Homiliae*. Edited by J. Fraipont. CCSL 122. Turnhout: Brepols, 1955, pp. 1–378.

————. *Homilies on the Gospels.* Edited and translated by Lawrence T. Martin and David Hurst. Kalamazoo, MI: Cistercian Publications, 1991.

————. *Hymni.* Edited by J. Fraipont. CCSL 122. Turnhout: Brepols, 1955, pp. 407–38.

————. *In Cantica Canticorum.* Edited by David Hurst. CCSL 119B. Turnhout: Brepols, 1983.

————. *In epistulas septem catholicas.* Edited by David Hurst. CCSL 121, pp. 179–342. Turnhout: Brepols, 1983.

————. *In Ezram et Neemiam.* Edited by David Hurst, CCSL 119A. Turnhout: Brepols, 1969.

————. *In Genesim. PL* 91:9.

————. *In Genesim.* Edited by Charles W. Jones. CCSL 118A. Turnhout: Brepols, 1967.

————. *In librum beati patris Tobiae.* Edited by David Hurst. CCSL 119B. Turnhout: Brepols, 1983.

————. *In Lucam.* Edited by David Hurst. CCSL 120. Turnhout: Brepols, 1960.

————. *In Regum XXX quaestiones.* CCSL 119. Turnhout: Brepols, 1962.

————. *In Tobiam.* Edited by David Hurst and J. E. Hudson. CCSL 119B. Turnhout: Brepols, 1983.

————. *On the Temple.* Translated by Seán Connolly. Liverpool: Liverpool University Press, 1995.

————. *On Tobit and On the Canticle of Habakkuk.* Translated by Seán Connolly. Dublin: Four Courts Press, 1997.

————. *Venerabilis Baedae opera historica.* Edited by Charles Plummer. 2 vols. Oxford: Clarendon Press, 1896.

Beer, Frances. *Women and Mystical Experience in the Middle Ages.* Woodbridge: Boydell, 1992.

Belting, Hans. *Likeness and Presence: A History of the Image before the Era of Art.* Chicago: University of Chicago Press, 1994.

Berkhout, Carl T. "Anglo-Saxon Studies in the Age of Shakespeare." *OEN* 19,2 (1986), A-28.

————. "*Beowulf* 2200–08: Mind the Gap." *ANQ* 15.2 (2002), 51–58.

————. "Laurence Nowell (1530–ca. 1570)." In *Medieval Scholarship: Biographical Studies on the Formation of a Discipline*, edited by Helen Damico, 2:3–17. New York: Garland, 1998.

Bernard of Clairvaux, Saint. *On the Song of Songs.* Edited by Kilian Walsh and Irene Edmonds. Kalamazoo, MI: Cistercian Publications, 1979.

————. *Sancti Bernardi opera.* Edited by J. LeClercq, C. H. Talbot, H. M. Rochais. Rome: Cisterican Editions, 1957.

Bernold of Constance. *Micrologus de ecclesiasticis observationibus. PL* 151.

Bertolini, Ottorino. *Roma di fronte a Bisanzio e ai Longobardi.* Bologna: L. Cappelli, 1941.

Biernoff, Suzannah. *Sight and Embodiment in the Middle Ages.* Basingstoke: Palgrave, 2003.

Biggs, Frederick M. "*Beowulf* and Some Fictions of the Geatish Succession." *ASE* 32 (2003), 55–77.

———. "Deor's Threatened 'Blame Poem.'" *Studies in Philology* 94/3 (1997), 297–320.

Billington, Sandra. *A Social History of the Fool.* New York: St. Martin's Press, 1984.

Binski, Paul, and Stella Panayotova, eds. *The Cambridge Illuminations: Ten Centuries of Book Production in the Medieval West.* London: Harvey Miller, 2005.

Bjork, Robert E. "Digressions and Episodes." In *A Beowulf Handbook.* Edited by Bjork, pp. 193–212. Lincoln: University of Nebraska Press, 1997.

———. "Unferth in the Hermeneutic Circle: A Reappraisal of James L. Rosier's 'Design for Treachery: The Unferth Perplex.'" *Papers on Language and Literature* 16 (1980), 133–41.

Blake, E. O., ed. *Liber Eliensis.* London: Office of the Royal Historical Society, 1962.

Blanton-Whetsell, Virginia. "Imagines Ætheldredae: Mapping Hagiographic Representations of Abbatial Power and Religious Patronage." *Studies in Iconography* 23 (2002), 55–107.

Bloomfield, Morton. "*Beowulf* and Christian Allegory: An Interpretation of Unferth." *Traditio* 7 (1949–51, 410–15.

Boccaccio, Giovanni. *The Decameron.* Translated by G. H. McWilliam. 2nd ed. Harmondsworth: Penguin Books, 1995.

Boinet, A., ed. *Les manuscrits a peintures de la Bibliothèque Sainte-Geneviève de Paris.* Bulletin de la Société française de reproductions de manuscrits a peintures 5. Paris, 1921.

Bolton, Whitney F. "Boethius, Alfred, and *Deor* Again." *Modern Philology* 69 (1972), 222–27.

———. "How Boethian Is Alfred's *Boethius?*" In *Studies in Earlier Old English Prose,* edited by Paul E. Szarmach, pp. 153–68. Albany: State University of New York Press, 1986.

Bonaventure, Saint. *Opera omnia.* 10 vols. Quarracchi: Colegii S. Bonaventura, 1882–1902.

———. *The Works of Bonaventure: Cardinal, Seraphic Doctor and Saint.* Translated by José de Vinck. Patterson, NJ: St. Anthony Guild, 1960.

Bonjour, Adrien. "Unferth: A Return to Orthodoxy." In *Twelve "Beowulf" Papers, 1940–1960, with Additional Comments.* Neuchâtel: Faculté des lettres, 1962.

Boren, James L. "The Design of the Old English *Deor*." In *Anglo-Saxon Poetry: Essays in Appreciation for John C. McGalliard,* edited by Lewis E. Nicholson and Dolores Warwick Frese, pp. 264–76. Notre Dame, IN: University of Notre Dame Press, 1975.

Bosworth, Joseph, and T. Northcote Toller, eds. *An Anglo-Saxon Dictionary.* London: Oxford University Press, 1898. Reprint, 1973.

Boulton, Maureen. "Digulleville's *Pèlerinage de Jésus Christ*: A Poem of Courtly Devotion." In *The Vernacular Spirit: Essays on Medieval Religious Literature,* edited by Renate Blumenfeld-Kosinski, Duncan Robertson, and Nancy Bradley Warren, pp. 125–44. New York: Palgrave, 2002.

Bradley, S. A. J., ed. and trans. *Anglo-Saxon Poetry.* London: Dent, 1982.

Brantley, Jessica. *Reading in the Wilderness: Private Devotion and Public Performance in Late Medieval England.* Chicago: University of Chicago Press, 2007.

———. "The Visual Environment of Carthusian Texts: Decoration and Illustration in Notre Dame 67." In *The Text in the Community: Essays on Medieval Works, Manuscripts, Authors, and Readers,* edited by Jill Mann and Maura Nolan, pp. 125–44. Notre Dame, IN: University of Notre Dame Press, 2006.

Brenk, Beat. "Kultgeschichte versus Stilgeschichte: von der 'Raison d'Être' des Bildes im 7. Jahrhundert in Rom." In *Umo e spazio nell; alto medioevo.* Setimane di studio del Centro italiano di Studi sull'Alto Medioevo 50, 2:971–1053. Spoleto: Centro itliano di Studi sull'Alto Medioevo, 2003.

———. "Papal Patronage in a Greek Church in Rome." In *Santa Maria Antiqua al Foro Romano cento anni dopo.* Atti del colloquio internazionale. Roma 5–6 maggio 2000, pp. 67–81. Rome: Campisano Editore, 2004.

Brodeur, Arthur Gilchrist. *The Art of Beowulf.* Berkeley: University of California Press, 1971.

Brooks, Nicholas P., and James Graham-Campbell. "Reflections on the Viking-Age Silver Hoard from Croydon, Surrey." In *Anglo-Saxon Monetary History,* edited by M. A. S. Blackburn, pp. 91–110. Leicester: Leicester University Press, 1986.

Brown, Michelle P. "Echoes: The *Book of Kells* and Southern English Manuscript Production." In *The Book of Kells: Proceedings of a Conference at Trinity College Dublin,* edited by Felicity O'Mahony, pp. 333–43. Aldershot: Scholar Press, 1994.

————. *The Lindisfarne Gospels: Society, Spirituality and the Scribe.* London: The British Library, 2003.

Brown, Ray. "The Begging Scop and the Generous King in *Widsith.*" *Neophilologus* 73 (1989), 281–92.

Brown, Raymond E., ed. *The Anchor Bible: The Gospel according to John (xiii–xxi).* Garden City, NY: Doubleday, 1970.

Brunn, Emilie Zum, and Georgette Epiney-Burgard. *Women Mystics in Medieval Europe.* New York: Paragon House, 1989.

Budny, Mildred. *Insular, Anglo-Saxon, and Early Anglo-Norman Manuscript Art at Corpus Christi College, Cambridge.* 2 vols. Kalamazoo, MI: Medieval Institute Publications, 1997.

Bugge, Sophus. "Studien über das Beowulfepos." *Beiträge zur Geschichte der deutschen Sprache und Literatur* 12 (1887), 1–112, 360–75.

Bulst, Walther, and M. L. Bulst-Thiele, eds. *Hilarii Aurelianensis versus et ludi, epistolae.* Leiden: E. J. Brill, 1989.

Burlin, R. B. "The Ruthwell Cross, *The Dream of the Rood,* and the Vita Contemplativa." *Studies in Philology* 65 (1968), 23–43.

Burrow, J. A. *The Ages of Man: A Study in Medieval Writing and Thought.* Oxford: Clarendon Press, 1986.

————. "An Approach to the *Dream of the Rood.*" *Neophilologus* 43 (1959), 123–33.

Butler, Edward Cuthbert. *Western Mysticism.* 2nd ed. New York: Harper & Row, 1966.

Bynum, Caroline Walker. *Holy Feast and Holy Fast: The Significance of Food to Medieval Women.* Berkeley: University of California Press, 1987.

————. *Jesus as Mother: Studies in the Spirituality of the High Middle Ages.* Berkeley: University of California Press, 1982.

————. Review of *Nuns as Artists: The Visual Culture of Medieval Convent,* by Jeffrey Hamburger. *History of Religions* 38 (1999), 407.

Calin, William. *The French Tradition and the Literature of Medieval England.* Toronto: University of Toronto Press, 1994.

Cameron, Kenneth. "Scandinavian Place-Names." In Cameron, *English Place-Names,* pp. 75–86. London: Batsford, 1961.

————. *Scandinavian Settlement in the Territory of the Five Boroughs: The Place-Name Evidence.* Inaugural lecture, University of Nottingham, 1965.

————. "Scandinavian Settlement in the Territory of the Five Boroughs: The Place-name Evidence. Part II, Place-names in Thorp." *Medieval Scandinavia* 3 (1970), 35–49;

————. "Scandinavian Settlement in the Territory of the Five Boroughs: The Place-name Evidence. Part III, the Grimston Hybrids." In *England before the Conquest: Studies in Primary Sources Presented to Dorothy Whitelock*, edited by Peter Clemoes and Kathleen Hughes, pp. 147–63. Cambridge: Cambridge University Press, 1971.

————. "The Scandinavians in Derbyshire: The Place-Name Evidence." *Nottingham Medieval Studies* 2 (1958), 86–118

————. "The Significance of English Place-names." *Proceedings of the British Academy* 62 (1976), 135–55.

Camille, Michael. "Before the Gaze: The Internal Senses and Late Medieval Practices of Seeing." In *Visuality before and beyond the Renaissance*, edited by Robert S. Nelson, pp. 197–223. Cambridge: Cambridge University Press, 2000.

————. "The Gregorian Definition Revisited: Writing and the Medieval Image." In *L'Image: fonctions et usages des images dans l'Occident médiéval*, edited by Jérôme Baschet and Jean-Claude Schmitt, pp. 89–101. Paris: Le Léopard d'Or, 1996.

————. "The Iconoclast's Desire: Deguileville's Idolatry in France and England." In *Images, Idolatry, and Iconoclasm in Late Medieval England: Textuality and the Visual Image*, edited by Jeremy Dimmick, James Simpson, Nicolette Zeeman, pp. 151–71. Oxford: Oxford University Press, 2002.

————. "The Illustrated Manuscripts of Guillaume de Deguileville's 'Pèlerinages,' 1330–1426." Ph.D. diss., University of Cambridge, 1985.

————. *Master of Death: The Lifeless Art of Pierre Remiet, Illuminator*. New Haven, CT: Yale University Press, 1996.

————. *The Medieval Art of Love*. New York: Harry N. Abrams, 1998.

————. "Reading the Printed Image: Illuminations and Woodcuts of the *Pèlerinage de la vie humaine* in the Fifteenth Century." In *Printing the Written Word: The Social History of Books, circa 1450–1520*, edited by Sandra L. Hindman, pp. 259–91. Ithaca, NY: Cornell University Press, 1991.

————. "Visionary Perception and Images of the Apocalypse in the Later Middle Ages." In *Apocalypse in the Middle Ages*, edited by Richard K. Emmerson and Bernard McGinn, pp. 276–89. Ithaca, NY: Cornell University Press, 1992.

Cantor, Paul A. "The Uncanonical Dante: The *Divine Comedy* and Islamic Philosophy." *Philosophy and Literature* 20 (1996), 138–53.

Caraffa, Filippo, et al., eds. *Bibliotheca Sanctorum*. 13 vols., 2 suppl. Rome: Istituto Giovanni XXIII nella Pontificia Università Lateranense, 1961–2000.

Carrington, Ann. "David Imagery and the Chase Motif in Pictish Sculpture." *Studia Celtica* 30 (1996), 147–58.

Carver, Martin. "An Iona of the East: The Early Medieval Monastery at Portmahomack, Tarbat Ness." *Medieval Archaeology* 48 (2004), 1–30.

———. *Portmahomack: Monastery of the Picts.* Edinburgh: Edinburgh University Press, 2007.

———. "Sculpture in Action: Contexts for Stone Carving on the Tarbat Peninsula, Easter Ross." In *Able Minds and Practiced Hands,* edited by Sally Foster, pp. 13–36. London: Society for Medieval Archaeology (Maney Publishing), 2005.

Cassian, John. *Iohannis Cassiani Conlationes XXIIII.* Edited by Michael Petschenig. CSEL 13. Vienna: Gerold, 1886.

———. *John Cassian. The Conferences.* Translated by Boniface Ramsey. New York: Newman Press, 1997.

Cassidy, Brendan, ed. *The Ruthwell Cross: Papers from the Colloquium Sponsored by the Index of Christian Art.* Princeton, NJ: Department of Art and Archaeology, Princeton University, 1993.

Catalogue of Additions to the Manuscripts in the British Museum in the Years 1888–93. London: British Museum, 1894.

Catalogue of Additions to the Manuscripts in the British Museum, 1900–1905. London: British Museum, 1907.

Catalogue of the Fifty Manuscripts and Printed Books Bequeathed to the British Museum by Alfred H. Huth. London: British Museum, 1912.

Cerulli, Enrico. *Il "Libro della Scala" e la questione delle fonti arabo-spagnole della Divina Commedia.* Vatican City: Biblioteca Apostolica Vaticana, 1949.

———. *Nuove ricerche sul Libro della Scala e la conoscenza dell'Islam in Occidente.* Vatican City: Biblioteca Apostolica Vaticana, 1972.

Chadwick, Henry. "Theodore, the English Church and the Monothelete Controversy." In *Archbishop Theodore: Commemorative Studies on his Life and Influence,* edited by Michael Lapidge, pp. 88–95. Cambridge: Cambridge University Press, 1995.

Chazelle, Celia M. "Memory, Instruction, Worship: 'Gregory's' Influence on Early Medieval Doctrines of the Artistic Image." In *Gregory the Great: A Symposium,* edited by John C. Cavadini, pp. 181–215. Notre Dame, IN: University of Notre Dame Press, 1995.

———. "Pictures, Books, and the Illiterate: Pope Gregory I's Letters to Serenus of Marseilles." *Word and Image* 6 (1990), 138–53.

Christiansen, Reiðar Th. *The Vikings and the Viking Wars in Irish and Gaelic Tradition.* Skrifter utgitt av det Norske Videnskaps-Akademi i Oslo, II Historisk-filosofisk klasse. Oslo: I kommisjan has J. Dybwad, 1931.

Church, A. P. "Beowulf's '*ane ben*' and the Rhetorical Context of the 'Hunferþ Episode.'" *Rhetorica* 18.1 (2000), 49–78.

Church of England. *The First and Second Prayer Books of Edward VI, 1549.* London: Dent, 1910.

Ciklamini, Marlene. "The Problem of Starkaðr." *Scandinavian Studies* 43 (1971), 169–88.

Clack, Peter A. G., and Brian H. Gill. "The Land-Divisions of County Durham in the Early Medieval Period (Fifth–Eleventh Centuries A.D.): The Uplands." In Medieval Village Research Group, *28th Annual Report (for 1980).* London: Medieval Village Research Group, 1981, 30–34.

Clancy, Tom. "Iona, Scotland and the *Céli Dé*." In *Scotland in Dark Age Britain,* edited by Barbara Crawford, pp. 111–130. Aberdeen: Scottish Cultural Press, 1996.

Clarke, D. E. Martin. "The Office of the Thyle in Beowulf." *Review of English Studies* 12 (1936), 61–68.

Clayton, Mary. *The Cult of the Virgin Mary in Anglo-Saxon England.* Cambridge: University Press, 1990.

Cleasby, Richard, and Guðbrandur Vigfússon, eds. *An Icelandic-English Dictionary.* 2nd ed., with a supplement by William A. Craigie. Oxford: Clarendon Press, 1957.

Clover, Carol J. "The Germanic Context of the Unferð Episode." *Speculum* 55 (1980), 444–68.

Coatsworth, Elizabeth. "The Decoration of the Durham Gospels." In *The Durham Gospels together with Fragments of a Gospel Book in Uncial, Durham Cathedral Library, MS A.II.17,* edited by Christopher D. Verey, T. Julian Brown, and Elizabeth Coatsworth, pp. 53–63. EEMF 20. Copenhagen: Rosenkilde and Bagger, 1980.

———. "The Iconography of the Crucifixion in pre-Conquest Sculpture in England." 2 vols. Ph.D. diss., Durham University, 1979.

———. "The 'Robed Christ' in Pre-Conquest Sculptures of the Crucifixion." *ASE* 29 (2000), 153–76.

Coggins, Dennis. *Upper Teesdale. The Archaeology of a North Pennine Valley.* Oxford: British Archaeological Reports, 1986.

Coggins, Dennis, Kenneth J. Fairless, and Colleen E. Batey. "Simy Folds: An Early Medieval Settlement in Upper Teesdale." *Medieval Archaeology* 27 (1981), 1–26.

Coleman, Joyce. *Public Reading and the Reading Public in Late Medieval England and France.* Cambridge: Cambridge University Press, 1996.

Colgrave, Bertram, ed and trans. *The Earliest Life of Gregory the Great by an Anonymous Monk of Whitby.* Cambridge: Cambridge University Press, 1968.

————, ed. *Felix's Life of Saint Guthlac*. Cambridge: Cambridge University Press, 1956.

Collingwood, W. G. *Northumbrian Crosses of the Pre-Norman Age*. London: Faber & Gwyer, 1927.

Conklin Akbari, Suzanne. "Islam and Islamic Culture." In *The Dante Encyclopedia*, edited by Richard Lansing, pp. 520–23. New York: Garland Publishing, 2000.

Conner, Patrick W. "The Section Numbers in the *Beowulf* Manuscript." *ANQ* 24.3–4 (1985), 33–38.

Corbin, Solange. *La déposition liturgique du Christ au vendredi saint*. Lisbon: Livraria Bertrand, 1960.

Corti, Maria. "La *Commedia* di Dante e l'oltretomba islamico." *Belfagor* 50.3 (31 maggio 1995), 301–24.

Courcelle, Pierre. *Les Confessions de saint Augustin dans la tradition littéraire*. Paris: Études Augustiniennes, 1963.

Cramp, Rosemary. "The Anglian Sculptures from Jedburgh," In *From the Stone Age to the 'Forty Five': Studies Presented to R. B. K. Stevenson*, edited by A. O'Connor and D. V. Clarke, pp. 269–284. Edinburgh: John Donald, 1983.

————."The Anglo-Saxon Period." In *Durham County and City with Teeside*, edited by John C. Dewdney, pp. 199–206. Durham: Local Executive Committee of the British Association, 1970.

————. *Durham and Northumberland*. Vol. 1 of *Corpus of Anglo-Saxon Stone Sculpture*. Oxford: Oxford University Press, 1984.

————. "Early Northumbrian Sculpture." In *Bede and His World: The Jarrow Lectures, 1958–1978*, with a preface by Michael Lapidge, 1:135–52. Aldershot: Variorum, 1994.

————. "Schools of Mercian Sculpture." In *Mercian Studies*, edited by Ann Dornier, pp. 191–233. Leicester: Leicester University Press, 1977.

————. "The Viking Image." In *The Vikings*, edited by Robert T. Farrell, pp. 8–19. Chichester: Phillamore, 1982.

————. *Wearmouth and Jarrow Monastic Sites*. 2 vols. Swindon: English Heritage, 2005–6.

Craster, H. H. Edmund. "The Patrimony of St Cuthbert." *English Historical Review* 69 (1954), 177–99.

Croquison J. "Les origines de l'iconographie Grégorienne." *Cahiers archéologiques* 12 (1962), 249–62.

Cross, J. E. "English Vernacular Saints' Lives before 1000 A.D." In *Hagiographies: histoire internationale de la littérature hagiographique latine et vernaculaire en Occident des origines à 1550*, edited by Guy Philippart, 2:413–27. Turnhout: Brepols, 1994.

Cubitt, Catherine. *Anglo-Saxon Church Councils c.650–c.850*. Leicester: Leicester University Press, 1995.

Cyprian, Saint. *Opera omnia*. Edited by Guilelmus Hartel. CSEL 3. Vienna: C. Geroldi, 1868–71.

———. *Testimoniorum libri tres adversus Judaeos*. PL 4:675–780.

Dagens, Claude. *Saint Grégoire le Grand: culture et expérience chrétiennes*. Paris: Études Augustiniennes, 1977.

Damico, Helen. "*Beowulf*'s Foreign Queen and the Politics of Eleventh-Century England." In *(Inter)texts: Studies in Early Insular Culture Presented to Paul E. Szarmach*, edited by Virginia Blanton and Helene Scheck, pp. 209–40. Medieval & Renaissance Texts & Studies 334. Tempe, AZ: ACMRS, 2008.

———. "*Sörlaþáttr* and the Hama Episode in *Beowulf*." *Scandinavian Studies* 55 (1983), 222–35.

D'Ancona, Alessandro. "La leggenda di Maometto in Occidente." In *Studi di critica e storia letteraria*. Bologna: Zanichelli, 1912, pp. 167–306.

Davidson, Clifford, ed. *Fools and Folly*. Kalamazoo, MI: Medieval Institute Publications, 1996.

Davis, Craig R. *Beowulf and the Demise of Germanic Legend in England*. New York: Garland, 1996.

de Blaauw, Sible. *Cultus et Decor: Liturgia e architettura nella Roma tardoantica e medievale: Basilica Salvatoris, Sanctae Mariae, Sancti Petri*. 2 vols. Vatican City: Biblioteca Apostolica Vaticana, 1994.

Dekkers, Eligius, and Emil Gaar. *Clavis Patrum Latinorum*. 3rd ed. Steenbrugge: in Abbatia Sancti Petri, 1995.

de Paor, Liam. "Some Vine Scrolls and Other Patterns in Embossed Metal from Dumfriesshire." *Proceedings of the Society of the Antiquaries of Scotland* 94 (1961), 184–95.

de Puniet, Pierre. "Les trois homélies catéchétiques du sacramentaire Gélasien pour la tradition des évangiles, du symbole et de l'oraison dominicale." *Revue d'histoire ecclésiastique* 5 (1904), 505–21 and 755–86; 6 (1905), 15–32 and 304–18.

Derolez, A. *Les Catalogues des Bibliothèques*. Turnhout: Brepols, 1979.

Deshman, Robert. *The Benedictional of Æthelwold*. Princeton, NJ: Princeton University Press, 1995.

———. "The Galba Psalter: Pictures, Texts and Context in an Early Medieval Prayerbook." *ASE* 26 (1999), 109–38.

Deshusses, Jean, ed. *Le Sacramentaire grégorien. Ses principales formes d'après les plus anciens manuscrits.* 3 vols. 2nd edition. Fribourg-en-Suisse: Éditions universitaires, 1979–82.

De Wolf, Anouk. "Pratique de la personification chez Guillaume de Digulleville et Philippe de Mézières." In *Ecriture et modes de pensée au Moyen Age (VIIIe–XVe siècles),* edited by Dominique Boutet and Laurence Harf-Lancner, pp. 125–47. Paris: Presses de l'Ecole normale supérieure, 1993.

Dickinson, S. "Bryant's Gill, Kentmere: Another 'Viking Period' Ribblehead?" In *The Scandinavians in Cumbria,* edited by J. R. Baldwin and I. D. Whyte, pp. 83–88. Edinburgh: Scottish Society for Northern Studies, 1985.

The Dictionary of Medieval Latin from British Sources. London: Oxford University Press, 1975–.

DiNapoli, Robert. "The Heart of Visionary Experience: *The Order of the World* and Its Place in the Old English Canon." *English Studies* 79 (1998), 97–108.

Doran, John. *History of Court Fools.* London: Richard Bentley, 1858.

Doyle, Ian. "English Carthusian Books Not Yet Linked with a Charterhouse." In *"A Miracle of Learning." Studies in Manuscripts and Irish Learning: Essays in Honour of William O'Sullivan,* edited by Toby Barnard et al., pp. 122–36. Aldershot: Ashgate, 1998.

Durandas of Mende, William. *Rationale Divinorum Officiorum.* In *Guillemi Duranti Rationale Divinorum Officiorum,* edited by Anselme Davril and Timothy M. Thibodeau, CCCM, 140–140B. 3 vols. Turnhout: Brepols, 1995–2000.

Egilsson, Sveinbjörn. See Sveinbjörn Egilsson

Eiríkr Magnússon. "Anmærkninger til I, 'Fornyrðadrápa' . . ." *Aarbøger for nordisk oldkyndighed og historie* 3 (1888), 322–40.

Eliason, Norman E. "Deor—a Begging Poem?" In *Medieval Literature and Civilization: Studies in Memory of G. N. Garmonsway,* edited by D. A. Pearsall and R. A Waldron, pp. 55–61. London: Athlone Press, 1969.

———. "The *Þyle* and *Scop* in *Beowulf.*" *Speculum* 38 (1963), 267–85.

———. "Two Old English Scop Poems." *PMLA* 81 (1966), 185–92.

Emmerson, Richard K. "The Apocalypse Cycle in the Bedford Book of Hours." *Traditio* 50 (1995), 173–98.

———. "Imagining and Imaging the End: Universal and Individual Eschatology in Two Carthursian Illustrated Manuscripts." In *The Morton W. Bloomfield Lectures, 1989–2005*, edited by Daniel Donoghue, James Simpson, and Nicholas Watson. Kalamazoo, MI: Medieval Institute Publications, 2010.

———. "'A Large Order of the Whole': Intertextuality and Interpictoriality in the *Hours of Isabella Stuart.*" *Studies in Iconography* 28 (2007), 51–110.

———. "Reading Gower in a Manuscript Culture: Latin and English in Illustrated Manuscripts of the *Confessio Amantis.*" *Studies in the Age of Chaucer* 21 (1999), 143–86.

Emmerson, Richard K., and Suzanne Lewis. "Census and Bibliography of Medieval Manuscripts Containing Apocalypse Illustrations, c. 800–1500." *Traditio* 41 (1985), 370–409.

Emmerson, Richard K., and Bernard McGinn, eds. *The Apocalypse in the Middle Ages.* Ithaca, NY: Cornell University Press, 1992.

Enright, Michael J. "The Warband Context of the Unferth Episode." *Speculum* 73.2 (1998), 297–337.

Erasumus. *Collected Works of Erasmus.* Vol. 34: *Adages II.vii.i to III.iii.100.* Edited, translated, and annotated by R. A. B. Mynors. Toronto: University of Toronto Press, 1992.

Evans, G. R. *The Thought of Gregory the Great.* Cambridge: Cambridge University Press, 1986.

Fajardo-Acosta, Fidel. "Intemperance, Fratricide and the Elusiveness of Grendel." *English Studies* 73 (1992), 205–10.

Faral, Edmond. "Guillaume de Digulleville, Jean Galloppes et Pierre Virgin." In *Études romanes dediées à Mario Roques par ses amis, collègues et élèves de France*, pp. 89–102. Paris: E. Droz, 1946.

———. "Guillaume de Deguileville, moine de Chaalis." In *Histoire Littéraire de la France*, 39:1–132. Paris: Imprimerie nationale, 1952.

Farmer, D. H., ed. and trans. *The Age of Bede.* Harmondsworth: Penguin, 1986.

Fellows-Jensen, Gillian. "Lancashire and Yorkshire Names." *Northern History* 19 (1983), 231–37.

———. "Place-Names and Settlement History: A Review." *Northern History* 13 (1977), 1–26.

———. "Place-Names and Settlement in the North Riding of Yorkshire." *Northern History* 14 (1978), 19–46.

———. "Place-Names Research and Northern History: A Survey." *Northern History* 8 (1973), 1–23.

————. *Scandinavian Settlement-Names in Yorkshire.* Copenhagen: Institute for Navneforskning, 1972.

————. "The Vikings in England: A Review." *ASE* 4 (1975), 181–206.

Ferrante, Joan. *To the Glory of Her Sex: Women's Roles in the Composition of Medieval Texts.* Bloomington: Indiana University Press, 1997.

Fidjestøl, Bjarne. "Bjarni Kolbeinsson." In *Medieval Scandinavia: An Encyclopedia,* edited by Phillip Pulsiano and Kirsten Wolf, p. 48. New York: Garland, 1993.

Finnur Jónsson, ed. *Den norsk-islandske skjaldedigtning.* 2 vols. Copenhagen: Gyldendal, 1915.

————. *Den oldnorske og oldislandske litteraturs historie.* 2nd ed. 3 vols. Copenhagen: G. E. C. Gad, 1923.

————. "Fornyrðadrápa (Málsháttakvæði)."*Aarbøger for nordisk oldkyndighed og historie* 5 (1890), 253–66.

————. "*Málsháttakvæði* eller *Fornyrðadrápa.*" In *Samfund til udgivelser af gammel nordisk litteratur,* pp. 283–88. Copenhagen: Thieles, 1889–91.

Fisher, Sally. *The Square Halo and Other Mysteries of Western Art: Images and the Stories That Inspired Them.* New York: Abrams, 1995.

Fleming, John V. "*The Dream of the Rood* and Anglo-Saxon Monasticism." *Traditio* 22 (1966), 43–72.

Fontes Anglo-Saxonici. http://fontes.english.ox.ac.uk

Forster, K. "Idiomenkommunikation." In *Lexikon für Theologie und Kirche,* edited by Josef Höfer and Karl Rahner. 2nd ed. 10 vols. Freiburg im Breisgau: Herder, 1957–67.

Foster, Sally. *Picts, Gaels and Scots: Early Historic Scotland.* London: Batsford, 1996.

Frank, Roberta. "'Mere' and 'Sund': Two Sea-Changes in *Beowulf.*" In *Modes of Interpretation in Old English Literature: Essays in Honour of Stanley B. Greenfield,* edited by Phyllis Rugg Brown, Georgia Ronan Crampton, and Fred C. Robinson, pp. 153–72. Toronto: University of Toronto Press, 1986.

————. "A Scandal in Toronto: *The Dating of "Beowulf"* a Quarter Century On." *Speculum* 82 (2007), 843–64.

————. "Sex, Lies, and *Málsháttakvæði*: A Norse Poem from Medieval Orkney." The Fell-Benedikz Lecture delivered in the University of Nottingham, 22 May 2003. In *Occasional Papers of the Centre for the Study of the Viking Age,* edited by Judith Jesch, 2:3–31. Nottingham: University of Nottingham, 2004.

Fraser, Constance, and Kenneth Emsley. "Durham and the Wapentake of Sadberge." *Transactions of the Architectural and Archaeological Soc. Durham and Northumberland* n. s. 2 (1970), 71–81.

Frazer, James G. *The Golden Bough.* 1890. Reprinted with a new foreword by Curtis Church. New York: Avenel Books, 1981.

Freeman, Ann, and Paul Meyvaert. "The Meaning of Theodulf's Apse Mosaic at Germigny-des-Prés." *Gesta* 40 (2001), 125–39.

Frénaud, Georges. "Le culte de Nôtre-Dame dans l'ancienne liturgie latine." In *Maria: Études sur la sainte Vierge,* edited by Hubert Du Manoir, 6:157–211. Paris: Beauchesne, 1949–71.

French, W. H. "*Widsith* and the Scop." *PMLA* 60 (1945), 623–30.

Friis-Jensen, Karsten, and James M. W. Willoughby, eds. *Peterborough Abbey.* Corpus of British Medieval Library Catalogues 8. London: British Library, 2001.

Fritzner, Johan. *Ordbog over det gamle norske Sprog I–III.* Oslo: Feilberg & Landmark, 1867.

Fry, Donald K. "Bede Fortunate in His Translator: The Barking Nuns." In *Studies in Earlier Old English Prose,* edited by Paul E. Szarmach, pp. 345–62. Albany: State University of New York Press, 1986.

Frye, Northrop. *The Secular Scripture: A Study of the Structure of Romance.* Cambridge: Cambridge University Press, 1976.

Fulk, R. D. "On Argumentation in Old English Philology, with Particular Reference to the Editing and Dating of *Beowulf*." *ASE* 32 (2003), 1–41.

———. "Some Contested Readings in the Beowulf Manuscript." *Review of English Studies* 56 (2005), 192–223.

———. "Unferth and His Name." *Modern Philology* 85.2 (1987), 113–27.

Fulton, Rachel. *From Judgment to Passion: Devotion to Christ and the Virgin Mary, 800–1200.* New York: Columbia University Press, 2002.

Gabrieli, Francesco. "Islam." In *Enciclopedia Dantesca,* 3:523–25. Rome: Istituto della Enciclopedia Italiana, 1984.

———. "Maometto." In *Enciclopedia Dantesca,* 3:815–16. Rome: Istituto della Enciclopedia Italiana, 1984.

Galloway, Andrew. "Dream-Theory in *The Dream of the Rood* and *The Wanderer*." *Review of English Studies* n.s. 45 (1994), 475–85.

Galpin, Stanley Leman. "On the Sources of Guillaume de Deguileville's *Pèlerinage de l'âme*." *PMLA* 25 (1910), 275–308.

Gameson, Richard. *The Manuscripts of Early Norman England (c. 1066–1130).* Oxford: Oxford University Press, 1999.

———. *The Role of Art in the Late Anglo-Saxon Church.* Oxford: Clarendon Press, 1995.

Gandolfo, Francesco. "La Basilica Sistina: I mosaici della navata e dell'arco triongale." In *Santa Maria Maggiore a Roma*, edited by Carlo Pietrangeli, pp. 85–123. Florence: Nardini, 1988.

Garrison, Mary, Janet Nelson, and Dominic Tweddle. *Alcuin and Charlemagne: The Golden Age of York.* York: The Yorkshire Museum, 2001.

Geiriadur Prifysgol Cymru. Edited by R. J. Thomas et al. Cardiff: University of Wales Press, 1950–2002.

Gem, Richard. "Documentary References to Anglo-Saxon Painted Architecture." In *Early Medieval Wall-Painting and Painted Sculpture in England*, edited by Sharon Cather, David Park, and Paul Williamson, pp. 1–16. Oxford: British Archaeological Reports, 1990.

Gerritsen, Johan. "Have with You to Lexington! The *Beowulf* Manuscript and *Beowulf.*" In *In Other Words: Transcultural Studies in Philology, Translation, and Lexicology Presented to Hans Heinrich Meier on the Occasion of His Sixty-fifth Birthday*, edited by J. Lachlan Mackenzie and Richard Todd, pp. 15–34. Dordrecht: Foris, 1989.

Gertrude of Helfta. *Gertrude of Helfta, The Herald of Divine Love.* Translated by Margaret Winkworth. New York: Paulist Press, 1993.

———. *The Herald of God's Loving-Kindness.* Translated by Alexandra Barratt. Books 1 and 2. Kalamazoo, MI: Cistercian Publications, 1991. Book 3. Kalamazoo, MI: Cistercian Publications, 1999.

Gingher, Robert S. "The Unferth Perplex." *Thoth* 14 (1974), 19–28.

Girard, René. *Violence and the Sacred.* Translated by Patrick Gregory. Baltimore: Johns Hopins University Press, 1977.

Gíslason, Konráð. See Konráð Gíslason.

Gjerløw, Lilli. *Adoratio Crucis: The Regularis Concordia and the Decreta Lanfranci.* Oslo: Norwegian University Press, 1961.

Gneuss, Helmut, ed. *Handlist of Anglo-Saxon Manuscripts: A List of Manuscripts and Manuscript Fragments Written or Owned in England up to 1100.* Tempe: Arizona Center for Medieval and Renaissance Studies, 2001.

———. "Liturgical Books in Anglo-Saxon England and Their Old English Terminology." In *Learning and Literature in Anglo-Saxon England: Studies Presented to Peter Clemoes on the Occasion of His Sixty-fifth Birthday*, edited by Michael Lapidge and Helmut Gneuss, pp. 91–141. Cambridge: Cambridge University Press, 1985.

Godden, Malcolm R. "Were It Not That I Have Bad Dreams: Gregory the Great and the Anglo-Saxons on the Dangers of Dreaming." In *Rome and the North: The Early Reception of Gregory the Great in Germanic Europe*, edited by Rolf H. Bremmer Jr., Kees Dekker, and David F. Johnson, pp. 93–113. Paris: Peeters, 2001.

Godfrey, J. "The Place of the Double-Monastery in the Anglo-Saxon Minster System." In *Famulus Christi: Essays in Commemoration of the Thirteenth Centenary of the Birth of the Venerable Bede*, edited by G. Bonner, pp. 344–50. London: SPCK, 1976.

Godman, Peter. *Alcuin: The Bishops, Kings, and Saints of York.* Oxford: Clarendon Press, 1982.

Goetinck, Glenys W., ed. *Historia Peredur vab Efrawc.* Cardiff: University of Wales Press, 1976.

Goscelin of Saint-Bertin. *The Book of Encouragement and Consolation (Liber Confortatorius).* Translated by Monika Otter. Cambridge: D. S. Brewer, 2004.

————. *The Hagiography of the Female Saints of Ely.* Edited and translated by Rosalind C. Love. Oxford: Clarendon Press, 2004.

————. *The Liber Confortatorius of Goscelin of Saint Bertin.* Edited by C. H. Talbot. Studia Anselmiana 37. Rome: Herder, 1955.

Gougaud, Louis. *Devotional and Ascetic Practices in the Middle Ages.* London: Burns Oates & Washbourne, 1927.

————. *Dévotions et pratiques ascétiques du Moyen Age.* Paris: Desclée, 1925.

————. "Le Coeur vulnéré du Sauveur dans la piété, l'iconographie et la liturgie." *La vie et les arts liturgiques* 8 (1921), 198–209.

Graham-Campbell, James. "The Archaeology of the Danelaw: An Introduction." In *Les mondes normands (VIII–XIIèmes siècles.)*, edited by H. Galiné, pp. 69–76. Caen: Société d'archéologie médiévale, 1989.

Gray, Douglas. "London, British Library, Additonal MS 37049—A Spiritual Encyclopedia." In *Text and Controversy from Wyclif to Bale: Essays in Honour of Anne Hudson*, edited by Helen Barr and Ann M. Hutchison, pp. 99–116. Turnhout: Brepols, 2005.

Gray, Theodosia, ed. *The Homilies of Saint Gregory the Great on the Book of the Prophet Ezekiel in English Translation.* Etna, CA: Center for Traditionalist Orthodox Studies, 1990.

Green, Eugene. *Anglo-Saxon Audiences.* New York: Peter Lang, 2001.

Green, Miranda. *Animals in Celtic Life and Myth.* London: Routledge, 1992.

Greenfield, Stanley B. *The Interpretation of Old English Poems.* London: Routledge & Kegan Paul, 1972.

Greenfield, Stanley B., and Daniel Calder. *A New Critical History of Old English Literature.* New York: New York University Press, 1986.

Greenhill, Eleanor. "The Child in the Tree: A Study of the Cosmological Tree in Christian Tradition." *Traditio* 10 (1954), 323–71.

Gregory the Great. *S. Gregorii Magni: Homiliae in Evangelia.* Edited by Raymond Étaix, CCSL 141. Turnhout: Brepols, 1999.

———. *S. Gregorii Magni: Moralia in Job.* Edited by Marc Adriaen. CCSL 143, 143A, 143B. Trunhout: Brepols. 1979.

———. *S. Gregorii Magni: Registrum Epistolarum.* Edited by Dag Norberg. CCSL 140A. Turnhout: Brepols, 1982.

Guðbrandur Vigfússon. See Vigfússon, Guðbrandur

Guerric of Igny. *Liturgical Sermons.* Translated by Monks of St. Bernard Abbey. Spencer, MA: Cistercian Publications, 1971.

Guillaume de Degulleville. *Le Pèlerinage de Jhésucrist.* Edited by J. J. Stürzinger. London: Roxburghe Club, 1897.

———. *Le Pèlerinage de l'âme.* Edited by J. J. Stürzinger. London: Roxburghe Club, 1895.

———. *Le Pèlerinage de la vie humaine de Guillaume de Deguileville.* Edited by J. J. Stürzinger. London: Roxburghe Club, 1893.

———. *The Pilgrimage of Human Life.* Translated by Eugene Clasby. New York: Garland, 1992.

Gurewich, Vladimir. "Observations on the Iconography of the Wound in Christ's Side, with Special Reference to Its Position." *Journal of the Warburg and Courtauld Institute* 20 (1957), 358–62.

Haddan, Arthur West, and William Stubbs, eds. *Councils and Ecclesiastical Documents Relating to Great Britain and Ireland.* 3 vols. Oxford: Clarendon Press, 1871.

Hagen, Susan K. *Allegorical Remembrance: A Study of The Pilgrimage of the Life of Man as a Medieval Treatise on Seeing and Remembering.* Athens: University of Georgia Press, 1990.

Hahn, Cynthia. "*Visio Dei*: Changes in Medieval Visuality." In *Visuality before and beyond the Renaissance,* edited by Robert S. Nelson, pp. 169–96. Cambridge: Cambridge University Press, 2000.

Hall, J. R. "Three Studies on the Manuscript Text of *Beowulf*: Lines 47b, 747b, and 2232b." In *Beatus Vir: Studies in Early English and Norse Manuscripts in Memory of Phillip Pulsiano,* edited by Nick Doane and Kirsten Wolfe, pp. 441–70. Tempe, AZ: ACMRS, 2006.

Hall, Thomas N. "The Cross as Green Tree in the *Vindicta Salvatoris* and the Green Rod of Moses in *Exodus.*" *English Studies* 72 (1991), 297–307.

———. "The Early English Manuscripts of Gregory the Great's *Homilies on the Gospel* and *Homilies on Ezechiel*: A Preliminary Survey." In *Rome and the North: The Early Reception of Gregory the Great in Germanic Europe,* edited by Rolf H. Bremmer Jr., Kees Dekker, and David F. Johnson, pp. 115–36. Paris: Peeters, 2001.

Hamburger, Jeffrey. *Nuns as Artists: The Visual Culture of a Medieval Convent.* Berkeley: University of California Press, 1997.

———. *The Rothschild Canticles; Art and Mysticism in Flanders and the Rhineland ca. 1300.* New Haven, CT: Yale University Press, 1990.

———. "Speculations on Speculation: Vision and Perception in the Theory and Practice of Mystical Devotion." In *Deutsche Mystik im abendländischen Zusammenhang: Neu erschlossene Texte, neue methodische Ansätze, neue theoretische Konzepte. Kolloquium, Kloster Fischingen 1998*, edited by Walter Haug and Wolfram Schneider-Lastin, pp. 353–408. Tübingen: Niemeyer, 2000.

———. *The Visual and the Visionary: Art and Female Spirituality in Late Medieval Germany.* New York: Zone Books, 1998.

Harbus, Antonina, "Dream and Symbol in *The Dream of the Rood.*" *Nottingham Medieval Studies* 40 (1996), 1–15.

Harris, Joseph. "Eddic Poetry as Oral Poetry: The Evidence of Parallel Passages in the Helgi Poems for Question of Confrontation and Performance." In *Edda: A Collection of Essays*, edited by Robert J. Glendinning and Haraldur Bessason, pp. 210–42. Winnipeg: University of Manitoba, 1983.

———. "The *Senna*: From Description to Literary Theory." *Michigan Germanic Studies* 5 (1979), 65–74.

Harris, P. R. *A History of the British Museum Library, 1753–1973.* London: The British Library, 1998.

Harrison, O. G. "The Formulas *ad virgines sacras*: A Study of the Sources." *Ephemerides Liturgica* 66 (1952), 252–73 and 352–66.

Hart, Cyril R. *The Early Charters of Northern England and the North Midlands.* Leicester: Leicester University Press, 1975.

Harthan, John. *The Book of Hours.* New York: Crowell, 1977.

Hawkes, Jane. "An Iconography of Identity? The Cross-Head from Mayo Abbey." In *From Ireland Coming: Irish Art from the Early Christian to the Late Gothic Period and its European Context*, edited by Colum Hourihane, pp. 261–75. Princeton, NJ: Princeton University Press, 2001.

Healey, Antonette diPaolo, ed. *The Complete Corpus of Old English in Electronic Form.* Dictionary of Old English Corpus, Dictionary of Old English Project. Toronto: Centre for Medieval Studies, University of Toronto, 2000.

Henderson, George. *Bede and the Visual Arts.* Jarrow Lecture, 1980. Jarrow: Jarrow Parish, 1980.

Henderson, Isabel. "The *Book of Kells* and the Snake-Boss Motif on Pictish Cross-Slabs and the Iona Crosses." In *Ireland and Insular Art: AD 500–1200*, edited by Michael Ryan, pp. 55–65. Dublin: Royal Irish Academy, 1987.

———. "'The David Cycle' in Pictish Art." In *Early Medieval Sculpture in Britain and Ireland*, edited by John Higgitt, pp. 87–123. Oxford: British Archaeological Reports, 1986.

———. *Hilton of Cadboll Chapel Site: Art-Historical Analysis of Sculpture Found during the Excavations of Summer 2001*. Historic Scotland: Ref. HS/C/53228/2972.

———. "Pictish Art and the *Book of Kells*." In *Ireland in Early Medieval Europe: Studies in Memory of Kathleen Hughes*, edited by Dorothy Whitelock, Rosamond. McKitterick and David N. Dumville, pp. 79–105. Cambridge: Cambridge University Press, 1982.

———. "Pictish Vine-Scroll Ornament." In *From the Stone Age to the 'Forty-Five': Studies Presented to R. B. K. Stevenson*, edited by by A. O'Connor and D. V. Clarke, pp. 243–68. Edinburgh: John Donald, 1983.

———. *The Picts*. London: Thames and Hudson, 1967.

———. "The Shape and Decoration of the Cross on Pictish Cross-Slabs Carved in Relief." In *The Age of Migrating Ideas: Early Medieval Art in Northern Britain and Ireland*, edited by R. Michael Spearman and John Higgitt, pp. 209–18. Edinburgh: National Museums of Scotland, 1993.

Hennessy, Marlene Villalobos. "Passion, Devotion, Penitential Reading, and the Manuscript Page: The 'Hours of the Cross' in London, British Library, Additional 37049." *Medieval Studies* 66 (2004), 213–52.

———. "The Remains of the Royal Dead in an English Carthusian Manuscript, London, British Library, MS Additional 37049." *Viator* 33 (2002), 310–49.

Henry, Avril. "The Illuminations in the Two Illustrated Middle English Manuscripts of the Prose *Pilgrimage of þe Lyfe of þe Manhode*." *Scriptorium* 37 (1983), 264–73.

———, ed. *The Pilgrimage of the Lyfe of the Manhode*. EETS 288, 292. London: EETS, 1985, 1988.

Henry, P. L. *The Early English and Celtic Lyric*. London: Allen & Unwin, 1966.

Hermann Pálsson. "A Florilegium in Norse from Medieval Orkney." In *The Northern and Western Isles in the Viking World*, edited by Alexander Fenton and Hermann Pálsson, pp. 258–64. Edinburgh: J. Donald, 1984.

Das Herz. 3 vols. Biberach: Karl Thomas, g.m.b.h., 1969.

Heslop, T. A. "The Production of *de luxe* Manuscripts and the Patronage of King Cnut and Queen Emma." *ASE* 19 (1990), 151–91.

Hicks, Carola. *Animals in Early Medieval Art.* Edinburgh: Edinburgh University Press, 1993.

Hieatt, Constance B. "Dream Frame and Verbal Echo in *The Dream of the Rood.*" *Neuphilologische Mitteilungen* 72 (1971), 251–63.

Higham, Nicholas. *The Northern Counties to AD 1000.* London: Longman, 1986.

Higley, Sarah Lynn. *Between Languages: The Uncooperative Text in Early Welsh and Old English Nature Poetry.* University Park: Pennsylvania State University Press, 1993.

Hilberg, Isidore, ed. *Sancti Eusebii Hieronymi Epistulae.* CSEL 54–56. Vienna: F. Tempsly, 1910–18.

Hildegard of Bingen. *Symphonia.* Edited by Barbara Newman. 2nd ed. Ithaca, NY: Cornell University Press, 1998.

Hill, John M. *The Cultural World in Beowulf.* Toronto: University of Toronto Press, 1994.

Hillgarth, J. N. "Ireland and Spain in the Seventh-Century." *Peritia* 3 (1984), 1–16.

———. "St. Julian of Toledo in the Middle Ages." *Journal of the Warburg and Courtauld Institutes* 21 (1958), 7–26.

———. "Visigothic Spain and Early Christian Ireland." *Proceedings of the Royal Irish Academy* 63:C5 (1962), 167–95.

Historia de sancto Cuthberto. Edited by Thomas Arnold. In *Symeonis monachi opera omnia,* 1:196–214. Rolls Series 75. London: HMSO, 1882.

Historia de sancto Cuthberto. Edited by J. Hodgson Hinde. In *Symeonis Dunelmensis opera et collectanea,* 1:138–52. Durham: Andrews & Co., 1868.

Hodges, C. C. "The Conyers Falchion." *Archaeologia Aeliana* 15 (1892), 214–17.

Hogg, James, ed. *An Illustrated Yorkshire Carthusian Religious Miscellany: British Library Additional MS 37049.* Analecta Cartusiana 95. Salzburg: Institut für Anglistik und Amerikanistik, Universität Salzburg, 1981.

Holcomb, Chris. *Mirth Making: The Rhetorical Discourse on Jesting in Early Modern England.* Columbia: University of South Carolina Press, 2001.

Hollis, Stephanie. *Anglo-Saxon Women and the Church: Sharing a Common Fate.* Woodbridge: Boydell, 1992.

Hollis, Stephanie, ed., with W. R. Barnes, Rebecca Hayward, Kathleen Loncar, and Michael Wright. *Writing the Wilton Women: Goscelin's Legend of Edith and "Liber confortatorius."* Turnhout: Brepols, 2004.

Hollowell, Ida Masters. "Unferð the *Þyle* in Beowulf." *Studies in Philology* 73 (1976), 239–65.

Horner, Shari. *The Discourse of Enclosure.* Albany: State University of New York Press, 2001.

Houghton, H. A. G. *Augustine's Text of John: Patristic Citations and Latin Gospel Manuscripts.* Oxford: Oxford University Press, 2008.

Howe, Eunice D. "Antoniazzo Romano, the 'Golden Legend' and a Madonna of Santa Maria Maggiore." *Burlington Magazine* 126 (1984): 417–19.

Howlett, David R. "Form and Genre in *Widsith*." *English Studies* 55 (1974), 505–11.

Hughes, Geoffrey. "Beowulf, Unferth and Hrunting: An Interpretation." *English Studies* 58 (1972), 385–95.

Hughes, Kathleen. "Evidence for Contacts between the Churches of the Irish and the English from the Synod of Whitby to the Viking Age." In *England before the Conquest: Studies in Primary Sources presented to Dorothy Whitelock*, edited by Peter Clemoes and Kathleen Hughes, pp. 49–67. Cambridge: Cambridge University Press, 1971.

Hunter Blair, Peter, ed. *The Moore Bede.* With a contribution by R. A. B. Mynors. EEMF 9. Copenhagen: Rosenkilde and Bagger, 1959.

Huot, Sylvia. *The Romance of the Rose and Its Medieval Readers.* Cambridge: Cambridge University Press, 1993.

Hurley, Michael. "Born Incorruptibly. The Third Canon of the Lateran Council, A.D. 649." *Heythrop Journal* 2 (1961), 216–36.

Hurst, David, ed. *Commentary on the Seven Catholic Epistles of Bede.* Kalamazoo, MI: Cistercian Publications, 1985.

Huws, Bleddyn Owen. *Canu Gofyn a Diolch, c. 1350–c.1630.* Cardiff: University of Wales Press, 1998.

Ihm, Christa. *Die Programme der christlichen Apsismalerei vom vierten Jahrhundert bis zur Mitte des achten Jahrhunderts.* Wiesbaden: Franz Steiner, 1960.

Innocent III. *De sacro altaris mysterio libri sex. PL* 217:773–916.

Irvine, Susan. "Adam or Christ? A Pronominal Pun in *The Dream of the Rood*." *Review of English Studies* n.s. 48 (1977), 433–47.

———. *The Anglo-Saxon Chronicle: A Collaborative Edition.* Vol. 7: *MS E.* Cambridge: D. S. Brewer, 2004.

Irving, Edward B., Jr. *Rereading Beowulf.* Philadelphia: University of Pennsylvania Press, 1989.

Isaacs, Neil. *Structural Principles in Old English Poetry.* Knoxville: University of Tennessee Press, 1968.

Isidore. *Allegoriae quaedem scripturae sacrae. PL* 83:97–130.

———. *Differentiarum libri duo.* II.19–21. *PL* 83:81–82.

———. *Isidori hispalensis episcopi ethymolgiarum siue originem libri XX.* Edited by W. M. Lindsay. 2 vols. Oxford: Clarendon Press, 1911.

———. *Quaestiones in vetus testamentum. PL* 83:207–424.

Jacob, W., and R. Hanslik, eds. *Cassiodori–Epiphanii Historia Ecclesiastica Tripartita.* CSEL 71. Vienna: Hoelder, Pinchler, Tempsky, 1952.

Jacobs, Nicholas. "The Old English Heroic Tradition in Light of the Welsh Evidence." In *Astudiaethau ar yr Hengerdd,* edited by Rachel Bromwich and R. Brinley Jones, pp. 165–78. Cardiff: University of Wales Press, 1978.

———. "The Old English Heroic Tradition in the Light of Welsh Evidence." *Cambridge Medieval Celtic Studies* 2 (Winter, 1981), 9–20.

Jackson, Peter "Ælfric and the Purpose of Christian Marriage: A Reconsideration of the *Life of Æthelthryth,* lines 120–30." *ASE* 29 (2000), 235–60.

Jackson, Peter, and Michael Lapidge. "The Contents of the Cotton-Corpus Legendary." In *Holy Men and Holy Women: Old English Prose Saints' Lives and Their Contexts,* edited by Paul E. Szarmach, pp. 131–46. Albany: State University of New York Press, 1996.

Jager, Eric. *The Book of the Heart.* Chicago: University of Chicago Press, 2000.

James, M. R., ed. *A Descriptive Catalogue of the Manuscripts in the Fitzwilliam Museum.* Cambridge: Cambridge University Press, 1895.

———. *A Descriptive Catalogue of the Manuscripts in the Library of Lambeth Palace.* Cambridge: Cambridge University Press, 1930–32.

———. *The Western Manuscripts in the Library of Trinity College, Cambridge: A Descriptive Catalogue.* 4 vols. Cambridge: Cambridge University Press, 1900–1904.

James, M. R., and Ellis H. Minns. *A Descriptive Catalogue of the Manuscripts in the Library of Pembroke College Cambridge.* Cambridge: Cambridge University Press, 1905.

Jerome. *S. Hieronymi Presbyteri Commentorium in Esaiam Libri XXIII.* Edited by Marc Adriaen. CCSL 73, 73A. Turnhout: Brepols, 1963.

———. *S. Hieronymi Presbyteri Hebraicae quaestiones in libros Geneseos.* Edited by Paul de LaGarde. CCSL 72. Turnhout: Brepols, 1959.

Jewell, R. H. I. "The Anglo-Saxon Friezes at Breedon-on-the Hill, Leicestershire." *Archaeologia* 108 (1986), 95–115.

Johnson, David F. "Old English Religious Poetry: *Christ and Satan* and *The Dream of the Rood.*" In *Companion to Old English Poetry,* edited by Henk Aertsen and Rolf H. Bremmer Jr, pp. 159–87. Amsterdam: VU University Press, 1994.

Johnson South, Ted. *Historia de Sancto Cuthberto. A History of Saint Cuthbert and a Record of His Patrimony.* Cambridge: Cambridge University Press, 2002.

——— [Theodore]. "The 'Historia de Sancto Cuthberto': A New Edition and Translation, with Discussions of the Surviving Manuscripts, the Text, and Northumbrian Estate Structure." Ph.D. diss., Cornell University, 1990.

———. "Toward a Model of the Landholdings of the Community of Saint Cuthbert in the Pre-Norman Period. The Evidence of the *Historia de Sancto Cuthberto.*" M.A. diss., Durham University, 1987.

Johnston, Dafydd, ed. *Gwaith Llywelyn Goch ap Meurig Hen.* Aberystwyth: Centre for Advanced Welsh and Celtic Studies, 1998.

Jones, Elin, ed. *Gwaith Llywarch ap Llywelyn.* In *Cyfres Beirdd y Tywysogion V,* pp. 279–84. Cardiff: University of Wales Press, 1991.

Jones, Nerys Ann, and Ann Parry Owen, eds. *Gwaith Cynddelw Brydydd Mawr II.* In *Cyfres Beirdd y Tywysogion IV.* Cardiff: University of Wales Press, 1995, pp. 174–219.

Jónsson, Finnur. See Finnur Jónsson.

Joret, Charles. *La rose dans l'antiquité et au moyen âge.* Paris: Bouillon, 1892.

Jucker, Andreas H., and Irma Taavitsamen. "Diachronic Speech Act Analysis: Insults from Flyting to Flaming." *Journal of Historical Pragmatics* 1.1 (2000), 67–95.

Julian of Norwich. *A Book of Showings to the Anchoress Julian of Norwich.* Edited by Edmund Colledge and James Walsh. Toronto: Pontifical Institute of Mediaeval Studies, 1978.

———. *Revelations of Divine Love.* Translated by Elizabeth Spearing. Harmondsworth: Penguin, 1998.

Julian of Toledo. *Sancti Juliani Toletanae Sedis Episcopi Opera,* pars 1. Edited by J. N. Hillgarth. CCSL 115. Turnhout: Brepols, 1976.

Jung, Carl. "Psychology and Literature." In *The Collected Works of C. G. Jung.* Vol. 15: *The Spirit in Man, Art, and Literature.* Translated by R. F. C. Hull, pp. 84–105. London: Routledge & Kegan Paul, 1966.

Jungmann, Josef A. *The Mass of the Roman Rite: Its Origins and Development (Missarum Sollemnia).* Translated by Francis Brunner. 2 vols. New York: Benziger, 1955. Reprint, Dublin: Four Courts Press, 1986.

Karkov, Catherine E. "Whitby, Jarrow and the Commemoration of Death in Northumbria." In *Northumbria's Golden Age,* edited by Jane Hawkes and Susan Mills, pp. 126–35. Stroud: Alan Sutton, 1999.

Keefer, Sarah Larratt. "'Either/And' as 'Style' in Anglo-Saxon Christian Verse." In *Anglo-Saxon Styles*, edited by Catherine E. Karkov and George H. Brown, pp. 179–200. Albany: State University of New York Press, 2003.

———. "Performance of the Cross in Anglo-Saxon England." In *Cross and Culture in Anglo-Saxon England*, edited by Karen L. Jolly, Catherine E. Karkov, and Sarah Larratt Keefer, pp. 203–41. Morgantown: West Virginia University Press, 2008.

———. "The Veneration of the Cross in Anglo-Saxon England." In *The Liturgy of the Late Anglo-Saxon Church*, edited by Helen Gittos and M. Bradford Bedingfield, pp. 143–84. Woodbridge: Boydell, 2005.

Kelly, John N. D. *Early Christian Creeds*. 3rd ed. London: Longman, 1972.

Kennedy, Victor L. *The Saints of the Canon of the Mass*. 2nd edition. Rome: Pontificio Istituto di archeologia cristiana, 1963.

Ker, N. R. *Catalogue of Manuscripts Containing Anglo-Saxon*. Oxford: Clarendon Press, 1957.

Kessler, Herbert L. *Spiritual Seeing: Picturing God's Invisibility in Medieval Art*. Philadelphia: University of Pennsylvania Press, 2000.

Kiernan, Kevin S. *Beowulf and the Beowulf Manuscript*. New Brunswick, NJ: Rutgers University Press, 1981. Rev. ed. Ann Arbor: University of Michigan Press, 1996.

———."Digital Image-Processing and the Beowulf Manuscript." *Literary and Linguistic Computing* 6.1 (April 1991), 20–27.

———. "The Eleventh-Century Origin of *Beowulf* and the *Beowulf* Manuscript." In *The Dating of Beowulf*, edited by Colin Chase, pp. 9–21. Toronto: University of Toronto Press, 1981.

———. "Old Manuscripts/New Technologies." In *Anglo-Saxon Manuscripts: Basic Readings*, edited by Mary P. Richards, pp. 37–54. New York: Garland Press, 1994. Paperback ed., New York: Routledge, 2001.

———. "The Palimpsest and the New Text of Folio 179." In *Beowulf and the Beowulf Manuscript*, ed. Kiernan, pp. 219–43.

———. "Remodeling Alfred's *Boethius* with *tol ond andweorc* of Edition Production Technology (EPT)." In *Making Sense: Constructing Meaning in Early English*, edited by Antonette diPaolo Healey and Kevin Kiernan, pp. 72–115. Publications of the Dictionary of Old English 7. Toronto: University of Toronto Press, 2007.

———. "The State of the *Beowulf* Manuscript 1882–1983." *ASE* 13 (1984): 23–42.

———. *The Thorkelin Transcripts of 'Beowulf.'* Anglistica 25. Copenhagen: Rosenkilde & Bagger, 1986.

Kiernan, Kevin S., with Andrew Prescott et al., eds. *Electronic Beowulf.* London: British Library; Ann Arbor: University of Michigan Press, 1999. Rev. ed., *Electronic Beowulf 2.0,* ed. Kevin S. Kiernan with Ionut Emil Iacob. London: British Library, 2004.

King, A. "Gauber High Pasture, Ribblehead—an Interim Report." In *Viking Age York and the North,* edited by Richard A. Hall, pp. 21–25. London: Council for British Archaeology, 1978.

Kirschbaum, Engelbert, and Wolfgang Braunfels, eds. *Lexikon der christlichen Ikonographie.* 8 vols. Rome: Herder, 1968–76.

Kittle, Gerhard, ed. *Theological Dictionary of the New Testament.* Grand Rapids, MI: Eerdmans, 1965.

Kitzinger, Ernst. "The Coffin-Reliquary." In *The Relics of Saint Cuthbert,* edited by C. F. Battiscombe, pp. 202–304. Oxford: Oxford University Press, 1956.

———. "Interlace and Icons: Form and Function in Early Insular Art." In *The Age of Migrating Ideas: Early Medieval Art in Northern Britain and Ireland,* edited by R. Michael Spearman and John Higgitt, pp. 3–15. Edinburgh: National Museum of Scotland, 1993.

Klaeber, Friedrich, ed. *Beowulf and the Fight at Finnsburg.* 1922. Reprint, 3rd ed. with first and second supplements. Lexington, MA: D. C. Heath and Company, 1950. *Klaeber's Beowulf and the Fight at Finnsburg,* edited with introduction, commentary, appendices, glossary, and bibliography by R. D. Fulk, Robert E. Bjork, and John D. Niles. Toronto Old English Series 21. Toronto: University of Toronto Press, 2008.

Klausner, David N. "Aspects of Time in the Battle Poetry of Early Britain." In *The Middle Ages in the North-west,* edited by P. Starkey and T. Scott, pp. 85–107. Liverpool: Leopard's Head Press, 1995.

———, ed. "Statud Gruffudd ap Cynan." In *Welsh Music History/Hanes Cerddoriaeth Cymru* 3 (1999), 282–98.

———. "The Topos of the Beasts of Battle in Early Welsh Poetry." In *The Centre and Its Compass: Studies in Medieval Literature in Honor of Professor John Leyerle,* edited by R. A. Taylor et al., pp. 247–63. Kalamazoo, MI: Medieval Institute Publications, 1993.

Klinck, Anne. *The Old English Elegies: A Critical Edition and Genre Study.* Montreal: McGill-Queen's University Press, 1992.

Knott, Eleanor, ed. *Togail Bruidne Da Derga.* Dublin: Dublin Institute for Advanced Studies, 1936.

Knowles, W. H. "Sockburn Church." *Transactions of the Architectural and Archaeological Soc. Durham and Northumberland* 5 (1896–1905), 99–120.

Koch, John, ed. *The Gododdin of Aneirin: Text and Context from Dark-Age North Britain.* Cardiff: University of Wales Press, 1997.

König, Eberhard. *The Bedford Hours: The Making of a Medieval Masterpiece.* London: British Library, 2007.

Konráð Gíslason. *Efterladte Skrifter.* Vol. 2. Copenhagen: Glydendal, 1897.

Kornexl, Lucia, ed. *Die Regularis Concordia und ihre altenglishche Interlinearversion.* Munich: Fink, 1993.

Krapp, George Philip, ed. *The Vercelli Book.* ASPR 2. New York: Columbia University Press, 1932.

Krapp, George Philip, and Elliott van Kirk Dobbie, eds. *The Exeter Book.* ASPR 3. New York: Columbia University Press, 1936.

Kristeva, Julia. "Stabat Mater." In *The Kristeva Reader,* edited by Toril Moi and translated by Lèon S. Roudiez, pp. 160–86. New York: Columbia University Press, 1986.

Kruger, Steven F. *Dreaming in the Middle Ages.* Cambridge: Cambridge University Press, 1992.

Lachance, Paul, ed. *Angela Foligno: Complete Works.* New York: Paulist Press, 1993.

Lang, James, ed. *Anglo-Saxon and Viking Age Sculpture.* Oxford: British Archaeological Reports, 1978.

———. "The Compilation of Design in Colonial Viking Sculpture." In *Festskrift til Thorleif Sjøvold,* edited by Charlotte Blindheim, pp. 125–37. Oslo: University of Oslo, 1985.

———. "The Distinctiveness of Viking Colonial Art." In *Sources of Anglo-Saxon Culture,* edited by Paul E. Szarmach, with V. D. Oggins, pp. 243–60. Kalamazoo, MI: Medieval Institute Publications, 1986.

———. "Fine Measurement Analysis of Viking Age Ornament." In *Beretning fra tredie tvaerfaglige Vikingesymposium,* edited by Gillian Fellows-Jensen and N. Lund, pp. 37–57. Højbjerg: Hikuin og afdeling for middelalderarkeologi, 1984.

———. "The Hogback. A Viking Colonial Monument." *Anglo-Saxon Studies in Archaeology and History* 3 (1984), 85–176.

———. "Illustrative Carvings of the Viking Period at Sockburn-on-Tees." *Archaeologia Aeliana,* 4th ser., 40 (1972), 235–48.

———. *Northern Yorkshire.* Vol. 6 of *Corpus of Anglo-Saxon Stone Sculpture.* Edited by Rosemary Cramp. Oxford: Oxford University Press, 2001.

———. "Principles of Design in Free-style Carving in the Irish Sea Province c. 800 to c. 950." In *Medieval Sculpture in Britain and Ireland,* edited by John Higgitt, pp. 153–74. Oxford: British Archaeological Reports, 1986.

————. "Recent Studies in the Pre-Conquest Sculpture of Northumbria." In *Studies in Medieval Sculpture*, edited by F. H. Thompson, pp. 177–89. London: Society of Antiquaries of London, 1983.

————. "Some Units of Linear Measurement in Insular Art." In *Keimelia: Studies in Medieval Archaeology In Memory of Tom Delaney*, edited by Gearóid Mac Niocaill and Patrick F. Wallace, pp. 95–101. Galway: Galway University Press, 1988.

————. *York and Eastern Yorkshire*. Vol. 3 of *Corpus of Anglo-Saxon Stone Sculpture*. Edited by Rosemary Cramp. Oxford: Oxford University Press, 1991.

Lang, James, and Christopher D. Morris. "Recent Finds of Pre-Norman Sculpture from Gilling West, N. Yorkshire." *Medieval Archaeology* 22 (1978), 127–30.

Lapidge, Michael. *The Anglo-Saxon Library*. Oxford: Oxford University Press, 2006.

————. "The Archetype of *Beowulf*." *ASE* 29 (2000), 5–41.

————. "The Career of Archbishop Theodore." In *Archbishop Theodore: Commemorative Studies on His Life and Influence*, edited by Michael Lapidge, pp. 1–29. Cambridge: Cambridge University Press, 1995.

————. "Surviving Booklists from Anglo-Saxon England." In *Learning and Literature in Anglo-Saxon England*, edited by Michael Lapidge and Helmut Gneuss, pp. 33–89. Cambridge: Cambridge University Press, 1985.

Lapidge, Michael, and Michael Herren, eds. and trans. *Aldhelm: The Prose Works*. Ipswich: Rowman and Littlefield, 1979.

Lapidge, M[ichael], and R[osalind] C. Love. "The Latin Hagiography of England and Wales (600–1550)." In *Hagiographies: histoire internationale de la littérature hagiographique latine et vernaculaire en Occident des origines à 1550*, edited by Guy Philippart, 3:203–325. Turnhout: Brepols, 2001.

Lawton, Lesley Suzanne. "Text and Image in Late Mediaeval English Vernacular Manuscripts." 4 vols. D.Phil. diss., Univ. of York, 1982.

Leclercq, Jean. "Messes pour la profession et l'oblation monastiques." *Archiv für Liturgiewissenschaft* 4 (1955), 93–96.

Lee, Alan A. *Gold-Hall and Earth-Dragon: Beowulf as Metaphor*. Toronto: University of Toronto Press, 1998.

Lees, Clare A., and Gillian R. Overing. "Birthing Bishops and Fathering Poets: Bede, Hild, and the Relations of Cultural Production." *Exemplaria* 6 (1994), 35–65.

————. *Double Agents: Women and Clerical Culture in Anglo-Saxon England*. Philadelphia: University of Pennsylvania Press, 2001.

Legaré, Anne-Marie. "La reception du *Pèlerinage de Vie humaine* de Guillaume de Digulleville dans le milieu angevin d'après les sources et les manuscripts conserves." In *Religion et mentalités au Moyen Âge: Mélanges en l'honneur d'Hervé Martin*, edited by Sophie Cassagnes-Brouquet et al., pp. 543–61. Rennes: Presses Universitaires de Rennes, 2003.

Lenker, Ursula. *Die westsächsische Evangelienversion und die Perikopenordnungen im angelsächsischen England.* Munich: Fink, 1997.

Leo the Great. *Sancti Leonis Magni Romani pontificis tractatus septem et nonaginta.* Edited by Antoine Chavasse. CCSL, 138, 138A. Turnhout: Brepols, 1973.

———. *Sermons.* Translated by Jane Freeland and Agnes Conway. Washington, DC: Catholic University of America Press, 1995.

L'Estrange, Elizabeth. *Holy Motherhood: Gender, Dynasty and Visual Culture in the Later Middle Ages.* Manchester: Manchester University Press, 2008.

Lewis, C. S. *The Allegory of Love.* London: Oxford University Press, 1936.

Lewis, Charlton, and Charles Short, eds. *A Latin Dictionary.* Oxford: Clarendon Press, 1975.

Lewis, Flora. "The Wound in Christ's Side and the Instruments of the Passion: Gendered Experience and Response." In *Women and the Book: Assessing the Visual Evidence*, edited by Leslie Smith and Jane H. M. Taylor, pp. 204–29. London: The British Library, 1996.

Lewis, Henry, Thomas Roberts, and Ifor Williams, eds. *Cywyddau Iolo Goch ac Eraill.* 2nd ed. Cardiff: University of Wales Press, 1972.

Lewis, Suzanne. *Reading Images: Narrative Discourse and Reception in the Thirteenth-Century Illuminated Apocalypse.* Cambridge: Cambridge University Press, 1995.

Lieb, Michael. *The Visionary Mode: Biblical Prophecy, Hermeneutics, and Cultural Change.* Ithaca, NY: Cornell Univ. Press, 1991.

Lieblang, Franz. *Grundfragen der mystischen Theologie nach Gregors des Grossen Moralia und Ezechielhomilien.* Freiburg-im-Breisgau: Herder, 1934.

Lochrie, Karma. "Mystical Acts, Queer Tendencies." In *Constructing Medieval Sexuality*, edited by Karma Lochrie and James A. Schulz, pp. 180–200. Minneapolis: University of Minnesota Press, 1997.

Lofthouse, Marion. "'Le Pèlerinage de vie humaine' by Guillaume de Deguileville, with Special Reference to the French MS. 2 of the John Rylands Library." *Bulletin of the John Rylands Library* 19 (1935), 170–215.

Lydgate, John. *The Pilgrimage of the Life of Man.* Edited by F. J. Furnivall. 3 vols., EETS e.s. 77, 83, 92. 1899, 1901, 1904. Reprint, New York: Kraus Reprint, 1973.

Lynch, Kathryn L. *The High Medieval Dream Vision: Poetry, Philosophy, and Literary Form.* Stanford, CA: Stanford University Press, 1988.

Lynch, Peredur, et al., eds. *Gwaith Dafydd Benfras ac Eraill.* In *Cyfres Beirdd y Tywysogion VI*, pp. 74–87. Cardiff: University of Wales Press, 1995.

Mac Airt, Seán, and Gearóid Mac Niocaill, eds. and trans. *The Annals of Ulster (to A.D. 1131).* Dublin: Dublin Institute for Advanced Studies, 1983.

Mackreth, D. F. "Peterborough from St Aethelwold to Martin de Bec c. 970–1155." In *Monasteries and Society in Medieval Britain: Proceedings of the 1994 Harlaxton Symposium*, edited by Benjamin Thompson, pp. 127–56. Stamford: Paul Watkins, 1999.

Mac Lean, Douglas. "Northumbrian Vine-Scroll Ornament and the *Book of Kells*." In *Northumbria's Golden Age*, edited by Jane Hawkes and Susan Mills, pp. 178–90. Stroud: Sutton, 1999.

———. "Snake-Bosses and Redemption at Iona and in Pictland." In *The Age of Migrating Ideas: Early Medieval Art in Northern Britain and Ireland*, edited by R. Michael Spearman and John Higgitt, pp. 245–53. Edinburgh: National Museum of Scotland, 1993.

Maddocks, Hilary. "'Me thowhte as I slepte that I was a pilgrime': Text and Illustration in Deguillevile's 'Pilgrimages' in the State Library of Victoria." *Latrobe Library Journal* 13, nos. 51/52 (October 1993), 60–69.

Magennis, Hugh. "The *Beowulf* Poet and His 'Druncne Dryhtguman.'" *Neuphilologische Mitteilungen* 86 (1985), 159–64.

———. "Images of Laughter in Old English Poetry, with Particular Reference to the 'Hleahtor Wera' of *The Seafarer*." *English Studies* 73 (1992), 193–204.

———. "Treatments of Treachery and Betrayal in Anglo-Saxon Texts." *English Studies* 76 (1995), 1–19.

Magnússon, Eiríkr. See Eiríkr Magnússon.

Mahler, Annemarie E. "*Lignum Domini* and the Opening Vision of *The Dream of the Rood*: A Viable Hypothesis?" *Speculum* 53 (1978), 441–59.

Mâle, Émile. *L'art religieux de la fin du Moyen Age en France.* Paris: Armand Colin, 1922.

Malone, Kemp, ed. *Deor.* Copenhagen: Rosenkilde and Bagger, 1962. Rev. ed. Exeter: Exeter University Press, 1977.

———, ed., *The Nowell Codex: British Museum Cotton Vitellius A. xv, Second MS.* EEMF 12. Copenhagen: Rosenkilde and Bagger, 1963.

———. "When Did Middle English Begin?" *Language: Journal of the Linguistic Society of America* 4 (1930): 10–17.

———, ed. *Widsith.* London: Methuen, 1936.

Manion, Margaret M., and Vera F. Vines, eds. *Medieval and Renaissance Illuminated Manuscripts in Australian Collections.* New York: Thames and Hudson, 1984.

Markland, Murry F. "Boethius, Alfred and *Deor.*" *Modern Philology* 66 (1968), 1–4.

Markus, R. A. *Gregory the Great and His World.* Cambridge: Cambridge University Press, 1997.

Martini, A. *Il Cosiddetto Pontificale di Poitiers.* Rome: Herder, 1979.

McGerr, Rosemarie Potz. "Editing the Self-Conscious Medieval Translator: Some Issues and Examples." *Text* 4 (1988), 147–61.

———, ed. *The Pilgrimage of the Soul: A Critical Edition of the Middle English Dream Vision.* New York: Garland, 1990.

McGinn, Bernard. "Contemplation in Gregory the Great." In *Gregory the Great: A Symposium,* edited by John C. Cavadini, pp. 146–67. Notre Dame, IN: University of Notre Dame Press, 1995.

———. *The Presence of God: A History of Western Christian Mysticism.* Vol. 2: *The Growth of Mysticism.* New York: Crossroads, 1994.

McKinnon, James W. *The Advent Project: The Later-Seventh-Century Creation of the Roman Mass Proper.* Berkeley: University of California Press, 2000.

McNally, R. "Isidorian Pseudepigraphia in the Early Middle-Ages." In *Isidoriana: Estudios sobre San Isidoro de Sevilla en el XIV Centenario de su Nacimiento,* edited by M. C. Diaz y Diaz, pp. 305–16. Leon: Centro de Estudios "San Isidoro," 1961.

McNamara, Jo Ann, and John E. Halborg, with E. Gordon Whatley, eds. *Sainted Women of the Dark Ages.* Durham, NC: Duke University Press, 1992.

Mechthild von Magdeburg. *Das fliessende Licht der Gottheit.* Edited by Margot Schmidt. Stuttgart: Bad Cannstatt, 1995.

Meehan, Bernard. *The Book of Kells: An Illustrated Introduction to the Manuscript in Trinity College Dublin.* London: Thames and Hudson, 1994.

Meiss, Millard. *French Painting in the Time of Jean de Berry.* Part 3: *The Limbourgs and Their Contemporaries.* London: Thames and Hudson, 1974.

Mellows, W. T., ed. *The Chronicle of Hugh Candidus.* London: Oxford University Press, 1949.

Ménager, A. "La contemplation d'après saint Grégoire le Grand." *La vie spirituelle* 9 (1923), 242–82.

———. "Les divers sens du mot 'contemplatio' chez saint Grégoire le Grand." *La vie spirituelle,* suppl. (June 1939), 145–69, and (July 1939), 39–56.

Menocal, María Rosa. *The Arabic Role in Medieval Literary History: A Forgotten Heritage.* Philadelphia: University of Pennsylvania Press, 1987.

Metzger, B. M. *The Canon of the New Testament: Its Origin, Development, and Significance.* Oxford: Oxford University Press, 1987.

Meyer, Kellie S. "Reading the Stones: The Pictish Class II Monuments on Tarbat Peninsula." Ph.D. diss., University of York, 2004.

Meyer, Kuno, ed. *Liadain and Curithir. An Irish Love-Story of the Ninth Century.* London: D. Nutt: 1902.

Meyvaert, Paul. "Bede and the Church Paintings at Wearmouth-Jarrow." *ASE* 8 (1979), 63–77.

Meyvaert, Paul, and Anselme Davril. "Théodulfe et Bède au sujet des blessures du Christ." *Revue bénédictine* 113 (2003), 71–79.

Miket, R., and M. Pocock. "An Anglo-Saxon Cemetery at Greenbank, Darlington." *Medieval Archaeology* 20 (1976), 62–74.

Miles, Margaret. "Vision: The Eye of the Body and the Eye of the Mind in Saint Augustine's *De trinitate* and *Confessions.*" *Journal of Religion* 63 (1983), 125–42.

Miller, Thomas, ed. *The Old English Version of Bede's Ecclesiastical History.* EETS o.s. 95, 96, 110, 111. Oxford: Oxford University Press, 1890–98. Reprint, 1959–63, 1996–97.

Mitchell, Bruce. *Old English Syntax.* Vol. 2. Oxford: Clarendon Press, 1985.

Mitchell, Bruce, and Fred C. Robinson, eds. *Beowulf: An Edition.* Oxford: Blackwell, 1998.

———, eds. *A Guide to Old English.* 6th ed. Oxford: Blackwell, 2001.

Möbius, Theodor. *Zeitschrift für deutsche Philologie. Ergänzungsband.* Halle: Buchdruckerei des Waisenhouses, 1874.

Mohlberg, Leo Cunibert, ed. *Die älteste erreichbare Gestalt des Liber Sacramentorum anni circuli der römischen Kirche (Cod. Pad. D.47, folios 11r–100r); Untersuchungen von Anton Baumstark.* Münster-im-Westfalen: Aschendorff, 1927.

Mohlberg, Leo Cunibert, Peter Siffrin, and Ludwig Eisenhöfer, eds. *Liber Sacramentorum Romanae Aeclesiae Ordinis Anni Circuli (Cod. Vat. Reg. lat. 316/Paris Bib. Nat. 7193, 41/56) (Sacramentarium Gelasianum).* 3rd edition, revised by Ludwig Eisenhöfer. Rome: Herder, 1981.

Mombritius, Boninus. *Sanctuarium seu vitae sanctorum.* 2 vols. Milan, 1479. Reprint, Paris, 1910; New York: Georg Olms Verlag, 1978.

Morel, Charles, ed. and trans. *Grégoire le Grand. Homélies sur Ézéchiel.* 2 vols. Paris: Éditions du Cerf, 1986, 1990.

Morris, Christopher D. "Aspects of Scandinavian Settlement in Northern England: A Review." *Northern History* 20 (1984), 3–22.

———. "Aycliffe and Its Pre-Norman Sculpture." In *Anglo-Saxon and Viking Age Sculpture and Its Context*, edited by James Lang, pp. 97–133. Oxford: British Archaeological Reports, 1978.

———. "Northumbria and the Viking Settlement: The Evidence for Landholding." *Archaeologia Aeliana*, 5th ser., 5 (1977), 81–103.

———. "Pre-Conquest Sculpture of the Tees Valley." *Medieval Archaeology* 20 (1976), 140–46.

———. "The Pre-Norman Sculpture of the Darlington Area." In *Darlington: A Topographical Study*, edited by Peter A. G. Clack and Nicholas F. Pearson, pp. 44–51. Durham: Northern Archaeological Survey, Dept. of Archaeology, University of Durham, 1978.

———. "Viking and Native in Northern England. A Case-Study." In *Proceedings of the Eighth Viking Congress, Århus 24–31 August 1977*, edited by Hans Bekker-Nielsen, Peter Foote, and Olaf Olsen, pp. 223–44. Odense: Odense University Press, 1981.

———. "The Vikings and Irish Monasteries." *Durham University Journal* 71 part 2 (1979), 175–86.

Morris, John, ed. and trans. *British History and the Welsh Annals*. London: Phillimore, 1980.

———, ed. *Domesday Book: Gloucestershire*. Chicester: Phillimore Publishing, 1982.

Morrison, Stephen. "The Figure of *Christus Sponsus* in Old English Prose." *Beiträge zur Deutschen Philologie* 58 (1984), 5–15.

Muzerelle, Denis, et al. *Manuscrits datés des bibliothèques de France*. Vol. 1. Paris: CNRS Editions, 2000.

Nagy, Michael S. "A Reassessment of Unferth's Fratricide in *Beowulf*." *Proceedings of the Medieval Association of the Midwest* 3 (1995), 15–30.

Nedoma, Robert. "The Legend of Wayland in *Deor*." *Zeitschrift für Anglistik und Amerikanistik* 38 (1990), 129–45.

Nelles, William. "Beowulf's sorhfullne sið with Breca." *Neophilologus* 83.2 (1999), 299–312.

Nestle, Eberhard, Erwin Nestle, and Kurt Aland, eds. *Nestle-Aland Novum Testamentum Graece et Latine*. 3rd ed. Stuttgart: Deutsche Bibelgesellschaft, 1994.

Neuss, Wilhelm. *Das Buch Ezechiel in Theologie und Kunst bis zum Ende des XII. Jahrhunderts*. Münster: Aschendorff, 1912.

Newman, Barbara. "What Did It Mean to Say 'I Saw'? The Clash between Theory and Practice in Medieval Visionary Culture." *Speculum* 80 (2005), 1–43.

Nicholson, Lewis E. "Hunlafing and the Point of the Sword." In *Anglo-Saxon Poetry: Essays in Appreciation for John C. McGalliard*, edited by Lewis E. Nicholson and Dolores Warwick Frese, pp. 50–65. Notre Dame, IN: University of Notre Dame Press, 1975.

Nieke, Margaret. "Penannular and Related Brooches: Secular Ornament or Symbol in Action?" In *The Age of Migrating Ideas: Early Medieval Art in Northern Britain and Ireland*, edited by R. Michael Spearman and John Higgitt, pp. 128–34. Edinburgh: National Museums of Scotland, 1993.

Noble, Thomas F. X. "The Vocabulary of Vision and Worship in the Early Carolingian Period." In *Seeing the Invisible in Late Antiquity and the Early Middle Ages: Papers from "Verbal and Pictorial Imaging: Representing and Accessing Experience of the Invisible, 400–1000." (Utrecht 11–13 December 2003)*, edited by Giselle de Nie, Karl F. Morrison, and Marco Mostert, pp. 213–37, Utrecht Studies in Medieval Literacy 14. Turnhout: Brepols, 2005.

Nordhagen, Per Jonas. "The Earliest Decorations in Santa Maria Antiqua and Their Date." *Acta ad Archaeologiam et Artium Historiam Pertinentia* 1 (1962), 53–72.

———. "S. Maria Antiqua: The Frescoes of the Seventh Century." *Acta ad Archaeologiam et Artium Historiam Pertinentia* 8 (1978), 89–142.

North, J. R. J. "Jeux d'esprit in *Deor*: Geat and Mæðhild." *Amsterdamer Beiträge zur älteren Germanistik* 27 (1988), 11–24.

Ó Carragáin, Éamonn. "The Annunciation of the Lord and His Passion: A Liturgical Topos from St Peter's on the Vatican in *The Dream of the Rood*, Thomas Cranmer and John Donne." In *Essays on Anglo-Saxon and Related Themes in Memory of Dr Lynne Grundy*, edited by Jane Roberts and Janet Nelson, pp. 339–81. London: King's College, 2000.

———. "Between Annunciation and Visitation: Spiritual Birth and the Cycles of the Sun on the Ruthwell Cross: A Response to Fred Orton." In *Theorizing Anglo-Saxon Stone Sculpture*, edited by Catherine E. Karkov and Fred Orton, pp. 131–87. Morgantown: West Virginia University Press, 2003.

———. *The City of Rome and the World of Bede*. Newcastle Upon Tyne: J. & P. Bealls Ltd., 1994.

———. "Liturgical Innovation Associated with Pope Sergius and the Iconography of the Ruthwell and Bewcastle Crosses." In *Bede and Anglo-Saxon England: Papers in Honour of the 1300th Anniversary of the Birth of Bede*, edited by Robert T. Farrell, pp. 131–47. Oxford: British Archaeological Reports, 1978.

———. "The Necessary Distance: *Imitatio Romae* and the Ruthwell Cross." In *Northumbria's Golden Age*, edited by Jane Hawkes and Susan Mills, pp. 191–203. Stroud: Sutton Publishing, 1999.

———. *Ritual and the Rood: Liturgical Images and the Old English Poems of the Dream of the Rood Tradition*. London: British Library, 2005.

———. "Rome, Ruthwell, Vercelli: *The Dream of the Rood* and the Italian Connection." In *Vercelli tra Oriente ed Occidente tra Tarda Antichita e Medioevo*, edited by Vittoria Dolcetti Corazza, pp. 59–100. Estratto: Edizioni dell'Orsino, 1999.

———. "The Ruthwell Crucifixion Poem in Its Iconographic and Liturgical Contexts." *Peritia* 6–7 (1987–88), 1–71.

———. "Sources or Analogues: Problems of Using Liturgical Evidence to Date *The Dream of the Rood*." In *Cross and Cruciform in the Anglo-Saxon World: Studies to Honor the Memory of Timothy Reuter*, edited by Sarah Larratt Keefer, Karen L. Jolly, and Catherine E. Karkov. Morgantown: West Virginia University Press, forthcoming.

———. "The Term *Porticus* and *Imitatio Romae* in Anglo-Saxon England." In *Text and Gloss: Studies in Insular Learning and Literature Presented to Joseph Donovan Pheifer*, edited by Helen Conrad O'Briain, Ann Marie D'Arcy, and John Scattergood, pp. 13–34. Dublin: Four Courts Press, 1999.

Ó Corráin, Donnchadh, ed. *The Annals of Ulster*. CELT: Corpus of Electronic Texts: University College Cork, 1997. http://www.ucc.ie/celt/online/G100001.

O'Daly, M., ed. and trans. *Cath Maige Mucrama*. Dublin: Irish Texts Society, 1975.

O'Donovan, John, and Eugene O'Curry, eds. *Ancient Laws of Ireland: Senchus Mor*. Vol. 1. 1865. Reprint, Buffalo, NY: W. S. Hein, 1983.

Ogilvy, J. D. A. "Mimi, Scurrae, Histriones: Entertainers of the Early Middle Ages." *Speculum* 38 (1963), 603–19.

———. "Unferth: Foil to Beowulf?" *PMLA* 79 (1964), 370–75.

O'Rahilly, Cecile, ed. and trans. *Táin Bó Cúailnge: Recension I*. Dublin: Irish Texts Society, 1976.

Orchard, Andy. *A Critical Companion to Beowulf*. Rochester, NY: D. S. Brewer, 2003.

Orchard, Nicholas, ed. *The Leofric Missal*. 2 vols. Henry Bradshaw Society 113, 114. London: Boydell, 2002.

———, ed. *The Sacramentary of Ratoldus*. Henry Bradshaw Society 116. London: Boydell, 2005.

O' Reilly, Jennifer. "Patristic and Insular Traditions of the Evangelists: Exegesis and Iconography." In *Le Isole britanniche e Roma in età Romanobar-
barica*, edited by A. M. Luiselli Fadda and Éamonn Ó Carragáin, pp.
49–94. Rome: Herder, 1998.

———. *Studies in the Iconography of the Virtues and Vices in the Middle Ages.* New
York: Garland Publishing, 1988.

———. "The Tree of Eden in Medieval Iconography." In *A Walk in the Gar-
den: Biblical, Iconographical and Literary Images of Eden*, edited by Paul
Morris and Deborah Sawyer, pp. 167–204. Sheffield: Journal for the
Study of the Old Testament Press, 1992.

Osborn, Marijane. "Some Uses of Ambiguity in Beowulf." *Thoth* 10 (1969),
18–35.

Osborne, John. "Images of the Mother of God in Early Medieval Rome." In
*Icon and Word: The Power of Images in Byzantium. Studies Presented to Robin
Cormack*, edited by Antony Eastmond and Liz James, pp. 135–51. Alder-
shot: Ashgate, 2003.

Otter, Monika. "The Temptation of St. Æthethryth." *Exemplaria* 9 (1997),
139–63.

Otto, Beatrice K. *Fools Are Everywhere: The Court Jester around the World.* Chicago: University of Chicago Press, 2001.

Owen, Morfydd, et al., eds. *Gwaith Llywelyn Fardd I ac Eraill.* In *Cyfres Beirdd y
Tywysogion II*, pp. 44–53. Cardiff: University of Wales Press, 1994.

Pächt, Otto, and J. J. G. Alexander. *Illuminated Manuscripts in the Bodleian
Library, Oxford.* 3 vols. Oxford: Oxford University Press, 1966.

Padelford, F. M. "Spenser and *The Pilgrimage of the Life of Man*." *Studies in
Philology* 28 (1931), 211–18.

Pálsson, Hermann. See Hermann Pálsson.

Paltsits, Victor Hugo. "The Petworth Manuscript of 'Grace Dieu' or 'The
Pilgrimage of the Soul.'" *Bulletin of the New York Public Library* 32 (1928),
715–20.

Parks, Ward. *Verbal Dueling in Heroic Narrative: The Homeric and Old English
Tradition.* Princeton, NJ: Princeton University Press, 1990.

Patch, Howard R. "Liturgical Influence in *The Dream of the Rood*." *PMLA* 34
(1919), 233–57.

Payne, Richard C. "Convention and Originality in the Vision Framework of
The Dream of the Rood." *Modern Philology* 73 (1976), 334–41.

Penna, Angelo. "Ebrei." In *Enciclopedia Dantesca*, 2:623. Rome: Istituto della
Enciclopedia Italiana, 1984.

Peters, Ursula. *Das Ich im Bild: Die Figur des Autors in volkssprachigen Bilder-
handschriften des 13. bis 16. Jahrhunderts.* Cologne: Böhlau Verlag, 2008.

Petroff, Elizabeth, ed. and trans. *Medieval Women's Visionary Literature.* Oxford: Oxford University Press, 1986.

Phillips, Helen. "Chaucer and Deguileville: The *ABC* in Context." *Medium Ævum* 62 (1993), 1–19.

Poole, Russell. "Ormr Steinþórsson and the *Snjófríðadrápa.*" *Arkiv för nordisk filologi* 97 (1982), 122–37.

Pope, John C. "*Beowulf* 505, 'gehedde,' and the Pretensions of Unferth." In *Modes of Interpretation in Old English Literature: Essays in Honour of Stanley B. Greenfield,* edited by Phyllis Rugg Brown, Georgia Ronan Crampton, and Fred C. Robinson, pp. 173–88. Toronto: University of Toronto Press, 1986.

———. "Paleography and Poetry: Some Solved and Unsolved Problems of the Exeter Book." In *Medieval Scribes, Manuscripts and Libraries: Essays Presented to N.R. Ker,* edited by M. B. Parkes and Andrew W. Watson, pp. 25–65. London: Scolar Press, 1978.

Pseudo-Jerome. *Expositio quattuor Evangeliorum. PL* 30:638B.

Quin, E. G., ed. *Dictionary of the Irish Language.* Compact Edition. Dublin: Royal Irish Academy, 1983.

Rabanus Maurus. *Allegoriae in universam sacrum scripturam. PL* 112:849–1088.

Radner, Joan Newton, ed. and trans. *Fragmentary Annals of Ireland.* Dublin: Irish Texts Society, 1978.

Raine, James, ed. *The Historians of the Church of York and Its Archbishops.* Rolls Series 71.1. London: Longman, 1879–94.

Ranisch, Wilhelm, ed. *Die Gautrekssaga.* Berlin: Mayer & Müller, 1900.

Raw, Barbara C. *Anglo-Saxon Crucifixion Iconography and the Art of the Monastic Revival.* CSASE 1. Cambridge: Cambridge University Press, 1990.

———. "*The Dream of the Rood* and Its Connections with Early Christian Art." *Medium Ævum* 39 (1970), 239–56.

Raymond of Capua. *The Life of Catherine of Siena.* Translated by Conleth Kearns. Wilmington, DE: Michael Glazier, 1980.

Reginald of Durham. *Reginaldi Monachi dunelmensis libellus de admirandis beati Cuthberti virtutibus quae novellis patratae sunt temporibus.* Edited by James Raine. London: J. B. Nichols and Son, 1835.

Reyner, Clement. *Apostolatus benedictinorum in Anglia sive disceptatio historica de antiquitate ordinis congregationisque monachorum nigrorum S. Benedicti in regno angliae.* Duaci: Laurentii Kellami, 1626.

Richstätter, K. *Medieval Devotions to the Sacred Heart.* London: Burns, Oates, 1925.

Ridyard, S. *The Royal Saints of Anglo-Saxon England: A Study of West Saxon and East Anglian Cults.* Cambridge: Cambridge University Press, 1988.

Riedinger, Rudolf, ed. *Concilium Lateranense a. 649 celebratum.* Berlin: De Gruyter, 1984.

Risden, E. L. "Heroic Humor in *Beowulf.*" In *Humour in Anglo-Saxon Literature,* edited by Jonathan Wilcox, pp. 71–78. Cambridge: D. S. Brewer, 2000.

Roberts, Alexander, and James Donaldson, eds. and trans. *The Ante-Nicene Fathers: Translations of the Writings of the Fathers down to A.D. 325.* 10 vols. Buffalo, NY: Christian Library Publishing Co., 1885–96.

Roberts, Brian K. *The Green Villages of County Durham.* Durham: Durham County Council, 1977.

———. *The Making of the English Village: A Study in Historical Geography.* Harlow: Longman Scientific & Technical, 1987.

———. "Man and Land in Upper Teesdale." In *Upper Teesdale: The Area and Its Natural History,* edited by A. R. Clapham, pp. 141–59. London: Collins, 1978.

Roberts, Brynley F., ed. *Gwaith Bleddyn Fardd ac Eraill.* In *Cyfres Beirdd y Tywysogion VII,* pp. 183–99. Cardiff: University of Wales Press, 1996.

Roberts, Jane. "Old English Un- 'Very' and Unferth." *English Studies* 61 (1980), 289–92.

———. "Some Relationships between *The Dream of the Rood* and the Cross at Ruthwell." *Studies in Medieval English Language and Literature* 15 (2000), 1–25.

Roberts, Thomas, ed. *Gwaith Tudur Penllyn ac Ieuan ap Tudur Penllyn.* Cardiff: University of Wales Press, 1958.

Robinson, Fred C. *Beowulf and the Appositive Style.* Knoxville: University of Tennessee Press, 1987.

———."Elements of the Marvelous in the Characterization of Beowulf: A Reconsideration of the Textual Evidence." In Fred C. Robinson, *The Tomb of Beowulf and Other Essays on Old English,* pp. 22–35. Oxford: Blackwell, 1993.

———. "Personal Names in Medieval Narrative and the Name of Unferth in *Beowulf.*" In Fred C. Robinson, *The Tomb of Beowulf and Other Essays on Old English,* pp. 219–23. Oxford: Blackwell, 1993.

Roll, Susan K. *Towards the Origins of Christmas.* Kampen: Kok Pharos, 1995.

Rosier, James L. "Design for Treachery: The Unferth Intrigue." *PMLA* 77 (1962), 1–7.

Roth, C. "New Light on Dante's Circle." *Modern Language Review* 48 (1953), 26–32.

Rothenberg, Albert. "Artistic Creation as Stimulated by Superimposed versus Combined-Composite Visual Images." *Journal of Personality and Social Psychology* 50 (1986), 370–81.

———. *Creativity and Madness: New Findings and Old Stereotypes.* Baltimore: Johns Hopkins University Press, 1990.

———. "Creativity and the Homospatial Process: Experimental Studies." *Psychiatric Clinics of North America* 2 (1988), 443–59.

———. "The Process of Janusian Thinking in Creativity." *Archives of General Psychiatry* 24 (1971), 195–205. Reprinted in *The Creativity Question,* edited by Albert Rothenberg and Carl R. Hausman, pp. 311–27. Durham, NC: Duke University Press, 1976.

Rothenberg, Albert, and Robert S. Sobel. "Creation of Literary Metaphors as Stimulated by Superimposed versus Separated Visual Images." *Journal of Mental Imagery* 4 (1980), 77–91.

Rubin, Miri. *Gentile Tales: The Narrative Assault on Late Medieval Jews.* New Haven, CT: Yale University Press, 1999.

Rushforth, Gordon McNeil. "The Church of S. Maria Antiqua." *Papers of the British School at Rome* 1 (1902), 1–123.

Rushforth, Rebecca. "The Eleventh- and Early Twelfth-Century Manuscripts of Bury St Edmunds Abbey." 2 vols. Ph.D. diss., Cambridge University, 2002.

Russell, Peter. "Assunzione celeste." In *Poetic Asides 1,* pp. 34–51. Salzburg: University of Salzburg, 1992.

———. "Dante e l'Islam." In *Poetic Asides 1,* pp. 5–23. Salzburg: University of Salzburg, 1992.

———. "Dante e l'Islam oggi." In *Poetic Asides 1,* pp. 24–33. Salzburg: University of Salzburg, 1992.

Ryan, Michael. "The Menagerie of the Derrynaflan Chalice." In *The Age of Migrating Ideas: Early Medieval Art in Northern Britain and Ireland,* edited by R. Michael Spearman and John Higgitt, pp. 151–61. Edinburgh: National Museum of Scotland, 1993.

Santorilli, Paola, ed. *La Vida Radegundis di Baudonivia.* Naples: D'Auria, 1999.

Saurma-Jeltsch, Lieselotte E. *Die Miniaturen im "Liber Scivias" der Hildegard von Bingen: Die Wucht der Vision und die Ordnung der Bilder.* Wiesbaden: Reichert, 1998.

Sawyer, Peter H. *The Age of the Vikings.* London: E. Arnold, 1962. 2nd ed., 1971.

———. *Anglo-Saxon Charters: An Annotated List and Bibliography.* London: Royal Historical Society, 1968.

————. "Baldersby, Borup and Bruges. The Rise of Northern Europe." *University of Leeds Review* 16 (1973), 75–96

————. "Conquest and Colonization: Scandinavians in the Danelaw and in Normandy." In *Proceedings of the Eighth Viking Congress, Århus 24–31 August 1977*, edited by Hans Bekker-Nielsen, Peter Foote, and Olaf Olsen, pp. 123–31. Odense: Odense University Press, 1981.

————. "The Density of the Danish Settlement in England." *University of Birmingham Historical Journal* 6 (1958), 1–17.

————. *From Roman Britain to Norman England.* London: Methuen, 1978.

————. *Kings and Vikings. Scandinavia and Europe AD 700–1100.* London: Methuen, 1982.

————. "Medieval English Settlement: New Interpretations." In *English Medieval Settlement*, edited by P. H. Sawyer, pp. 1–8. London: E. Arnold, 1979.

Sawyer, Peter H., et al. "The Two Viking Ages of Britain: A Discussion." *Medieval Scandinavia* 2 (1969), 163–207.

Saxer, Victor. *Sainte-Marie-Majeure, une basilique de Rome dans l'histoire de la ville et de son église.* Collection de l'École française de Rome 283. Rome: École française de Rome, 2001.

Schaff, Phillip, and Henry Wace, eds. and trans. *Nicene and Post-Nicene Fathers.* 2nd ser. 14 vols. Grand Rapids, MI: Eerdmans, 1983.

Schiller, Gertrud. *Iconography of Christian Art.* Translated by Janet Seligman. Vol. 2: *The Passion of Jesus Christ.* Greenwich, CT: New York Graphic Society, 1971–72.

Schipperges, Heinrich. *The World of Hildegard of Bingen.* Collegeville, MN: Liturgical Press, 1998.

Schlauch, Margaret. "Widsith, Víthförull, and Some Other Analogues." *PMLA* 46 (1931), 969–87.

Schwab, Ute. "Das Traumgesicht vom Kreuzesbaum: ein ikonologischer Interpretationsansatz zu dem ags. Dream of the Rood." In *Philologische Studien: Gedenkschrift für Richard Kienast*, edited by Ute Schwab and Elfriede Stutz, pp. 131–92. Heidelberg: Carl Winter, 1978.

Schwartz, Eduard, and Theodor Mommsen, eds. *Eusebius Werke.* Vol. 2: *Die Kirchengeschichte.* Leipzig: J. C. Hinrichs'sche Buchhandlung, 1903–08.

Scott, Kathleen L., ed. *Later Gothic Manuscripts 1390–1490.* 2 vols. London: Harvey Miller, 1996.

Scragg, D. G., ed. *The Vercelli Homilies and Related Texts.* EETS o.s. 300. Oxford: Oxford University Press, 1992.

Sherley-Price, Leo, trans. *Bede: A History of the English Church and People.* Harmondsworth: Penguin, 1955. Reprint, 1979.

Shippey, Thomas A. *Beowulf.* London: Edward Arnold, 1978.

————.‟Grim Wordplay': Folly and Wisdom in Anglo-Saxon Humor." In *Humour in Anglo-Saxon Literature,* edited by Jonathan Wilcox, pp. 33–48. Cambridge: D. S. Brewer, 2000.

Silber, Patricia. "Hunferth and the Paths of Exile." *In Geardagum* 17 (1996), 15–29.

————. "Rhetoric as Prowess in the Unferð Episode." *Texas Studies in Literature and Language* 23 (1981), 471–83.

————. "Unferth: Another Look at the Emendation." *Names* 28 (1980), 101–11.

Sims-Williams, Patrick. "'Is it fog or smoke or warriors fighting?': Irish and Welsh Parallels to the *Finnsburg* Fragment." *Bulletin of the Board of Celtic Studies* 27 (1978), 505–14.

————. "Some Functions of Origin Stories in Early Medieval Wales." In *History and Heroic Tales: A Symposium,* edited by Tore Nyberg et al., pp. 97–132. Odense: Odense University Press, 1985.

Singleton, Charles S. "The Irreducible Dove." *Comparative Literature* 9 (1957), 129–35.

Smetana, Cyril J., OSA. "Aelfric and the Early Medieval Homilary." *Traditio* 15 (1959), 163–204.

Smith, A. H. "The Photography of Manuscripts." *London Mediæval Studies* 1 (1938), 179–207.

Sobel, Robert S., and Albert Rothenberg. "Artistic Creation as Stimulated by Superimposed versus Separated Visual Images." *Journal of Personality and Social Psychology* 39 (1980), 953–61.

Sola Buil, Ricardo J. "The Dream Vision as a Literary Convention: A Tradition." In *Papers from the IVth International Conference of the Spanish Society for Medieval English Language and Literature,* edited by Teresa Fanego Lema, pp. 273–83. Santiago de Compostela: Universidade de Santiago de Compostela, 1993.

South, Ted Johnson. See Johnson South, Ted.

Southern, R. W. *Western Views of Islam in the Middle Ages.* Cambridge, MA: Harvard University Press, 1962.

Southworth, John. *Fools and Jesters at the English Court.* Thrupp: Sutton Publishing, 1998.

Steiner, Emily. *Documentary Culture and the Making of Medieval English Literature.* Cambridge: Cambridge University Press, 2003.

Stenton, Frank. *Anglo-Saxon England.* 3rd edition. Oxford: Oxford University Press, 1971.

Stevens, J., ed. *Bede's Ecclesiastical History of the English Nation.* London: Dent, 1965.

Stevenson, R. B. K. "The Chronology and Relationships of Some Irish and Scottish Crosses." *Journal of the Royal Society of Antiquaries of Ireland* 86–87 (1956–57), 84–96.

———. "Sculpture in Scotland in the 6th–9th Centuries AD." In *Kolloquium über Spätanitike und Frümittelalterliche Sculptur,* edited by V. Milojcic, pp. 65–74. Mainz: Verlag Philipp von Zabern, 1971.

Stierli, Josef, ed. *Heart of the Saviour.* New York: Herder, 1957.

Stratford, Jenny. *The Bedford Inventories: The Worldly Goods of John, Duke of Bedford, Regent of France, 1389–1435.* London: Society of Antiquaries, 1993.

Suso, Henry. *Büchlein der Weisheit.* In *Deutsche Schriften,* edited by Karl Bihlmeyer. Stuttgart: W. Kohlhammer, 1907.

———. *The Exemplar: Life and Writings of Blessed Henry Suso, O.P.* Translated by M. Ann Edward. Dubuque, IA: Priory Press, 1962.

Sutherland, Elizabeth. *In Search of the Picts.* London: Constable, 1994.

Sveinbjörn Egilsson. *Lexicon poeticum antiquae linguae septentrionalis.* Copenhagen: J. D. Qvist, 1854–60.

Swain, Barbara. *Fools and Folly during the Middle Ages and the Renaissance.* New York: Columbia University Press, 1932.

Swanton, Michael, ed. *The Anglo-Saxon Chronicle.* London: J. M. Dent, 1996.

———. *The Dream of the Rood.* Manchester: Manchester University Press, 1970. Reprinted with minor corrections and a supplementary bibliography, 1978.

Swenson, Karen. *Performing Definitions: Two Genres of Insult in Old Norse Literature.* Columbia, SC: Camden House, 1991.

Symeon of Durham. *Historia Regum.* Edited by Thomas Arnold in *Symeonis Monachi opera omnia,* 2:3–283. Rolls Series 75. London: HMSO, 1885.

Symons, Dom Thomas, ed. and trans. *The Monastic Agreement of the Monks and Nuns of the English Nation (Regularis Concordia anglicae nationis monachorum sanctimonialiumque).* London: Nelson, 1953.

Szarmach, Paul E. "Ælfric and the Problem of Women." In *Essays on Anglo-Saxon and Related Themes in Memory of Lynne Grundy,* edited by Jane Roberts and Janet Nelson, pp. 571–90. London: King's College London, Centre for Late Antique & Medieval Studies, 2000.

———. "Ælfric, the Prose Vision, and *The Dream of the Rood.*" In *Studies in Honour of René Derolez,* edited by A. M. Simon-Vandenbergen, pp. 592–602. Ghent: Seminarie voor Engelse en Oud-Germaanse Taalkunde, R.U.G., 1987. Reprinted in *Old English Prose: Basic Readings,* edited by Paul E. Szarmach, pp. 327–38. New York: Garland Publishing, 2000.

————. "The Poetic Turn of Mind of the Translator of the *OE Bede*." In *Anglo-Saxons: Studies Presented to Cyril Hart*, edited by Simon Keynes and Alfred P. Smyth, pp.56–68. Dublin: Four Courts Press, 2006.

Talley, Thomas J. *The Origins of the Liturgical Year*. New York: Pueblo Publishing Co., 1986.

Tarbat Discovery Programme. Bulletins 1–6. University of York, 1995–2000. http//:york.ac.uk/dept/arch/staff/sites/tarbat.

Tatlock, J. S. P. "Mohammed and His Followers in Dante." *Modern Language Review* 27 (1932), 186–95.

Taylor, Andrew. "Into His Secret Chamber: Reading and Privacy in Late Medieval England." In *The Practice and Representation of Reading in England*, edited by James Raven, Helen Small, and Naomi Tadnor, pp. 41–61. Cambridge: Cambridge University Press, 1996.

Taylor, H. M., and Joan Taylor. *Anglo-Saxon Architecture*. 2 vols. Cambridge: Cambridge University Press, 1965.

Taylor, Simon. "Place-Names and the Early Church in Eastern Scotland." In *Scotland in Dark Age Britain*, edited by Barbara Crawford, pp. 93–110. Aberdeen: Scottish Cultural Press, 1996.

Thompson, Edward Maunde. *Handbook of Greek and Latin Palæography*. London: Kegan Paul, Trench, Trübner & Co., 1893.

————. *An Introduction to Greek and Latin Palaeography*. Oxford: Oxford University Press, 1912. Reprint, New York: B. Franklin, 1965.

Thompson, Pauline A. "St. Æthelthryth: The Making of History from Hagiography." In *Studies in English Language and Literature: 'doubt wisely': Papers in Honour of E. G. Stanley*, edited by M. J. Toswell and E. M. Tyler, pp. 475–92. London: Routledge, 1996.

Thompson, Pauline A., and Elizabeth Stevens. "Gregory of Ely's Verse Life and Miracles of St. Æthelthryth." *Analecta Bollandiana* 106 (1988), 333–90.

Tolan, John, ed. *Medieval Christian Perceptions of Islam: A Book of Essays*. New York: Garland, 1996.

Tomasch, Sylvia. "Judecca, Dante's Satan, and the *Dis*-placed Jew." In *Text and Territory: Geographical Imagination in the European Middle Ages*, edited by Sylvia Tomasch and Sealy Gilles, pp. 247–67. Philadelphia: University of Pennsylvania Press, 1998.

Torrance, E. Paul. *Why Fly? A Philosophy of Creativity*. Norwood, NJ: Ablex, 1995.

Toswell, Jane. "St Martial and the Dating of Late Anglo-Saxon Manuscripts." *Scriptorium* 51 (1997), 3–14.

Treharne, Elaine M. "'Hiht waes geniwad': Rebirth in *The Dream of the Rood.*" In *The Place of the Cross in Anglo-Saxon England,* edited by Catherine E. Karkov, Sarah Larratt Keefer, and Karen Louise Jolly, pp. 145–57. Woodbridge: Boydell, 2006.

————. *The Old English Life of St Nicholas with the Old English Life of St Giles.* Leeds Texts and Monographs n.s. 15. Leeds: University of Leeds Press, 1997.

Tripp, Raymond P., Jr. "Humor, Wordplay, and Semantic Resonance in *Beowulf.*" In *Humour in Anglo-Saxon Literature,* edited by Jonathan Wilcox, pp. 49–69. Cambridge: D. S. Brewer, 2000.

Tromp, S. "De Nativitate Ecclesiae ex Corde Iesu in Cruce." *Gregorianum* 13 (1932), 489–527.

Tronzo, William. "The Shape of Narrative: A Problem in the Mural Decoration of Early Medieval Rome." *Roma nell'alto medioevo: Settimane di studio del Centro italiano di studi sull'Alto Medioevo* 48, 1:457–92. 2 vols. Spoleto, 2001.

Tuve, Rosemond. *Allegorical Imagery: Some Mediaeval Books and Their Posterity.* Princeton, NJ: Princeton University Press, 1966.

Van Beek, Cornelius I. M., ed. *Passio Sanctarum Perpetuae et Felicitatis.* Nijmegen: Dekker and Van de Vegt, 1936.

Vaughan, Míeál F. "A Reconsideration of 'Unferð.'" *Neuphilologische Mitteilungen* 77 (1976), 32–48.

Veelenturf, Kees. *Dia Brátha: Eschatological Theophanies and Irish High Crosses.* Amsterdam: Stichting Amsterdamse Historische Reeks, 1997.

Ventura, Alberto. "Presenze islamiche nell'opera di Dante." *Islàm: storia e civiltà* 4.1 (Jan.–Mar., 1985), 31–41.

Vigfússon, Guðbrandur, ed. *Icelandic-English Dictionary.* Oxford: Clarendon Press, 1874.

Vigfússon, Guðbrandur, and F. York Powell. *Corpus Poeticum Boreale: The Poetry of the Old Northern Tongue.* Oxford, 1883. Reprint, New York: Russell & Russell, 1965.

Virgil. *Aeneid.* Edited and translated by H. Rushton Fairclough. Cambridge, MA: Harvard University Press, 1967.

Voaden, Rosalynn. "All Girls Together: Community, Gender and Vision at Helfta." In *Medieval Women in Their Communities,* edited by Diane Watt, pp. 72–91. Cardiff: University of Wales Press, 1997.

Waddell, Helen. *Poetry in the Dark Ages.* Glasgow: Jackson, 1948.

Wainwright, Geoffrey. *Eucharist and Eschatology.* London: Epworth Press, 1971.

Waite, Gregory George. *Old English Prose Translations of King Alfred's Reign.* Cambridge: D. S. Brewer, 2000.

——. "The Vocabulary of the Old English Version of Bede's *Historia Ecclesiastica.*" Ph.D. diss., University of Toronto, 1994.

Wall, John. "The Conyers Falchion." *Durham Archaeological Journal* 2 (1986), 77–83.

Wallace-Hadrill, J. M. *Bede's Ecclesiastical History of the English People: A Historical Commentary.* Oxford: Clarendon Press, 1988. Reprint, 1991.

Walls, K. M. M. "Did Lydgate Translate the *Pèlerinage de vie humaine?*" *Notes & Queries* 24 (1977), 1033–35.

Ward, H. L. D., ed. *Catalogue of Romances in the Department of Manuscripts in the British Museum.* 2 vols. London: British Museum, 1893.

Warner, George, ed. and trans. *The Stowe Missal.* 2 vols. Henry Bradshaw Society 31 and 32. London, 1906–15.

Warren, F. E. *The Liturgy and Ritual of the Celtic Church.* Oxford: Oxford University Press, 1881.

Watson, Nicholas "Censorship and Cultural Change in Late-Medieval England: Vernacular Theology, the Oxford Translation Debate, and Arundel's Constitutions of 1409." *Speculum* 70 (1995), 822–64.

Watts, Victor E. "Comment on 'The Evidence of Place-Names' by Margaret Gelling." In *Medieval Settlement. Continuity and Change,* edited by Peter H. Sawyer, pp. 212–22. London: Edward Arnold, 1976. Reprinted. as "The Evidence of Place-Names II," in *English Medieval Settlement,* edited by P. H. Sawyer, pp. 122–32. London: Edward Arnold, 1979.

——. "Place-Name Evidence." In *The Archaeology of the Coal-Measures and the Magnesian Limestone Escarpment in Co. Durham: A Preliminary Survey,* edited by Percival Turnbull and Rick F. J. Jones, pp. 223–33. Barnard Castle: Bowes Museum, 1978.

——. "Place-Names." In *Durham County and City with Teesside,* edited by John C. Dewdney, pp. 251–65. Durham: Local Executive Committee of the British Association, 1970.

——. "The Place-Names of County Durham." *Transactions of the Durham and Northumberland Architectural and Archaeological Society* 11 (1958–65), 319–33.

——. "Place-Names of the Darlington Area." In *Darlington: A Topographical Study,* edited by Peter A. G. Clack and Nicholas F. Pearson, pp. 40–43. Durham: Northern Archaeological Survey, Dept. of Archaeology, University of Durham, 1978.

——. "Scandinavian Settlement-Names in County Durham." *Nomina* 12 (1988–89), 17–63.

Webber, Teresa. *Scribes and Scholars at Salisbury Cathedral c. 1075–c. 1125.* Oxford: Clarendon Press, 1992.

Welsford, Enid. *The Fool: His Social and Literary History.* London: Faber and Faber, 1935.

Wenzel, Siegfried. "The Pilgrimage of Life as a Late Medieval Genre." *Mediaeval Studies* 35 (1973), 370–88.

Werner, Martin. "The Cross-Carpet Page in the Book of Durrow: The Cult of the True Cross, Adomnán, and Iona." *Art Bulletin* 72 (1990), 174–223.

Westphalen, Tilman. *Beowulf 3150–55: Textkritik- und Editionsgeschichte.* Munich: Wilhelm Fink, 1967.

Whatley, E. Gordon. "Acta Sanctorum." In *Sources of Anglo-Saxon Literary Culture.* Vol. 1: *Abbo of Fleury, Abbo of Saint-Germain-des-Prés, and Acta Sanctorum,* edited by Frederick M. Biggs, Thomas D. Hill, Paul E. Szarmach, and E. Gordon Whatley, pp. 22–486. Kalamazoo, MI: Medieval Institute Publications, 2001.

———. "Hagiography in England, ca. 950–1150." In *Hagiographies: histoire internationale de la littérature hagiographique latine et vernaculaire en Occident des origines à 1550,* edited by Guy Philippart, 2:429–99. Turnhout: Brepols, 1994.

———. "An Introduction to the Study of Old English Prose Hagiography: Sources and Resources." In *Holy Men and Holy Women,* edited by Paul E. Szarmach, pp. 3–32. Albany: State University of New York Press, 1996.

Whitaker, Edward Charles, trans. *Documents of the Baptismal Liturgy.* 2nd edition. London: SPCK, 1970.

Whitbread, Leslie. "The Pattern of Misfortune in *Deor* and Other Old English Poems." *Neophilologus* 54 (1970), 167–83.

White, Carolinne. *Early Christian Latin Poets.* London: Routledge, 2000.

Whitelock, Dorothy, ed. *English Historical Documents c. 500–1042.* London: Eyre and Spottiswoode, 1968.

Whitelock, Dorothy, with D. C. Douglas and S. I. Tucker, eds. and trans. *The Anglo-Saxon Chronicle. A Revised Translation.* 2nd impression. London: Eyre and Spottiswoode, 1965.

Wilcox, Jonathan, ed. *Humour in Anglo-Saxon Literature.* Cambridge: D. S. Brewer, 2000.

Willeford, William. *The Fool and His Scepter.* Evanston, IL: Northwestern University Press, 1969.

William of Malmesbury. *Gesta Regum Anglorum.* Edited by R. A. B. Mynors, R. M. Thomson, and M. Winterbottom. 2 vols. Oxford: Clarendon Press, 1998–99.

William of St. Thierry. *La Contemplation de Dieu.* Edited by Jacques Hourlier. Paris: Édition de Cerfs, 1959.

———. *On Contemplating God.* Vol. 1 of *The Works of William of St. Thierry.* Translated by Sr. Penelope. Kalamazoo, MI: Cistercian Publications, 1971.

Williams, Ifor, ed. *The Poems of Taliesin.* English version by J. E. Caerwyn Williams. Dublin: Dublin Institute for Advanced Study, 1968.

Williams, Ifor, and Thomas Roberts, eds. *Cywyddau Dafydd ap Gwilym a'e Gyfoeswyr.* Cardiff: University of Wales Press, 1935.

Wilmart, André, ed. "La légende de Ste Edith en prose et vers par le moine Goscellin." *Analecta Bollandiana* 56 (1938), 5–101, 307.

Wilson, David M. "The Scandinavians in England." In *The Archaeology of Anglo-Saxon England,* edited by David M. Wilson, pp. 393–403. London: Methuen, 1976.

Wilson, H. A., ed. *The Benedictional of Archbishop Robert.* London: Harrison and Sons, 1903.

———. *The Missal of Robert of Jumièges.* Henry Bradshaw Society 11. London: Henry Bradshaw Society, 1896.

Wogan-Browne, Jocelyn. *Saints' Lives and Women's Literary Culture.* Oxford: Oxford University Press, 2001.

Wogan-Browne, Jocelyn, Nicholas Watson, Andrew Taylor, and Ruth Evans, eds. *The Idea of the Vernacular: An Anthology of Middle English Literary Theory, 1280–1520.* University Park: Pennsylvania State University Press, 1999.

Wolf, Gerhard P. *Salus Populi Romani. Die Geschichte römischer Kultbilder im Mittelalter.* Weinheim: VCH, 1990.

Woolf, Rosemary. "Doctrinal Influences on *The Dream of the Rood.*" *Medium Ævum* 27 (1958), 137–53. Reprinted in Woolf, *Art and Doctrine: Essays on Medieval Literature,* edited by Heather O'Donaghue, pp. 29–48. London: Hambledon Press, 1986.

Wormald, Francis, and Phyllis M. Giles, eds. *Illuminated Manuscripts in the Fitzwilliam Museum.* Cambridge: Fitzwilliam Museum, 1966.

Wormald, Patrick. "The Emergence of the *Regnum Scottorum:* A Carolingian Hegemony?" In *Scotland in Dark Age Britain,* edited by Barbara Crawford, pp. 131–60. Aberdeen: Scottish Cultural Press, 1996.

Wrenn, C. L. *Beowulf, with the Finnesburg Fragment.* 3rd ed. Revised by W. F. Bolton. New York: St. Martin's Press, 1973.

Wright, Robert Edward. "Art and the Incarnate Word: Medieval Christologies and the Problem of Literary Inexpressibility." Ph.D. diss., Duke University, 1986.

Wright, Stephen K. "Deguileville's *Pèlerinage de vie humaine* as 'Contrepartie Edifiante' of the *Roman de la Rose.*" *Philological Quarterly* 68 (1989), 399–422.

Wright, Thomas, and R. P. Wülcker. *Anglo-Saxon and Old English Vocabularies.* 2nd ed. Edited by. R. P. Wülcker. London: Tübner, 1884. Reprint New York: Gordon Press, 1978.

Wulfstan. *The Homilies of Wulfstan.* Edited by Dorothy Bethurum. Oxford: Clarendon Press, 1957.

Zijderveld, Anton C. *Reality in a Looking-Glass: Rationality through and Analysis of Traditional Folly.* London: Routledge & Kegan Paul, 1982.

Zupitza, Julius, ed. *Beowulf, Reproduced in Facsimile from the Unique Manuscript British Museum MS. Cotton Vitellius A. xv, with a Transliteration and Notes by Julius Zupitza.* 2nd ed., containing a new reproduction of the manuscript with an introductory note by Norman Davis. EETS 245. London: Oxford University Press 1959.

CONTRIBUTORS

GEORGE HARDIN BROWN is professor emeritus of English at Stanford University.

PATRICK W. CONNER is professor of English at West Virginia University.

LESLIE A. DONOVAN is an associate professor in the University Honors Program at the University of New Mexico.

RICHARD K. EMMERSON is dean of the School of Arts at Manhattan College.

ROBERTA FRANK is Douglas Tracy Smith Professor of English at Yale University. She has published widely on both Old English and Old Norse poetry and culture and is a past president of the Medieval Academy of America.

THOMAS N. HALL teaches in the English Department and the Medieval Institute at the University of Notre Dame.

CATHERINE E. KARKOV is Chair of Art History and Head of the School of Fine Art, University of Leeds.

SARAH LARRATT KEEFER is professor of English at Trent University.

KEVIN KIERNAN is professor emeritus of English at the University of Kentucky.

DAVID N. KLAUSNER is Professor of English and Vice-Dean of Interdisciplinary Affairs, University of Toronto.

CHRISTOPHER KLEINHENZ is professor emeritus of Italian at the University of Wisconsin–Madison.

KELLIE S. MEYER teaches in the English Department at the University of New Mexico.

CHRISTOPHER D. MORRIS is professor emeritus of Archaeology and honorary professorial research fellow at the University of Glasgow.

KATHERINE O'BRIEN O'KEEFFE is professor of English at the University of California, Berkeley.

ÉAMONN Ó CARRAGÁIN is professor emeritus in the English Department at University College Cork. He has published on many aspects of Anglo-Saxon and medieval art and literature.

PAUL E. SZARMACH is executive director of the Medieval Academy of America.

INDEX OF MANUSCRIPTS

General Index

Typeset in 10/13 ITC New Baskerville
Designed by Linda K. Judy
Composed by Tom Krol
Manufactured by Cushing-Malloy, Inc.

Medieval Institute Publications
College of Arts and Sciences
Western Michigan University
1903 W. Michigan Avenue
Kalamazoo, MI 49008-5432
http: //www.wmich.edu/medieval/mip

 WESTERN MICHIGAN UNIVERSITY